ZAGATSURVEY®

2003

AMERICA'S TOP GOLF COURSES

Golf Editors: Jim Gorant, Joe Passov and Evan Rothman
Editor: Betsy Andrews

Published and distributed by
ZAGAT SURVEY, LLC
4 Columbus Circle
New York, New York 10019
Tel: 212 977 6000
E-mail: golf@zagat.com
Web site: www.zagat.com

Acknowledgments

For their invaluable assistance in the creation of this guide, we thank Audobon International, the Golf Channel, the Golf Course Superintendents Association of America, GOLFONLINE, the National Golf Foundation and the World Golf Hall of Fame. We are also grateful to John Angelo, William Dougherty, William O. Grabe, Jack D. Gunther, Jr., Karin Anne Henderson, Franklin W. Hobbes, David C. Hodgson, Nick Nicholas, Betsy Ryan Passov, Brad Race and Peter J. Solomon.

This guide would not have been possible without the hard work of our staff, especially Erika Boudreau-Harris, Al Cadalzo, Reni Chin, Anna Chlumsky, Jamie Clark, Anne Cole, Steve DeLorenzo, Griff Foxley, Shelley Gallagher, Randi Gollin, Katherine Harris, Gail Horwood, Natalie Lebert, Charles Levine, Mike Liao, Dave Makulec, Donna Marino, Patrick O'Toole, Rob Poole, Benjamin Schmerler, Troy Segal, Liliana Valderrama, Wei Wu, Sharon Yates and Kyle Zolner.

Contents

About This Survey

For 24 years, Zagat Survey has reported on the shared experiences of diners and travelers. Recently, we've expanded our scope to include nightlife, shopping and movies. Now we've teamed up with **ESPN**, the worldwide leader in sports, to bring you what we believe is the ultimate golfer's guide, covering 1,049 public, semi-private and resort courses in the USA, including the Virgin Islands and Puerto Rico.

To help you find the right course for your next round, we have prepared a number of lists – see Most Popular (page 9) and Top Ratings (pages 10–19) – as well as 40+ handy indexes, plus information on urban driving ranges and 100 leading private courses. We've also provided a tournament guide.

Thanks to our 5,311 reviewers, you have the benefit of your fellow golfers' experiences at virtually every course you may want to play. Our participants played an average of eight rounds per month. With their ratings and reviews, we think we've achieved a uniquely reliable guide for golfers of every stripe.

Of our surveyors, 86% are men, 14% women; the breakdown by age is 11% in their 20s, 28% in their 30s, 25% in their 40s, 24% in their 50s and 12% in their 60s and above. Our editors have done their best to summarize these surveyors' opinions, with their exact comments shown in quotation marks. Thus, the real authors of this guide are the avid golfers who shared their experiences with us. We thank each and every one of them – this guide is really theirs.

We are especially grateful to our editing team, Evan Rothman, senior editor at *Travel & Leisure Golf*, Joe Passov, author of *The Unofficial Guide to Golf Vacations in the Eastern U.S.*, and Jim Gorant, who's written for *Sports Illustrated* and *Golf Magazine*, among others.

As companions to this guide, we also publish *Top U.S. Hotels, Resorts & Spas* and *America's Top Restaurants*, in which you can find nearby good food and lodging if the course you're playing doesn't provide these amenities.

To join our next *Golf Survey* or any of our upcoming *Surveys*, just register at zagat.com. Since this is a first-time effort, we would appreciate your comments, suggestions and even criticisms so that we can improve future editions. Please contact us at golf@zagat.com. We look forward to hearing from you.

New York, NY
November 18, 2002

Nina and Tim Zagat

What's New

With the rise of Tiger Woods, Americans have become increasingly fascinated with golf. They want to know more about the sport and where to play it. This new *Zagat Survey* is designed to steer golfers toward the most beautiful and challenging U.S. courses accessible to the public.

Instant Classics: Pacific Dunes' July 2001 unveiling in Coos Bay, Oregon, was the biggest since its sister, Bandon Dunes, opened in 1998. Many of our surveyors rate this duo as this book's strongest one-two punch. Other newcomers certain to become institutions include Cowboys Golf Club in Texas, The Glen Club in Illinois and Pinehills Golf Club in Massachusetts.

Navel Gazing: Golf design's most recent obsession is the recreation of classic layouts. Las Vegas' Royal Links and Texas' Tribute Golf Club pay homage to great holes in the U.K., Texas' two Tour 18 courses crib from the PGA Tour and noted Golden Age designers are celebrated by the new Architects Golf Club in New Jersey, where each hole is a paean to the likes of C.B. MacDonald and Donald Ross. Today's designers even laud their own prior work, e.g. at Bear's Best in Las Vegas and its new sibling in Atlanta, Jack Nicklaus has recreated some of his better-known holes.

If You Rebuild It, They Will Come: The multimillion-dollar renovations at Long Island's Bethpage Black in preparation for the 2002 U.S. Open and at Torrey Pines South in San Diego in hopes of attracting the Open in the future were the highest-profile recent overhauls. Pete Dye tweaked his own work at Harbour Town on Hilton Head Island and the Ocean Course at Kiawah Island. Finally, projects like that at Palmetto Dunes' Robert Trent Jones course have restored and enhanced classic designs of yesteryear.

Chain Links: Trees seem *so* five minutes ago. We're seeing a wave of new, open links-style designs, including The Links at Gettysburg in Pennsylvania, The Links at Pointe West in Florida and Twisted Dunes in New Jersey, all of which give a sense of what play is like at British Isles classics.

Trail Mix: The success of the budget-priced Robert Trent Jones Golf Trail in Alabama is spawning a mini-wave of loosely affiliated reasonably priced courses, including Louisiana's Audubon Golf Trail, Tennessee's Bear Trace and the Texas Golf Trail.

Going Low: The country's economic downturn and years of course overdevelopment have caught up to the golf business. The famed Greenlefe Resort in Florida went into bankruptcy and a handful of other tracks closed, but the most common symptom has been a boon for golfers: a decrease in greens fees at many fine layouts. At an average of $101 for a high-season weekend round, that's a welcome trend.

New York, NY   Evan Rothman
November 18, 2002

ESPN Golf Travel Tips

Leave Your Sticks at Home: That's right, leave 'em in the garage. Consider using rental sets for trips with fewer than three rounds. Rental quality has improved in recent years, "borrowed-club syndrome" dictates you'll play better with someone else's clubs, and you'll save yourself heavy lifting. If you must bring your clubs but don't trust the airlines, consider a club-shipping service.

Get the Best Rates: It's all about the discounts. Check into special rates via corporate affiliations, affinity groups, senior citizenship and frequent-flier clubs. With resorts, when a rate is quoted, always ask: "Is this the lowest price you have?" Usually, calling resorts directly rather than a chain's toll-free number can score you lower rates.

Research Online: The Internet can be your best friend when it comes to getting the lowdown on the links. A wealth of player forums and informational sites provide descriptions, photos and course maps – and you'll often find online-only bargains too. Throughout the guide, you'll find Web site addresses for courses.

Go Against the Grain: Sometimes following the crowd will cost you a pretty penny. If you go to Palm Springs or Scottsdale in the middle of winter, it's a good bet you'll pay top dollar. Don't be afraid to travel during shoulder seasons or to try some less well-known destinations. It doesn't have to be 85 degrees and sunny to play great golf.

Don't Count On a Career Round: Don't expect to score well your first time on any course. GPS, yardage books and pin position sheets can only do so much. Consider planning two rounds at a track you're excited about, or if you're with a group, try a scramble format or a betting game that keeps everyone interested. Remember, golf is supposed to be fun, especially when you're on vacation!

Flash a Little Green: Sometimes, to be treated like a king you need to show the money. Golf isn't a high-paying industry unless your name is Tiger or Jack, so a few bucks' tip should get you the help you need.

Tap-Ins – A Few Final Thoughts: Don't forget the rain gear. Getting stuck on the back nine during a downpour without a jacket can ruin any round. A good travel planner can also make your life easier. So will calling the course a few days in advance to double-check your tee time, make sure the greens aren't being aerated that day and so on.

Lastly, and we can't stress this enough – leave a little time to get lost, and enjoy yourself no matter how you play. After all, it sure beats working!

For more golf news and information, log on to ESPN.com.

Key to Ratings/Symbols

Name, Address, Phone Number, Web Site, Yardage, USGA Rating, Slope

Caddies Available, Carts Only, Restricted Tee Times

Zagat Ratings

	C	F	S	V	$
	17	19	15	18	$195

Tim & Nina's Hole-in-One Resort, Swamp 🏃🛺🕐 ▽

4 Columbus Circle; 212-977-6000; www.zagat.com; 6100/5000; 65.7/63.4; 119/105

◪ "It ain't Pebble Beach", but "play is kinda rocky" anyway at this "rodent-infested" urban course near "scenic" Central Park, where "hackers" and "aging caddies" "duck errant balls"; since "its best hole is the 19th", golfers who gush over "gorgeous links" aren't referring to the "weedy greens" – they mean the "killer hot dogs" from the "snack carts that are always in the way."

Review, with surveyors' comments in quotes

Properties throughout Tops lists are followed by nearest major city/area. The alphabetical index at the back of the book lists their page numbers.

Courses with the highest overall ratings and greatest popularity and importance are printed in CAPITAL LETTERS.

Before each review a symbol indicates whether responses were uniform ■ or mixed ◪.

🏃 Caddies Available
🛺 Carts Only
🕐 Restricted Tee Times (call ahead for public hours)

Reviews note resort courses that are guests-only.

Ratings: Course, Facilities, Service and Value are rated on a scale of **0** to **30**.

C	Course	F	Facilities	S	Service	V	Value
17		19		15		18	

0–9 poor to fair
10–15 fair to good
16–19 good to very good

20–25 very good to excellent
26–30 extraordinary to perfection
▽ low response/less reliable

Price ($) is the cost per non-member or non-guest to play 18 holes on a weekend in high season, excluding the extra cost of a cart. **This is the highest possible price of play.**

Most Popular Courses

Each of our reviewers has been asked to name his or her five favorite courses. The courses most frequently named, in order of their popularity, are:

1. Pebble Beach, *Monterey Peninsula, CA*
2. Bethpage State Park, Black, *Long Island, NY*
3. Spyglass Hill, *Monterey Peninsula, CA*
4. Montauk Downs State Park, *Long Island, NY*
5. Kiawah Island, Ocean, *Charleston, SC*
6. Spanish Bay, *Monterey Peninsula, CA*
7. Aviara, *San Diego, CA*
8. Pinehurst, No. 2, *Pinehurst, NC*
9. Bethpage State Park, Red, *Long Island, NY*
10. Troon North, Monument, *Scottsdale, AZ*
11. Centennial Golf Club, *NYC Metro Area*
12. Pasatiempo, *Santa Cruz, CA*
13. TPC at Sawgrass, Stadium, *Jacksonville, FL*
14. Kapalua, Plantation, *Maui, HI*
15. Crystal Springs, Ballyowen, *NYC Metro Area*
16. Blackwolf Run, River, *Kohler, WI*
17. Torrey Pines, South, *San Diego, CA*
18. Bethpage State Park, Blue, *Long Island, NY*
19. Doral Resort, Blue Monster, *Miami, FL*
20. Poppy Hills, *Monterey Peninsula, CA*
21. Ojai Valley Inn, *Los Angeles, CA*
22. Long Island National, *Long Island, NY*
23. Pelican Hill, Ocean North, *Orange County, CA*
24. Harbour Town Golf Links, *Hilton Head, SC*
25. Whistling Straits, Straits, *Kohler, WI*
26. Challenge at Manele, *Lanai, HI*
27. La Quinta, Mountain, *Palm Springs, CA*
28. World Woods, Pine Barrens, *Tampa, FL*
29. Hominy Hill, *Freehold, NJ*
30. Princeville, Prince, *Kauai, HI**
31. Richter Park, *Danbury, CT*
32. Torrey Pines, North, *San Diego, CA*
33. Boulders, North, *Scottsdale, AZ*
34. Bandon Dunes, Bandon Dunes Course, *Coos Bay, OR*
35. Seaview Marriott, Bay, *Atlantic City, NJ*
36. Cog Hill, No. 4 (Dubsdread), *Chicago, IL*
37. PGA West, TPC Stadium, *Palm Springs, CA*
38. Bethpage State Park, Green, *Long Island, NY*
39. Garrison, *Hudson Valley, NY*
40. Sandpiper, *Santa Barbara, CA**
41. Presidio, *San Francisco Bay Area, CA*
42. Grayhawk, *Raptor, Scottsdale, AZ*
43. Emerald Dunes, *Palm Beach, FL*
44. Bay Hill, *Orlando, FL*
45. Experience at Koele, *Lanai, HI*
46. Great River, *Danbury, CT**
47. Harbor Links, *Long Island, NY**
48. Mansion Ridge, *NYC Metro Area**
49. Caledonia, *Pawleys Island, SC*
50. Poipu Bay, *Kauai, HI**

---

* Tied with course directly above it

Top Ratings

Top 50 Courses

30 Bandon Dunes, Bandon Dunes Course, *Coos Bay, OR*
29 Pebble Beach, *Monterey Peninsula, CA*
Bulle Rock, *Baltimore, MD*
Bethpage State Park, Black, *Long Island, NY*
TPC at Sawgrass, Stadium, *Jacksonville, FL*
Crumpin-Fox Club, *Berkshires, MA*
Whistling Straits, Straits, *Kohler, WI*
Blackwolf Run, River, *Kohler, WI*
Bandon Dunes, Pacific Dunes, *Coos Bay, OR*
Kiawah Island, Ocean, *Charleston, SC*
World Woods, Pine Barrens, *Tampa, FL*
Cowboys, *Dallas, TX*
Shadow Creek, *Las Vegas, NV*
Spyglass Hill, *Monterey Peninsula, CA*
Pinehurst, No. 2, *Pinehurst, NC*
Capitol Hill, Judge, *Montgomery, AL*
Reynolds Plantation, Great Waters, *Lake Oconee, GA*
28 Longaberger, *Columbus, OH*
Edgewood Tahoe, *Reno, NV*
Princeville, Prince, *Kauai, HI*
Troon North, Monument, *Scottsdale, AZ*
Gold Mountain, Olympic, *Bremerton, WA*
Kapalua, Plantation, *Maui, HI*
Barefoot Resort, Fazio, *Myrtle Beach, SC*
Reflection Bay, *Las Vegas, NV*
Eagle Ridge, The General, *Galena, IL*
Challenge at Manele, *Lanai, HI*
Arcadia Bluffs, *Traverse City, MI*
Pinehills, Jones, *Boston, MA**
Homestead, Cascades, *Roanoke, VA*
PGA Oak Valley, Champions, *San Bernardino, CA*
Troon North, Pinnacle, *Scottsdale, AZ*
Caledonia Golf & Fish Club, *Pawleys Island, SC*
Ridge at Castle Pines North, *Denver, CO**
Harbour Town Golf Links, *Hilton Head, SC*
Silver Lakes, *Anniston, AL*
Sugarloaf, *Central ME*
Primm Valley, Lakes, *Las Vegas, NV*
Pasatiempo, *Santa Cruz, CA*
Country Club of New Seabury, Ocean, *Cape Cod, MA*
Tanglewood Park, Championship, *Winston-Salem, NC*
World Golf Village, King & Bear, *Jacksonville, FL*
Barton Creek, Fazio Canyons, *Austin, TX*
Cog Hill, No. 4 (Dubsdread), *Chicago, IL**
Falls Resort & Club, *Houston, TX*
Glen Club, The, *Chicago, IL*
La Purisima, *Santa Barbara, CA*
Pine Needles Lodge, *Pinehurst, NC*
Bay Hill, *Orlando, FL*
Carolina National, *Myrtle Beach Area*

---

* Tied with course directly above it

Top Courses by Region

Arizona
- **28** Troon North, Monument, *Scottsdale*
  Troon North, Pinnacle, *Scottsdale*
  We-Ko-Pa, *Scottsdale*
- **27** Grayhawk, Talon, *Scottsdale*
  Ventana Canyon, Mountain, *Tucson*
  Boulders, North, *Scottsdale*
  Grayhawk, Raptor, *Scottsdale*
  Arizona National, *Tucson*
  Boulders, South, *Scottsdale*
- **26** Ventana Canyon, Canyon, *Tucson*

California
- **29** Pebble Beach, *Monterey Peninsula*
  Spyglass Hill, *Monterey Peninsula*
- **28** PGA Oak Valley, Champions, *San Bernardino*
  Pasatiempo, *Santa Cruz*
  La Purisima, *Santa Barbara*
- **27** Maderas, *San Diego*
  Torrey Pines, South, *San Diego*
  Marriott Shadow Ridge, *Palm Springs*
  Desert Willow, Firecliff, *Palm Springs*
- **26** Pelican Hill, Ocean North, *Orange County*

Florida
- **29** TPC at Sawgrass, Stadium, *Jacksonville*
  World Woods, Pine Barrens, *Tampa*
- **28** World Golf Village, King & Bear, *Jacksonville*
  Bay Hill, *Orlando*
- **27** Orange County National, Panther Lake, *Orlando*
  World Woods, Rolling Oaks, *Tampa*
  Ocean Hammock, *Daytona Beach*
  Emerald Dunes, *Palm Beach*
- **26** El Diablo, *Ocala*
  PGA Golf Club, North, *Port St. Lucie*

Hawaii
- **28** Princeville, Prince, *Kauai*
  Kapalua, Plantation, *Maui*
  Challenge at Manele, *Lanai*
- **27** Mauna Kea, *Big Island*
  Kauai Lagoons, Kiele, *Kauai*
  Poipu Bay, *Kauai*
- **26** Experience at Koele, *Lanai*
  Mauna Lani, North, *Big Island*
  Hualalai Golf Club, *Big Island*
  Mauna Lani, South, *Big Island*

Mid-Atlantic (DC, DE, MD, PA, VA, WV)
- **29** Bulle Rock, *Baltimore, MD*
- **28** Homestead, Cascades, *Roanoke, VA*
- **27** Links at Lighthouse Sound, *Ocean City, MD*
  Golden Horseshoe, Gold, *Williamsburg, VA*
  Whiskey Creek, *Frederick, VA*
  Atlantic Golf At Queenstown Harbor, River, *Easton, MD*
  Rum Pointe Seaside Golf Links, *Ocean City, MD*
  Kingsmill Resort, River, *Williamsburg, VA*
- **26** Augustine, *DC Metro Area*
  Nemacolin Woodlands, Mystic Rock, *Pittsburgh, PA*

Midwest (IL, IN, KS, MI, MN, MO, OH, OK, WI)
29 Whistling Straits, Straits, *Kohler, WI*
Blackwolf Run, River, *Kohler, WI*
28 Longaberger, *Columbus, OH*
Eagle Ridge, The General, *Galena, IL*
Arcadia Bluffs, *Traverse City, MI*
Cog Hill, No. 4 (Dubsdread), *Chicago, IL*
Glen Club, *Chicago, IL*
Chaska Town, *Minneapolis, MN*
27 University Ridge, *Madison, WI*
Bay Harbor, *Petoskey, MI*

New England (MA, ME, NH, RI, VT)
29 Crumpin-Fox Club, *Berkshires, MA*
28 Pinehills, Jones, *Boston, MA*
Sugarloaf, *Central ME*
Country Club of New Seabury, Ocean, *Cape Cod, MA*
26 Taconic, *Berkshires, MA*
Balsams Panorama, *Colebrook, NH*
Farm Neck, *Martha's Vineyard, MA*
Waverly Oaks, Championship, *Boston, MA*
25 Samoset, *Southern ME*
Green Mountain National, *Southern VT*

New York & Environs (CT, NJ, NY)
29 Bethpage State Park, Black, *Long Island, NY*
27 Richter Park, *Danbury, CT*
Seven Oaks, *Finger Lakes, NY*
Hominy Hill, *Freehold, NJ*
Great River, *Danbury, CT*
Pine Hill, *Cape May, NJ*
Leatherstocking, *Albany, NY*
Crystal Springs, Ballyowen, *NYC Metro Area*
26 Links at Hiawatha Landing, *Finger Lakes, NY*
Sand Barrens, *Cape May, NJ*

Pacific Northwest (OR, WA)
30 Bandon Dunes, Bandon Dunes Course, *Coos Bay, OR*
29 Bandon Dunes, Pacific Dunes, *Coos Bay, OR*
28 Gold Mountain, Olympic, *Bremerton, WA*
27 Sunriver, Crosswater, *Bend, OR*
Desert Canyon, *Wenatchee, WA*
Pumpkin Ridge, Ghost Creek, *Portland, OR*
25 Tokatee, *Eugene, OR*
McCormick Woods, *Bremerton, WA*
23 Black Butte Ranch, Big Meadow, *Bend, OR*
22 Washington National, *Seattle, WA*

Rocky Mountains (CO, ID, MT, NV, UT, WY)
29 Shadow Creek, *Las Vegas, NV*
28 Edgewood Tahoe, *Reno, NV*
Reflection Bay, *Las Vegas, NV*
Ridge at Castle Pines North, *Denver, CO*
Primm Valley, Lakes, *Las Vegas, NV*
Entrada at Snow Canyon, *St. George, UT*
27 Thanksgiving Point, *Salt Lake City, UT*
Coeur d'Alene Resort, *Coeur d'Alene, ID*
Primm Valley, Desert, *Las Vegas, NV*
26 Las Vegas Paiute Resort, Snow Mountain, *Las Vegas, NV*

Southeast (AL, AR, GA, KY, LA, MS, NC, SC, TN)

29 Kiawah Island, Ocean, *Charleston, SC*
Pinehurst, No. 2, *Pinehurst, NC*
Capitol Hill, Judge, *Montgomery, AL*
Reynolds Plantation, Great Waters, *Lake Oconee, GA*
28 Barefoot, Fazio, *Myrtle Beach Area*
Caledonia Golf & Fish Club, *Pawleys Island, SC*
Harbour Town Golf Links, *Hilton Head, SC*
Silver Lakes, *Anniston, AL*
Tanglewood Park, Championship, *Winston-Salem, NC*
Pine Needles Lodge, *Pinehurst, NC*

Southwest (NM, TX)

29 Cowboys, *Dallas*
28 Barton Creek, Fazio Canyons, *Austin*
Falls Resort & Club, *Houston*
La Cantera, Palmer, *San Antonio*
27 Barton Creek, Fazio Foothills, *Austin*
Woodlands Resort, TPC, *Houston*
Four Seasons Las Colinas, TPC, *Dallas*
La Cantera, Resort, *San Antonio*
26 Four Seasons Las Colinas, Cottonwood Valley, *Dallas*
Horseshoe Bay, Ram Rock, *Austin*

Tops by Special Feature

In some categories, clubs with more than one course are listed only once, according to their highest Course rating.

Budget ($40 and under)
29 Bethpage State Park, Black, *Long Island, NY*
25 Tokatee, *Eugene, OR*
Montauk Downs State Park, *Long Island, NY*
Riverdale, Dunes, *Denver, CO*
23 Buffalo Run, *Denver, CO*
22 Heron Lakes, Great Blue, *Portland, OR*
21 Ridgeview Ranch, *Dallas, TX*
19 Pacific Grove, *Monterey Peninsula, CA*

Conditioning
30 Bandon Dunes, Bandon Dunes Course, *Coos Bay, OR*
29 Bethpage State Park, Black, *Long Island, NY*
Whistling Straits, Straits, *Kohler, WI*
28 Longaberger, *Columbus, OH*
Princeville, Prince, *Kauai, HI*
Troon North, Monument, *Scottsdale, AZ*
27 Couer d'Alene Resort, *Coeur d'Alene, ID*
26 Pinehurst, No. 8, *Pinehurst, NC*

Environmentally Friendly
29 TPC at Sawgrass, *Jacksonville, FL*
Pumpkin Ridge, *Portland, OR*
Reynolds Plantation, *Lake Oconee, GA*
28 Pasatiempo, *Santa Cruz, CA*
Barton Creek, *Austin, TX*
26 Broadmoor, *Colorado Springs, CO*
23 Regatta Bay, *Panhandle, FL*
20 Widow's Walk, *Boston, MA*

Expense Account ($200 and over)
29 Pebble Beach, *Monterey Peninsula, CA*
TPC at Sawgrass, Stadium, *Jacksonville, FL*
Whistling Straits, Straits, *Kohler, WI*
Kiawah Island, Ocean, *Charleston, SC*
Shadow Creek, *Las Vegas, NV*
Spyglass Hill, *Monterey Peninsula, CA*
Pinehurst, No. 2, *Pinehurst, NC*
28 Troon North, Monument, *Scottsdale, AZ*

Fine Food Too
29 Pebble Beach, *Monterey Peninsula, CA*
Whistling Straits/Blackwolf Run, *Kohler, WI*
26 Experience at Koele, *Lanai, HI*
Aviara, *San Diego, CA*
Greenbrier, *White Sulphur Springs, WV*
Broadmoor, *Colorado Springs, CO*
23 Sea Island, *Lowcountry, GA*
Bali Hai, *Las Vegas, NV*

Instruction
28 Reflection Bay, *Las Vegas, NV*
PGA at Oak Valley, *San Bernardino, CA*
27 Whiskey Creek, *Frederick, MD*
Treetops, *Traverse City, MI*
26 Doral, *Miami, FL*
Rio Secco, *Las Vegas, NV*
Wyncote, *Philadelphia, PA*
22 ChampionsGate, *Orlando, FL*

Newcomers/Rated

29 Cowboys, *Dallas, TX*
28 Pinehills, Jones, *Boston, MA*
    Glen Club, The, *Chicago, IL*
    We-Ko-Pa, *Scottsdale, AZ*
25 Architects, *Trenton, NJ*
    Branton Woods, *Hudson Valley, NY*
    Black Gold, *Yorba Linda, CA*
    CrossCreek, *Temecula, CA*

Newcomers/Unrated

    Bear Trace at Ross Creek Landing, *Nashville, TN*
    Belterra, *Cincinnati Area*
    Eagle Ranch, *Vail, CO*
    Grande Dunes, *Myrtle Beach Area*
    Independence, *Richmond, VA*
    Redlands Mesa, *Denver, CO*
    RiverTowne, *Charleston, SC*
    Wolf Creek, *Las Vegas, NV*

19th Holes

29 TPC at Sawgrass, *Jacksonville, FL*
    Kiawah Island, *Charleston, SC*
28 Homestead, *Roanoke, VA*
    Harbour Town Golf Links, *Hilton Head, SC*
    We-Ko-Pa, *Scottsdale, AZ*
26 Spanish Bay, *Monterey Peninsula, CA*
    Doral, *Miami, FL*
25 Ojai Valley Inn, *Los Angeles, CA*

Player-Friendly

27 Coeur d'Alene Resort, *Coeur d'Alene, ID*
25 Long Island Nat'l, *Long Island, NY*
24 Eaglesticks, *Columbus, OH*
23 Doral Resort, Great White, *Miami, FL*
    Captains, Port, *Cape Cod, MA*
    Cog Hill, No. 2, *Chicago, IL*
22 Kingsmill Resort, Plantation, *Williamsburg, VA*
    Pinehurst, No. 1, *Pinehurst, NC*

Practice Facilities

29 TPC at Sawgrass, *Jacksonville, FL*
    World Woods, *Tampa, FL*
    Pinehurst, *Pinehurst, NC*
28 Longaberger, *Columbus, OH*
27 Grayhawk, *Scottsdale, AZ*
    Four Seasons at Las Colinas, *Dallas, TX*
25 PGA Golf Club, *Port St. Lucie, FL*
    PGA West, *Palm Springs, CA*

Pro Shops

30 Bandon Dunes, *Coos Bay, OR*
29 Pebble Beach, *Monterey Peninsula, CA*
    TPC at Sawgrass, *Jacksonville, FL*
    Pinehurst, *Pinehurst, NC*
28 Troon North, *Scottsdale, AZ*
    La Cantera, *San Antonio, TX*
25 Wailea, *Maui, HI*
23 Marriott Desert Springs, *Palms Springs, CA*

Resorts

29 Pebble Beach, *Monterey Peninsula, CA*
    Whistling Straits/Blackwolf Run, *Kohler, WI*
    Pinehurst, *Pinehurst, SC*
    Reynolds Plantation, *Lake Oconee, GA*
28 Troon North, *Scottsdale, AZ*
    Challenge at Manele, *Lanai, HI*
26 Aviara, *San Diego, CA*
    Hualalai, *Big Island, HI*

Scenic

30 Bandon Dunes, Bandon Dunes Course, *Coos Bay, OR*
29 Pebble Beach, *Monterey Peninsula, CA*
28 Edgewood Tahoe, *Reno, NV*
    Challenge at Manele, *Lanai, HI*
    Ridge at Castle Pines North, *Denver, CO*
    Sugarloaf, *Central ME*
    Entrada at Snow Canyon, *St. George, UT*
27 Boulders, North, *Scottsdale, AZ*

Toughest

30 Bandon Dunes, Bandon Dunes Course, *Coos Bay, OR*
29 Bulle Rock, *Baltimore, MD*
    Bethpage State Park, Black, *Long Island, NY*
    TPC at Sawgrass, Stadium, *Jacksonville, FL*
    Whistling Straits, Straits, *Kohler, WI*
    Blackwolf Run, River, *Kohler, WI*
    Kiawah Island, Ocean, *Charleston, SC*
    Spyglass Hill, *Monterey Peninsula, CA*

Women-Friendly

28 Pine Needles, *Pinehurst, NC*
26 Spanish Bay Inn, *Monterey Peninsula, CA*
    LPGA International, Legends, *Daytona Beach, FL*
    Broadmoor, East, *Boulder, CO*
25 Legacy Ridge, *Boulder, CO*
    Wailea, Emerald, *Maui, HI*
    Twelve Bridges, *Sacramento, CA*
23 Deer Creek, *Ft. Lauderdale, FL*

Top 50 Facilities

Facilities includes clubhouses, pro shops, practice areas, restaurants and, at resorts, lodging and other amenities. Clubs with more than one course are listed only once, according to their highest rating.

29 Longaberger, *Columbus, OH*
Greenbrier, *White Sulphur Springs, WV*
Whistling Straits/Blackwolf Run, *Kohler, WI*
Bay Harbor, *Petoskey, MI*
Shadow Creek, *Las Vegas, NV*
28 Broadmoor, *Boulder, CO*
Golf Club at Newcastle, *Seattle, WA*
Pinehurst, *Pinehurst, NC*
Four Seasons Las Colinas, *Dallas, TX*
Silver Lakes, *Anniston, AL*
Grand National, *Auburn, AL*
27 TPC at Sawgrass, *Jacksonville, FL*
Links at Lighthouse Sound, *Ocean City, MD*
Capitol Hill, *Montgomery, AL*
Great River, *Danbury, CT*
World Golf Village, *Jacksonville, FL*
Bulle Rock, *Baltimore, MD*
Pinehills, *Boston, MA*
Pebble Beach, *Monterey Peninsula, CA*
Glen Club, The, *Chicago, IL*
Boulders, *Scottsdale, AZ*
Grand National, *Auburn, AL*
Hualalai, *Big Island, HI*
Princeville, *Kauai, HI*
Kapalua, *Maui , HI*
Aviara, *San Diego, CA*
Kingsmill, *Williamsburg, VA*
Grayhawk, *Scottsdale, AZ*
Coeur d'Alene Resort, *Coeur d'Alene, ID*
Troon North, *Scottsdale, AZ*
Bandon Dunes, *Coos Bay, OR*
Grayhawk, *Scottsdale, AZ*
Pumpkin Ridge, *Portland, OR*
Reflection Bay, *Las Vegas, NV*
26 Spanish Bay, *Monterey Peninsula, CA*
La Cantera, *San Antonio, TX*
Grand Cypress, *Orlando, FL*
Experience at Koele, *Lanai, HI*
Cowboys, *Dallas, TX*
Ridge at Castle Pines, *Denver, CO*
Tiburon, *Naples, FL*
Challenge at Manele, *Lanai, HI*
Barton Creek, *Austin, TX*
Grand Traverse Resort, *Traverse City, MI*
Arcadia Bluffs, *Traverse City, MI*
Hyatt Hill, *San Antonio, TX*
Orange County National, *Orlando, FL*
Eagle Ridge, *Galena, IL*
Mauna Lani, *Big Island, HI*
Eagle Ridge, The General, *Galena, IL*

Top 50 Service

Clubs with more than one course are listed only once, according to their highest rating.

29 Silver Lakes, *Anniston, AL*
Longaberger, *Columbus, OH*
28 Whistling Straits/Blackwolf Run, *Kohler, WI*
Shadow Creek, *Las Vegas, NV*
Greenbrier, *White Sulphur Springs, WV*
Bulle Rock, *Baltimore, MD*
27 Hualalai Golf Club, *Big Island, HI*
Boulders, *Scottsdale, AZ*
Experience at Koele, *Lanai, HI*
Golf Club at Newcastle, *Seattle, WA*
Pinehurst, *Pinehurst, NC*
Bandon Dunes, *Coos Bay, OR*
Four Seasons Las Colinas, *Dallas, TX*
Boulders, *Scottsdale, AZ*
Grayhawk, *Scottsdale, AZ*
Cowboys, *Dallas, TX*
Bay Harbor, *Petoskey, MI*
Broadmoor, *Boulder, CO*
Coeur d'Alene Resort, *Coeur d'Alene, ID*
Primm Valley, *Las Vegas, NV*
Pebble Beach, *Monterey Peninsula, CA*
26 Raven at South Mountain, *Phoenix, AZ*
Kapalua, *Maui, HI*
Links at Lighthouse Sound, *Ocean City, MD*
Pinehills, *Boston, MA*
World Golf Village, *Jacksonville, FL*
Challenge at Manele, *Lanai, HI*
Tiburon, *Naples, FL*
La Cantera, *San Antonio, TX*
Troon North, *Scottsdale, AZ*
Grand National, *Auburn, AL*
Spanish Bay, *Monterey Peninsula, CA*
Bay Hill, *Orlando, FL*
Homestead, *Roanoke, VA*
Cambrian Ridge, *Montgomery, AL*
Rio Secco, *Las Vegas, NV*
Pine Lakes International, *Myrtle Beach, SC*
Princeville, *Kauai, HI*
Grand National, *Auburn, AL*
Aviara, *San Diego, CA*
Ojai Valley Inn, *Los Angeles, CA*
PGA Golf Club, *Port St. Lucie, FL*
Mauna Lani, *Big Island, HI*
Great River, *Stamford, CT*
We-Ko-Pa, *Scottsdale, AZ*
Oxmoor Valley, *Birmingham, AL*
25 Capitol Hill, *Montgomery, AL*
Lost Canyons, *Los Angeles, CA*
Balsams Panorama, *Colebrook, NH*
Grand Cypress, *Orlando, FL*

Top 50 Values

29 Bethpage State Park, Black, *Long Island, NY*
28 Capitol Hill, Judge, *Montgomery, AL*
Grand National, Links, *Auburn, AL*
Bethpage State Park, Red, *Long Island, NY*
Silver Lakes, *Anniston, AL*
Cambrian Ridge, *Montgomery, AL*
Gold Mountain, Olympic, *Bremerton, WA*
Tanglewood Park, Championship, *Winston-Salem, NC*
Capitol Hill, Senator, *Montgomery, AL*
27 PGA Golf Club, South, *Port St. Lucie, FL*
Bethpage State Park, Blue, *Long Island, NY*
Pacific Grove, *Monterey Peninsula, CA*
PGA Golf Club, North, *Port St. Lucie, FL*
Poppy Ridge, *San Francisco Bay Area, CA*
Bethpage State Park, Green, *Long Island, NY*
26 Grand National, Lake, *Auburn, AL*
Hominy Hill, *Freehold, NJ*
Univ. of New Mexico Championship, *Albuquerque, NM*
PGA Golf Club, Pete Dye, *Port St. Lucie, FL*
Bandon Dunes, Pacific Dunes, *Coos Bay, OR*
Heritage Bluffs, *Chicago, IL*
Montauk Downs State Park, *Long Island, NY*
Tokatee, *Eugene, OR*
Bandon Dunes, Bandon Dunes Course, *Coos Bay, OR*
25 Capitol Hill, Legislator, *Montgomery, AL*
Shenandoah Valley, *Front Royal, VA*
PGA Oak Valley, Legends, *San Bernardino, CA*
Seven Oaks, *Finger Lakes, NY*
Oxmoor Valley, Ridge, *Birmingham, AL*
World Woods, Pine Barrens, *Tampa, FL*
Orange County National, Crooked Cat, *Orlando, FL*
Riverdale, Dunes, *Boulder, CO*
World Woods, Rolling Oaks, *Tampa, FL*
Flanders Valley, White/Blue, *NYC Metro Area*
Windmill Lakes, *Akron, OH*
Meadows Farms, *DC Metro Area*
PGA Oak Valley, Champions, *San Bernardino, CA*
Howell Park, *Freehold, NJ*
Mission Inn, El Campeon, *Orlando, FL*
Gold Creek, *Atlanta, GA*
La Purisima, *Santa Barbara, CA*
Buffalo Run, *Boulder, CO*
Memorial Park, *Houston, TX*
Links at Hiawatha Landing, *Finger Lakes, NY*
24 Duke University, *Raleigh-Durham, NC*
Flanders Valley, Red/Gold, *NYC Metro Area*
University Ridge, *Madison, WI*
Oxmoor Valley, Valley, *Birmingham, AL*
LPGA International, Legends, *Daytona Beach, FL*
Primm Valley, Desert, *Las Vegas, NV*

Top Tournaments Guide

Programming schedules are subject to change. Check your local listings for details.

Dates	Tournament	Television	Course	Location
February 26-March 2	Accenture Match Play Championship	ESPN/ABC	La Costa Resort and Spa	Carlsbad, CA
March 27-30	THE PLAYERS Championship	ESPN/NBC	TPC at Sawgrass	Ponte Vedra Beach, FL
March 27-30	Kraft Nabisco Championship	ESPN/ABC	Mission Hills Country Club	Rancho Mirage, CA
April 10-13	The Masters	USA/CBS	Augusta National Golf Club	Augusta, GA
June 5-8	McDonald's LPGA Championship	CBS	The DuPont Country Club	Wilmington, DE
June 5-8	Senior PGA Championship	ESPN/NBC	Aronimink Golf Club	Newtown Square, PA
June 12-15	U.S. Open	ESPN/NBC	Olympia Fields Country Club	Olympia Fields, IL
June 26-29	U.S. Senior Open	ESPN/NBC	Inverness Club	Toledo, OH
July 3-6	U.S. Women's Open	ESPN/NBC	Pumpkin Ridge Golf Club	North Plains, OR
July 17-20	British Open	TNT/ABC	Royal St. George's Golf Club	Kent, England
July 24-27	Senior British Open	TNT/ABC	Turnberry	Ayrshire, Scotland
July 31-August 3	Women's British Open	TNT/ABC	Royal Lytham St. Annes	Lancashire, England
August 14-17	PGA Championship	TNT/CBS	Oak Hill Country Club	Rochester, NY
August 21-24	NEC Invitational	ESPN/CBS	Firestone Country Club	Akron, OH
October 2-5	American Express Championship	ESPN/ABC	The Capital City Club	Atlanta, GA
November 6-9	THE TOUR Championship	ESPN/ABC	Champions Golf Club	Houston, TX
November 13-16	EMC World Cup	ESPN/ABC	The Ocean Course	Kiawah Island, SC
November 21-23	The President's Cup	TNT/NBC	The Links at Fancourt	George, South Africa

Course Directory

Alabama

Anniston

SILVER LAKES   28 | 28 | 29 | 28 | $60
1 Sunbelt Pkwy., Glencoe; 256-892-3268; www.rtjgolf.com
Backbreaker/Heartbreaker: 7674/4865; 78.2/68.8; 152/124
Heartbreaker/Mindbreaker: 7207/4685; 77.1/68.3; 142/122
Mindbreaker/Backbreaker: 7225/4686; 76.1/67.5; 148/118

■ 'Backbreaker', 'Mindbreaker', 'Heartbreaker': "take these names seriously" warn angst-ridden roundsmen on this "beautiful", forested Robert Trent Jones Trail "test" with 27 "excellent" holes that'll "scare the pants off you" east of Birmingham near the Georgia border; "it doesn't matter which order you play the nines – they are all hard", though most masochists consider the one that shatters your heart the toughest and the one that blows your mind the easiest, and while some pampered putters moan "the greens are too undulating", the "low pricing" for excellent service and facilities isn't sadistic at all.

Auburn

GRAND NATIONAL, LAKE   26 | 28 | 26 | 26 | $57
3000 Sunbelt Pkwy., Opelika; 334-749-9011; 800-949-4444;
www.rtjgolf.com; 7149/4910; 74.9/68.7; 138/117

■ "Promise me you'll scatter my ashes" at this "golfer's dream", plead players pondering that great fairway in the sky; "even in the rain", the "Robert Trent Jones Trail jewel" shines with "beautiful scenery" and "multi-tiered, large greens"; those who say it's "not as good as the Links course" have to agree that Alabama's No. 1–rated Facilities offer "outstanding value."

GRAND NATIONAL, LINKS   27 | 27 | 26 | 28 | $57
3000 Sunbelt Pkwy., Opelika; 334-749-9011; 800-949-4444;
www.rtjgolf.com; 7311/4843; 74.9/69.6; 141/113

◪ Thanks to "tall fescue" roughs and a "killer finishing hole", this "testy" track might be "both the most frustrating and the most fulfilling course you ever play", and at prices like these, "what a steal of a deal" it is; a macho minority mashes RTJ's "elevated" greens as "a little too Micky Mouse for their taste."

Birmingham

Oxmoor Valley, Ridge   26 | 25 | 24 | 25 | $57
100 Sunbelt Pkwy.; 205-942-1177; 800-949-4444; www.rtjgolf.com;
7055/4974; 73.5/69.1; 140/122

■ "Well worth the trip to Alabama!" gush enthusiasts of this "hilly", "demanding" "must-stop" on the Robert Trent Jones Trail; voted Most Popular in Alabama, it offers "incredible value" on many "breathtakingly beautiful holes" at "surprising" elevations, leading aerobicizers to suggest "walk it if you want to burn 6,000 calories."

Oxmoor Valley, Valley   25 | 25 | 25 | 24 | $57
100 Sunbelt Pkwy.; 205-942-1177; 800-949-4444; www.rtjgolf.com;
7292/4899; 73.9/69.4; 135/122

◪ Putting pals proclaim just 'cause it's "much easier than its partner", don't fool yourself that the "low country–style course"

"at this Birmingham complex" isn't a "challenge" – "if you think that
the putting green is tough, wait until you see some of the actual
ones"; club-wielding critics counter there are "some fairly good
holes, but others are pretty forgettable."

Huntsville

Hampton Cove, Highlands   ∇ 21 | 24 | 23 | 24 | $60
450 Old Hwy. 431, Owens Cross Roads; 256-551-1818; 800-949-4444;
www.rtjgolf.com; 7262/4765; 75/68.3; 133/113
■ Golfers make their deals with this devil in Owens Cross Roads in
northeast Alabama; it's "nicely laid out", but "if you are not accurate
with your approach shots, it can be very tough", as "the sand
bunkers are placed exactly where your irons would come up
short in the shot to the green"; laced with Japanese black pines,
dogwoods, oaks, crepe myrtles and creeks, it wows ball-whacking
worshipers who swear "you haven't golfed until you've played the
Robert Trent Jones Trail."

Hampton Cove, River   ∇ 19 | 23 | 24 | 23 | $60
450 Old Hwy. 431, Owens Cross Roads; 256-551-1818; 800-949-4444;
www.rtjgolf.com; 7667/5278; 76/70.4; 130/119
■ "All can enjoy" this Robert Trent Jones Sr. Trailster; fashioned on
former soybean fields with loads of water and massive, old oaks
but not a single home or bunker in sight, it's a swim downstream
under "top-rate course conditions", with "five sets of tee boxes"
and large, elevated greens at "a great value."

Mobile

Craft Farms, Cotton Creek   21 | 20 | 21 | 19 | $70
3840 Cotton Creek Blvd., Gulf Shores; 251-968-7500; 800-327-2657;
www.craftfarms.com; 7028/5175; 74.1/70.9; 136/122
◪ Club-wielders take a cotton to this Gulf Coast Arnold Palmer
layout because it "allows you room for error on drive and approach
shots" on rolling hills and undulating dance floors with plenty of
risk/reward choices at a "well-handled, big operation" with a "very
friendly staff"; contrarians creak that it's "starting to show its age
a little", with "almost crusty greens" and "overbooking, just like
the airline" you took to get down here.

Craft Farms, Cypress Bend   ∇ 16 | 19 | 21 | 20 | $70
3840 Cotton Creek Blvd., Gulf Shores; 251-968-7500; 800-327-2657;
www.craftfarms.com; 6848/5048; 72.4/68.4; 127/112
◪ The newest of the Craft Farms trio, designed by Arnold Palmer,
is "a very nice course that is fair and fun to play" as it winds wide
open through hills, lakes, ponds and lots of large bunkers; putting
pollyannas praise "excellent customer service", while belligerent
ball wallopers bend the other way, bawling "something went
wrong" on "way too many" dizzying doglegs, "nondescript par 3s"
and "greens in such bad shape that the $75 fee should be $7.50."

Craft Farms, The Woodlands   ∇ 20 | 19 | 22 | 23 | $70
3840 Cotton Creek Blvd., Gulf Shores; 251-968-7500; 800-327-2657;
www.craftfarms.com; 6484/5145; 70.8/67.9; 123/109
■ "Ladies and gentlemen, if you're traveling through southern
Alabama, put this course on the menu" say self-made golf guides

of this layout "for the average hack who wants to enjoy the day and shoot a decent score" at a decent price; "wetlands, pines and 100-year-old oaks" do "require accuracy" because "errant shots enter snake territory."

Kiva Dunes   25 | 20 | 22 | 18 | $96

815 Plantation Rd., Gulf Shores; 251-540-7000;
7092/5006; 73.9/68.5; 132/115
■ You'll "love the dunes" say beach buffs of this "gem" "on a peninsula with the Atlantic Ocean on one side and Mobile Bay on the other" that's sculpted through "beautiful natural" areas filled with lakes and a whole "lot of sand"; you might want to wear protective goggles and you should "expect to add a few strokes" and "use your full bag" "in windy conditions", while on "the one day of the year with no gusts", "the gnats will carry you off", if the "marshals who treat golfers like chess pieces" don't get to you first.

Peninsula Golf & Racquet ⚲   26 | 25 | 23 | 22 | $82

20 Peninsula Blvd., Gulf Shores; 251-968-8009;
www.peninsulagolfclub.com
Cypress/Lakes: 7055/4978; 74/69.6; 131/121
Lakes/Marsh: 7026/5072; 73.8/68.7; 130/115
Marsh/Cypress: 7179/5080; 74.7/70.1; 133/120
◨ Surrounded by the Bon Secour Wildlife Preserve on the shores of Mobile Bay, "the setting is an oasis that is worth coming back to every year" sigh nature lovers lobbing golf balls on this "beautiful" 27-hole course with "water, water everywhere", and apparently much of it to drink at the bar in the "excellent clubhouse"; given "Tour conditions", a bang-up practice area and a "staff that treats you right", it's "well worth the price", even though all those back-to-the-land types tsk it "was much better before the houses showed up" along the fairways.

Rock Creek   ▽ 26 | 25 | 23 | 25 | $63

140 Clubhouse Dr., Fairhope; 251-928-4223; www.rockcreekgolf.com;
6920/5157; 72.2/69.2; 129/123
■ "Set in a residential community" on Mobile Bay's eastern shore, this "relatively undiscovered gem" poses a "hell of a challenge", dramatically designed with "rolling hills, uneven terrain" and "beautiful trees lining great golf holes"; those who know it say it's a "well-maintained" "must-play" where a staff that "treats you just like family" embodies Southern hospitality.

TimberCreek   20 | 19 | 19 | 21 | $55

9650 Timbercreek Blvd., Daphne; 334-621-9900; 888-621-9980;
www.golftimbercreek.com
Dogwood/Magnolia: 7062/4885; 72.2/66.7; 130/106
Magnolia/Pines: 7090/4990; 72.2/67.8; 126/107
Pines/Dogwood: 6928/4911; 71.8/66.7; 122/105
■ "Almost as good as Rock Creek", this is "a great second course to play on a golf trip to the Mobile area" say savvy surveyors of this 27-holer that features a fine clubhouse, a multitude of wildlife and tremendous elevation changes as it zigzags through forests; Dogwood/Magnolia is often cited as the "toughest combination of the three" nines, but all of the track "stays in great shape year round for you snowbirds."

Montgomery

CAMBRIAN RIDGE
27 | 26 | 26 | 28 | $57

101 Sunbelt Pkwy., Greenville; 334-382-9787; www.rtjgolf.com
Canyon/Sherling: 7325/4857; 73.3/68.0; 141/127
Loblolly/Canyon: 7297/4772; 74.5/67.7; 139/124
Sherling/Loblolly: 7130/4785; 73.8/66.9; 132/119

■ "The best all-around value on the Robert Trent Jones Trail" can be had on the "challenging", "visually stunning Canyon/Sherling combo" at this "out-of-the-way" 27-hole venue that's "well worth the trip" 40 miles south of Montgomery; bring your vertigo pills for the "unbelievable elevation changes" on "great terrain" that is peppered with dramatic bunkers, towering trees and "memorable holes", even on the easier Loblolly nine.

CAPITOL HILL, JUDGE 🏖
29 | 27 | 25 | 28 | $80

2600 Constitution Ave., Prattville; 334-285-1114; www.rtjgolf.com;
7719/4968; 77.8/68.3; 144/121

■ "The spectacular first hole alone is worth the price of admission" to the "best course on the RTJ Trail", judged Alabama's No. 1 for its "impossible par 3s" and a 700-plus-yard par 5 that make some feel they're "playing a U.S. Open course"; situated 10 miles from Montgomery alongside the Alabama River, it's a capital "bayou adventure" where "winding, elevation drops" put players through a "magnificent", "relentless" "test of skill and strength."

Capitol Hill, Legislator 🏖
25 | 26 | 25 | 25 | $70

2600 Constitution Ave., Prattville; 334-285-1114; www.rtjgolf.com;
7323/5414; 74.1/71.5; 126/119

☑ Supporters say it might not wield as much power as the Senator or the Judge, but this "awesome", traditional Carolinas-style spread carved amid huge pines is still "nice" and "challenging", and the facilities and service are "excellent" at the business-friendly resort; putters in the opposing party are "disappointed", voting it "ordinary" and speculating that "Jones Sr. didn't have enough room for this third 18."

CAPITOL HILL, SENATOR 🏖
26 | 27 | 26 | 28 | $70

2600 Constitution Ave., Prattville; 334-285-1114; www.rtjgolf.com;
7726/5122; 76.6/67.6; 131/115

■ "Scottish links in Alabama – never thought it was possible", and yet here they are at this "lovely, windswept" Robert Trent Jones Trail track with "stunning" towering mounds, 150-plus pot bunkers and "many blind shots"; "be ready with a case of balls" because scoring might be "impossible", though an "outstanding value" means that paying for it isn't.

Alaska

Anchorage

Eagleglen
– | – | – | – | $35

4414 First St.; 907-552-3821; www.elmendorfservices.com;
6687/5307; 71.6/70.9; 127/123

Long heralded as a top Alaska track, this 1973 RTJ Jr. design on the Elmendorf Air Force Base just north of Anchorage occupies a handsome setting on Ship Creek and features the usual assortment of Jones family large greens and well-placed bunkers; it's nicely maintained given its location and short season, but as you drop your balls into its holes, beware the geese and moose.

Fairbanks

Chena Bend   _ | _ | _ | _ | $30
2092 Gaffney Rd., Fort Wainwright; 907-353-6223;
7025/5316; 73.6/71.6; 128/117
With its abundance of pine trees, standing water, rivers and mosquitos, Fairbanks resembles central Minnesota, so it makes sense that a hardy Midwesterner, golf architect Jerry Matthews, was called upon in 1994 to redesign the Fort Wainright nine that the Army built adjacent to the Chena River in 1942; it's now a full, well-bunkered, challenging 18 with relatively flat fairways and greens, water on seven holes and wildlife at every bend on the course.

Arizona

★ **Best in State**
28 Troon North, Monument, *Scottsdale*
     Troon North, Pinnacle, *Scottsdale*
     We-Ko-Pa, *Scottsdale*
27 Grayhawk, Talon, *Scottsdale*
     Ventana, Canyon Mountain, *Tucson*
     Boulders, North, *Scottsdale*
     Grayhawk, Raptor, *Scottsdale*
     Arizona National, *Tucson*
     Boulders, South, *Scottsdale*
26 Ventana Canyon, Canyon, *Tucson*

Flagstaff

Lake Powell National 🏌   _ | _ | _ | _ | $63
400 Clubhouse Dr., Page; 928-645-2023; www.lakepowellgolf.com;
7064/5097; 73.4/68.0; 139/122
Knock a few in on the doorstep of the Grand Canyon at this "striking design" adjacent to the Glen Canyon Dam where bright blue Lake Powell puddles; one of the outstanding remote outposts in American golf, the "beautiful course" boasts a par-3 12th with views of the Wahweap Lodge and Marina and a par-3 15th that plunges almost two stories downhill, and all of its holes can be played at "very affordable" rates.

Phoenix

Arizona Biltmore, Adobe 🏌   18 | 21 | 22 | 15 | $165
2400 E. Missouri Ave.; 602-955-9655; www.arizonabiltmore.com;
6449/5796; 70.1/72.2; 119/118
◪ "You think Frank Lloyd Wright might yell 'fore' at any moment" on this "park-like" "classic" adjacent to the über-architect's Arizona Biltmore Hotel, an institution with a celeb-studded pedigree; "you may have an 80-year-old in front of you and an eight-year-old behind", as the "back-and-forth straight holes" are "forgiving to even the newest beginner", which makes them "rather dull" for aces who rate the track "not up to today's standards."

Arizona Biltmore, Links 🏌　　20 | 22 | 20 | 16 |$165
2400 E. Missouri Ave.; 602-955-9655; www.arizonabiltmore.com;
6300/4747; 69.7/66.5; 126/106
☑ Urbanites cheer this "beautiful" "non-desert" layout "in the heart
of the city" for "great views from high points", including the
"signature par 3 on the back that makes this one worth playing",
"more so than its sister"; however, the fabled resort's "snooty staff"
"falls short of expectations", and claustrophes complain that "so
many" "huge houses" "surround the fairways that it feels like you're
playing through someone's backyard."

Coyote Lakes 🏌　　▽ 18 | 18 | 16 | 22 | $50
18800 N. Coyote Lakes Pkwy., Surprise; 623-566-2323;
6159/4708; 69.2/55.8; 117/110
■ It's located in the town of Surprise, but the only shock you'll
get here is from the howlingly "reasonable prices", even in high
season, at this "good" desert course where "beginners" in the
pack "always have fun", particularly because the "short driving
range" makes them feel like John Daly.

Dove Valley Ranch 🏌　　20 | 18 | 18 | 17 |$125
33244 N. Black Mountain Pkwy., Cave Creek; 480-473-1444;
www.dovevalleyranch.com; 7011/5337; 72.7/70.5; 131/114
☑ "Score early and hold on" advise savvy card-and-pencil types
who acknowledge the Jekyll-and-Hyde "open front nine" and
"more difficult" "desert back" at this RTJ Jr. mountain-surrounded
"sleeper" north of Phoenix; you may warm to the "nice staff", grass
driving range and "cool carts with GPS computers", but "issues
with conditioning" leave some cold.

Estrella Mountain Ranch　　23 | 21 | 21 | 19 |$120
11800 S. Golf Club Dr., Goodyear; 623-386-2600;
www.estrellamtnranch.com; 7139/5124; 73.6/68.2; 136/115
☑ In a live-and-lob community in the Sierra Estrella foothills, this
"awesome", boldly bunkered "desert layout" by rising star Jack
Nicklaus II is "more upscale than your average public course",
"rivaling north Scottsdale in beauty"; Phoenix folks accustomed to
teeing off just around the corner crack "you need to leave the night
before or own a Lear jet to get there", and when you do, the "winter
seeding" might make you sigh "oh, if only the greens had grass!"

500 Club　　▽ 17 | 14 | 16 | 23 | $56
4707 W. Pinnacle Peak Rd., Glendale; 623-492-9500;
www.the500club.com; 6897/5601; 71.5/69.8; 121/112
☑ Co-owned and co-designed by former Indianapolis 500 winner
Tom Sneva, this "mountainous" northeast Phoenix desert track is
"very scenic and well maintained", with a "secluded feel even
though it's in the city"; some in the judge's stand feel it deserves a
second-place finish, as "three goofy, little cement ponds" and "flat"
holes with "marginal conditions" "keep it from being a fine" winner.

Gold Canyon,　　26 | 18 | 20 | 21 |$170
Dinosaur Mountain 🏌
6100 S. Kings Ranch Rd., Gold Canyon; 480-982-9449;
800-624-6445; www.gcgr.com; 6653/4833; 71.3/67.4; 143/115
■ "Bring your A game and your camera" gush nature lovers at this
"out of the way, but worth it" resort track amid the ghost towns east

of Phoenix that delights the eye with "huge elevation changes" and splendid "high-desert views" "of the Superstition Mountains"; even zoologists would admit "it's a challenge keeping your eye on the ball while watching" "roadrunners, bobcats, javelinas" and "more jackrabbits than an Easter special" "frolic in the fairway", but besides the critters, there's "no one on the course."

Gold Canyon, Sidewinder   20 | 20 | 20 | 22 | $100

6100 S. Kings Ranch Rd., Gold Canyon; 480-982-9449; 800-624-6445; www.gcgr.com; 6630/4527; 71.9/66.5; 130/111

☑ Though it offers "good", "reasonably priced" "fun" for the weekend golfer, ambitious aces hiss that this sister layout is "too easy from the reds" and thus "not on par with Dinosaur Mountain"; it certainly is "scenic", except for a couple of power lines" bisecting the vista, and though they frown at the holes that "smell of the stables" where the mounts for dudes on holiday are kept, fauna fans fawn over "lots of wildlife" including "rattlesnakes – that's cool!"

Las Sendas 🏌   24 | 21 | 20 | 20 | $160

7555 E. Eagle Crest Dr., Mesa; 480-396-4000; www.lassendas.com; 6874/5100; 73.8/69.9; 149/128

■ "Tough! tough! tough!" huff hackers on this "tight layout" where "crowned fairways and greens that force slightly off-line shots into unplayable rocks and cacti" are par for the "penal" course for designer Robert Trent Jones Jr.; with "unique holes" "meandering around a pinnacle", it's a "must-play for anyone visiting the Valley of the Sun" "on the outskirts of Phoenix", though "without local knowledge", surviving this desert design can be "brutal."

Legend at Arrowhead, The   20 | 16 | 17 | 20 | $85

21027 N. 67th Ave., Glendale; 623-561-0953; www.americangolf.com; 7005/5233; 73.0/71.2; 129/119

■ "Northern" sports chortle it's "my kind of course" over this "tough", "clean, crisp" Arnold Palmer layout amid the foothills, lakes and orange groves of northwest Phoenix where the "great atmosphere" and "mountain views" are reminiscent of colder climes; while "it's very good for every level", Grand Canyon Staters will tell you that familiarity is helpful in navigating those lush, "heavily contoured" greens, so play it twice.

Los Caballeros   ▽ 26 | 18 | 21 | 25 | $120

1551 S. Vulture Mine Rd., Wickenburg; 928-684-2704; www.loscaballerosgolf.com; 6952/5264; 73.5/71.2; 138/124

■ A "gem" was dropped "out in the country, but by a stroke of genius", it landed "next to a wonderful resort" say treasure hunters who've stumbled upon this guests-only desert "challenge"; long hitters say "hats off" to a "fantastic" design where "you can really let the shaft out", though a few say flatly there are "more hills than you can deal with", adding "look out for rattlesnakes", and Republicans – "ex-Vice President Dan Quayle plays here."

Marriott Wildfire,   ▽ 21 | 21 | 22 | 22 | $145
Faldo Championship

5225 E. Pathfinder Dr.; 480-473-0205; www.wildfiregolf.com; 6800/5500; 71.6/69.6; 127/120

■ One of the anchors of the upcoming JW Marriott Desert Ridge (slated to be the state's largest luxe resort) is this "great new course" with magnificent views of the McDowell Mountains; fashioned with an Australian flair by PGA Tour vet Nick Faldo, it features 106 bunkers, plus elevated tees and hard-to-hit greens.

Marriott Wildfire, Palmer Signature
24 | 22 | 23 | 23 | $145

5225 E. Pathfinder Dr.; 480-473-0205; www.wildfiregolf.com;
7100/5500; 73.3/67.9; 135/119

■ "A real challenge" that's "honest and playable", this youngish Palmer desert beauty is "not as well known as its neighbors", but it's making its mark as the first of two ambitious Wildfire layouts, with spectacular views of Camelback Mountain and Squaw Peak, superb conditioning and a forgiving design with solid bunkering and generous landing areas; though the clubhouse is "still under construction", the track is bound to please vacationers who check into the JW Marriott when it opens in November 2002.

Ocotillo Golf Club
24 | 22 | 21 | 21 | $155

3751 S. Clubhouse Dr., Chandler; 480-917-6660; 888-624-8899;
www.ocotillogolf.com
Gold/Blue: 6729/5128; 71.3/71.3; 131/128
Gold/White: 6612/5124; 71.4/68.4; 128/122
White/Blue: 6533/5134; 70.8/71.0; 128/127

■ "Water, water, everywhere" . . . "in Arizona?" – "bring plenty of extra balls" gurgle aquaphobes dipping into "about 22 or more" liquid-laden holes on these three "outstanding" nines afloat amid "exquisite landscaping" that's "better manicured than the toes on your wife", or your wife-to-be – it's a lush location for a lavish wedding catered by the elegant on-course eatery, Bernard's; try it in the summer, when it's cheap compared with spring.

Palm Valley, Palms
▽ 19 | 16 | 17 | 23 | $45

2211 N. Litchfield Rd., Goodyear; 623-935-2500;
www.palmvalleygolf.com; 7015/6160; 73.4/62.4; 133/126

■ Just about "the best value in metro Phoenix" can be had at this "pretty" "sleeper" "in the West Valley" 25 minutes or so from downtown; the facility sports an Arthur Hills championship track and a Hale Irwin–designed executive layout, "both of which are worth playing", plus a lighted nine-hole par-3 course, making it one of Arizona's premier sites for junior and family golfing.

Papago Municipal
19 | 11 | 13 | 24 | $35

5595 E. Moreland St.; 602-275-8428; 7068/5937; 73.3/72.4; 132/119

◪ "Best bang for the buck" in Phoenix, insist spendthrift swingers clamoring for "tough-to-get tee times" and "crowding" onto this "old-fashioned" muni for a "somewhat challenging" round; though public putters proudly proclaim that the "conditions are good" for a track that's "taken so much hard play", high-rollers accustomed to the "aesthetics of the resort courses" crank "the city has let it go to hell."

Pointe Hilton at Tapatio Cliffs, Lookout Mountain 🏌
21 | 20 | 20 | 17 | $159

11111 N. Seventh St.; 602-866-6356; 6617/4557; 71.2/65.3; 135/113

◪ Overheated hookers "love when they bring icy towels for your neck in summer while you're playing" the Hilton's "target mountain" layout with "great views of the valley", and of your balls careening down into it; "bring lots of 'em" to cover your losses on a track that "has some interesting tricks", even though seasoned swingers call it "grossly overpriced"; non-golfers in the clan find the family resort's water park universally exciting.

Raven at South Mountain   25 | 24 | 26 | 20 | $170

3636 E. Baseline Rd.; 602-243-3636; www.ravengolf.com; 7100/5800; 73.9/72.9; 133/124

■ "Mango-scented, ice-cold towels, mmm!" – "from the time you drop your clubs to the time you leave the parking lot", the "superb" staff "treats you like you are a member" of a "country club" at this "upscale" design dishing out "understated elegance" near the airport on Phoenix's south side; it's an "impeccably conditioned" "Midwestern-style course plopped down in the middle of the desert", where "lush" "fairways lined with pines" make a shady home for the Arizona Diamondbacks, who are pleased to putt when they're not at bat.

Sedona Golf Resort   23 | 22 | 21 | 20 | $99

35 Ridge Trail Dr., Sedona; 928-284-9355; 877-733-9888; www.sedonagolfresort.com; 6646/5059; 70.3/67.0; 129/114

■ "Surrounded by the red rocks", New Agers and old golfers alike harmonize about one of Arizona's "most picturesque courses" where "the views will soothe you as the traps frustrate you"; indeed, it's "hard to keep your head down" amid "the sheer beauty" surrounding the "hilly, challenging but doable" layout, though gallery goers and crystal collectors would tell you to look up long enough to "enjoy the town after your round", "especially at sunset."

Stonecreek 🏞   17 | 16 | 17 | 19 | $105

4435 E. Paradise Village Pkwy. S.; 602-953-9111; www.americangolf.com; 6871/5018; 72.8/68.4; 131/119

☑ It might "not be to your liking" if you're looking for "your typical desert course", but this "links" layout with "really tight" routing and many mounds designed by Roy Dye, Pete's brother, and redone in stones and creeks by Arthur Hills is "challenging and fun" if you're not a stickler for Southwestern style; a "staff that works hard to make sure you enjoy yourself" flips the "best flapjacks west of the Mississippi" and may even "send you a plaque, the ball" and your scorecard if you "get a hole-in-one."

Superstition Springs 🏞   20 | 20 | 19 | 21 | $105

6542 E. Baseline Rd., Mesa; 480-985-5622; 800-468-7918; www.americangolf.com; 7005/5328; 74.1/70.7; 135/117

■ If you're "sick of the desert, go here" say fans of the Floridian feel at this "PGA-quality" layout that's "long" on yardage and "water", with unique twisted hurricane palms that make you feel you're in the Southeast rather than the Southwest; vets vie for their balls to fly over "sand traps like World War II bunkers", though the greens they land on are "still coming back from a major makeover" a few years ago.

Wigwam, Blue   19 | 22 | 21 | 19 | $120

451 N. Litchfield Rd., Litchfield Park; 623-935-9414; www.wigwamresort.com; 6085/5178; 69.1/69.1; 122/118

☑ Parts of this "old-style" layout date to the 1930s, when the toddler Wigwam resort boasted the only golf west of Phoenix; in the late

1950s Robert Trent Jones Sr. polished up the twentysomething, crafting "a short gem" that's "enjoyable" for lightweights; heavy hitters sing the blues over the "oftentimes boring" track that's "nothing special" compared with its "incredible" namesake hotel.

Wigwam, Gold | 22 | 24 | 21 | 18 | $120

451 N. Litchfield Rd., Litchfield Park; 623-935-9414;
www.wigwamresort.com; 7074/5663; 74.1/72.1; 133/125
☑ "If a traditional-looking course is to your liking", the strong bunkering and "elevated, volcano-like greens" might have you hailing this "longstanding great" design by longstanding great Robert Trent Jones Sr. as "the best open to the public on the west side" of Phoenix; newfangled foozlers who find the "toughest of the three" at Wigwam to be "nice but not spectacular" suggest that "time has passed it by" and it's lost its glitter.

Wigwam, Red | ▽ 17 | 23 | 22 | 20 | $120

451 N. Litchfield Rd., Litchfield Park; 623-935-9414;
www.wigwamresort.com; 6865/5808; 72.4/71.8; 126/118
☑ Across the road to the west of its cousins, this mid-'70s layout is named for its architect, Red Lawrence, who designed some desert winners; despite a challenging closing stretch, however, this traditional, tree-lined flatty serves up only "so-so golf"; better to skip the round and go straight for the "great facilities", including the innovative Arizona Kitchen restaurant at the adjacent hotel.

San Carlos

Apache Stronghold | ▽ 24 | 17 | 17 | 23 | $70

Hwy. 70 (4 mi. east of Hwy. 77); 928-475-4653; 800-272-2438;
www.apachegoldcasinoresort.com; 7519/5535; 74.9/70.4; 138/123
☑ It's "very cool" to see a "bronze statue" of an Apache warrior "looking down on the 9th" cry warriors battling this "wonderful" lay-of-the-land course 90 miles east of Phoenix on the San Carlos Apache Indian Reservation; it's "not in the best of shape", but it offers "a great value" as it tumbles over rolling desert terrain with valley-like holes on the front and distant mountain backdrops on the back.

Scottsdale

BOULDERS, NORTH ⊕ | 27 | 27 | 27 | 19 | $230

34631 N. Tom Darlington Dr., Carefree; 480-488-9028;
www.wyndham.com; 6811/5440; 72.6/71.1; 137/126
■ "Sand and cacti", "clean, crisp air", "spectacular views" and, true to its name, "those boulders" come together in a "wonderful desert setting" for "a unique round of golf" on "lush fairways" at this "heaven"-in-the-"heat" resort boasting the new Golden Door spa; "warm, personal" Service rates Arizona's No. 1 but doesn't include snake charming, so "bring an extra sleeve" of balls because "you don't want to fight the rattlers for 'em in the washes."

BOULDERS, SOUTH ⊕ | 27 | 27 | 27 | 20 | $230

34631 N. Tom Darlington Dr., Carefree; 480-488-9028;
www.wyndham.com; 6726/5151; 71.9/71.1; 140/125
■ "The scenery alone is worth the price of admission", which is as "steep" as the "breathtaking rock formations throughout" this

"classic desert layout" designed by Jay Morrish to "wind through" one of "Arizona's best resorts"; the state's No. 1–rated Facilities are in "immaculate condition", so "wow", "go, go, go", preferably in the spring, when amenities include particularly "beautiful" weather.

Camelback, Club 🏌 | 19 | 22 | 22 | 18 | $105 |
7847 N. Mockingbird Ln.; 480-948-1700; 800-242-2635;
www.camelbackgolf.com; 7014/5917; 72.6/71.5; 122/118
◪ "Apart from the occasional cactus", this "forgiving" "course in the middle of Phoenix" is "without too many challenges", so it's "good golf" for "novices", who can rest assured the "friendliest of staffs" will "treat 'em right"; beauty is in the eye of the club holder, however, where "fragrant desert flowers lining the fairways" have some hackers hailing the "lush" "cutie", while other duffers dis it as "flat and uninteresting."

Camelback, Resort 🏌 | 19 | 22 | 21 | 18 | $145 |
7847 N. Mockingbird Ln.; 480-948-1700; 800-242-2635;
www.camelbackgolf.com; 6868/5069; 72.8/68.6; 132/114
◪ "Bring your credit cards", shoppers, because the "fine facilities" at this "ok desert course" include "one of the best pro shops around"; as for the layout, gruff golfers grumble that designer Arthur Hills' "traditional" "holes have a sameness to them", making for "an unremarkable adventure" that recent "remodeling" only made more "gimmicky."

Eagle Mountain 🏌 | 22 | 20 | 22 | 19 | $175 |
14915 E. Eagle Mountain Pkwy., Fountain Hills; 480-816-1234;
www.eaglemtn.com; 6763/5065; 71.7/68.2; 139/118
◼ If you need a confidence boost as "a great warm-up to your Scottsdale golf vacation", this "mountain track" with "gorgeous valley views" is so "player-friendly that all shots bounce back to the center of the fairway"; with "dramatic elevation changes" and healthy carries from the back tees, it's a "challenging but not penal" "test for long hitters as well as short players", while gripes about "greens that need work and holes that drain poorly" should be nipped in the bud by a summer 2002 overhaul.

GRAYHAWK, RAPTOR | 27 | 27 | 26 | 18 | $205 |
8620 E. Thompson Peak Pkwy.; 480-502-1800; 800-472-9429;
www.grayhawk.com; 7135/5309; 74.1/71.3; 143/127
◼ Desert golf "doesn't get much better than" at this "exceptional" resort course, "a perfect all-around experience" with "U.S. Open" greens, "'70s rock music in the practice area" and "a Zen-style golf book at the end of the round" to pore over over a pour at the "outstanding" Phil's Grill, named for Grayhawk Touring Pro Phil Mickelson; everything here is "stunningly beautiful", including the "drink-cart girls who themselves are worth the price of admission", which is so sky-high, "you'll feel as if a raptor has eaten your wallet."

Grayhawk, Talon | 27 | 27 | 27 | 19 | $205 |
8620 E. Thompson Peak Pkwy.; 480-502-1800; 800-472-9429;
www.grayhawk.com; 6973/5143; 73.6/70.0; 143/121
◼ "They treat you like a king", though it wouldn't hurt to have Midas' touch at this "pricey", "tough, but playable" "beauty" that's "better manicured than the nails of a Beverly Hills trophy wife" (with a

"cart-path-only" rule that keeps it that way); the "top-notch" staff will "clean your clubs on the range" and mix you "a cold one" afterward at the "great" 19th hole; budget birdies: if you can book on the fly, their last-minute summer promotions might hook you – cheap, cheap.

Kierland 村 🏠
20 | 21 | 21 | 19 | $165

15636 N. Clubgate Dr.; 480-922-9283; www.kierlandgolf.com
Acacia/Ironwood: 7017/5017; 73.3/69.4; 133/120
Ironwood/Mesquite: 6974/4985; 72.9/69.2; 130/116
Mesquite/Acacia: 6913/4898; 72.6/69.0; 133/117

☑ "A new clubhouse opened" in summer 2002 and "an awesome new Westin resort is opening the fall" that follows, both of which promise to enhance this "very nice" 27-holer that, "for the money", is "a good alternative to the known courses"; artistic aces argue it's "not a very imaginative layout" because "this hole goes straight, that hole goes straight, this hole you pretty much get what you see."

Legend Trail
23 | 21 | 22 | 18 | $170

9462 E. Legendary Ln.; 480-488-7434; www.legendtrailgc.com;
6845/5001; 73.2/68.2; 135/122

■ "Incredible shot values" explain the fatal attraction to this Rees Jones "target"-style track, which is "pretty" and "plush" but "challenging" in a schizophrenic way, with "front and back nines like two different worlds"; given a "staff that's not all stuck-up" and "nice practice facilities", even the "many long carries over the desert" and the "added housing developments" don't dissuade daredevils who declare that they "like it much better than" its swankier, saner neighbors.

McCormick Ranch, Palm 🏠
18 | 20 | 20 | 19 | $140

7505 E. McCormick Pkwy.; 480-948-0260;
www.mccormickranchgolf.com; 7044/5057; 73.7/68.6; 137/114

■ "Old" and "established" by area standards, this thirtysomething spread at the Millennium Resort "is not your normal desert course, but it's an ok" "traditional" with a "great backdrop" of mountains, lakes and palm trees; it's renowned as "great fun for scrambles and best-ball tournaments", and gregarious golfers gush "had an outing here and the staff was helpful and accommodating."

McCormick Ranch, Pine 🏠
18 | 20 | 18 | 19 | $140

7505 E. McCormick Pkwy.; 480-948-0260;
www.mccormickranchgolf.com; 7137/5333; 74.4/69.9; 135/117

■ "Both McCormick Ranch courses offer good fun and a fair value" say local yokels who like this track's "convenient" heart-of-Scottsdale location, its "open" fairways and "good conditions with fast greens"; while some slicers snicker that the 29-year-old "is a little past its prime", the majority says the experience is nothing but "a good [old?] time."

Phoenician, The 🏠
21 | 26 | 24 | 17 | $170

6000 E. Camelback Rd.; 480-941-8200; www.thephoenician.com
Canyon/Desert: 6300/4777; 69.4/67.7; 131/114
Desert/Oasis: 6310/5024; 70.3/69.7; 130/113
Oasis/Canyon: 6258/4871; 70.1/69.1; 130/111

☑ "The only thing more pampered than the greens and fairways is you" at this "expensive", "outstanding, all-inclusive resort" with

27 "beautifully maintained" holes, a super-luxe spa and Mary Elaine's *fabuleux* French fare; "amid the serene desert" at the base of Camelback Mountain, late tee-timers risk "rattlesnakes" to "see the most beautiful sunset"; as for the layout, long-gamers "ho-hum" "lots of short holes", which are "too cute" and "not very challenging" – "they needed more land to squeeze in the course."

SunRidge Canyon   26 | 21 | 22 | 21 | $175

13100 N. Sunridge Dr., Fountain Hills; 480-837-5100; 800-562-5178; www.sunridgegolf.com; 6823/5141; 73.4/70.1; 140/123

■ With "breathtaking views" of Four Peaks and a "nice blend of desert and mountain styles", this "real beaut" "starts out friendly" but "begins to show its teeth at the turn" – "you'll be ready for the 19th hole after the back side's" 300-ft. elevation change "leaves you exhausted"; high-energy low-handicappers call it "a joy to play", sighing "I could live here" in one of the "homes that surround the front side", even though wilderness buffs say the buildings "detract from the experience."

Talking Stick, North   21 | 20 | 21 | 18 | $140

9998 E. Indian Bend Rd.; 480-860-2221; www.talkingstickgolfclub.com; 7133/5532; 73.8/70; 125/116

☑ "An unusual course for Arizona", this "challenging but fair test" owned by the Salt River Pima-Maricopa Indian Community was "designed after traditional Scottish links" by Bill Coore and Ben Crenshaw; "play off-season and take advantage of twilight rates" for an "area bargain" boasting "hard fairways" and deep, sprawling bunkers, even if yipsters yawn that the "most interesting features" in the "flat", "uninspiring" setting are the occasional sightings of "palominos" and "Charles Barkley at the driving range."

Talking Stick, South   21 | 20 | 20 | 19 | $140

9998 E. Indian Bend Rd.; 480-860-2221; www.talkingstickgolfclub.com; 6833/5429; 72.7/69.1; 129/118

☑ For a "walk that's easy" on the feet and the wallet, Talking Stick North's "wide", tree-lined "desert" sister is "somewhat flat compared with other Scottsdale courses" and "not too pricey"; noting that the five-year-old "needs a lot of maturity", old-timers gulping firewater in the Native American–themed clubhouse opine that it "may grow up someday", though there might not be as much hope for the "stuck-up" staff.

TPC of Scottsdale, Desert   19 | 22 | 21 | 22 | $53

17020 N. Hayden Rd.; 480-585-4334; www.tpc.com; 6423/4612; 71.4/65.9; 112/105

☑ "Bring a beat-up club to use" on both your ball and the "rattlers" "when you hit out of the fairways" at this "sandbox" of a "little brother to the Stadium"; "playable for every level", the "fun" "ride through some interesting holes" is a "great value for the money" and a "very nice" "way to begin a week of golf" in the "desert" with a stay at the Marriott McDowell Mountain Ranch beside the course.

TPC of Scottsdale, Stadium ⚐   24 | 26 | 23 | 17 | $214

17020 N. Hayden Rd.; 480-585-4334; www.tpc.com; 7070/6049; 74.4/71.6; 133/122

☑ "Imagine the gallery cheering you on" as you "try to relive Tiger's hole-in-one" at the "expensive" "home of the Phoenix Open", where the "friendly staff" in the "great practice area", "very nice pro shop" and top-notch Fairmont Scottsdale Princess hotel pamper pros and novices alike; "humongous water hazards" and "an excellent mix of short and long holes" "requiring accuracy" make this "one of the better TPC layouts", so divas "try to keep in mind" the "barren" setting, cart-path-only rule and "aggressive" marshals are geared to accommodate "TV" and "big crowds."

TROON NORTH, MONUMENT   28 | 27 | 26 | 19 | $240
10320 E. Dynamite Blvd.; 480-585-5300; www.troonnorthgolf.com; 7028/5050; 73.3/68.5; 147/117

■ Believers rejoice in this "religious experience", Arizona's No. 1–rated Course and Most Popular "jewel", where the choir of angelic staffers sings "may I wipe your brow, sir?"; "fairways manicured to perfection are almost too nice to play on", but if you do, "be accurate" or the "cacti will literally swallow your balls"; the "gorgeous scenery", "memorable par 3s" and lavish clubhouse are undeniably "expensive", especially "in winter", but even "spanked snowbirds" on a course "surrounded by house after house after condo" cry "this is what golf heaven looks like" (and fittingly, the lodging and dining are at the Four Seasons).

TROON NORTH, PINNACLE   28 | 26 | 26 | 18 | $240
10320 E. Dynamite Blvd.; 480-585-5300; www.troonnorthgolf.com; 7044/4980; 73.4/68.6; 147/120

■ Proclaiming Arizona's No. 2–rated Course "just as good as its more famous sister", players partial to this "very demanding, very lovely" pinnacle of "must-plays" are "awed" by "lush fairways and true greens in a pristine desert setting" with "magnificent views"; "no request is too small" for the "professional staff" at this "truly first-class" facility with a stellar spa and fitness center where "every amenity imaginable" is on hand.

We-Ko-Pa   28 | 26 | 25 | 24 | $165
18200 E. TohVee Circle, Fountain Hills; 480-836-9000; www.wekopa.com; 7225/5337; 72.5/69.1; 130/119

■ The Yavapai Indian Nation "is in the process of developing a world-class" facility, and its "new course" is "killer" already, with "interesting varied terrain and elevation changes", an "excellent practice area" and a "nice clubhouse with a wonderful patio for drinking" down cocktails and drinking in "unbelievable views" of namesake Four Peaks Mountain; "the best part is there's no housing", and the land-loving folks here insist there never will be, making it the "best value in the Valley" for nature seekers.

Tempe

ASU Karsten   19 | 19 | 19 | 21 | $93
1125 E. Rio Salado Pkwy.; 480-921-8070; www.asukarsten.com; 7026/4765; 73.7/67.7; 132/115

■ "Very imaginative" say Sun Devils swinging under the devilish sun at their home course, which "smacks of NCAA tournament play" on nutty professor Pete Dye's mounded, "forgiving fairways" and "huge pot bunkers" "right in the middle of Tempe"; it's "a great challenge when played from the tips", but those "Arizona State University kids in fancy socks" and "Payne Stewart knickers" are "extremely helpful", so ask them for pointers, and try not to study the "super-ugly" "power plant", "planes" and "highway" that make up the vista.

Tucson

Arizona National 🏌   27 | 24 | 25 | 22 | $170
9777 E. Sabino Greens Dr.; 520-749-3636; 6776/4733; 73.2/67.7; 146/113

■ "You're guaranteed to spot wildlife", and we're not just referring to the U of A golf team at their new home, "probably the most scenic course in Tucson", with "great elevation changes" affording "mountain and city views"; given "long carries over desert rough" and "a million cacti surrounding the fairways", play can be prickly, but the "friendly" staffers in the "great pro shop" and a "private-club" ambiance cushion the pain of the "forced risk/reward decisions" on a RTJ Jr. layout so "spectacular", you "must see it to believe it."

El Conquistador, Cañada 🏌   22 | 22 | 22 | 22 | $105
10555 N. La Cañada Dr.; 520-544-1985; 6713/5093; 71.9/70.8; 130/125

■ It "can be more prickly than a cactus", but don't let this "great resort course" connected to the same-named Sheraton conquer you; just take in the rolling desert landscape and handsome Santa Catalina Mountains, don't get stuck on the elevated, well-bunkered greens of the front nine and make your way to the back, which is more forgiving; the "great service" is an added balm to your wounds, and if you don't score well, blame Cañada.

El Conquistador, Conquistador 🏌   21 | 22 | 20 | 20 | $105
10555 N. La Cañada Dr.; 520-544-1985; 6801/4821; 72.7/69.0; 126/121

■ In a "nice location in Tucson", with panoramic mountain vistas, this "good value for Arizona resort courses" is more wide open than its sister, but there's also more housing attached to it, so it can be "an oasis if you hit long and straight", but if you're sloppy, you'd better bring a ladder to retrieve your "wayward drives" off the "rooftops."

La Paloma Country Club 🏌   24 | 24 | 23 | 18 | $195
3660 E. Sunrise Dr.; 520-299-1500; 800-222-1249
Canyon/Hill: 6453/5057; 72.2/70.6; 152/126
Hill/Ridge: 6464/4878; 72.0/68.5; 150/123
Ridge/Canyon: 6635/5075; 72.2/70.6; 152/126

■ "Now this is what desert golf is all about" coo lovers of 'The Dove', a "magnificent", "well-maintained" Jack Nicklaus 27-holer at a "stunning facility" where some of "the highest slope ratings possible are well deserved"; for the privilege of tackling the rugged site laced with cacti, canyons and "many holes too severe for average players", you have to check into the Westin La Paloma Resort and Spa, but it's a "fabulous getaway" "even if you're not a golfer", so bring the family, and maybe the kids can help you "look for expensive balls" "in the rough."

San Ignacio 🏌   ▽ 19 | 16 | 17 | 21 | $69
4201 S. Camino del Sol, Green Valley; 520-648-3468;
6288/5865; 69.8/70.5; 130/125

■ Located a cool 3,000 feet above sea level, this "solid and fun" Arthur Hills layout 20 miles south of Tucson has "tough, narrow fairways" lined with mesquite trees that ribbon through "desert washes" teeming with natural wildlife; praising extreme elevation changes, numerous hazards and panoramic views of the Santa Rita Mountains, locals implore take an "extra day if you've got one" while you're on vacation to tee it up at this Green Valley oasis.

Starr Pass ⌂   24 | 23 | 20 | 21 | $149
3645 W. Starr Pass Blvd.; 520-670-0400; 800-503-2898;
www.starrpasstucson.com; 6910/5071; 74.8/70.0; 144/129
■ "Hit it straight" or else, pardner, on this "fun desert course" in the "Old Pueblo", where your ball giddyaps down a "historic stagecoach pass on the 15th hole" and "some of the greatest par 5s around" lie in ambush; to make it out alive, "you have to concentrate on the challenge" rather than "the drop-dead gorgeous valley views" at the "former TPC" and Tucson Open stop that's "not as crowded" as the more amenity-heavy rounds in town.

Ventana Canyon, Canyon   26 | 25 | 25 | 20 | $199
6200 N. Club House Ln.; 520-577-4061; 6819/4919; 72.6/70.2; 140/119
■ Thanks to holes with "breathtaking views", such as Nos. 3, 4 and 5, winding through Esperrero Canyon, the 10th, which abuts Whaleback Rock, and the 18th, backdropped by a waterfall and striking hotel, this "top-notch" Tom Fazio desert design is a "terrific visual setting for a round" that's "more wide open and easier" than play on its companion course; those who remember it when say the greens are "a little worn" and the pro shop is so "poorly stocked."

Ventana Canyon, Mountain   27 | 25 | 24 | 20 | $199
6200 N. Club House Ln.; 520-577-4061; 6907/4709; 73.0/68.3; 147/119
■ She "slaps hackers around worse than a grumpy mother", and the "rattlers and gila monsters" join in the "very tough" fun; this "beautiful" but "unforgiving" "desert test" is "like mini-golf on a broad scale", where only "accurate shotmaking and creativity" will save you from the "must-see 3rd hole" "in the foothills"; after a "wonderful" workout like this, relax in the "great clubhouse" and the lavish adjacent hotels, the Loews and the Lodge.

Vistoso   24 | 22 | 24 | 21 | $155
955 W. Vistoso Highlands Dr., Oro Valley; 520-797-7900;
www.vistosogolf.com; 6932/5962; 72.1/68.0; 147/126
■ It's "target" "desert golf at its finest" on this "must for visitors to the Tucson area", where Tom Weiskopf has crafted a "tasteful co-existence of housing and golf"; it's "almost impossible from the tips", and if you "try to be a he-man on No. 8, you will end up all wet", but it's "playable" and "enjoyable" nonetheless – just "beware snakes" and "cart-path-only days."

Arkansas

Fairfield Bay

Mountain Ranch Golf Club   – | – | – | – | $57
820 Lost Creek Pkwy.; 501-884-3400; www.mountainranchgolf.com;
6780/5325; 72.8/66.2; 140/126
Arkansas isn't blessed with a multitude of top-ranked public courses, but this 1983 track rolling through the Ozark Mountains

some 80 miles north of Little Rock is an acclaimed exception
to the rule; a friendly staff, several blind tee shots and two
remarkable par 5s on Nos. 2 and 14 are guaranteed to bring ball-
launching bubbas back.

Hot Springs

Glenwood Country Club   – | – | – | – | $42
584 Hwy. 70, Glenwood; 870-356-4422; 800-833-3110;
www.glenwoodcountryclub.com; 6550/5076; 70.8/64.1; 128/114
Thirty minutes southwest of Hot Springs sits a pleasant, comfy and
affordable layout beside a cozy, 12-room lodge on rolling terrain
surrounded by wilderness; it's not too tough from any set of tees,
but locals are hog wild about its rock-solid collection of par 3s,
including two surrounded by water.

Mt. Home

Big Creek Golf & Country Club   – | – | – | – | $55
452 Country Club Dr., Mountain Home; 870-425-0333;
www.bigcreekgolf.com; 7820/5068; 75.1/69.7; 133/120
Northern Arkansas is hardly known for its upscale residential golf
communities, but this layout southeast of Bull Shoals Lake near
the Missouri border may convert disbelievers; renowned for its
outstanding service, good grooming and uncrowded rounds, this
big, yet playable course features a blend of open and tree-lined
holes, interesting creek-laced risk/reward par 5s and a rugged
uphill par-4 finish.

California

★ **Best in State**
29 Pebble Beach, *Monterey Peninsula*
     Spyglass Hill, *Monterey Peninsula*
28 PGA Oak Valley, Champions, *San Bernardino*
     Pasatiempo, *San Jose*
     La Purisima, *Santa Barbara*
27 Maderas, *San Diego*
     Torrey Pines, South, *San Diego*
     Marriott Shadow Ridge, *Palm Springs*
     Desert Willow, Firecliff, *Palm Springs*
26 Pelican Hill, Ocean North, *Orange County*

Lake Tahoe

Golf Club At Whitehawk Ranch   26 | 20 | 22 | 18 | $125
1137 Hwy. 89, Clio; 530-836-0394; 800-332-4295;
www.golfwhitehawk.com; 6928/4816; 72.4/64.2; 130/115
■ It's "a beautiful ride to and from" this "high-altitude" "Sierra
favorite" where former ranch pasture lands were transformed
into "one of the most beautiful, serene golf settings" in California;
"buried north of Truckee in a growing hotbed of courses", the
resort track is "very impressive" compared with its neighbors, with
a "well-maintained" layout and "fabulous practice area"; the
"marshals even offer you bug spray to keep the mosquitos" from
eating you, while you yourself can dine on a delicious meal in
the lodge restaurant.

Graeagle Meadows　　　　　17 | 14 | 15 | 19 | $45
107 Hwy. 89, Graeagle; 530-836-2323; www.playgraeagle.com;
6725/5589; 72.1/71.1; 129/127

▣ In an old lumber town in the Sierras is a resort wrung in alpine lakes with a "great boomer course for guys who like to use their driver and play army golf"; in other words, it's "wide open" for taking it "nice" and "easy" in a "beautiful" "mountain" setting overlooking the Feather River – "otherwise, it's undistinguished."

Lake Tahoe Golf Course　　　19 | 18 | 19 | 21 | $70
2500 Emerald Bay Rd., South Lake Tahoe; 530-577-0788;
www.americangolf.com; 6741/5654; 70.8/70.1; 126/115

■ The "snow-covered Sierras" form the "breathtaking backdrop" of this "pleasant", "flat" course overlooking Lake Tahoe that offers "great value" after losses at "nearby gambling meccas"; while the "creek that meanders through" is "irritating" to those who "lose balls" in it, others sigh, with a setting like this "who cares"?

Northstar-At-Tahoe　　　　19 | 19 | 18 | 16 | $95
168 Basque Dr., Truckee; 530-562-2490; www.boothcreek.com;
6897/5470; 72.4/71.2; 137/134

▣ It's a tale of two nines at this "mountain course" in a ski resort, where the "windy", "wide-open" front end that "winds through a meadowland" is a "great contrast" to the "woodsy", "narrow" back where you'll "lose a few balls" in the pines; it's the best of times for those who find a "good challenge" and a "very friendly staff", but it may be the worst of times for others who uncover a "relatively bland" venue that seems "overpriced and under-maintained."

Resort At Squaw Creek 🏌　22 | 23 | 22 | 16 | $115
400 Squaw Creek Rd., Olympic Valley; 530-581-6637; 800-327-3353;
www.squawcreek.com; 7001/5097; 72.9/68.9; 143/127

▣ A "priceless view": watching your ball fly against the backdrop of the "spectacular Sierras" is one reward on this "short-season" RTJ Jr. ski resort course, and the fine dining and the water garden are others; the track opens "alpine"-style, then "meanders through a meadow", "from canyons to marshes", and "if you can't hit it straight, don't bother" say swingers braving "afternoon winds" and "thunderstorms" to enjoy their "solitude" here.

Tahoe Donner ⊕　　　　▽ 17 | 11 | 15 | 18 | $130
12850 Northwoods Blvd., Truckee; 530-587-9443;
www.tahoedonner.com; 6917/6032; 72.4/73.1; 133/138

▣ It's "worth the trip and the money" say fans flubbing it on this "tough" but "fun" track whose "interesting greens" and "narrow fairways" "run through the mountains" "near Truckee" at a resort where riding, skiing and camping are also on offer; naysayers needle the "layout in the pines" as "boring" with "poor drainage."

Los Angeles

Lost Canyons, Shadow 🏌　26 | 24 | 25 | 19 | $120
3301 Lost Canyon Dr., Simi Valley; 805-522-4653;
www.lostcanyons.com; 7005/4795; 75.0/64.1; 149/125

■ "Not for the faint of heart" huzzah harried hoofers of this tough, "majestic" course "built into the mountains" where it "seems like every hole is uphill"; it may be "perilous without a forecaddie" and "excruciatingly expensive with one", but the "serene setting" "close to LA", "awesome vistas", "great risk/reward", "good twilight deals" and "the best Bloody Marys around" have most deeming this "new addition" an "absolute must-play."

Lost Canyons, Sky 🏌   26 24 25 20 $120
3301 Lost Canyon Dr., Simi Valley; 805-522-4653;
www.lostcanyons.com; 7250/4885; 76.1/70.0; 149/120
■ It's "like playing on the moon" proclaim enthusiasts of this "pristine and incredible" Pete Dye course that sends them into orbit, thanks to "country club–quality service" and a "beautiful but brutal layout" "carved out of a canyon", where "forecaddies are a nice touch"; some find it more "fun" than its sister, Shadow, but advise "bring an extra bucket of balls", as there are "blind shots galore."

Los Verdes   20 13 12 24 $27
7000 Los Verdes Dr., Rancho Palos Verdes; 310-377-7888;
www.americangolf.com; 6617/5772; 71.1/67.7; 122/112
◪ If it weren't for "spectacular" Pacific "views on every hole", this would be "just another muni" and a very "slooow" one at that, since weary wedgers warn "be ready for a six- to seven-hour round" behind "crowds" of "fivesomes" – and that's after you've weathered the "pure hell" of getting a tee time ("locals and regulars get preference"); still, the "great value" and location trumps all, so even though every putt seems to "break toward the ocean", it's worth "sleeping in your car" for a shot at this one.

Malibu Country Club   18 14 16 16 $80
901 Encinal Canyon Rd., Malibu; 818-889-6680;
www.malibucountryclub.net; 6631/5523; 70.5/71.4; 125/120
◪ Surfers-turned-swingers "get away" to this "steep" "canyon course" "nestled in the Santa Monica Mountains"; fans feel "it's well worth the trek" along the "winding drive" to get to its "tight fairways" and work on "accuracy"; still, snobs sneer with "weekend play slower than molasses", "a few batting cages" for practice facilities, "rinky-dink holes" and a "horrible snack bar" with "inflated prices", it "fails to live up to par."

Ocean Trails Golf Club 🏌   19 21 19 15 $120
1 Ocean Trail Dr., Rancho Palos Verdes; 310-265-5525;
877-799-4659; www.oceantrails.com; 6821/5313; 72.6/68.9; 146/133
◪ Incredulous ball launchers blurt "how Pete Dye ever squeezed a course into this land is a thing to behold", but in fact, he didn't – before its opening the cliff crumbled, the "18th slid into the ocean" and "two adjacent holes were closed", so now this "beautiful" spread in posh Palos Verdes is "the best 15 you can play"; it's a "weird" setup, but the Pacific views are "awesome", the "facilities top-notch" and the "service excellent" – "golf it now" before new owner Donald Trump repairs it and it "becomes a $300 course."

OJAI VALLEY INN AND SPA   25 25 26 20 $135
905 Country Club Rd., Ojai; 805-646-2420; 800-422-6524;
www.golfojai.com; 6305/5244; 70.7/71.2; 125/130
■ "Tradition oozes" at this 1923 "gem", perhaps "the most relaxing, spiritual golf experience in Southern California"; wayward hitters who tangle with "ball-grabbing oaks" on the "green rolling hills" at this Senior PGA event host can recover their faith at the "very nice"

resort's "fabulous spa", while transcendence is on hand at the "wonderful restaurant and terrific pro shop" with "unbeatable service", where "clubs are cleaned and shoes shined."

Pacific Palms, Babe Didrikson Zaharias   23 | 18 | 17 | 19 | $89

1 Industry Hills Pkwy., City of Industry; 626-810-4653; www.pacificpalmsresort.com; 6600/5363; 72.5/72.4; 134/133

☑ This Babe is no lady according to survivors of the "tough, tough, tough" "challenge" where an "extremely narrow" layout and "tricky greens" carved out of the hills are "way too difficult for the average player"; the resort's "great facilities" include an Olympic-size pool, lighted tennis courts and a "good pro shop and restaurant", though it's "difficult to get snacks during play" with all those "conventioneers" and "foreign business visitors" from the adjacent Sheraton crowding the drink carts during "hot summers."

Pacific Palms, Eisenhower   23 | 19 | 17 | 19 | $89

1 Industry Hills Pkwy., City of Industry; 626-810-4653; www.pacificpalmsresort.com; 6735/5589; 72.9/73.1; 136/135

☑ "Ike is awesome" salute supporters of this "challenging beyond belief" "oasis in the middle of a heavily industrialized area" that "tests all of your skills" and causes "plenty of trouble"; foes fret it's "wicked long", "smoggy in mid-summer" ("bring your gas mask") and "eats golf balls alive, just like its sister course"; but if you're looking to "learn humility", this one helps you "find out how good [or bad] you are."

Palos Verdes Golf Club 🏨 ⏱   23 | 19 | 18 | 21 | $205

3301 Via Campesina, Palos Verdes Estates; 310-375-2533; 6219/4696; 70.5/69.2; 129/126

☑ "There's no shortage of charm" at this "great old" semi-private "built in the '20s" that's "tucked into an exclusive enclave" amid "huge eucalyptus groves" where "each tee shot requires not only accuracy but a deep breath" to take in the "absolutely gorgeous views" of "the Pacific Ocean and West Los Angeles", including the fabled Hollywood sign; "play it with a member for better value" and more access, and take its "run-down facilities" for Norma Desmond–style glamour.

Robinson Ranch, Mountain   24 | 20 | 21 | 18 | $125

27734 Sand Canyon Rd., Santa Clarita; 661-252-7666; www.robinsonranchgolf.com; 6508/5076; 72.1/69.5; 133/121

■ "The truest greens around" "test putters" on this "tough but forgiving", "picture-perfect" track "set amid gorgeous rolling hills and oaks" at a "great complex" built and run by the eponymous Teds Sr. and Jr. with "nice practice and banquet facilities" and a waterfall-draped clubhouse that's "one of the most beautiful in the world"; it's a "great getaway from crowded city courses", but "some funky holes" lead critics to complain it's "too tricked up for my taste", so "don't bring a box of balls – bring a crate."

Robinson Ranch, Valley   24 | 20 | 20 | 18 | $125

27734 Sand Canyon Rd., Santa Clarita; 661-252-7666; www.robinsonranchgolf.com; 6903/5408; 74.5/72.2; 140/126

■ If you see "Michael Bolton" here and he's "sans do", it may be due to the "frequent wind factor" at this "bitchin' layout with many forced carries" and "greens like Augusta", where celebrities like the formerly hirsute musician and "Marcus Allen" "bring their guts" to "play from the tips"; despite the "silly" "massive oak in the middle of No. 9", it "uses the natural terrain wonderfully."

Monterey Peninsula

Bayonet & Black Horse, Bayonet 矛
25 | 16 | 17 | 23 | $95

1 McClure Way, Seaside; 831-899-7271; www.bayonetblackhorse.com; 7117/5763; 75.6/69.2; 136/123

☑ "It's a long march", weapons drawn, to the "aptly named Combat Corner" on the 11th–15th holes at this "brutal" battlefield which, "true to its military heritage", is like a soldier: "stern, unforgiving", "in terrific condition" and bound to be a "killer"; host of the Buy.com Tour and PGA Tour Qualifiers, it's "hidden at old Fort Ord", where "very mature firs lining fairways" will "eat your lunch", though you won't mind skipping a meal, since the grill and other facilities "leave a bit to be desired" in comparison with high-end neighbors; still, the "awesome views" of Monterey Bay are way cheaper here than at Spyglass.

Bayonet & Black Horse, Black Horse 矛
23 | 16 | 19 | 22 | $95

1 McClure Way, Seaside; 831-899-7271; www.bayonetblackhorse.com; 7009/5648; 74.9/73.0; 137/126

■ Amid "fog, wind and trees that block the view" of the Pacific Ocean, golfers gallop "up and downhill", trying to "stay out of the rough" on this "tremendous track" that's a "real value for the area"; critics of its arboreal abundance argue "bring a chainsaw to deal with all the firs", but everyone agrees if "Bayonet's little brother" is "good enough for [PGA Tour] Q-School, it's good enough for me."

Carmel Valley Ranch 🔊 ⏲
20 | 22 | 23 | 18 | $180

1 Old Ranch Rd., Carmel; 831-626-2519; 800-432-7635; www.cvrgolf.com; 6515/5088; 70.1/69.6; 124/135

■ "The deer meet you at the doorstep" with "wild turkeys" right behind them at this "short", "tranquil" and "pretty" Pete Dye design "on the sunny side of Carmel", where "weather is better and prices lower than Pebble Beach"; it slinks through oaks and along the river on the front, then "plays in the hills" "with a spectacular set of mountain holes" on the back nine; while dissenters dis a couple of "goofy", "tricked-up" spots, there's nothing inane about the "great" Wyndham hotel next door, the "helpful staff" and the "excellent restaurant."

Del Monte Golf Course 矛
16 | 15 | 18 | 18 | $95

1300 Sylvan Rd., Monterey; 831-373-2700; www.pebblebeach.com; 6357/6052; 70.8/69.5; 123/121

■ "Picture yourself at the turn of the century playing the U.S. Amateur" rhapsodize nostalgics who "love" this "contoured classic" from 1897 that's "flat" and "easy" enough to make it "fun to play with the family" for a "respite" from the "beating you receive" at "nearby" "big names" "in the Pebble Beach empire"; it's "a good walk" through "history", but "cost is high" for "service that could be better" on a track that "bores" modernists.

PACIFIC GROVE GOLF COURSE | 19 | 11 | 14 | 27 | $38 |

77 Asilomar Blvd., Pacific Grove; 831-648-5775;
5732/5305; 67.5/70.5; 117/114

■ "Flying balls don't seem to faze" the "pheasants and deer roaming through" this municipal "treasure"; take a cue from the wildlife and "by all means walk it if you can" because, though the front nine is a "pretty straightforward meander through the neighborhood", the back is a "heavenly" pay-off with "plenty of iceplants", sand dunes and "spectacular ocean views" of the Point Piños lighthouse; built in 1932, this "short, poor man's Pebble Beach" has been the "best value in the famous Monterey area" for many, many years.

PEBBLE BEACH 🏌️ | 29 | 27 | 27 | 16 | $350 |

1700 17-Mile Dr., Pebble Beach; 831-624-3811; 800-654-9300;
www.pebblebeach.com; 6719/5198; 73.8/71.9; 142/130

■ "Beg, borrow, steal" or "mortgage your first born" to "make the pilgrimage" "once before you die" and tee off on the "most gorgeous stretch of golf on earth"; the "plush" dining and "gold-standard" accommodations are "nirvana" enough, while this *Survey*'s Most Popular course is "like playing baseball in Yankee Stadium or football at the Rose Bowl"; amid "barking seals" and crashing waves, the clifftop "national treasure" "makes grown men drop to their knees" and "throw frugality to the wind" as they walk in the "mystical" footsteps of "Nicklaus, Watson and Woods."

POPPY HILLS 🏌️ | 25 | 22 | 22 | 24 | $150 |

3200 Lopez Rd., Pebble Beach; 831-625-1513; 6822/5372; 74.6/71.6; 144/131

■ "Stay out of the pine trees" warn Hansels and Gretels, as you "escape into this beautiful course" on the 17-Mile Drive that is "far enough from the water to be sheltered from the wind" but close enough to "hear the seals"; "one of the best deals on the planet", Poppy Ridge's cousin is a "fair but stern test" where, if the "scenery doesn't distract you", the "deer in the fairways" "at dusk will."

SPANISH BAY 🏌️ | 26 | 26 | 26 | 17 | $215 |

2700 17-Mile Dr., Pebble Beach; 831-647-7500; 800-654-9300;
www.pebblebeach.com; 6821/5332; 73.8/71.9; 142/130

☑ Putting princes proclaim this "striking" seaside Cinderella the "undervalued stepchild" of "the Pebble Beach trio", with a "very women-friendly", "off-the-charts" "links" layout amid "gorgeous ocean views", "sand dunes, forest" and "deer in your face"; check into the "top-notch hotel", "have a drink", groove to the "sundown bagpiper" and try to ignore the "nose-bleed prices" and "lack of practice facilities."

SPYGLASS HILL 🏌️ | 29 | 21 | 24 | 18 | $260 |

Spyglass Hill Rd., Pebble Beach; 831-625-8563; 800-654-9300;
www.pebblebeach.com; 6862/5380; 75.3/73.7; 148/133

☑ "I've never had so much fun getting crushed" cry muff-a-lot masochists at this "unmatched challenge" by Robert Trent Jones Sr. where the "almost perfect" "exhaustion" comes from hazards such as "ice plants", "towering trees" and "the grazing deer you play right next to who don't budge an inch" on a "links by the beach" "in the fog"; "even given the extraordinary fees", it's "cheaper than Pebble Beach", so while nitpickers tsk over "moderate clubhouse facilities" and driving range "mats", those pondering that eternal play-and-stay deal say "scatter my ashes down No. 1 at Spyglass."

Orange County

Coyote Hills ⛳   20 | 20 | 21 | 17 |$106
1440 E. Bastanchury Rd., Fullerton; 714-672-6800;
6510/4437; 71.1/64.2; 128/108
☑ Wily women golfers catch the birdie on this "tight, hilly" "sleeper" that's so "favorable for play from the forward tees" that deflated male egos moan it's "one of the few courses where my wife actually beat me scratch"; "on days with good-to-moderate air", the views of Catalina Island and LA are "spectacular" from the "elevated greens" "built ingeniously on an oil field", though at closer range, visions of "drilling apparatuses" "take away from the golf" at what clowning club-wielders call "Coyote Wells."

Monarch Beach   22 | 20 | 21 | 15 |$175
33033 Niguel Rd., Dana Point; 949-240-8247;
www.monarchbeachgolf.com; 6344/5046; 71.4/70.4; 134/125
☑ It's "hard to concentrate on shots" when "the Pacific's within reach" at this "challenging and beautiful" Robert Trent Jones Jr. design that has "lots of bunkers", ridges and slopes; but with "only two ocean holes" and a "very ordinary back nine", some say the designer "missed the boat", concluding they "expected more from a course that borders the new St. Regis and the Ritz-Carlton."

Oak Creek ⛳   20 | 21 | 21 | 15 |$135
1 Golf Club Dr., Irvine; 949-653-7300; www.oakcreekgolfclub.com;
6850/5621; 72.7/71.2; 132/121
■ If you're stuck in traffic on the San Diego or Santa Ana freeway, "a solid choice" would be to exit at this "super Tom Fazio design" with "wide-open fairways" and a "tough back nine" that "demands some distance and good putting"; the "excellent practice facilities and friendly staff" will ease your road rage, though – "wow and ouch!" – the "way-too-expensive" greens fees might leave you with little gas money to get home.

PELICAN HILL, OCEAN NORTH ⛳   26 | 25 | 24 | 15 |$270
22651 Pelican Hill Rd., Newport Coast; 949-760-0707;
www.pelicanhill.com; 6856/4950; 73.3/67.6; 133/112
☑ "It's like a dream in Orange County, overlooking the ocean" sigh starry-eyed swingers on this "pretty but pricey" "home run" that touches every base with a "hilly", "challenging" Tom Fazio layout "not for the duffer", a "superb" staff, "terrific food and wine" and blufftop views of "the gorgeous Pacific"; though misers cry about "Rolls-Royce prices for a Cadillac round", workaholic wagglers insist it's "worth taking the day off to play", especially provided "someone else is paying."

Pelican Hill, Ocean South ⛳   26 | 24 | 24 | 14 |$270
22651 Pelican Hill Rd., Newport Coast; 949-760-0707;
www.pelicanhill.com; 6634/4712; 72.1/68.7; 130/116
■ "Great photo ops" pop up all over this "spectacular venue" that boasts "stunning" "seaside views" from nearly every hole, including the "back-to-back par 3s"; situated "a shuttle bus ride

from the Ritz-Carlton in Laguna Niguel", with a Four Seasons eatery and an "extensive pro shop", it's in "great shape" all the way through to its "wonderful final four finishers", but bring oxygen at check-in because the "prices will take your breath away."

Strawberry Farms
| 20 | 20 | 20 | 15 | $195 |

11 Strawberry Farms Rd., Irvine; 949-551-1811;
www.strawberryfarmsgolf.com; 6700/4832; 12.7/68.7; 134/114

✓ "You get a tranquil feeling" on at least half the holes at this "schizophrenic" yet "beautiful course" with a "narrow" "packed-in" front and a "superb back nine" 30 minutes from John Wayne Airport; "the rates are a little out of synch with a layout" that's "built around an environmentally protected area where you lose balls", but you gain a few pounds because the "nice staff" in the "clubhouse offers a good burger with fries" and just about "the best club sandwich you'll ever have."

Talega 🏨
| 25 | 18 | 20 | 17 | $120 |

990 Avenida Talega, San Clemente; 949-369-6226; www.talega.com;
6951/5569; 73.6/71.1; 137/121

✓ "Once you get away from the homes" around it, this "beautiful new course in the hills" not far from Nixon's Western White House offers "one of the most pleasant golf experiences in California"; it's "well maintained", with a "killer back nine" overlooking canyons, marshes and lakes, but it's "still young", and there is "no driving range" yet, so it's "pricey" for a place where you can't "warm up."

Tijeras Creek
| 23 | 19 | 20 | 18 | $115 |

29082 Tijeras Creek, Rancho Santa Margarita; 949-589-9793;
www.tijerascreek.com; 6918/5130; 73.4/69.8; 136/120

■ "You never get bored with" these "fun-filled holes" duffers declare after the "basic condo-golf front nine" "got them cocky" and before the "narrow" "target" back nine strapped them in for a "stunning", "scary" "trip through the canyon"; now that new black tee boxes have been laid down, even aces agree that what they used to call a "Kaufman & Broad nightmare" of a first half is much less "uninteresting" than it was, and a course that can now stretch to 6918 might have hackers tucking their tails before they tee it up on No. 1.

Tustin Ranch 🏌
| 19 | 20 | 20 | 15 | $135 |

12442 Tustin Ranch Rd., Tustin; 714-730-1611; www.tustinranchgolf.com;
6803/5263; 72.4/70.3; 129/118

✓ "Experience the value of caddies" (call ahead) or "hit the ball well" all by your lonesome at this "nice", "flat" track spread out among lakes in a "gated community", where the "gorgeous landscaping" looks "easy" but "the rough will get you every time"; however, it charges like it "wants to be a private club", and comics crack "if you like condo golf, this is your place . . . please take it."

Palm Springs

Cimarron
| 23 | 22 | 19 | 21 | $95 |

67603 30th Ave., Cathedral City; 760-770-6060;
www.cimarrongolf.com; 6858/5127; 73.9/69.7; 124/117

■ Somnambulant swingers sigh "I dream about my next visit" to this "interesting" desert layout where "the contrast between the velvety green grass and the sandy scrub is beautiful"; it's "short", but nature helps with "good risk/reward" "challenges", from the "havoc of a windy day" to "a huge expanse of hardpan flanking the holes" to – "watch out" – "those jackrabbits everywhere"; it's "arid" and "treeless" out there, so it's a good thing the "energetic staff" "always" has the "refreshment cart in sight."

Desert Dunes ⛳ 22 | 19 | 19 | 19 | $100
19300 Palm Dr., Desert Hot Springs; 760-251-5367;
6876/5359; 73.8/70.7; 142/122
■ Tee off, "hold onto your hat" and you'll "know why there are windmills" in the Valley at this "links-style" "Q-school qualifying course" "in the middle of the desert"; it "doesn't get quite the attention that others receive" in the area, so it's "usually not too crowded" for a "challenging but fair" round on Robert Trent Jones Jr.'s "good mix of holes", including two lined with Tamarisk trees to stand under during "very hot afternoons."

Desert Falls ⛳ 22 | 20 | 21 | 20 | $180
1111 Desert Falls Pkwy., Palm Desert; 760-340-4653;
7017/5013; 75.0/71.7; 145/124
■ Prairie dogs "go for the gusto" at this "diamond-in-the-rough" "desert favorite" "you can usually get on"; the "ever-changing" layout is always "perfect for all handicaps", the pro staff is "friendly" and the "excellent amenities" include a "great 19th hole" where "lunch on the outside deck is wonderful and the lake with mountains in the background is breathtaking."

Desert Willow, Firecliff ⛳ 27 | 25 | 24 | 21 | $165
38995 Desert Willow Dr., Palm Desert; 760-346-7060; 800-323-3323;
www.desertwillow.com; 7056/5079; 74.1/69.0; 138/120
■ The only course ever featured on the cover of *Smithsonian Magazine,* this "environmentally sound", "superbly" photogenic city-owned stretch backdropped by the Santa Rosas might be "the best value in Palm Desert"; "well-manicured fairways" carved out amid "sand dunes" and "bunkers galore" delight inland duffers "looking for a day at the beach" ("if they don't bump into a cactus"), and while the resort "facilities are not completed" yet, the "great" staffers in the "first-rate pro shop" do their best to deliver the "trappings of a private club."

Desert Willow, Mountain View ⛳ 25 | 23 | 22 | 20 | $165
38995 Desert Willow Dr., Palm Desert; 760-346-7060; 800-323-3323;
www.desertwillow.com; 6913/5040; 73.4/69.0; 129/116
■ "More user-friendly" "than its sister course, Firecliff", this "wonderful test of golf" "amid beautiful surroundings" offers a "good mix of interesting holes"; "don't trust the computer caddie, look for yardages on the course", "choose the proper set of tees and you'll have a ball."

Heritage Palms ⛳ 19 | 19 | 18 | 19 | $100
44291 Heritage Palms Dr. S., Indio; 760-772-7334;
6727/5577; 71.4/66; 119/106
◪ It's "beautiful in the morning" say dew-sweepers swinging on this "fair" Arthur Hills design that's "playable for all golfers", until it "gets windy in the afternoon"; with "lightning greens" and "very good practice facilities" laid down "amid a retirement community"

in the Coachella Valley 15 miles east of Palm Springs, it's a "no-frills", "well-maintained" "alternative" "if you can't get a tee time" at any of the "numerous great" "resort" tracks; nonetheless, religious rounders hankering for "trees" tsk "when God created average he invented this course."

Indian Wells, East 🏊   19 | 20 | 19 | 16 | $120

44500 Indian Wells Ln., Indian Wells; 760-346-4653;
www.indianwells.org/golf; 6631/5516; 71.7/71.5; 122/113
■ "The setting may distract you" at this "elegantly landscaped" layout "within a beautiful resort" boasting panoramic vistas of the Santa Rosa Mountains, but the design is "fair" enough to be "confidence-building" anyway; it's a "high-class outfit" with a "good pro shop and restaurant", but you'd better "bring an air conditioner and 12 quarts of water to survive the heat", which might really be the only difficult thing about a course that's "too easy" not to "bore" low handicappers.

Indian Wells, West 🏊   21 | 20 | 19 | 17 | $120

44500 Indian Wells Ln., Indian Wells; 760-346-4653;
www.indianwells.org/golf; 6500/5408; 70.7/71.0; 120/127
☑ "It's startling how enjoyable the entire experience is here" say vacationers on the multi-tiered greens and watery par-3 13th at this "beautiful course" that "winds its way around" the Hyatt Grand Champions and the Renaissance Esmeralda; the "service is great", the "facilities are good" and the track is "well groomed" – now if they could just do something to make it more difficult so seasoned swingers don't ask "why do so many pay so much for so little" to challenge them?

La Quinta, Dunes 🏌   23 | 24 | 23 | 18 | $145

50200 Vista Bonita, La Quinta; 760-564-7610; www.laquintaresort.com;
6747/4997; 73.1/68.0; 137/114
☑ "They can't do more for you" on this course at a "wonderful", casita-dotted resort where "La Quinta service" comes with "lots of smiles and thank-yous"; while the majority applauds the "plush", "challenging layout" in a "gorgeous setting" "on a small piece of property that follows the canal out and back" to "the great clubhouse", a handful of hookers snickers that it's "typical Pete Dye", so they've "seen all these holes elsewhere."

LA QUINTA, MOUNTAIN 🏌   25 | 24 | 23 | 18 | $235

50200 Vista Bonita, La Quinta; 760-564-7610; www.laquintaresort.com;
6756/5005; 74.1/71.0; 140/123
■ "Unbelievable beauty" surrounds "dramatic holes" on this "deceptively difficult" "mountainside course" that's enhanced by resort facilities "rich in old-world charms", including Native American spa treatments; Pete Dye's "memorable layout" winds through a "well-manicured", "lunar landscape" toward the "stellar back nine", while a "first-rate" staff does "what you want without being asked"; it may be pricey, but it's "worth every penny."

Marriott Desert Springs, Palm 🏊   23 | 25 | 24 | 18 | $150

74855 Country Club Dr., Palm Desert; 760-341-2211; 800-331-3112;
www.desertspringsresort.com; 6761/5492; 72.1/70.8; 130/116
■ There are "generous amounts of water and sand" at this "truly picturesque" course at the foot of the Santa Rosa Mountains; a

"great value in summer", even if you have to "bring a bucket of ice and sunscreen" to brave the "inferno", it's "highly recommended for vacation play", especially when you can get a "package deal" and cool off in one of the resort's ample pools afterward.

Marriott Desert Springs, Valley ⛳
20 | 23 | 22 | 17 | $150

74855 Country Club Dr., Palm Desert; 760-341-2211; 800-331-3112; www.desertspringsresort.com; 6627/5262; 71.5/69.6; 127/110

◪ "Memorable water features" highlight this "well-maintained" course "in the desert" with "gorgeous" palm-framed, multi-tiered greens that's the "less played", "better paced" of the lagoon-laden Marriott's two; grumblers grouse about the "relatively flat" layout that's "not nearly as good as the Palm", but they still get to enjoy the "first-class pro shop and restaurants."

Marriott Shadow Ridge ⛳
27 | 25 | 24 | 20 | $145

9002 Shadow Ridge Rd., Palm Desert; 760-674-2700; 6923/6114; 73.9/69.2; 134/124

■ Designer Nick Faldo "did a great job" on this new "visually stunning" and "deceptive" course in an Australian sandbelt style with "deeep bunkering", "ample fairways" and "approach shots that require great precision"; "it feels like a private club" with a "friendly, attentive staff", "excellent practice facilities" and "quality throughout", so admirers assure "you won't regret playing here."

Mesquite
17 | 15 | 16 | 19 | $75

2700 E. Mesquite Ave.; 760-323-9377; www.americangolf.com; 6328/5281; 72.8/70.8; 122/120

■ "A welcome oasis" set amid the namesake trees with "beautiful views of the San Jacinto and Santa Rosa Mountains", this "very accommodating, well-maintained and well-priced" layout is "especially user-friendly for ladies"; "distances appropriately long without being intimidating" "can make you work, but you can also have fun" say women golfers, even though you'll "suffer from slow play at peak" hours.

PGA West, Greg Norman ⛳
22 | 23 | 22 | 16 | $235

56150 PGA Blvd., La Quinta; 760-564-7170; 800-742-9378; www.pgawest.com; 7156/5281; 75.1/71.0; 139/122

■ "Fun to play, hard to score on and worth a visit" sums up the sentiments of shotmakers on this "beautifully challenging" "true desert" "target course" that "severely penalizes mediocrity"; designed by its namesake Australian superstar in the "gravel and brush" of the Coachella Valley 40 feet below sea level, it's a "great value in the hot summer months", but it "takes an acquired taste" akin to Neil Armstrong's to "contend with" an environment that's like "golfing on the moon."

PGA West, Jack Nicklaus Tournament ⛳
25 | 25 | 23 | 17 | $235

56150 PGA Blvd., La Quinta; 760-564-7170; 800-742-9378; www.pgawest.com; 7204/5023; 74.7/69.9; 139/121

■ "Long, longer, longest" moan power-deprived mortals of this "tough", "visually intimidating" layout "for big boys only" that "will kick your butt" with its large lakes, steep drop-offs where "Jack punishes you for missing fairways" and the "deepest pot bunkers ever"; "precision golf is the key to excelling" on an "exciting, picturesque" course that "has everything", including "superb practice facilities" and "beautiful mountain views."

PGA WEST, TPC STADIUM ⛳ 25 │ 25 │ 22 │ 16 │ $235

56150 PGA Blvd., La Quinta; 760-564-7170; 800-742-9378; www.pgawest.com; 7266/5092; 75.9/70.0; 150/124

☑ "The course everyone loves to hate" is "the hardest inland layout ever designed", "where every shot must be played to perfection" according to veterans who have "finished on and lived to tell about" the "diabolical" Pete Dye's "devilish greens, monster bunkers" and par-3 17th "island green, 'Alcatraz'"; given all this and "facilities that can't be beat", most model swingers are "truly mesmerized by the difficult, beautiful" pro-event host, even if dollar-wise duffers dis it as "expensive", "tricky" and "unfair."

Tahquitz Creek, Legend 20 │ 19 │ 20 │ 21 │ $70

1885 Golf Club Dr.; 760-328-1956; 800-743-2211; www.palmergolf.com; 6775/5861; 72.3/71.9; 118/120

■ "It's a desert out there, so watch out for rabbits and roadrunners", and steer clear of the 40-some new bunkers on this "fun and challenging" municipal "secret"; "when you don't want to shell out for the big-ticket Palm Desert courses", this "basic" "old favorite" "will give you your fix without emptying your wallet."

Tahquitz Creek, Resort ⛳ 18 │ 16 │ 17 │ 20 │ $95

1885 Golf Club Dr.; 760-328-1956; 800-743-2211; www.palmergolf.com; 6705/5206; 71.8/70.0; 125/119

■ It's "no frills", but the price is right as you "golf your way through this quiet neighborhood" on a "decent desert course" that's "great for players of all levels"; the Arnold Palmer–managed muni earns kudos as "possibly the area's best value in summer", "if you can stand the heat" and the bargain-hunting hackers – it's "just like Sunday driving: relaxing, but painfully slow"; N.B. despite its name, there's no lodging at the facility, though they do offer stay-and-play packages with nearby hotels.

Westin Mission Hills, Gary Player ⛳ 23 │ 23 │ 22 │ 18 │ $145

70-705 Ramon Rd., Rancho Mirage; 760-770-9496; 800-358-2211; www.troongolf.com; 7082/4907; 73.9/68.0; 134/118

■ "Many great holes, several extraordinary ones" lure linksters to the Dye course's sibling, nestled amid desert flora and fauna a six-mile drive from the convention-oriented, newly-redone hotel amid "extremely beautiful" views of the San Jacinto Mountains; "it can be very windy in the afternoon", so it's "best to play in the morning", but "it's well-conditioned", "pretty" and "enjoyable" any time of day, despite "the addition of home sites that have deteriorated the feel."

Westin Mission Hills, Pete Dye ⛳ 22 │ 23 │ 22 │ 18 │ $145

71501 Dinah Shore Dr., Rancho Mirage; 760-328-3198; 800-358-2211; www.troongolf.com; 6706/4841; 73.5/67.4; 137/107

■ Aces aim for "target approaches" at this Dye layout that "wraps through the Mission Hills development" before concluding with a "long, narrow 18th fairway along the water that's a round maker or breaker" at the Westin resort; "it's not the most challenging course", though the "diabolical" designer still dishes up some difficulty on a track that features "excellent conditioning and superb practice areas."

Riverside

Hidden Valley 🏌   21 | 18 | 18 | 17 | $95
10 Clubhouse Dr., Norco; 909-737-1010; 800-822-0101; www.hiddenvalleygolf.com; 6721/4649; 73.3/66.6; 140/116
☑ "Fantasy-golf-calendar holes" with "incredible vistas from the elevated tees" make this "short but interesting layout" a pinup favorite for "mountain climbers"; "bring an extra sleeve of balls" and a "snake bite kit" with you because it's an "out-of-control target" test where not only your Titleist, but you yourself can "get lost on the first hole"; environmentalists who insist "this course should stay hidden" protest "new housing developments along the fairways of the back nine" that they say "ruin what used to be spectacular nature views."

Landmark at Oak Quarry 🏌   25 | 22 | 23 | 22 | $90
7151 Sierra Ave.; 909-685-1440; www.oakquarrygolfclub.com; 7002/5408; 73.9/75.4; 137/131
■ "You'll want to come back" to this newish "gorgeous" course carved into the abandoned, historic Jensen Quarry that's got "amazing par 3s" and an especially "memorable 14th"; just "bring your A game" and "watch out for the wind", "water hazards, huge bunkers and elevated greens" because a "lot of thought" went into this "solid" design where it's "hard to recover from your mistakes"; don't miss the best part: a "drink in the clubhouse watching others attempt their tee shots on the 17th."

Moreno Valley Ranch 🏌   23 | 20 | 20 | 23 | $65
28095 John F. Kennedy Dr., Moreno Valley; 909-924-4444; www.mvrgolf.com
Lake/Mountain: 6684/5108; 73.1/69.6; 139/121
Lake/Valley: 6898/5196; 74.1/70.1; 138/122
Mountain/Valley: 6880/5196; 74.2/70.1; 140/122
■ "A gem in the middle of nowhere", this "sharp", "must-play" 27-hole Pete Dye design has "great valley views on the Mountain nine", especially from the signature par-3 7th, where it "feels like you're on top of the world" – just watch out for the "lizards hanging off the big boulders."

Sacramento

Diablo Grande, Legends West 🏌   25 | 22 | 22 | 22 | $100
10001 Oak Flat Rd., Patterson; 209-892-4653; www.diablogrande.com; 7112/4905; 74.4/69.3; 147/123
■ "If it weren't in East Jesus", this "great golf complex would be hugely popular" declare Bay Area drivers who deem the Jack Nicklaus/Gene Sarazen collaboration "an absolute wonder" "worth the two-hour trip" all the way out into the Central Valley; if its developers realize their plans, one day it will be the anchor of an enormous, well-populated residential community, but for now, it's still "out in the boonies" surrounded by the vineyards and the hills, so it's "never crowded", and its "challenging holes" feel like "wonderful hideaways."

Diablo Grande, Ranch　　22 │ 21 │ 20 │ 23 │ $85
10001 Oak Flat Rd., Patterson; 209-892-4653;
www.diablogrande.com; 7246/5026; 75.1/69.5; 141/120
◪ "Tough, long, narrow but fair", this "big brother" to Legends
West is a "beautiful" layout lined with creeks and 400-year-old
oaks, bordered by a vineyard and sporting "a couple of strange
par 5s"; you "must like snakes, heat, wind" and "a good drive
from the city", but "it's a pleasure" if you do, and a "good value",
particularly combined with its sister at the "36-hole price"; stop
at the Diablo Grande Vineyards for a post-round wine tasting.

Twelve Bridges Golf Club　　25 │ 22 │ 21 │ 22 │ $80
3075 Twelve Bridges Dr., Lincoln; 916-645-7200; 888-893-5832;
www.twelvebridges.com; 7150/5328; 74.2/71.0; 146/123
◪ It "knocks your socks off" declare drivers dressed down by this
"great, great, great" LPGA Tour host where "beautiful oak trees line
fairways" on the rolling hills "just north of Cowtown"; "the design
demands accuracy" off the tees, and "even the pros have a tough
time with the large, undulating greens", but they can relax later in
the "women-friendly" environs of the "outstanding clubhouse" and
ignore lazy lofters who lament the "cart-path-only rule", speed
freaks who fuss that "play can be slow" and whimps who whine
over "snakes and summer heat."

San Bernardino

Empire Lakes　　19 │ 17 │ 17 │ 17 │ $90
11015 Sixth St., Rancho Cucamonga; 909-481-6663;
www.empirelakes.com; 6923/5200; 73.4/70.5; 133/125
■ "If you hit it good, it will reward you" lilt lofters who "love" the
"beautiful" setting in a "windy" "arroyo between industrial parks"
at this "very playable" Palmer design 40 miles east of LA; it's
"friendly for all handicaps", but perhaps not for all pocketbooks –
financially needy neophytes natter "it's a little overpriced for what
you get", which includes "many ridiculously blind tee shots where
first-timers are sure to find trouble."

Oak Valley　　25 │ 19 │ 20 │ 23 │ $79
1888 Golf Club Dr., Beaumont; 909-769-7200;
www.oakvalleygolf.com; 7003/5349; 74.0/71.9; 138/128
■ "Best desert course that nobody's heard of" claim reticent
reviewers of this "gem" "on the way to Palm Springs" that's
"beautiful and competitive" at a price "you can afford"; the
"clubhouse and range are small", but "play the course and you
won't be sorry", as it gives "very good golf" and has "great
character without beating you up."

PGA OF SOUTHERN CALIFORNIA　28 │ 24 │ 24 │ 25 │ $79
AT OAK VALLEY, CHAMPIONS
36211 Champions Dr., Calimesa; 877-742-2500;
7377/5274; 76.5/72.4; 141/128
■ "Best combination of challenging golf and value in Southern
California" gush surveyors smitten with this "beautiful course",
its "classy facilities" and its "immaculate conditions"; though
touted as a "long-hitter's dream" and menaced by "brutal wind at
times", it's a rolling links track that's a "real find" for players at all
levels, even if the PGA pros call it home.

PGA of Southern California at   26 | 24 | 23 | 25 | $79
Oak Valley, Legends
36211 Champions Dr., Calimesa; 877-742-2500;
7442/5169; 76.6/70.9; 144/130

■ "It's well worth the drive" east to this "great course for great golfers" that all agree is an "outstanding value"; the "interesting layout" ribbons through woodlands where some "blind shots and hidden hazards" lurk, so "be careful of the rattlers" if you "venture off the fairways" and, as on its sister, "watch out for wind."

San Diego

AVIARA 🏳   26 | 27 | 26 | 17 | $195
7447 Batiquitos Dr., Carlsbad; 760-603-6900;
www.fourseasons.com; 7007/5007; 74.2/69.1; 137/119

■ "Four Seasons golf . . . you should know what to expect": "superb service", "beautiful facilities", "great views" and "supreme conditions" on "one of the best, most challenging courses in Southern California" at an "opulent" resort amid "waterscapes, statues" and "florabunda galore"; of course, "beauty has its price", so "bring your trust fund" for putting privileges on Arnold Palmer's "Texas-size greens" at this "botanical garden"/"golfing nirvana", and go for broke by "ending your day with a massage at the spa."

Barona Creek 🏌   23 | 18 | 21 | 22 | $75
1932 Wildcat Canyon Rd., Lakeside; 619-387-7018; 888-722-7662;
www.barona.com; 7088/5296; 74.5/70.6; 139/126

■ Just like a game of bacarat at the casino slated for its corner of the Barona Indian Reservation, this "wonderful new track" "makes you think" about your "strategic options"; on a "fun, beautiful" layout, the "fastest greens in the Southwest" are also "difficult to read", and "a little difficult to get to" – swingers suffering the "long drive from North County" or San Diego say "once the hotel is complete" next door, "it will be a great weekend destination."

Carlton Oaks   20 | 14 | 16 | 20 | $75
9200 Inwood Dr., Santee; 619-448-4242; 800-831-6757;
www.carltonoaksgolf.com; 7100/5600; 74.6/73.1; 137/128

◪ You're not needy – you just want "a place to stay, to play, to eat, to drink" and "to sneak out onto during weekdays", and you'll find it at this "decent" "value" "you can usually get on"; "sure, it has an interstate next to it, but if you look past that", it's "one heck" of a "powerhouse" where "mature trees", "large waste bunkers" and a "creek" dish out "trouble if you want to take chances"; though "Santee heat can be unbearable", critics don't warm to what they call "deteriorated", "nondescript holes."

CrossCreek   25 | 12 | 20 | 19 | $85
43860 Glenn Meadows Rd., Temecula; 909-506-3402;
www.crosscreekgolfclub.com; 6833/6310; 74.1/71.6; 142/136

◪ "Step back in time" on this "great new" Arthur Hills layout where each knickered, Hogan-capped staff member personifies a different historical golf figure; it can "be extremely difficult when the wind is blowing" your ball into those oak and sycamore groves, particularly if your stomach is grumbling, but now that the clubhouse is completed, you can order lunch from the grill and leave your old-fashioned picnic at home.

Eagle Crest 🏌️   18 | 12 | 14 | 18 | $65

2492 Old Ranch Rd., Escondido; 760-737-9762;
www.americangolf.com; 6417/4941; 71.6/69.9; 136/123

■ "Keep quiet about this hidden gem" "tucked away in the San Pasqual Valley" plead purse-lipped partisans of a layout that's "kept in good condition" and is "tougher than you think" – "bring your straight ball" and don't get distracted by the "great mountain views" north of San Diego; "they treat seniors right", as long as the oldsters come appropriately dressed, because there is "no locker room" attached to the "unknown course" that, "with a little work, could be great."

Encinitas Ranch   18 | 13 | 16 | 19 | $85

1275 Quail Gardens Dr., Encinitas; 760-944-1936;
6523/5235; 71.2/70.0; 127/118

■ "Spectacular views of the Pacific" come "at a modest price" on this "beautiful, young" muni at a former flower ranch that wanders "uphill, downhill" on red sandstone bluffs north of San Diego; it will "test your game", and your concentration, since "ongoing housing development can be distracting", but it can't tax your taste buds because there is "no dining" beyond your basic snack bar fare yet – "it will probably be better when the permanent clubhouse is built" and the course "matures."

La Costa, North 🏌️🏌️   – | – | – | – | $195

2100 Costa Del Mar Rd., Carlsbad; 760-438-9111; 800-854-5000;
www.lacosta.com; 7021/5939; 74.8/76.3; 137/137

Thanks to a world-class spa, superb restaurants and a tournament tennis complex, there are plenty of vacationers who check into this lavish resort but never golf; that's a shame because the caddied experience, while it costs aplenty, is excellent; Nos. 1–3 and 13–18 make up the front nine of the composite used in PGA Tour competitions, such as the rainy play-off at the 1997 Mercedes Championships that Tiger Woods won by nearly acing the gorgeous, watery par-3 16th.

La Costa, South 🏌️🏌️   – | – | – | – | $195

2100 Costa Del Mar Rd., Carlsbad; 760-438-9111; 800-854-5000;
www.lacosta.com; 7004/5612; 74.4/74.0; 138/134

A bit tighter but equally challenging and attractive as its sister, the South is better known, thanks to the televised coverage of its back nine every year when the PGA Tour tackles this classy, sternly bunkered, tree-lined resort course 30 miles north of San Diego and a couple of miles inland from the Pacific Ocean; the final four holes, three intriguing par 4s and the lovely lake-lined par-5 17th, are called "Golf's Longest Mile", as they head straight into westerly breezes.

Maderas 🏌️🏌️   27 | 18 | 22 | 21 | $120

17750 Old Coach Rd., Poway; 858-726-4653; www.troongolf.com;
www.maderasgolf.com; 7115/5100; 75.2/70.0; 143/128

■ After they "spoil you to death" at this "beautifully manicured" "modern layout in the hills" outside San Diego, you'll ascend to "golf heaven", where there are "fast but fair greens", "some easy par 4s for the mid-handicapper" and a "new clubhouse that looks great"; you'll "hit every club in your bag", so bring 'em all to this newish "bargain" with "outstanding potential."

Mt. Woodson Country Club 🏌 | 24 | 16 | 19 | 21 | $80 |
16422 N. Woodson Dr., Ramona; 760-788-3555;
www.mtwoodson.com; 6113/4441; 68.3/65.9; 130/116
■ Granite "boulders", towering oaks, "soaring hawks", a "long" wooden bridge to No. 3 and lots of "quirky", "creative design" lead some loyalists to label this "Willy Wonka's golf factory"; it certainly "keeps you on your toes" with all those "blind shots" toward "poles instead of fairways" and "short but tight" holes, but even those who say the "greens could use some extra grooming" are "still chuckling at the fun layout."

Pala Mesa Resort | 20 | 17 | 19 | 20 | $80 |
2001 Old Hwy. 395, Fallbrook; 760-728-5881; www.palamesa.com;
6502/5632; 72.0/74.0; 131/134
☑ "Enjoy the serene hillside vistas during your perfect outing" ooh and aah admirers of this "beautiful layout" amid "lots of trees" in the Palomar Mountain foothills, where the "narrow, sloping fairways" are "full of challenges for all levels"; despite "wonderful food and atmosphere", activities ranging from horseshoes to hot-air ballooning plus "outstanding package deals" at this "hidden gem as far as resorts go", faultfinders scoff at "gimmicky greens with impossible pins" and "marginal practice facilities."

Rams Hill | ▽ 18 | 15 | 13 | 17 | $40 |
1881 Rams Hill Rd., Borrego Springs; 760-767-5125; 800-292-2944;
www.ramshillgolf.com; 6866/5694; 72.9/73.4; 130/128
■ It's "a cool ride to a very good course" say roving reviewers of this Ted Robinson layout two hours northeast of San Diego with "great scenery" of the majestic Santa Rosa Mountains and Anza Borrego Desert State Park; "in good condition" with seven lakes, waterfalls and its share of sand, it's "usually easy to get a tee time", making it even "worth the trip from Palm Springs", particularly if you stay over in a rental home.

Rancho Bernardo Inn | 18 | 22 | 23 | 18 | $110 |
17550 Bernardo Oaks Dr.; 858-487-1611; www.jcgolf.com;
6458/4945; 70.4/68.5; 129/119
☑ Statistically challenged chippers give it "a five on a scale of one to three" – this "very mature" layout "up and through canyons" 25 minutes north of San Diego is a "tight" "challenge" with "excellent greens" attached to a large "inn worth staying at" for its "fabulous dining room" and staff that "takes very good care of you"; it makes for a "wonderful weekend", even though gruff golfers grumble that there are "not many memorable holes" and the "greens could use some work" on the "overpriced" former PGA and LPGA host.

RedHawk 🏌 | 22 | 17 | 18 | 20 | $70 |
45100 Redhawk Pkwy., Temecula; 909-302-3850; 800-451-4295;
www.redhawkgolfcourse.com; 7175/5515; 75.7/72.0; 149/124
☑ "Better bring the big dog if you're going to succeed" on this "classy", "nicely manicured" "target" track that "plays long" "for substantial ego deflation" in a "beautiful" "oasis in the valley" at the foothills of the Palomar Mountains; it's a long way from Disneyland, but a vocal opposition scoffs at "some Mickey Mouse holes" with "goofy" "tiered greens", cranking "even the practice putting area is torture."

SCGA Members Club
23 | 15 | 19 | 24 | $78

38275 Murrieta Hot Springs Rd., Murrieta; 909-677-7446; 800-752-9724;
www.scga.org/mbr_club; 7060/5355; 74.4/71.7; 137/128

◩ It "keeps getting better and better" proclaim partisans of this inland "shotmakers'" RTJ Sr. layout about an hour southeast of LA where a recent "makeover" by its owner, the Southern California Golf Association, "enhanced several holes"; SCGA members who dig their deep discounts here say this "straightforward" test is "a pleasure to play", even though creatures of comfort complain its "ambiance is missing" amid "nearby construction."

Singing Hills, Oak Glen
18 | 18 | 18 | 21 | $50

3007 Dehesa Rd., El Cajon; 619-442-3425; 800-457-5568;
www.singinghills.com; 6489/5549; 71.1/71.4; 128/124

■ The hills are alive with the sound of swinging at this "average", "straightforward" guests-only spread built on an old vineyard at the Sycuan Tribe's casino and resort, a "great value" for "a mini-vacation" 20 miles east of San Diego; "open and forgiving", it's an "old-style course" with "smallish greens" run by "nice people."

Singing Hills, Willow Glen
18 | 18 | 18 | 21 | $50

3007 Dehesa Rd., El Cajon; 619-442-3425; 800-457-5568;
www.singinghills.com; 6605/5585; 72.3/72.5; 129/127

◩ "Nicely groomed fairways await your good tee shot" at this guests-only resort "layout in desert canyons" surrounded by mountains, oaks, sycamores and "flowers" at a pleasant "weekend getaway"; it's got "great practice facilities", and "like its sister, Oak Glen", you "can't beat it for value", though intellectual inlanders insist it's "not an interesting layout."

Steele Canyon Golf Course 🏡
21 | 17 | 18 | 18 | $85

3199 Stonefield Dr., Jamul; 619-441-6900; www.steelecanyon.com
Canyon/Meadow: 6672/4813; 72.2/67.9; 134/118
Meadow/Ranch: 7001/5026; 74.0/69.5; 137/125
Ranch/Canyon: 6741/4655; 72.7/66.6; 135/112

■ "Make sure your cart has good brakes because you're gonna need them" on this "outstanding Gary Player" 27-holer with "lots of terrain changes" "from mountainous to valley"; nitpickers who want their nines just so say "Canyon is too tricked up and Meadow is too benign", plus it's "a looooong way out there" from downtown San Diego, but insiders insist "don't miss out playing here before it goes private in the next couple of years."

Temecula Creek Inn
21 | 18 | 19 | 21 | $80

44501 Rainbow Canyon Rd., Temecula; 909-676-2405; 800-962-7335;
www.temeculacreekinn.com
Creek/Oaks: 6784/5737; 72.2/72.8; 126/118
Stonehouse/Creek: 6605/5686; 71.4/72.8; 129/120
Stonehouse/Oaks: 6693/5683; 72.2/73.1; 128/123

◩ Buckle your seatbelt because, with "dramatic, unbelievable, obscured holes", the "Stonehouse nine is a wild ride" at this "very challenging" track in "beautiful surroundings" at a "nice inn with an excellent restaurant" where gastronomic golfers gush that the "nightly meals included in [various package] rates are some of the best I've ever eaten"; it's a "good destination resort" just a short drive inland from San Diego, even though faultfinders fuss over "quirky fairways" and "tricky greens."

Temeku   ▽ 18 | 14 | 13 | 16 | $58

41687 Temeku Dr., Temecula; 909-693-1440;
www.temekuhills.com; 6636/5113; 72.4/68.8; 131/109

■ Nestled in the hills of a wine-producing valley near the Wild West storefronts of Old Town Temecula is a "fun little" "mix of holes" that "makes you think your way around", or read your way around – you "need a yardage book the first time" out on its rolling fairways and tiered greens; while you might "play every club in your bag", and you'll get a "good value" if you're a "senior", "don't expect too much" else, "and you'll be pleased."

TORREY PINES, NORTH   25 | 17 | 17 | 23 | $85

11480 N. Torrey Pines Rd., La Jolla; 858-452-3226; 800-985-4653;
www.torreypinesgolfcourse.com; 6874/6122; 72.1/75.4; 129/134

■ "It's worth camping out" to get on the holes "where the best congregate" for the PGA Tour's Buick Invitational at this "spectacular" "muni rarity" on La Jolla's "best ocean bluffs"; it's "less dramatic" and "shorter than the South", but it's "more scenic", with "amazing views of the nude beach from the 7th tee"; that and the newly redone Craftsman-style lodge and spa on the 18th fairway "help keep traffic busy" so "it's very hard to get on unless" you book a room to guarantee your tee time.

TORREY PINES, SOUTH   27 | 17 | 17 | 24 | $75

11480 N. Torrey Pines Rd., La Jolla; 858-452-3226; 800-985-4653;
www.torreypinesgolfcourse.com; 7607/5542; 78.1/73.5; 143/128

■ It's hard to find a "bigger ego deflator" than this Buick co-host and rumored "future U.S. Open venue" that "plays like a monster", "especially since a remodel" "added 600 more yards"; along "gorgeous coastline" in "SoCal weather", "hang gliders soar overhead as you reach for the sky with your driver" – "what better way to spend a day" "after you've slept in your car overnight just to get on" the "crowded" "beauty"?; N.B. don't even think about playing the blacks – they're open to pros only.

San Francisco Bay

Bridges 矛   19 | 22 | 20 | 13 | $95

9000 S. Gale Ridge Rd., San Ramon; 925-735-4253;
www.thebridgesgolf.com; 7081/5274; 74.5/71.4; 134/123

☑ It's 'risk/reward/risk again' on "the toughest course you'll love to play", a "beautiful but difficult" track where you better "take a caddie", as "many shots are not intuitively obvious"; the "fairways are almost cut like greens", but there's "no first or second grade of rough", so if you're "out of bounds", "you're in deep yogurt", and "high-handicappers" forced to eat it groan that designer Johnny Miller "squeezed the fun out" of the "tricked-up" layout.

Half Moon Bay, Ocean   24 | 20 | 21 | 16 | $145

2 Miramontes Point Rd., Half Moon Bay; 650-726-4438;
www.halfmoonbaygolf.com; 6732/5109; 71.8/71.6; 125/119

☑ "On a clear day you want to play forever" to savor the "beautiful, open" "ocean course" when it's "a piece of cake", but on a day of "wind, fog and cold", even "layers of attire" won't keep you from "crying for mercy" on Arthur Hills' "sweet" but "challenging" "must-play" links 45 minutes from downtown SF; despite the low brow "view of the mobile home park", it's a bit "hard on the wallet", though well-heeled 19th-holers do cough up the dough, "skipping the clubhouse bar and walking over to the new Ritz-Carlton for drinks" by the cliffside fire pit.

Half Moon Bay, Old Course   22 | 20 | 21 | 16 | $145

2 Miramontes Point Rd., Half Moon Bay; 650-726-4438;
www.halfmoonbaygolf.com; 7131/5769; 75.0/73.3; 135/128

☑ "The 18th hole alone is worth the greens fee" for its "breathtaking views of the coastline" (at least when it's not "foggy") gush golfers gaga over this "windy" "jewel" that's "quite a looker after the [recent] renovation and the Ritz-Carlton" opening; "nestled in and out of" a housing development, "it's like playing pinball off the adjacent homes if you're not accurate", and the "lack of practice area or driving range" won't help you learn to shoot straight.

Mare Island   17 | 8 | 14 | 22 | $48

1800 Club Dr., Mare Island, Vallejo; 707-562-4653;
6150/4832; 69.8/71.8; 124/117

■ "Awesome value" reels in wallet-watchers at this former Navy shipyard turned "low-traffic" links "hidden away" on an islet across the channel from Vallejo; it combines the "small greens" of an "old, traditional tree-lined" front nine with a newer, "open and hilly" back sporting "fabulous views" "on a clear day" of "majestic" San Pablo Bay; as in its past, working the iron here "can be brutal" if the "afternoon wind kicks up", but it's still "a pleasant surprise."

Oakmont Golf Club   18 | 20 | 18 | 23 | $47

7025 Oakmont Dr., Santa Rosa; 707-539-0415;
www.oakmontgc.com; 6379/5573; 71.1/71.8; 124/125

☑ "Old and elegant", this "hilly" Valley of the Moon layout with the "Sonoma-Napa Mountains" for a backdrop is "surprisingly nice", with "fast greens" "hidden within the Oakmont Village retirement community"; it's "pleasant" tailed by a meal at its "top" restaurant, the Quail Inn, but the homes creeping in on it lead critics to crack it's "good if you like to look into backyards for gardening tips."

Paradise Valley   18 | 18 | 17 | 23 | $45

3950 Paradise Valley Rd., Fairfield; 707-426-1600; www.fairfield-golf.com;
6704/5413; 70.1/71.1; 135/119

■ "Big, friendly greens" and big, friendly "discounts" greet golfers of "all handicaps" on this "playable", "walkable", "wide-open" muni; could Rancho Solano's sister sound more "nice and easy"? – it is, until the "wind" starts blowing and you have to "swing hard" and aim around those big, lone oaks.

POPPY RIDGE   23 | 23 | 22 | 27 | $70

4280 Greenville Rd., Livermore; 925-447-6779; www.poppyridgegolf.com
Chardonnay/Merlot: 7106/5212; 74.8/70.2; 141/120
Merlot/Zinfandel: 7128/5265; 74.8/70.2; 141/120
Zinfandel/Chardonnay: 7048/5267; 74.8/70.2; 141/120

■ The "treeless" Chardonnay, Merlot and Zinfandel nines make up this "interesting" Rees Jones 27-holer "surrounded by vineyards in the Livermore Valley" with views of Mt. Diablo; like fine wine, "as it matures, it's becoming top-notch" say devotees who drink up "the best deal in the Bay Area", particularly if they're members of the Northern California Golf Association, which runs the joint – either way, they "play in the morning before the wind starts howling."

PRESIDIO GOLF COURSE   20 | 16 | 16 | 18 | $72
300 Finley Rd., San Francisco; 415-561-4670; www.presidiogolf.com;
6477/5785; 72.2/69.2; 136/127
☑ "It is a draft-dodger's dream to play this excellent, former
military" course "in the heart of America's most beautiful city"; its
"great holes framed by eucalyptus trees" have "difficult sideway
slopes", but "even in the fog, it's a beauty"; sadly, all that "cold,
wet" "wind" results in "soggy" fairways "inundated with daisies",
which get "muddy in winter", and it's "crowded", even on a "range
that looks like they're trying to starve cows."

Rancho Solano   18 | 16 | 17 | 22 | $45
3250 Rancho Solano Pkwy., Fairfield; 707-429-4653;
www.ranchosolanoclub.com; 6616/5201; 72.1/69.6; 128/117
■ There are "more three- and four-putts than Phil Mickelson on
Sunday" on the "largest greens around" with "some subtle breaks"
tut twitchy tapsters on this "nice" muni with "more variety of holes"
than its sister, Paradise Valley; it's wallet-friendly, "women-friendly"
and "wide open", so ladies, "bring your driver and let it rip", but
if your hair's long, tie it up, as it's "wind, wind, windy" here.

Rio Vista Golf Club   19 | 19 | 18 | 22 | $49
1000 Summerset Dr., Rio Vista; 707-374-2900;
www.riovistagolf.com; 6800/5330; 73.9/72.4; 126/117
■ "In the middle of nowhere" near the Sacramento River delta is a
"retirement community" "in a pretty setting" with a "challenging
layout" that's "easy on the wallet" but "a butt kicker in the afternoon
wind" – "hit it straight" so you don't have to go diving in the many
"lakes" along the holes; fussy foozlers find it "flat, but wet and
sandy", and it might have been called 'Casa Vista', since "too
many homes line the fairways."

Roddy Ranch   22 | 10 | 15 | 18 | $80
1 Tour Way, Antioch; 925-978-4653; www.roddyranch.com;
6945/5390; 74.3/71.7; 131/120
☑ A "hidden gem", this millennial "pseudo-link" "laid out on rolling
pasture" has some ready ranchers "tested from the first hole"; you
pay a "ridiculous price considering" the clubhouse is still "just a
bunch of trailers" say survivalists who suggest that when you're
"in the middle of windswept nowhere" with "no running water"
and "no bathroom" save a "port-a-potty", the "key is to sweat"
or risk having to irrigate those "cement-hard greens."

Sonoma National 🏌   24 | 21 | 20 | 15 | $125
17700 Arnold Dr., Sonoma; 707-996-0300;
www.sonomamissioninn.com; 7087/5511; 74.1/71.8; 132/125
☑ "If you're a golfer visiting wine country, this is the only place to
play" say oenophilic swingers of this "country clubesque" "old
course" in a "beautiful setting" amid the vineyards; though it may be
one of the Bay Area's "prettiest and best", since being purchased
by the nearby Sonoma Mission Inn, it's now "for resort guests" only.

StoneTree   23 | 24 | 24 | 15 | $115
9 Stone Tree Ln., Novato; 415-209-6090; www.stonetreegolf.com;
6810/5232; 72.7/71.2; 137/127
☑ "A great way to spend a Sunday" "within 30 minutes of SF",
say Robert Louis Stevenson fans, is on this "new", "upscale"

suburbanite that's a schizophrenic "thrill to play": the front is "boring", but if the high-priced "hot dogs at the turn feel like a punch in the stomach", they do prepare you for a "back nine that can eat you up and spit you out"; you might land on a "miniature golf"–style green wondering "where the windmills [or the nonexistent driving range] are", but the "great clubhouse", "top-notch dining" and "wonderful staff" will have you coming back to be menaced all over again.

Wente Vineyards   23 | 22 | 23 | 16 | $120
5050 Arroyo Rd., Livermore; 925-456-2475; 800-999-2885;
www.wentegolf.com; 6934/4975; 74.0/69.4; 146/122
■ "The vineyards add to the enjoyment" both during and after your round at this "majestic beauty" that "weaves" through Wente's wine operations; "Greg Norman did a great job" on "creative elevation changes", "tight, punitive fairways" and "true but tough greens" with "incredible views" of the ripening grapes, while the "outstanding" restaurant matches his skill – just "don't drink before you play", warn golfing gourmands, because the "unfortunate rules" dictate that "balls cannot be hit out of the vines."

San Luis Obispo

BlackLake Resort   21 | 17 | 20 | 21 | $55
1490 Golf Course Ln., Nipomo; 805-343-1214; www.blacklake.com
Canyon/Lake: 6401/5638; 70.9/72; 123/120
Lake/Oaks: 6185/5760; 69.7/69.7; 121/117
Oaks/Canyon: 6034/5047; 69.3/69.5; 121/116
■ "You could get lost trying to find" these three "immaculate" nines "in the middle of nowhere" a couple of hours up the coast from LA, but it's "worth the long drive" because "the quiet is wonderful", particularly if you "play in the morning"; Canyon/Lake is the "best combo", but they're all a "very good value for the money", so carnivorous club-wielders suggest with dollars you save, "after your round head to Shell Beach for a great steak at McClintock's."

Hunter Ranch   23 | 18 | 19 | 23 | $60
4041 E. Hwy. 46, Paso Robles; 805-237-7444;
www.hunterranchgolf.com; 6741/5639; 72.8/72.8; 136/132
■ On-course oenophiles delight in "great golf in the morning and great wine in the afternoon" at this "beautiful layout" nestled "amid the vineyards" and "live oaks" in the "rolling hills of the Santa Lucia Mountains"; the "tough little Central California course" is "worth the trip" in itself despite its "lacking facilities", but if you've come to the area mainly to sip of the vine, "stop if you have the time" for a "challenging" bit of tee totaling.

Santa Barbara

Glen Annie   17 | 17 | 19 | 17 | $85
405 Glen Annie Rd., Goleta; 805-968-6400; www.glenanniegolf.com;
6420/5036; 71.1/69.5; 122/118
☑ "Test your driving power while activating your sense of sight" on this "short" but "hilly layout" just north of Santa Barbara where the "breathtaking views" of the Pacific and the Channel Islands are "delightfully distracting"; the "air is clean", the atmosphere is

"peaceful" and "it's a very nice facility", but size queens sneer "they ran out of room" and made it "bumpy" to "mask the lack."

LA PURISIMA ⛳   28 | 17 | 17 | 25 | $75
3455 E. Hwy. 246, Lompoc; 805-735-8395; www.lapurisimagolf.com; 7105/5763; 74.9/74.3; 143/131

■ "It's the purest" proclaim back-to-the-basics ball hitters of this "relatively uncrowded" "golfer's paradise" "always in country club condition" with "no homes or condos lining fairways" overlooking the "pristine" Lompoc, Valley where "you can lose a fistful of balls" to "the teeth of a stiff wind"; with "no frills, no food to speak of and no service", it's "perfect" if you want to "play a properly priced" but "inexhaustible set of challenging", "hilly" holes in "isolation."

Rancho San Marcos ⛳   24 | 19 | 21 | 20 | $139
4600 Hwy. 154; 805-683-6334; 877-766-1804; www.rsm1804.com; 6801/5018; 73.1/69.2; 135/117

■ "Hit the wineries after your round" at this "first-rate" "beauty along the Santa Ynez River", a little "off the beaten path"; outdoorsy types appreciate Robert Trent Jones Jr.'s "routing through vintage rolling hills and oaks" with "views of valley, lake" and "tumultuous mountains that inspire the tremendous tee shots needed"; if you must brush up on your drives, the "top-notch staff" can tell you that the "fantastic practice areas" "have golf written all over them."

River Course at Alisal   18 | 17 | 18 | 19 | $55
150 Alisal Rd., Solvang; 805-688-6042; www.rivercourse.com; 6830/5815; 73.1/73.4; 126/127

■ Posses of duffers canter into this horsey dude resort along the Santa Ynez River near the old Ronald Reagan Ranch for "great family tournaments" on a "nice track" where mom, pop and all the kids will find it "easy to score well"; gramps might hoot "that the 17th hole is a bomb shell, but ooh so much fun", while granny will say it won't be "great till the trees grow up in another 10 years", though she'll "truly love" tooling around in those "state-of-the-art computerized carts."

SANDPIPER   25 | 16 | 17 | 20 | $118
7925 Hollister Ave., Goleta; 805-968-1541; www.sandpipergolf.com; 7068/5725; 74.5/73.3; 134/125

◪ "There's nothing better than the ocean breeze blowing through your hair while you make a putt" pipe short-gamers sweet on this "wonderful seaside experience", "near the beautiful Bacara Resort" on "coastal bluffs", where you can "whale-watch between shots" on the back nine's "true oceanfront holes"; while the spa is stellar and "the views alone are worth the price of admission" "when it's not fogged in", penny-pinchers proclaim it "pricey" for "spotty conditions" and "limited dining."

Santa Cruz

Delaveaga   20 | 15 | 15 | 22 | $48
401 Upper Park Rd.; 831-423-7214; www.delaveagagolf.com; 6010/5331; 70.4/70.6; 133/125

■ With "lots of hills and gullies" leading to "strange lies", "poison oak out of bounds" and none of that Santa Cruz touchy-feeliness, this muni in the shadow of "Pasatiempo, its well-known country club neighbor", is "one wicked course for the money"; "leave your driver in the bag" and expect to "use your 5-iron through wedge a lot" as you "wind through the forest" on a "tight" "ride" with holes that "will bring you to your knees."

PASATIEMPO ♞   28 | 19 | 20 | 20 | $150

18 Clubhouse Rd.; 831-459-9155; www.pasatiempo.com; 6445/5629; 72.7/73.6; 141/135
■ Club-wielding kingmakers crown this "incredible" 1929 "Alister MacKenzie masterpiece" "in the beautiful Santa Cruz Mountains" "one of California's finest", thanks to a "narrow front nine", "classic back", "difficult sloped greens" and "interesting bunkering"; "steeped in history", it's a "respected", "unmatched beauty" that's withstood the passing of time, making it "a worthy side trip from Pebble Beach" an hour to the south and a "must-play" at least "once for golf buffs" who fully understand why it's so "expensive."

San Juan Oaks   25 | 24 | 22 | 21 | $80

3825 Union Rd., Hollister; 831-636-6118; 800-453-8337; www.sanjuanoaks.com; 7133/4770; 75.6/64.5; 145/115
■ "Oh, what fun" exclaim thrill-seekers on this "deceptively hard" "Fred Couples signature" "in beautiful farm country" not far from Monterey that's "first-class from top to bottom" "in and out of the canyons"; with "risk/reward opportunities" amid "afternoon winds", it "requires distance and finesse" as "errant tee shots exact a heavy toll" in "protected marshes" and "hay fields they call rough"; the payoff includes "superb hospitality" with stay-and-play deals at hotels in nearby San Juan Bautista, home of the 200-year-old mission.

Santa Rosa

Bodega Harbour Golf Links   22 | 16 | 19 | 19 | $90

21301 Heron Dr., Bodega Bay; 707-875-3538; www.bodegaharbourgolf.com; 6265/4749; 72.4/69.7; 134/120
■ "Frankly my dear, this one's gone with the wind" sigh Santa Rosa swingers turned scarlet over this Robert Trent Jones Jr. "quirky design" with "Jekyll-and-Hyde front and back nines", "awesome" finishing holes and "ocean and harbor" vistas "too beautiful for words" – just hold onto your visor, as "more gusts than a Kansas tornado" make it like "playing in pea soup"; try to ignore the "embarrassment" of the "driving range in a batting cage", smooth down your hairdo and calm your rattled nerves at the "amazing" Bodega Bay Lodge, where such "good food" means you'll never go hungry again.

Sea Ranch Lodge & Golf Links   19 | 10 | 13 | 17 | $70

42000 Hwy. 1, Sea Ranch; 707-785-2468; www.888searanch.com; 6616/4837; 73.2/71.5; 136/123
■ "Play nine with your honey and stay at the lodge", which is integrated into its natural setting, but "take lots of balls" because one of the first "Scottish links" in the West has "high" club-grabbing rough; don't forget foul-weather gear, as "nasty winds" make it "cold" on the "beautiful bluffs of the rugged Sonoma Coast", where "the views are spectacular" and the hazards include "lots" of intransigent "deer" – "I hit one and it didn't move" marvels one stray shooter.

Windsor Golf Club, The 20 | 16 | 18 | 23 | $51
1340 19th Hole Dr., Windsor; 707-838-7888; 6650/5116; 71.7/69.3; 128/112
■ "It's a sweetheart of a course" say Sonoma slicers of this "dreamboat" that's "gentle, pretty and easy if you know where the soft spots are" and "challenging" if you don't; in other words, "local knowledge will benefit you" on the "old home of the Nike Tour", and here's two neighborhood tidbits: "watch the corn silo guarding the left side on the 3rd hole", and "don't expect miracles" with the "hard-to-get starting times."

Stockton

Lockeford Springs ▽ 18 | 18 | 17 | 27 | $22
16360 N. Hwy. 88, Lodi; 209-333-6275; www.lockefordsprings.com; 6861/5951; 73.8/74.0; 130/123
■ "For the price, course conditions are excellent" bellow bargain-shopping ball hitters on this "long course" in central California's wine country 35 miles southeast of Sacramento featuring "lots of grassy bunkers", "very deep rough" and a risk/reward, dogleg-left, par-5 18th with a handsome waterfall; those grapes need their sunshine, so if you're walking rather than riding, "play early or in the cooler seasons."

Saddle Creek 24 | 20 | 20 | 18 | $90
3840 Little John Rd., Copperopolis; 209-785-3700; 888-852-5787; www.saddlecreek.com; 6829/4488; 73.0/65.4; 132/111
☑ There's "hidden treasure in the Sierra Nevada foothills", and it's on this "terrific", "pristine" layout where some of designer Jay Morrish's holes are "totally wonderful" and "unique" and his "bunkering is both intelligent and beautiful"; you "gotta try the bungalows" for a night, though locals would rather you not stay longer, as "new homes are beginning to ruin" this "foothills beauty" that takes some flak for a "carts-on-the-path-only rule" that makes for a "long", "hot" day in the saddle.

Stevinson Ranch 24 | 19 | 22 | 22 | $85
2700 N. Van Clief Rd., Stevinson; 209-668-8200; 877-752-9276; www.stevinsonranch.com; 7205/5461; 74.3/71.9; 140/124
☑ "How they built this gem in the middle of nowhere still boggles the mind" say city slickers willing to "stay in a cabin and make a weekend of it" at these "excellent" "links" on former dairy farmland in the San Joaquin Valley; the "great greens and fast fairways" come at a "bargain price", but "be prepared for summer heat" and "bring gallons of mosquito repellent" to grapple with wetland pests on the first track in California to be certified as an Audubon International Signature Course for environmental friendliness.

Yorba Linda

Black Gold 25 | 24 | 24 | 21 | $95
17681 Lakeview Ave.; 714-961-0060; www.blackgoldgolf.com; 6756/4936; 73.3/69.3; 133/124
☑ "Two thumbs up" for this "unique, picturesque" Arthur Hills newcomer, a "beautiful layout in the heights of Yorba Linda" where a clear day dishes up "great views" of Catalina Island; it's so "hilly that if you don't take a cart, you'll need mouth-to-mouth at the end", and a "staff that wants you to feel like it's a private

club" just might oblige you, though Nicklaus/Flick instructor Seth Glasco should offer an "anger management class" on the weekend, when play on "OC's best addition" is oh-so-"very slow."

Colorado

★ **Best in State**
28 Ridge at Castle Pines North, The, *Denver*
26 Broadmoor, East, *Colorado Springs*
25 Riverdale, Dunes, *Denver*
　　 Murphy Creek, *Denver*
　　 Legacy Ridge, *Denver*

Aspen

Aspen Golf Club
▽ 20 | 17 | 18 | 20 | $80

39551 Hwy. 82; 970-925-2145; www.aspengov.com/golf;
7136/5222; 73.7/69.1; 133/119

☑ There are "views of the mountains on every hole" at this "great" municipal course with lush fairways and "well-maintained greens" amid aspen, spruce and willow groves in the middle of the ski capital of the U.S.; "service is top-notch" and it's "close to town", but "the bad news" is you pay "Aspen prices" for a "not-so-special course" that's "too flat" for its pedigree.

Boulder

Coal Creek
19 | 15 | 15 | 19 | $41

585 W. Dillon Rd., Louisville; 303-666-7888;
www.coalcreekgolf.com; 1028/5185; 72.4/67.3; 136/118

☑ Oh, those "views of the Rockies" – where the other half lives in a residential community on the outskirts of Boulder, there's a "nicely matured", "pretty" "parklander" with priceless Colorado views; the homes themselves can be priced, however, so "if you like whacking drives into half-million dollar houses, it's enjoyable."

Indian Peaks
23 | 17 | 18 | 23 | $40

2300 Indian Peaks Trail, Lafayette; 303-666-4706;
www.cityoflafayette.com; 7083/5468; 73.9/70.8; 134/122

■ "One of the favorites" of fussbudget foozlers is this year-round muni with "awesome views" from the foothills of the snowcapped Rockies; Hale Irwin has designed a wide-open layout with few trees, native grass, half a dozen lakes and a hilly back nine that is "challenging", "great fun" and "easy to walk"; with an impressive pro shop, it's just about the "best value" around; N.B. if you bonk a pedestrian strolling the community trail that intersects the course, you were forewarned.

Mariana Butte
24 | 16 | 18 | 24 | $33

701 Clubhouse Dr., Loveland; 970-667-8308;
6604/5420; 70.8/70.0; 130/121

☑ "They found all the holes" on this "great piece of land", and hopefully you will too at a "beautiful, beautiful" course that's "one of everybody's favorites" in the "Denver metro area"; its "fine" layout is well "integrated with the Big Thompson River" and the "spectacular" surrounding scenery, and it's in "good condition", but it's "a bit short", with "slow play."

Colorado Springs

BROADMOOR, EAST ⛳   26 27 26 21 $160
1 Lake Circle; 719-577-5790; www.broadmoor.com;
7091/5847; 73.0/72.7; 129/139
■ "Wow, what a course" exclaim enthusiasts of this "1918 Donald
Ross gem" with RTJ Sr. additions where the "great conditioning
and challenges" live up to their "historic" reputation at a recently
redone resort and spa, "one of America's best for a stay-and-
play"; though the high-altitude "views are breathtaking", it's the
"downright scary", "fastest-ever" greens that leave you gasping
for that "mountain air" – just ask 1959 U.S. Amateur champ Jack
Nicklaus or 1995 U.S. Women's Open winner Annika Sorenstam.

BROADMOOR, WEST ⛳   25 28 27 19 $160
1 Lake Circle; 719-577-5790; www.broadmoor.com;
6937/5375; 73.0/70.5; 133/127
■ "It starts out tame enough, but soon you work up into narrow,
tough holes in high country" at this "classic" Donald Ross design
with "some fun stuff added" in the 1950s by Robert Trent Jones
Sr.; at a "five-star resort" offering the No. 1 Facilities and Service
in Colorado, this "pleasurable experience" may be "a notch below"
its sister, the East course", but you really "should not miss" the
chance to tee off in the shadow of Cheyenne Mountain, where big-
timers Bob Hope, Bing Crosby and Jackie Gleason long ago
traded quips and chips.

Walking Stick   ▽ 24 17 17 27 $29
4301 Walking Stick Dr., Pueblo; 719-584-3400;
7147/5181; 73.5/68.5; 131/121
■ "It's real easy to sabotage a good score" on the "devastatingly
fast, undulating greens" or in the "penalizing rough" of this "long
hitter's" 18 south of Colorado Springs; "there's nothing there except
the golf facility, but it's well worth the trip" for a "solid" "links-style"
"test" "well designed" by Arthur Hills and Keith Foster offering
"one of the best values" per "difficulty" around, and "if the course
doesn't get you, maybe the rattlers will."

Denver

Arrowhead ⛳   23 16 16 17 $120
10850 Sundown Trail, Littleton; 303-973-9614;
6682/5465; 70.9/71.1; 134/127
☑ "Drive till you think you're lost, then go another half-hour and
you're there" say explorers about a course so "striking", it almost
"doesn't look real" as it winds its "postcard"-perfect way through
"wonderful red-rock formations" where "all sorts of wildlife"
roams; "watch for the black bear who sometimes chases balls at
the signature par 3" where you "drop"-"shoot into a mini-canyon",
but also beware "spotty" conditions that critics grouse "don't
justify" the "very high price of admission."

Buffalo Run   23 21 18 25 $38
15700 E. 112th Ave., Commerce City; 303-289-1500;
www.golfexperience.com/buffalorun; 7411/5227; 74.3/68.8; 129/117
■ Denver drivers "love" this "very entertaining, true links-style
muni" because "it's very close for day travelers", it's "easier than

most local courses to get a tee time" and at "under $50 with a cart", it's a "fantastic bargain" near Denver International Airport; Keith Foster has styled a "straight-up challenge" where "the wind can really blow" on rolling prairies with "great views" of the Front Range foothills not far from the airport; spinning on their après-round barstools in the "beautiful clubhouse", golfers gush "what a find!"

Fox Hollow at Lakewood   24 | 22 | 21 | 23 | $45
13410 Morrison Rd., Lakewood; 303-986-7888
Canyon/Links: 7030/5291; 72.9/69.8; 132/123
Canyon/Meadow: 6808/5203; 71.7/67.9; 133/122
Links/Meadow: 6888/5396; 72.0/69.7; 131/123
■ "Well-done, well-run", "solid and fun" rave rhymin' roundsmen on the "three excellent nines" at this muni "challenge"; "the wind can be a large factor on the Links", but the other two-thirds makes the "best combo", with "great scenery" plunging into a steep ravine on the Canyon's last four holes; if you're not a resident, "greens fees are high" and "tee times are hard to get", but it's worth a shot at the nation's first course to have incorporated the requirements of the Americans With Disabilities Act.

Legacy Ridge   25 | 20 | 19 | 23 | $55
10801 Legacy Ridge Pkwy., Westminster; 303-438-8997;
www.ci.westminster.co.us; 7212/5315; 74.0/70.6; 144/122
☑ Female pros "hit every shot in the bag" at the LPGA's Colorado Women's Futures Classic on Arthur Hills' "suburban" muni built around a "wildlife sanctuary" just north of Denver; there are "lots of very good holes" here with "tough" forced carries and hazards, but there are also "a couple of dogs", and the ribbits and tweets of the critters in those protected areas just might translate: "will the construction ever be done" on the "ambiance-killing" "homes being built around the course"?

Lone Tree   ▽ 19 | 20 | 16 | 15 | $54
9808 Sunningdale Blvd., Littleton; 303-799-9940; www.sspr.org;
7054/5288; 72.1/70.6; 127/120
☑ Arnold Palmer designed this "very nice" layout, which was private until the South Suburban Parks Department purchased it; it remains a well-bunkered test with undulating greens and appealing views of the cityscape and Front Range at a facility featuring luxury suites, a pool and tennis courts, but it seems to have been "eclipsed by newer courses in the area", and it's "overpriced" for a muni.

Murphy Creek   25 | 25 | 21 | 24 | $38
1700 S. Old Tom Morris Rd., Aurora; 303-361-7300;
www.golfaurora.com; 7456/5335; 74.6/68.7; 131/120
■ For that "old homestead feel", mosey over to the high prairie east of Denver, where "Ken Kavanaugh has shaped a gem on a great piece of land" for "links-style" lofters bound to use "every shot in the bag" on "marvelous" holes framed in "tall fescues and extravagant, rugged bunkering"; amid "old farm-style barns and silos" and "simple, rustic signage", you'd never know a "super practice facility" lurked, making it the "new" "best-kept secret" for drivers on the downlow, despite all the "dust and noise from construction of homes."

Pole Creek   ▽ 27 | 18 | 20 | 23 | $80
County Rd. 51, Winter Park; 970-726-8847; 800-511-5076;
www.polecreekgolf.com
Meadow/Ranch: 7106/5008; 73.7/68.5; 145/130
Ranch/Ridge: 7173/5058; 73.8/69.2; 142/128
Ridge/Meadow: 7062/5082; 73.3/67.9; 139/132
■ In a "breathtaking" valley on the southwestern edge of the Rocky Mountain National Park 67 miles from Denver is the off-the-beaten-path ski town of Winter Park and its acclaimed 27-hole course that climbs into lodgepole pine country and descends onto flatter ground, where the namesake creek comes into play; while the Meadow/Ranch combination might be your first choice to play, all three of these high-altitude nines offer challenge and scenery.

Red Hawk Ridge   ▽ 23 | 17 | 18 | 19 | $58
2156 Red Hawk Ridge Dr., Castle Rock; 303-663-7150;
www.redhawkridge.com; 6942/4636; 71.6/67.5; 129/107
■ It's "like playing on a private course", and yet it's a municipal – "awesome conditions" and a well-"enforced pace" lure locals to this newish "short but beautiful" layout with "amazing elevation changes" and a "nice finishing hole" with a pond-guarded green; unhappy hawks harrumph at "too many housing developments lining the fairways" and an "inexperienced staff" that "needs to focus more attention on each guest."

RIDGE AT   28 | 26 | 24 | 18 | $120
CASTLE PINES NORTH
1414 Castle Pines Pkwy., Castle Rock; 303-688-0100; www.troongolf.com;
7013/5001; 71.8/67.6; 143/123
■ It's "worth every penny" to purchase that "CCFAD (country club for a day) feel" at the No. 1–rated Course in Colorado, an "awesome" Tom Weiskopf "half links, half mountain" layout with "amazing holes", "many elevation changes" and "spectacular views" of Pike's Peak and Devil's Head; you'll be treated like the king of the Castle with the "best customer service" at this "beautiful and demanding" princess of the Rockies.

Riverdale, Dunes   25 | 15 | 16 | 25 | $37
13300 Riverdale Rd., Brighton; 303-659-6700; www.riverdalegolf.com;
7030/4903; 72.1/67.5; 129/109
■ "The rough eats you alive", and the "railroad ties" won't spare you either along Pete and P.B. Dye's "great links-style" "bentgrass greens and fairways"; the "conditions are what you'd expect from a country club", and now that the clubhouse is completed, at "under $40" it's just about "the greatest bargain you'll ever find."

Saddle Rock 🏃   22 | 19 | 19 | 21 | $40
21705 E. Arapahoe Rd., Aurora; 303-699-3939; www.auroragolf.org;
7351/5407; 73.7/70.9; 136/126
☑ You had better "think before you hit" say reflective reviewers ruminating over the "elevation changes" on this "long" and "testy" Dick Phelps layout that winds through natural wetlands among age-old trees; while cheery chippers chat up the former Colorado Open host as having "the best starter, pro shop and teaching staff" in the Denver metropolitan area, some scoff it's "tricked-up in places", including where "teenagers are blaring rap music from their fairway homes."

Durango

Tamarron Resort 🏌   ▽ 23 | 21 | 21 | 20 |$125|
40292 Hwy. 550; 970-259-2000; www.tamarron.com;
6885/5330; 73.0/70.6; 142/124
■ You might "see a couple of deer, beavers and even a gray wolf
trotting across the fairway" on the "spectacular" "huge drops"
and "straight uphills" of Arthur Hills' "awesome" 18 perched 7,500
feet up "in the rugged San Juan Mountains"; go a round with the
"wildlife" while your kids take a "scenic ride" on the nearby
"famous" Durango & Silverton Narrow Gauge Railroad, dine
afterward on "a superb meal" at the "excellent resort" and "don't
forget to pick up a jar of homemade chokecherry jelly on your way
home" – it's as big "a local treat" as the course.

Grand Junction

Redlands Mesa   – | – | – | – |$59|
2325 W. Ridges Blvd; 970-263-9270; www.redlandsmesa.com;
7007/4916; 71.7/68.6; 135/113
One of 2001's most highly lauded new courses is splashed across
the basement floor of a stunning, high-desert canyon rimmed with
buttes and bluffs and backdropped by the red-rock sandstone
formations of the Colorado National Monument, 240 miles west of
Denver; cliff-top, drop-shot par 3s, greens tucked in box canyons
and tee boxes etched into slender mesas, all at an affordable price,
make this a modern must-play.

Vail

Beaver Creek Golf Club 🏌⏱   20 | 21 | 21 | 15 |$160|
103 Offerson Rd., Beaver Creek; 970-845-5775;
6784/5088; 71.0/69.3; 140/131
☑ "You'll forget skiing in a hurry" on this "stunning" RTJ Jr. track at
a posh resort west of Denver, where "mountains frame each hole";
"awesome views" at "steep elevations" will have you craning your
neck, but you'd better "keep your body in the cart or you might
end up in a stream", or a construction site – naturalists dish that
the "snooty" spread is being "spoiled by real estate", though
vacationers still appreciate the buildings that house the new Inn
at Beaver Creek and the all-suite Beaver Creek Lodge.

Breckenridge Golf Club   24 | 18 | 18 | 20 |$95|
200 Clubhouse Dr., Breckenridge; 970-453-9104;
www.breckenridgegolfclub.com
Bear/Beaver: 7276/5063; 73.3/69.2; 150/124
Beaver/Elk: 7145/4978; 73.0/68.9; 148/131
Elk/Bear: 7257/5115; 73.5/69.3; 143/132
■ Now that they've added another nine to this "tough Golden Bear
beauty", the summering ski bums of Breckenridge boast it's "the
only 27-hole Nicklaus muni" in the world, so "why wouldn't you
want to play it?"; as "mountain golfers" gleefully attest, balls sail
farther at such "high altitude", so "take advantage of being 9,000
feet up, and you'll feel like you are John Daly teeing off" onto "tight,
sloped" fairways on a "top-notch" track, where the only drawback
is the very "good chance of an afternoon thunderstorm"; area
lodging ranges from condos to chalets to hotels.

C | F | S | V | $

Cordillera, Mountain 🏌

▽ 25 | 27 | 26 | 19 | $235

650 Club House Dr., Edwards; 970-926-5117; www.cordillera-vail.com;
7413/5226; 74.7/68.9; 145/130

■ "Macho doesn't work, so don't try it from the tips", plus it's "impossible to walk because it's unbelievably hilly, so relax, ride along, enjoy the views" and "have a caddie" accompany you for an "ego-stroking" handholding through several "blind shots" and lots of "frustrating" greens; do all that, figure out how to pay for it and you just might find this "beautiful course" at a luxurious chateau with "first-rate facilities" to be "absolutely wonderful" for a "pricey" round, but only late May–October when open.

Cordillera, Summit 🏌 🚡

– | – | – | – | $235

650 Club House Dr., Edwards; 970-926-5117; www.cordillera-vail.com;
7413/5226; 74.7/68.9; 145/130

"Scenery, scenery, scenery" are three reasons to get out on this short-season Nicklaus creation carved from aspens, wetlands and meadows, where "it's all about golf and the scenery", which "are both breathtaking"; with 360-degree views of the Rockies at 9,200 dizzying feet above sea level, it's either "blind shots" or "vertigo at every turn" – in other words, "mountain goat city", and they sure as heck won't let you walk it; recover your balance afterward at the highly acclaimed spa and restaurant.

Cordillera, Valley 🏌

▽ 25 | 24 | 24 | 15 | $235

650 Club House Dr., Edwards; 970-926-5117; www.cordillera-vail.com;
7005/5162; 72.2/69.4; 130/128

☑ A Tom Fazio work of alpine art that is dramatically different from sister courses Summit and Mountain, this "great, great course" 2,100 feet lower in elevation is open for a longer playing season; its "solid" Vail Valley layout is "part links and part mountain", with "some interesting holes", but given all the postcard-perfect vistas at other area tracks, "a view of the highway" does not quite rate the "overpricing" here.

Eagle Ranch

– | – | – | – | $107

50 Lime Park Rd., Eagle; 970-328-2882; 866-328-2882;
www.eagleranchgolf.com; 7575/5504; 74.8/69.8; 141/126

The first daily-fee course built in Eagle County near Vail since 1975 is a dandy, designed by Arnold Palmer and stretching to a King-size 7,575 yards from the tips, a distance rendered more manageable by the 6,600-ft. altitude; blessed with panoramas of the surrounding Sawatch Mountains, the easily walkable layout meanders through the Brush Creek Valley and features bookend Nos. 9 and 18, a pair of lake-menaced par 4s, and the unique, twin greens of the par-5 12th hole.

Eagle Vail

20 | 15 | 17 | 18 | $105

431 Eagle Dr., Avon; 970-949-5267; 800-341-8051;
6819/4856; 71.3/67.4; 131/123

☑ "Watch the ball soar in the air" as your "280-yard drive goes 350" at this sky-high "mountain golf beauty" along Eagle River with "fantastic views" and "huge drops off the tee"; despite a "sweet, efficient staff" critics complain this Eagle crash-lands on "ridiculously unfair" holes riddled with "blind shots and hidden hazards", including "condominiums", so "bring plenty of balls and insurance for the windows you may break."

Keystone Ranch, Ranch Course   23 | 21 | 21 | 17 | $140

39 Keystone Ranch Rd., Keystone; 970-496-4250;
www.keystoneresort.com; 7090/5532; 71.9/69.9; 130/128

■ "Views, views and more views" are the highlight of both courses at this action-packed family resort boasting a 64-year-old "beauty" of a log clubhouse with a stellar restaurant; Robert Trent Jones Jr. crafted the Ranch Course in 1980, and though it's "a mountain favorite, it actually plays as a links course for 16 of the 18 holes" as it hopscotches streams, ponds and bunkers in an alpine meadow, following two openers in the Ponderosa pines.

Keystone Ranch, River   23 | 21 | 21 | 17 | $140

39 Keystone Ranch Rd., Keystone; 970-496-4250;
www.keystoneresort.com; 6886/4762; 70.3/64.5; 131/114

■ "Everything about this place is beautiful, from the clubhouse to every last hole" gasp golfers on this women-friendly, two-year-old layout that starts off at 9,300 feet on the front nine with wide-open, nicely mounded holes framed by wildflowers and crisscrossed by the Snake River, then climbs into the mountains on the back end, affording at least a half-dozen off-the-top-of-the-world tee shots; while it's considered "easier" than the Ranch Course, both are "expensive" but "worth it."

Sonnenalp   ∇ 25 | 18 | 22 | 16 | $160

1265 Berry Creek Rd., Edwards; 970-477-5370;
www.sonnenalp.com; 7059/5293; 73.1/69.4; 139/125

■ "Put on your thinking cap because you'll need it on most of the holes" at what "might be the best layout in all of Vail Valley"; the sun certainly shines on this Jay Morrish/Robert Cupp course with "great views" of mountains and meadows, sagebrush and streams at a tiny jewel of a luxury resort and spa with a sister facility in Bavaria, but as you'd expect, "it's expensive to play."

Connecticut

Danbury

GREAT RIVER   27 | 27 | 25 | 17 | $125

130 Coram Ln., Milford; 203-876-8051; 877-478-7470;
www.greatrivergolfclub.com; 7209/4975; 75.5/70.7; 152/125

■ You're in for either a "championship-level" "day to remember" or a "butt kicking", so "bring your A-game, or your anti-depressants", and "don't even think of playing from the tips" at this "spectacular layout along the Housatonic River"; on "outstanding food and service", "top-notch practice facilities" and a track that's "superior to most private clubs", the owners "spared no expense", and neither will you – it's "not for your regular Saturday round unless you have big bucks."

H. Smith Richardson   18 | 12 | 12 | 20 | $40

2425 Morehouse Hwy., Fairfield; 203-255-7300;
6676/5764; 72.1/73.9; 126/127

☑ "Views of Long Island Sound from the back nine" add to the appeal of this "super-duper", "well-kept" muni just over an hour out of NYC, which "receives a tremendous amount of play" because it's an "excellent value"; outsiders "stepping into the Kmart-esque clubhouse" warn about "minimal amenities" and an "old boys' club mentality", perhaps in part because they're sore that it's "tough to get a tee time if you're not a town resident."

Lyman Orchards, Gary Player ⛳   22 | 20 | 19 | 18 | $48
Rte. 157/Lyman Rd., Middlefield; 860-349-8055; 888-995-9626; www.lymanorchards.com; 6600/4900; 73/68.7; 135/119
■ "Both courses are good" at this "central Connecticut" facility, "but the Player course is much tougher", with a "narrow", "tricky, thought-provoking" layout sporting "scenic views" "through apple orchards" with multiple doglegs, blind shots and "four holes set around a big hill"; it's in "great shape", with a "spacious range and short-game area" and "extremely friendly" personnel, all at a price that won't "break the bank."

Lyman Orchards, Robert Trent Jones   22 | 20 | 19 | 18 | $48
Rte. 157/Lyman Rd., Middlefield; 860-349-8055; 888-995-9626; www.lymanorchards.com; 7011/5812; 73.5/72.0; 129/124
■ "Two excellent courses" that "have their own unique qualities" coincide at this complex 15 miles from New Haven, where a slew of slicers prefer the 34-year-old Jones because it's "open, fair" and "you can easily walk it", navigating around "many water hazards"; the track, its "wonderful practice facility", fine "service" and "spectacular views of the Lyman farm" and the countryside all come at "affordable rates."

RICHTER PARK   27 | 16 | 15 | 24 | $53
100 Aunt Hack Rd.; 203-792-2552; www.richterpark.com; 6744/5114; 73.3/69.8; 134/126
☑ "Phenomenal" squeal linksters lucky enough to play this "charming" city-owned spread that's rated Most Popular, Best Course and Best Value in Connecticut due to its "tremendous", "challenging", low-cost layout that's "always in great condition", with "water all over the place" and "many scenic holes"; alas, like most munis, it's "difficult for non-residents to get on", and the "facilities need to be updated."

Ridgefield Golf Course   19 | 12 | 15 | 20 | $45
545 Ridgebury Rd., Ridgefield; 203-748-7008; 6444/5295; 70.9/70.6; 123/119
☑ "If you're looking for a country course" that's "good for walking" and "gorgeous in foliage season" thanks to an abundance of hills and forests, try this "above-average", "short-but-tough" muni that was designed in the early '70s by those famous Fazios; though the "back nine is strong", a few cranky club carriers think "one or two holes could use a redesign", as the front can be "uninteresting."

Sterling Farms   19 | 15 | 14 | 21 | $45
1349 Newfield Ave., Stamford; 203-329-7888; 6327/5409; 71.4/72.8; 126/125
☑ This municipal "course keeps getting better" claim Nutmeggers in-the-know of this "neatly designed", "well-maintained" Geoffrey Cornish layout on a "small patch of land" in Stamford; it's "a local's delight", but "good luck getting on" if you live elsewhere, and with "five-and-a-half- to six-hour rounds", "a beverage cart would be a nice touch."

Waterbury

Crestbrook Park   ▽ 17 | 12 | 15 | 20 | $34

834 Northfield Rd., Watertown; 860-945-5249; 6915/5696; 73.6/73.8; 128/128

☑ "Tough greens, sloped fairways and long drives up and down hills" make this "well-maintained" track "much more challenging than one would expect in a sleepy, middle Connecticut town"; "any track you can walk 18 holes any day of the week for under $35" appeals to New England thriftiness, but it's still not all Yankee Doodle Dandy with "grumpy rangers roving the course" and a "restaurant that's not great."

Delaware

Rehoboth Beach

Baywood Greens   ▽ 27 | 24 | 22 | 23 | $88

Long Neck Rd., Long Neck; 302-947-9800; 888-844-2254; www.baywoodgreens.com; 6983/3539; 73.2/60.5; 129/100

■ They've "spared no expense" at "one of the most beautiful courses on the East Coast" assert aesthetes acing it on this "great" track "off the beaten path" 15 minutes from Rehoboth where "perfect greens and fairways" are "landscaped like a garden" with over 200,000 flowers, shrubs and trees; especially friendly to women and juniors, it's a "real test from the back tees" but "great fun from the white" at "a steal" of a greens fee, "if you can find it."

Bear Trap Dunes   24 | 20 | 21 | 19 | $90

R.R. 2 at Central Ave., Ocean View; 302-537-5600; 877-232-7872; www.beartrapdunes.com
Black Bear/Codiack: 6853/5748; 72.4/69.8; 130/120
Grizzly/Black Bear: 6901/5721; 72.7/69.8; 130/120
Grizzly/Codiack: 6834/5817; 72.1/69.8; 126/120

■ It's "right in the middle of the beach", so of course it's "relatively flat with many dunes" and grassy hollows that are a bear "when wind is blowing" off the ocean; "awesome" variety, a "wonderful staff and a great facility" add up to "an enjoyable day", though you might feel trapped by "crowds" and "pricey" fees; N.B. there's more room now that they've added a third nine, called Black Bear.

Rookery, The   ▽ 18 | 13 | 18 | 18 | $54

R.R. 3, Milton; 302-684-3000; www.rookerygolf.com; 6461/4785; 70.5/67.0; 117/116

☑ Named for a nearby heron rookery, this "all-around golf course" is a "surprisingly well-kept" "challenge" for "mid- and low-handicappers"; while some surveyors feel "it's a pleasure to play", reviewers with ruffled feathers squawk "you won't rave" over a "piece of land with not much character", at least not compared to the over-the-top putt-putts on the nearby amusement strip.

Wilmington

Back Creek   ▽ 22 | 11 | 16 | 18 | $62

101 Back Creek Dr., Middletown; 302-378-6499; www.backcreekgc.com; 7003/5014; 74.2/69.3; 134/115

☑ Farmland once owned by Delaware's first governor is now a "great" course on which "you have to run the ball up instead of trying to hit the green in the air", i.e. it "plays British-style", which means it's "great for walking, and even better for bringing a beer", though in a "golf cart, not a pull cart", because the latter is "not allowed"; despite that "strange" rule, the "staff is very friendly", but there is "no clubhouse or locker", and thrill-seekers say the layout is "pretty run-of-the-mill."

Florida

★ Best in State
29 TPC at Sawgrass, Stadium, *Jacksonville*
World Woods, Pine Barrens, *Tampa*
28 World Golf Village, King & Bear, *Jacksonville*
Bay Hill, *Orlando*
27 Orange County National, Panther Lake, *Orlando*
World Woods, Rolling Oaks, *Tampa*
Ocean Hammock, *Daytona Beach*
Emerald Dunes, *Palm Beach*
26 El Diablo, *Ocala*
PGA Golf Club, North, *Vero Beach*

Daytona Beach

Halifax Plantation   ∇ 17 | 14 | 14 | 24 | $40
3400 Halifax Clubhouse Dr., Ormond Beach; 386-676-9600;
800-672-0445; www.halifaxplantation.com;
7101/4922; 74.1/68.3; 128/118
■ "In February, you might see some NASCAR boys" on this "fair mix of holes" with wide fairways and large, undulating greens cut through pines and century-old oaks in a live-and-play community north of Daytona; it's a "beautiful stretch" that "circles back to the clubhouse", which "should keep happy any golfer" who doesn't enjoy being stranded on the finish; ho-hum hookers say it's "nothing special, but you could do a lot worse for yourself" than teeing up after a foursome of famous speedsters.

LPGA International,   23 | 25 | 23 | 21 | $90
Champions ⚑
1000 Champions Dr.; 904-274-5742; www.lpgainternational.com;
7088/5131; 74.0/68.9; 134/122
■ It "gets better each time you play" at the home of the LPGA say "recreational" roundspersons on this "beautifully landscaped" Rees Jones layout with "generous landing areas" and "medium-to-large greens" built on a former pine tree farm; "throw in" a "terrific facility that includes a three-hole practice course" and "one of the best clubhouse restaurants in Central Florida", and you've got a real Daytona winner.

LPGA International, Legends ⚑   26 | 24 | 24 | 24 | $90
1000 Champions Dr.; 904-274-5742; www.lpgainternational.com;
6984/5131; 74.5/70.2; 138/123
■ Both male and female golfers "can lose several balls" on the "forced carries" over "water hazards" into "tight landing areas" "as narrow as your hallway" at this Arthur Hills course where "a strong variety" of holes "challenges" both "the seasoned player and beginner fairly"; it's "a great day away from the busy beaches", "even though I was really hungover" says one guzzling golfer.

Ocean Hammock   27 | 16 | 21 | 15 | $195

101 16th Rd., Palm Coast; 386-446-5584; 888-515-4579;
www.oceanhammockgolf.com; 7201/5115; 77.0/71.5; 147/131
■ "One of the most stunning new layouts in America", this millennial "masterpiece" by Jack Nicklaus is "almost half along the [Atlantic] coast", affording "no breaks" to beachside ball whackers, especially when you "add wind"; "stay-and-play package" putters proclaim there's "something special about every hole", particularly the 7th, where you can order lunch, and the 9th, where you pick it up – just don't plan on dinner at the clubhouse after, because it's "still under construction."

Ft. Lauderdale

Colony West, Championship ⛳   20 | 14 | 15 | 20 | $95

6800 NW 88th Ave., Tamarac; 954-726-8430;
www.colonywestcc.com; 7312/4415; 75.5/71.6; 140/127
☑ "Small planes can land on the tee boxes" at this well-bunkered "tough test" of a muni the faithful claim is an "excellent mix of challenging and easy" shots; "why don't they start with a longer opener" than the par-5 621 yarder, snipe sarcastic swingers who prefer an easier introduction – maybe that No. 1 stretch accounts for the "five-hour rounds waiting behind seniors"; try the Glades executive course if you need a quickie.

Deer Creek   23 | 20 | 19 | 17 | $135

2801 Country Club Blvd., Deerfield Beach; 954-429-0006;
www.deercreekflorida.com; 7038/5319; 74.8/71.6; 133/120
☑ A "beautifully kept, scenic" "challenge requiring finesse", this former host to the LPGA Mazda Classic is "a real dream to play"; "check out the pro shop" "stocked" with an "unusually fantastic selection", as well as Scampi's restaurant for "good food" with a Key West vibe; those in-the-know advise "go during off-snowbird hours", as it's "pricey" in season and "too crowded, both with people and condos", the latter of which don't budge, but at least they don't slow down play either.

Emerald Hills ⛳   24 | 20 | 18 | 19 | $150

4100 N. Hills Dr., Hollywood; 954-961-4000;
7117/5032; 74.6/70.1; 142/116
☑ Best known for its "fast, undulating greens" this formerly private "hidden gem" south of Ft. Lauderdale is "a great challenge"; while the majority applauds the "exceptional conditions" and "unusual variety of holes where "long, errant shots are harshly punished", style snobs sniff that the "tacky" "'70s clubhouse needs a face-lift" while lackluster "service leaves a lot to be desired."

Inverrary, East ⛳   18 | 16 | 16 | 17 | $99

3840 Inverrary Blvd., Lauderhill; 954-733-7550;
www.inverrarygolf.com; 7040/5444; 73.3/71.7; 132/119
☑ Even "the peacocks" have pedigrees on the legendary home of the Jackie Gleason Inverrary Classic and host to 15 LPGA and PGA Tour events from which the likes of Jack Nicklaus, Johnny Miller and Lee Trevino took trophies; though the "old" Robert Trent Jones "jewel" is a "nice layout", it's "starting to show its age", and hackers who say the honeymoon's over imagine The Great One "rolling over in his grave about how they let his course slide."

Jacaranda, East 🏌
20 │ 18 │ 18 │ 18 │ $99

9200 W. Broward Blvd., Plantation; 954-472-5836; www.scratch-golf.com; 7195/5638; 74/72.3; 130/124

◪ "Beautifully landscaped around rare old trees and gorgeous houses" at a "very nice club" 15 minutes from Ft. Lauderdale, this "immaculate", "fair" track is a "good weekend hacker's" "challenge"; more serious golfers gripe it's "playable", yes, but "commercial" and "nothing special."

Jacaranda, West 🏌
22 │ 20 │ 19 │ 19 │ $99

9200 W. Broward Blvd., Plantation; 954-472-5836; www.scratch-golf.com; 6729/5314; 72.5/71.1; 132/118

◪ With water on 16 holes and banyan, ficus and live oak trees framing approaches, this "mature layout is "a good test for the low-handicap golfer" who can make "skillful fairway shots"; the few who've flubbed some here praise the "very good facilities" it shares as "fun counterpart" to sister East.

TPC at Heron Bay 🏌
20 │ 23 │ 21 │ 15 │ $130

11801 Heron Bay Blvd., Coral Springs; 954-796-2000; 800-511-6616; www.tpc.com; 7268/4961; 74.9/68.7; 133/113

◪ "Bring a camel" with you because "there are sand bunkers everywhere" say sultans of swing sweating it out on the "former home of the Honda Classic"; though a few fans find the "wide-open" fairways and "perfect rolling" greens "a pleasure" to go with "impressive facilities", "disappointed" drivers declare it "one of the most boring designs in the world" that "plays like a wet, swampy football field"; if all that seems fishy to you, wait till you see what the ships brought in at neighborhood restaurants like highly-rated Hobo's Fish Joint.

Jacksonville

Amelia Island Plantation, Long Point
24 │ 22 │ 22 │ 19 │ $160

6800 First Coast Hwy., Amelia Island; 904-261-6161; 888-261-6161; www.aipfl.com; 6775/4927; 73.0/70.2; 135/123

◪ "Choose this one" suggest scramblers coughing up "extra" for the "best Amelia Island design"; the "inland holes are great", but for a real punch, "prepare to hit knockdowns" on the "cute, oceanside" back-to-back par 3s on a guests-only track "playable for golfers of every level"; though fussbudgets "feel the price is off the charts considering the amount of good courses within 10 minutes", moms and pops will find that the resort's youth programs make it a fabulous family destination.

Amelia Island Plantation, Oak Marsh
20 │ 22 │ 21 │ 17 │ $140

6800 First Coast Hwy., Amelia Island; 904-261-6161; 888-261-6161; www.aipfl.com; 6502/4983; 71.7/69.9; 130/124

■ "Check out the last par 3" urge salty dogs of the long forced carry from tee to green "over the Intracoastal Waterway wetlands" at this soupy, "interesting" track set amid heritage oaks; an early Pete Dye design, it may be "short" and "soft for his standards", but that only makes for a more relaxing round enhanced by "excellent facilities" and "terrific service" at a "fabulous resort" you must stay at to play at.

Amelia Island Plantation, Ocean Links
23 | 22 | 21 | 18 | $140

6800 First Coast Hwy., Amelia Island; 904-261-6161; 888-261-6161; www.aipfl.com; 6301/4550; 70.3/66.4; 134/115

■ It's "short", but it "grows on you" say size-queens keen on this "quirky, shoehorned" "beauty" of a Pete Dye course where "scenic" "holes squished by the ocean" demand "accurate iron shots"; "during a Nor'easter", the guests-only track really "claims links status", turning "windy", "foggy and cold as St. Andrews" – warm up with a heat treatment at the spa après-round.

Ponce De Leon Resort 🏠 ⏱
17 | 17 | 18 | 19 | $70

4000 US Hwy. 1 N., St. Augustine; 904-824-5314; 888-829-5314; www.theponce.com; 6823/5308; 72.9/70.6; 131/121

▣ First opened in 1916, a mere 351 years after America's Oldest City was founded, this "classic" designed by Donald Ross "conjures a bygone era", just not the one chockablock with Spanish explorers; the "links-style" front runs along "old marshland on the river", "the back winds through century-old oaks", and with "spectacular wildlife, awesome views and not a single house around", you can sightsee and "slice to your heart's content"; the Southern charmer suffers from "age and neglect", however – it needs a fountain of youth's worth of "TLC and money" to return it to "greatness."

Ravines Inn
22 | 17 | 19 | 22 | $70

2932 Ravines Rd., Middleburg; 904-282-7888; www.theravines.com; 6733/4817; 72.4/67.4; 133/120

■ "What a change for Florida" cry "mountain climbers" clamoring up and down the "ravines" at this "unique", "superb" "challenge" with "plenty of elevation changes" that "look more like the Carolinas" than Jacksonville; "bring all your game" and "extra balls" because it's "hard", but boy, is it "lots of fun", despite the "dumpy clubhouse" and "goofy parking."

TPC AT SAWGRASS, STADIUM
29 | 27 | 25 | 19 | $260

110 TPC Blvd., Ponte Vedra Beach; 904-273-3230; www.tpc.com; 6954/5000; 75.0/65.3; 149/125

■ They charge so much, they "should include a free set of clubs", but short-gamers "shivering at No. 17's island green" say it's "worth it" for "every hair-raising minute" on this guests-only "masterpiece" by "Pete Dye at his nastiest"; Florida's No. 1–rated Course and the host of the PGA Tour's Players Championship is "hard as hell", but it "seduces you" with "its combo of incredibly fast, undulating greens", "demanding length", "wind and water"; "at one of the world's most luxurious beaches", its "amazing practice areas", "wonderful pro shop" and "excellent dining" help make it "a must-play" at least "once in your life."

TPC at Sawgrass, Valley
25 | 27 | 24 | 20 | $130

110 TPC Blvd., Ponte Vedra Beach; 904-273-3230; www.tpc.com; 6864/5126; 72.8/68.7; 130/120

■ "I wasn't worthy to play this fine course" say humbled hackers of the "lesser known" Pete Dye tournament layout that sits right next to the "wonderful Sawgrass Marriott Resort"; with "plenty of elevation changes", "large greens" and a "good mix of wide and narrow landing areas", the "Stadium Course minus steroids" is a guests-only, "friendly" "complement" to its "big brother."

Windsor Parke 🏌️ ⊕   21 | 18 | 20 | 19 | $70

13823 Sutton Park Dr. N.; 904-223-4653; www.windsorparke.com;
6765/5206; 72.4/70.4; 136/125

☑ Arthur "Hills did a good job here" cheer chippers chuckling over "all the usual Florida quirks" on this "outstanding" track: tight, tree-lined fairways, lakes, bunkers and, unfortunately, "somewhat despoiling recent development"; though "dollar for dollar" it offers Jacksonville's "best public play", sober swingers snort there are "too many distractions", including a drink-cart attendee who's so "nice" you might want her to "do shots with your foresome."

WORLD GOLF VILLAGE,   28 | 27 | 26 | 20 | $170
KING & BEAR

2 World Golf Pl., St. Augustine; 904-940-6100; www.wgv.com;
7279/5119; 75.2/70.1; 141/123

■ "Play this course, you'll love it!" gush golf groupies of this "must-see", the "only course in the world co-designed by Hall of Famers Arnold Palmer and Jack Nicklaus"; indeed, "there's no better place" for "immersion in the game" than on the "wide fairways" and "contoured greens" of this "superb" resort layout that's "short but challenge-packed"; pecking at the "fresh fruit offered at the first tee", inner children chirp that the knickered staff's "unparalleled service" is "better than mom's", and the "superb practice facilities" help make it "worth returning to year after year."

World Golf Village,   24 | 27 | 24 | 18 | $170
Slammer & Squire

2 World Golf Pl., St. Augustine; 904-940-6100; www.wgv.com;
6939/4996; 73.8/69.1; 135/116

■ "It's a religious experience" to play "in the shadow of the World Golf Hall of Fame", the "mecca" where "pilgrims" pay homage to legends of the links; with "big fairways" and "well-bunkered greens", it's "forgiving" of fans flubbing it in the throes of "disbelief" over the "terrific accommodations" and "helpful" service at a facility that's simply "outstanding", "as it should be for the price."

Miami

Biltmore   18 | 18 | 17 | 19 | $53

1210 Anastasia Ave., Coral Gables; 305-460-5364;
www.biltmorehotel.com; 6624/5292; 71.5/71.2; 119/116

☑ Laid out in 1924 by Donald Ross, this "classic" "elegantly set" beside a historic and "beautiful hotel" "provides an enjoyable round to all skill levels"; in fact, it's so "tame", it's "easy to let your clients beat you" on it, and at the end of their ego-stroking, it's "great coming home on the 18th" with the "spectacular" "Biltmore in the background"; nevertheless, the city-owned course "may not appeal to those who are finicky about conditioning" and who might find that "the best thing about it is its proximity to the pool bar", where "lunch is nice" beside the "fantastic" shimmering water.

DORAL RESORT,   26 | 25 | 23 | 17 | $275
BLUE MONSTER 🏌️

4400 NW 87th Ave.; 305-592-2030; 800-713-6725;
www.doralresort.com; 7125/5392; 74.5/73.0; 130/124

☑ Sure, "the Monster can eat you alive", but "it's a thrill to play" this "Miami showpiece", host to PGA Tour events since 1962 and part of a "spectacular" resort with a "wonderful pro shop", "awesome spa" and a host of other facilities; "what a hole, that 18th" cheer champs of the behemoth with "lots of water" and "murderous" bunkers "bigger than your house"; it's even "better after renovations", but tightwads tut over "monstrous prices."

Doral Resort, Gold 🏌   22 | 25 | 23 | 18 | $250

4400 NW 87th Ave.; 305-592-2030; 800-713-6725;
www.doralresort.com; 6602/5179; 73.3/71.4; 129/123

☑ "For those who fear the Monster", this "Doral winner" offers a "sporty, fun" layout that's "not as famous but just as memorable", with "great services and facilities" that "can't be beat"; though "easier" than its blue sib, this "tough, challenging" golden girl still has her "real teeth", though a few suitors sigh that while she's "perfectly maintained", she's "not as pretty" as they'd like her to be.

Doral Resort, Great White 🏌   23 | 25 | 23 | 16 | $275

4400 NW 87th Ave.; 305-592-2030; 800-713-6725;
www.doralresort.com; 6208/5286; 69.7/70.1; 117/116

☑ "It's The Shark and then some" fawn fervent fans of this great, white desert-scape that "looks like it belongs in Arizona", with firmly packed coquina shells and pot bunkers everywhere; Greg Norman's ambitious design provides "wonderful" "diversity to South Florida's multitude of similarity" with "deceptively difficult" holes "in excellent condition"; conservative critics carp that it's "frustrating", with "too many gimmicks."

Doral Resort, Red 🏌   19 | 25 | 23 | 17 | $250

4400 NW 87th Ave.; 305-592-2030; 800-713-6725;
www.doralresort.com; 6214/5216; 69.9/70.6; 118/118

☑ "A super place to go if you're a beginner", this former host to the LPGA Office Depot Tournament is a "nice" 'n' "easy", "all-around course" that's "always fun to play"; but long hitters complain that its tips are "like playing from the ladies' tee box", and they see red over "Blue Monster prices", contending that the Doral's other choices are "much better."

Doral Resort, Silver 🏌   19 | 22 | 21 | 17 | $250

5001 NW 104th Ave.; 305-592-2030; 800-713-6725;
www.doralresort.com; 6567/5589; 72.5/68.7; 131/123

☑ "Got water?" quip aficionados of this "better than average" Doral daughter that boasts "menacing" H_2O "on every hole"; just a short shuttle ride from "the main resort", it's "a nice change" of pace "when you spend a weekend of golf" here; still, some fail to find the silver lining, deriding the layout as "dated" and "expensive."

International Links Miami 🏌   ∇ 17 | 11 | 11 | 18 | $98

1802 NW 37th Ave.; 305-633-4583; www.pcmgolf.com/melreese;
7173/5534; 73.4/72.4; 128/122

☑ Sure "it's in the flight plan of Miami International Airport", and yes, "you see major highways as you golf", but "for a quick round" before your plane takes off, "you can't beat" this "wonderful course in the middle of the city" on five lakes and cypress wetlands; there's "quite a lot going on" to distract you, so get one of the "excellent teachers" to give you pointers on concentration, and plan to dine on that in-flight meal, as "the clubhouse in a trailer" offers only sandwiches.

Naples

Eastwood
▽ 22 | 17 | 17 | 24 | $60

4600 Bruce Herd Ln., Ft. Myers; 941-275-4848; 6772/5116; 72.3/68.9; 130/120

☑ "How much to cut off" on No. 10's "drive across water" and other questions "keep you thinking" on this "challenging mix of holes" with a "lovable old Florida feel"; if you can't find the answers, the course is "forgiving" enough to be "enjoyable", and your wallet needs no excuses for "great value" rates; priced for crowds, it's "hard to get on", and the "practice area could be nicer."

Gateway ⛳
▽ 22 | 20 | 20 | 19 | $85

11360 Championship Dr., Ft. Myers; 941-561-1010; www.gatewaygolf.com; 6974/5323; 74.1/70.8; 129/123

☑ A "nice" "place to play on your way in or out of" the gates at Southwest Florida International is this "long" Fazio layout in close "proximity to the airport"; its "mounds, undulations" and Cape Cod bunkers are the "best conditioned in the area", and the "staff is always courteous and helpful"; the home course of a planned community, it "winds around condos", so despite the native cypress trees, it's "not much for natural beauty", and make sure you leave plenty of time before your flight because rounds "can be slow."

Lely Resort, Flamingo
22 | 19 | 21 | 21 | $140

8004 Lely Resort Blvd.; 941-793-2600; 800-388-4653; www.lely-resort.com; 7171/5377; 75.0/71.4; 136/123

☑ "Summertime prices can't be beat" beam bargain birdie hunters on this "sneaky tough" RTJ Sr. spread chock-full of Sabal palms, pines, mounds and bunkers 30 minutes south of Ft. Myers; though there's "a great deal of opportunity for scoring" on the "windy" resort course, "dumb holes and lotsa bugs" have critics itching to play the "many other options available" in the area.

Lely Resort, Mustang
22 | 20 | 20 | 22 | $140

8004 Lely Resort Blvd.; 941-793-2600; 800-388-4653; www.lely-resort.com; 7217/5197; 75.2/70.5; 141/120

■ As you'd expect at a course 15 minutes from the beach, there's a "fair amount of water" and sand bordering the forgiving fairways of this "long, rambling" layout by PGA Senior legend Lee Trevino; the lucky handful of hookers who have hacked up the greens here rate their ride on the Mustang "a good challenge."

Tiburon, Black
– | – | – | – | $80

2620 Tiburon Dr.; 941-594-2040; www.wcigolf.com; 7005/5065; 74.2/69.6; 147/119

Greg Norman has crafted a fourth nine at this retreat, and it might be the most challenging of all; it's been combined with the former South nine as its back, with pine-lined fairways, sod-wall bunkers, lakes, coquina-shell waste areas and an exciting risk/reward par-5 closing hole; stay at the new Ritz-Carlton here and you'll have access to its sister hotel's beach.

Tiburon, Gold
– | – | – | – | $80

2620 Tiburon Dr.; 941-594-2040; www.wcigolf.com; 7288/5148; 74.7/69.2; 137/113

The club's name is Spanish for 'shark', so it's no surprise that this course comprised of the old North and West nines by the Great

White One himself, Greg Norman, is a killer with "shaved"-down tall grass forming "fringe around the greens that extends 50 yards"; locals warn "no rough means no end to the Florida flora your ball will be introduced to", while thrifty types call it "a very expensive round in season", but what do you expect when there's a "top-notch" "Ritz-Carlton on-site" where they "treat you like a prince"?

Ocala

El Diablo 🏌️   26 | 13 | 17 | 24 | $59

10405 N. Sherman Dr., Citrus Springs; 352-465-0986; 877-353-4225; 7045/5144; 75.3/69.8; 147/117

■ "Wow!" – what "a Fazio course" this "tough", but "outstanding" devil 20 minutes from Ocala is; surrounded by thick pines with rolling fairways, "ample, curse-causing sand and waste areas" and "faaast", "hellaciously sloping greens", the "tremendous challenge with equally tremendous conditions" is the "best Central Florida track for the money, bar none."

Orlando

Bay Hill 🏌️   28 | 25 | 26 | 21 | $199

9000 Bay Hill Blvd.; 407-876-2429; www.bayhill.com; 6407/5235; 72.4/70.6; 130/122

■ "The Hill is a thrill" cheer legions of Arnie's Army who salute this "AAA+" guests-only "masterpiece" "fit for The King", where they treat you like royalty at the "elegantly run clubhouse and lodge"; "more challenging than ever" "after last year's refit", this "ultimate golf experience" near all the Orlando attractions comes complete with sprawling bunkers, expansive water hazards and a brutal finishing hole, and it's "rich in PGA tournament history", making you feel like a pro; N.B. there's also a nine-holer here for a quickie.

Baytree National 🏌️   21 | 21 | 20 | 20 | $75

8207 National Dr., Melbourne; 321-259-9060; www.golfbaytree.com; 7043/4803; 74.0/68.6; 135/118

■ "I play it every chance I get" say obsessives of this "gorgeous" Gary Player course offering "solid" "fun" "on the Atlantic and Intracoastal Waterway" 45 minutes from Orlando; though it "can be damp" and the "clubhouse isn't much", its length, many bunkers, large greens and red shale waste areas "provide for a challenge", and fanatics foam that they'd only skip it "during a hurricane."

Black Bear   20 | 17 | 17 | 21 | $65

24505 Calusa Blvd., Eustis; 352-357-4732; 800-423-2118; www.blackbeargolfclub.com; 7002/5044; 74.7/70.5; 134/121

■ "You can almost forget you're playing in Florida" navigating this "very hilly", "windswept" P.B. Dye design that weaves around high sandy dunes, "challenging all levels"; such "incredibly undulating" fairways are quite "unknown elsewhere" in the Sunshine State, and a few critics find them "a little too gimmicky."

ChampionsGate, International 🏌️ 20 | 21 | 22 | 15 | $125

1400 Masters Blvd., Champions Gate; 407-787-4653; 888-558-9301; www.championsgategolf.com; 7406/5682; 76.3/72.3; 143/123

■ "Challenging, fun and totally different", this "visually intimidating" track just south of Disney World sports "the look of a links course from across the pond" with an ostentatious Aussie touch; modeled after one of The Shark's homeland favorites – Royal Melbourne – this deeply bunkered, "rugged" and almost treeless terrain is a "test for any golfer", but be warned: "don't hunt for wayward balls, as alligators and copperheads await"; N.B. there's also a David Ledbetter academy on the grounds.

ChampionsGate, National 🏌   22 | 24 | 24 | 16 | $125

1400 Masters Blvd., Champions Gate; 407-787-4653; 888-558-9301; www.championsgategolf.com; 7048/4994; 75.1/69.8; 133/122

■ "More traditional" than its International sister, this Greg Norman newcomer poses an "excellent challenge", with "lots of wildlife roaming" the "well-manicured fairways" and rolling hills amid orange groves, oaks and pines; after a round, enjoy a meal with "private club–like service" in the "large, beautiful clubhouse"; the whole kit-and-kaboodle is "expensive but outstanding", and it "will only get better with time."

Cypress Creek 🏌   19 | 17 | 17 | 17 | $50

5353 Vineland Rd.; 407-351-2187; www.cypresscreekcc.com; 7014/6429; 73.6/70.6; 126/120

■ An errant shot's length from Universal Studios is this "pleasant surprise": a "tough", "gorgeous layout" loaded with "lots of hazards", including oaks, pines and the namesake trees, plus "water everywhere"; an "aged course with plenty of experience" at pro events, it's "not for the high-handicapper", but the women of the LPGA's Orlando Classic sure have enjoyed themselves on its "great greens."

DeBary Golf Club 🏌 ☺   20 | 17 | 19 | 23 | $65

300 Plantation Club Dr., DeBary; 386-668-1705; www.debarycc.com; 6776/5060; 72.7/69.3; 134/123

☑ "Bring your long, straight driver" to this wooded, "well-regarded course in southwest Volusia County", 20 miles north of Orlando, that offers "great value" with rolling hills and picturesque fairways that are "usually well kept"; if your idea of a good time is fishing for your ball, note the "strong finishing holes on both the front and back nines" boast the track's "only water", and rusty roundsmen rate it as having "not the greatest practice facilities."

Diamondback 🏌   22 | 14 | 19 | 19 | $85

6501 State Rd. 544 E., Haines City; 863-421-0437; 800-222-5629; www.diamondbackgc.com; 6805/5061; 73.3/70.3; 138/122

■ "How do you think they got the name?" quip enthusiasts of this "well-kept secret" 30 minutes outside of Orlando; "cut in the wild and left that way", this Jungle Cruise–like layout snaking through "beautiful flora and fauna" is "tough", "tight" and boldly bunkered, and the "first four holes" can rattle you so much they'll "break your day", so "take along a lot of balls" and remember, when you lose 'em "don't get out in the woods to look."

EastWood 🏌   18 | 15 | 15 | 19 | $65

13950 Golfway Blvd.; 407-281-4653; www.eastwoodgolf.com; 6528/5393; 71.7/76.7; 131/130

■ "A nice round of golf" can be had at this "solid track in south Orlando" that's "flat but has a few good moments", with water in play on 10 holes for an "overall good test from the regular men's tees"; you "can't ever tell what the conditions will be, however", and for a "mostly beginner course", the service can be intimidatingly "nasty."

Falcon's Fire 🏌   23 | 22 | 22 | 20 | $130
3200 Seralago Blvd., Kissimmee; 407-239-5445; 877-878-3473;
www.falconsfire.com; 6901/5417; 73.8/71.6; 138/126
■ Good thing the "satellite GPS" "gives you the yardage to all but the snack bar", because it's "needed to avoid hazards, gators, marsh, sand, lakes, etc." at Rees Jones' "first-rate" "treat"; fans are fired up by a "super-friendly staff" that outfits "the backs of carts" with "handy" "club covers for unpredictable thunderstorms."

Forest Lake 🏌   21 | 17 | 16 | 22 | $70
10521 Clarcona Ocoee Rd., Ocoee; 407-654-4653;
www.forestlakegolf.com; 7113/5773; 74.7/69.4; 128/117
☑ "The price is right" on this "local favorite", an "excellent layout" that's "often overlooked" by tourists and ignored by developers – there are "no homes along fairways" that roll through woods and lake-laced fields; it's a "strong test" "enhanced" by "nice greens", which you can train for at the "solid short-game practice area" while steering clear of staff that may be "grumpy" over conditions that are "sometimes good and sometimes terrible."

Golden Bear at Keene's Point 🏌   ▽ 23 | 23 | 24 | 18 | $125
6300 Jack Nicklaus Pkwy., Windermere; 407-876-5775;
www.thegoldenbearclub.com; 7173/5071; 74.8/69.1; 136/118
■ "It's nice that not many people have found" this "newer" Nicklaus residential track touting "tons of sand and big greens" bordered by live oaks and magnolias; in-the-know locals who "love" it say the Bear deserves a hug for an environmentally sensitive, "playable" "challenge" that management keeps "well maintained" with "beautiful facilities"; just "watch your speed when driving", not on it but to it, as local "cops seem to generate the entire city budget with tickets", and the greens fee itself is "steep" enough.

Grand Cypress 🏌 ⏰   24 | 26 | 25 | 19 | $225
1 N. Jacaranda St.; 407-239-4700; 800-835-7377; www.grandcypress.com
East/North: 6955/5056; 75.0/69.1; 139/114
North/South: 6983/5322; 75.1/71.1; 137/119
South/East: 6896/5120; 74.7/70.2; 138/123
■ "It doesn't matter which nines you play, they're all great" coo converts to this 27-hole, heavily mounded "Nicklaus circa-1980s" design, which is code for "bring your A-game" because it's "really different" from and "substantially less forgiving than the New course"; Hyatt Regency or Villas of Grand Cypress guests say it's "worth" the "hideous" resort prices for "well-trained staffers who turn off their mowers when you approach", the Academy of Golf, the "amazing" Black Swan restaurant and the equestrian center.

Grand Cypress, New 🏌 ⏰   25 | 26 | 25 | 20 | $225
1 N. Jacaranda St.; 407-239-4700; 800-835-7377;
www.grandcypress.com; 6773/5314; 72.2/69.8; 122/117
■ "St. Andrews with a suntan" "sans knickers and haggis", Jack Nicklaus' "replica" has lots of Scots mistaking it for the famous "Old Course" across the ocean, with "deep pot bunkers", pesky burns, "double greens" and even an old stone bridge; "you can smack

the ball wherever you want and still be in bounds" on its "wide-open fairways" at a resort where the "exceptionally gracious staff" and "awesome facilities" (including a "terrific golf academy" and a Hyatt Regency) provide a "heavenly" "head-clearing after the suffocation of the Magic Kingdom."

Hunter's Creek 🏌

19 | 15 | 15 | 20 | $75

14401 Sports Club Way; 407-240-6003; 7432/5755; 76.1/72.5; 137/120

■ "Work out before playing" this very "l-o-o-o-ng" track that's "fun" "from the tips" for power lofters and "tough" for weaker wallopers; convenient to all the area attractions but "off the beaten path", it's a "great vacation" course that's "not as flashy" but also "not as crowded" or expensive as more "well-known" Orlando spreads, though "bargain" hunters bemoan "poor conditions and service."

Legacy Club at Alaqua Lakes 🏌

25 | 23 | 23 | 22 | $59

1700 Alaqua Lakes Blvd., Longwood; 407-444-9995; www.legacyclubgolf.com; 7160/5055; 74.5/69.1; 132/112

■ The "best course north of Orlando", according to the few fortunate foozlers who "know about it", is this "gorgeous" Tom Fazio "gem hidden" "in a high-end residential development in Seminole County", where the "wonderful staff" oversees "beautiful practice facilities"; a precocious toddler, the track "looks and plays like it's 50 years old", with "long", lush fairways lined in hardwoods and "lots of bunkers", and if you find it "pricey during season", try summer twilight hours for a "must-play" bargain.

MetroWest 🏌

19 | 18 | 17 | 18 | $115

2100 S. Hiawassee Rd.; 407-299-8800; www.metrowestorlando.com; 7051/5325; 74.1/70.3; 132/122

■ "Stay out of the rough, or the long Bermuda will stop your iron dead" gasp grasshoppers at this late-vintage Robert Trent Jones Sr. track with "wide-open" rolling fairways, cavernous bunkers and "great greens" near all the area's vacation offerings; it's "always in immaculate shape", the "service is exceptional" and the "clubhouse and restaurant are great", but on-course critics crab that there are "too many houses" and "not enough variety" to make it more than "decent."

Mission Inn, El Campeon

26 | 25 | 25 | 25 | $125

10400 County Rd. 48, Howey-in-the-Hills; 352-324-3101; 800-874-9053; www.missioninnresort.com; 6923/4811; 73.6/67.3; 133/118

■ "Thankfully, not too many people know of this little gem" sigh nostalgics knocking a few on this "oldie but goodie" built in 1926 by Troon, Scotland's Charles E. Clarke with "significant elevation changes" and "panoramic views" amid lakes, rolling hills and "majestic" pines at a grande dame of a resort "in the middle of nowhere"; with "superior service" and a "beautiful hotel and clubhouse" where you can pig out on the "excellent Saturday night buffet", it's perfect for putters hungry for "golf, golf and more golf."

Mission Inn, Las Colinas

20 | 25 | 24 | 23 | $105

10400 County Rd. 48, Howey-in-the-Hills; 352-324-3101; 800-874-9053; www.missioninnresort.com; 6820/4665; 73.0/67.3; 131/110

▨ "The staff makes you feel like you're the only one playing" on this "much more wide-open" "addition at a great resort"; "forgiving" and friendly to the ladies, the "above-average" layout "has its moments", but old-school swingers say "it goes to show that newer isn't always better" because "it just can't hold a candle to its venerable sister."

Orange County National, Crooked Cat 🏌

25 | 25 | 22 | 25 | $125

16301 Phil Ritson Way, Winter Garden; 407-656-2626; 888-727-3672; www.ocngolf.com; 7277/5262; 75.4/70.3; 140/120

■ "You're only 30 minutes from Mouseland, but it might as well be a different world" at this "brilliant track" "out in orange grove territory" where it's "all golf" (and some citrus) with "no housing developments"; the resort offers "outstanding service", but that might not include an escort, as intrepid players prowling the Cat's "fast, firm fairways" and "tough finishing holes" say they "still couldn't find the location with a flashlight and a road map."

Orange County National, Panther Lake 🏌

27 | 26 | 23 | 24 | $125

16301 Phil Ritson Way, Winter Garden; 407-656-2626; 888-727-3672; www.ocngolf.com; 7295/5097; 75.7/71.5; 137/125

■ "Awesome" purr satisfied surveyors of this "first-class" native beauty slinking its "unforgiving", "superbly conditioned" way across rolling grasslands, meadows and wetlands; the "fantastic staff" helps make "one of the best-kept secrets in Florida" a "great value", "even giving you a towel to use in the locker room when the round is over."

Palisades

▽ 18 | 18 | 18 | 20 | $60

16510 Palisades Blvd., Clermont; 352-394-0085; 7004/5524; 73.8/72.1; 127/122

■ "Cut into the rolling hills" west of Orlando with "homes set well off the course", this "fun" local "favorite" has "a feel and look you wouldn't expect" in the Sunshine State; there's "not too much water" and the "greens are small", but "plenty of length from the back tees" makes it "tough" enough, while views of Lake Minneola would make it "something else, if it were better conditioned."

Remington 🏌

▽ 20 | 18 | 18 | 23 | $65

2995 Remington Blvd., Kissimmee; 407-344-4004; www.remington-gc.com; 7111/5178; 73.9/69.8; 134/118

■ Practice, play and stuff your face as much as you like for an all-you-can-golf-and-eat "four-star value" at a "very nice course" with "good" facilities 20 minutes from Disney World; "unlike most area tracks, water is not the only hazard" to tackle here, and with "enough challenge to keep you honest, it's fun" going, but the "best thing about it is the price."

Resort Course at Orange Lake 🏌

17 | 20 | 20 | 19 | $75

8505 W. Irlo Bronson Memorial Hwy, Kissimmee; 407-239-1050; 800-887-6522; www.orangelake.com
Cypress/Lake: 6621/4656; 72.3/72.1; 131/129
Lake/Orange: 6531/5289; 72.2/71.1; 132/130
Orange/Cypress: 6670/4667; 72.6/72.6; 131/129

☑ It's "beautiful", but it's "tough for the distance" say hackers huffing their way across this 27-holer where they're bound to be treated well by the "really friendly staff"; "all three nines are built

around a busy time-share community", so they're "basically
narrow but occasionally fun to play" off-season, when you won't
risk bonking a winter resident on the head; even so, "die-hard
serious golfers" might want to "look elsewhere."

Southern Dunes ⛳   25 │ 18 │ 16 │ 20 │ $100
2888 Southern Dunes Blvd., Haines City; 863-421-4653; 1-800-632-6400;
www.southerndunes.com; 7727/5200; 74.7/72.4; 135/126
■ "The operative word here is 'dunes'" say swingers swallowed
by "probably some of the largest bunkers in the world" guarding
"huge" greens at this "great, long, sand-filled lot"; if you're bored
of flat tracks, the "very interesting elevation changes" here "don't
fit the Florida mold", though "too many houses around the fairways"
are an all-too-familiar Sunshine State foible.

Stoneybrook West ⛳   ▽ 22 │ 17 │ 19 │ 19 │ $40
15501 Towne Commons Blvd., Winter Garden; 407-877-8533;
www.stoneybrookgolf.com; 7101/5173; 74.8/70.1; 135/117
☑ Formerly a citrus grove just off the turnpike on the west side of
Orlando, this Arthur Hills–designed, modern risk/reward layout runs
through natural habitat with rolling, mounded fairways and speedy
greens, and it's a "fun track" if the typical high winds aren't blowing;
snobs sniff the "people are friendly" here, but the "clubhouse is
still a mobile home."

Timacuan   ▽ 19 │ 18 │ 16 │ 16 │ $94
550 Timacuan Blvd., Lake Mary; 407-321-0010; www.golftimacuan.com;
7019/5401; 72.1/73.5; 123/137
☑ "Very popular with the local folks", this "favorite" a tee shot
northeast of Orlando is fair to all skill levels with hilly, wide-open
fairways and "lots of sand"; "interestingly", "the front and back
have different feelings", with links-style Nos. 1–9 and a watery,
woodsy Carolina-esque finish; if you're not from down-home, "you
need a yardage book to know where to hit some shots", and even
the neighbors "can't tell you when it'll be in good or bad shape."

Walt Disney World, Eagle Pines   23 │ 25 │ 24 │ 19 │ $150
1950 W. Magnolia-Palm Dr., Lake Buena Vista; 407-939-4653;
www.golf.disneyworld.com; 6772/4838; 72.5/68.0; 135/111
☑ "Leave the kids with the Mouse and treat yourself" to "a fine
example of Pete Dye design" that's "big, open and lush", with vast
sandy wastelands, pine-straw rough and "water everywhere";
because "Disney does it right", it's "always" in "beautiful shape",
with "great service" and "locker facilities" at its "top-notch
clubhouse"; noting it "doesn't drain too well", however, humid
hookers harrumph it's a "moist and muggy" "Minnie course with
a Mickey price."

Walt Disney World,   20 │ 22 │ 23 │ 16 │ $125
Lake Buena Vista
1950 W. Magnolia-Palm Dr., Lake Buena Vista; 407-939-4653;
www.golf.disneyworld.com; 6819/5194; 72.7/69.4; 128/120
☑ This "easiest of the Disney" layouts is "more accessible for
beginners", but it's still "no walk on the beach"; its "wide variety" of
"well-groomed" holes amid "plenty of flowering and leaf-changing
trees" are "delightful to play in early spring or fall" and "the people
here are great to families" any season of the year, but serious

swingers sigh "I should have brought a pillow and a shaver" to bed down beside those "ugly condos" while waiting for all the "high-handicap" "tourists" to sink their balls.

Walt Disney World, Magnolia   23   23   23   17 $135
1950 W. Magnolia-Palm Dr., Lake Buena Vista; 407-939-4653;
www.golf.disneyworld.com; 7190/5232; 73.9/70.5; 133/123
☑ "Check out the Mickey-shaped bunker" in front of the 6th green where "you may find Goofy waiting for you to putt" at this "over-the-top" classic graced with magnolia trees, "generous greens", "lots of sand and water" and real "animals (gators, deer and wild turkey) running all over the place"; while most agree the PGA Tour's National Car Rental Golf Classic host is "well maintained for the high amount of play it receives", faultfinders feel it's "dated", drawling "who cares about mouse ears for tee box markers when it's costing this much and taking this long?"

Walt Disney World, Osprey Ridge   26   25   25   20 $175
1950 W. Magnolia-Palm Dr., Lake Buena Vista; 407-939-4653;
www.golf.disneyworld.com; 7101/5402; 73.9/70.5; 135/122
■ Tom Fazio's "magic" leaves "you wanting more" of this "harder-than-it-looks" "sleeper" "peacefully set among scrub oaks and pines", where "you need to hit all types of shots to score well"; with dramatic "elevation changes", "huge, contoured greens" and "great locker rooms", there's nothing "Mickey Mouse" about the "highly regarded layout" except perhaps the "cute" mouse ear–shaped putting area and the "Disney-like greens fees."

Walt Disney World, Palm   23   22   24   18 $125
1950 W. Magnolia-Palm Dr., Lake Buena Vista; 407-939-4653;
www.golf.disneyworld.com; 6957/5311; 73.0/70.4; 133/124
■ "Forget the Alaskan cruise" and head south to this Magic Kingdom "marvel" winding through wetlands lined with mature pines and palms, where you can "play golf cart polo" with "old gators" or gaze "at Cinderella's castle" in the near distance; although the "friendly and helpful staff" will assist you "with anything you might need" at the "picturesque" "favorite" where the PGA Tour plays, penny-wise princes say the "high price" of this glass slipper doesn't fit the budgets of vacationing families.

Palm Beach

Atlantis Country Club 🏳   17   15   17   17 $77
190 Atlantis Blvd., Atlantis; 561-965-7700; 6610/5242; 71.5/70.9; 129/123
☑ Rising as if from undersea, this "lovely place" has had some holes "recently renovated and beautifully done" say tale-tellers on the "very enjoyable" layout where "the golfing is good" because it's "not overcrowded" and the "staff is friendly and helpful"; that's a myth, say nonbelievers who find the "mediocre landscaping" "around housing communities" with "postage stamp–size greens" "uninspiring" and the "facilities still in the '50s."

Boca Dunes 🏳   17   17   16   18 $63
1400 Country Club Dr., Boca Raton; 561-451-1600; www.bocadunes.com;
7100/5743; 73.1/71.1; 134/121
☑ "Walk out the door of the resort and there you are", smack dab in the middle of "a great day of golf" "that's not too heavy on

your wallet" say senior snowbirds smiling at a "good, flat", "well-maintained" layout with "lots of water everywhere" and a "beautiful new clubhouse"; younger yipsters yap "in season, it's a struggle to get through a round in under four hours behind all the oxygen bottles" chugging across the "just ok" course with "homes so close" a "swimming pool might swallow your ball."

Boca Raton Resort, Resort Course
– | – | – | – | $185

501 E. Camino Real, Boca Raton; 561-447-3000; 800-327-0101; www.bocaresort.com; 6253/4503; 69.3/65.5; 128/112
Even the golf carts are pretty in pink at the grande dame of Boca resorts where this diminutive but demanding course from the Roaring Twenties has been spruced up for 21st-century tastes; amid rock gardens, waterfalls and palms, tee off where celebs of yore tackled the par-3 13th beside a banyan-covered islet on a narrow layout that now sports faster greens, improved chipping areas and a healthy dose of mounding; you have to book a room to play, but who wouldn't want to relax on their own beachside lanai or take in a treatment at the Palazzo spa after a round?

Breakers, The, Ocean Course 🏌
– | – | – | – | $165

2 South County Rd.; 561-659-8407; www.thebreakers.com; 6167/5254; 68.1/69.0; 127/123
Along with the resort itself, Florida's oldest course has had a face-lift – the new layout is compact but complicated, with sand traps aplenty, contouring and more movement on the greens; you can see the ocean from only one hole, but you can feel it all over the guests-only course, where breezes rattle the coconuts and push your ball around; aprés-golf, relax at the new beach club or smooth your hairdo, gussy up and break the bank on a fabulous New French meal at the top-notch L'Escalier.

Champions Club at Summerfield 🏌
19 | 15 | 17 | 19 | $65

3400 SE Summerfield Way, Stuart; 772-283-1500; www.thechampionsclub.com; 6809/4941; 73.0/69.2; 131/117
☑ It's "tough scoring" on this "well-designed" Tom "Fazio layout", but it helps if you avoid "the edge" of the "marsh"-bordered "army-helmet greens" where shots "bounce into the water"; "spread out over" a "nature preserve with lots of birds and wildlife" "next to a pig farm", it's "beautiful" to look at, but "the aroma does keep players moving along", and there's just an "ordinary lunch" on offer, which, given the unsavory neighbors, "is ok" – try a steak at the well-regarded Flagler Grill in downtown Stuart instead.

EMERALD DUNES 🏌
27 | 21 | 21 | 17 | $150

2100 Emerald Dunes Dr., West Palm Beach; 561-684-5902; www.emeralddunes.com; 7006/4676; 73.8/67.1; 133/115
☑ "They treat you like a member" at this "top-shelf", "beautifully maintained" facility notorious for Tom Fazio's 50-ft.-tall Super Dune, which "creates nice elevation changes for a Florida course"; indeed, "other tracks pale in comparison" to the "gorgeous holes" with "waterfalls" that even local "private club members want to play"; while penny-pinchers scoff that "nobody can afford" this "over-glitzed and over-glammed" West Palm Beacher, defenders retort it's a "special place" "worth the money if you can spare it."

PGA National, Champion ⛳   25 | 24 | 22 | 18 | $280

400 Ave. of the Champions, West Palm Beach; 561-627-1800;
800-633-9150; www.pga-resorts.com; 7022/5377; 74.7/71.1; 142/123

☑ "The best of the courses at PGA National" is this "gorgeous" guests-only winner redesigned in 1990 by Jack Nicklaus, where the "brutally hard closing holes live up to their reputation", proving "quite tough on choppers"; despite some "great-value off-season" packages, sensitive, cent-counting swingers call it a "rip-off", insisting the "uncaring staff" lets the course fall into "poor condition except during" tournaments such as the 1987 Ryder Cup, the 1987 PGA Championships and, until 2000, the PGA Seniors Championship.

PGA National, Estates ⛳   21 | 17 | 20 | 20 | $150

400 Ave. of the Champions, West Palm Beach; 561-627-1800;
800-633-9150; www.pga-resorts.com; 6784/4903; 73.4/68.4; 131/118

■ If you're feeling overwhelmed by the nine pools, eight restaurants and 19 tennis courts at this large and luxe resort, step "a bit off property" and go a peaceful round on its "super", "little" guests-only course that's "easier" and "quieter compared with its neighbors"; despite being well-"used" and "a little on the flat side", it's kept in "pretty good condition", and there's enough drink to drop in here to make things interesting.

PGA National, General ⛳   24 | 25 | 24 | 20 | $150

400 Ave. of the Champions, West Palm Beach; 561-627-1800;
800-633-9150; www.pga-resorts.com; 6768/5324; 73.0/71.0; 130/122

☑ "An 18-gun salute for the General" fire Arnie's Army over this "fantastic Palmer design" that's "hard for beginners", due to the breeze across the links-like moguls and swales and to the water on nearly every hole, including the "great 18th", a par 5 with a soup-lined fairway where, "if the wind is in your face, forget about it"; aesthetes checked in so they can tee off at the "great, all-inclusive resort" say it's "not the prettiest" of the lot.

PGA National, Haig ⛳   22 | 25 | 25 | 20 | $150

400 Ave. of the Champions, West Palm Beach; 561-627-1800;
800-633-9150; www.pga-resorts.com; 6806/5645; 73.0/72.5; 130/121

☑ "Walter would be proud" of this "exciting" track designed by the Fazios in memory of five-time PGA Champion Hagen, because it "tests the entire bag"; straight shooters take solace that "accuracy is more important here than at the other" guests-only courses run by the pros, but snobby slicers "stay away", writing it off as "nothing special" and spending their days at the resort spa instead.

PGA National, Squire ⛳   21 | 24 | 24 | 19 | $150

400 Ave. of the Champions, West Palm Beach; 561-627-1800;
800-633-9150; www.pga-resorts.com; 6478/4982; 71.3/69.8; 127/123

■ Like its namesake, former PGA Champion Gene 'The Squire' Sarazen, this "good" guests-only resort course is "kind and gentle", and polite putters proclaim it the "most fun of the bunch" at PGA National; claustrophobes complain there are "too many houses too close" to it, but "water, water, water on 17 out of 18 holes, excellent conditions and fast greens" keep most of the crowd concentrating on their clubs and trotting over to one of the three driving ranges and six putting greens to brush up between rounds on the short Tom Fazio layout.

Polo Trace ⛳   23 | 20 | 20 | 17 | $139
*13481 Polo Trace Dr., Delray Beach; 561-495-5300; 866-465-3765;
www.polotracegolf.com; 7182/5445; 74.8/71.6; 139/125*
■ "You feel like you're in Scotland except the food is better" burp
boosters of this "little jewel of a links course in west Delray" where
"rolling hills and dunes" are "fun to play for every handicap";
however, "when the wind blows", this "eye-candy" lamb turns into
"a tiger", and swashbucklers suggest "bringing a swing blade to
get out of the rough" at the "overpriced" place.

Panhandle

Emerald Bay ⛳   ∇ 18 | 20 | 19 | 18 | $100
*4781 Clubhouse Dr., Destin; 850-837-5197; www.emeraldbaydestin.com;
6802/5184; 73.2/70.1; 140/122*
☑ On Choctawhatchee Bay, this track is chock-full of "water,
pines, Bermuda grass and palmettos"; play on its "large greens"
set amid forests and ponds laced with cattails and lily pads "moves
at a good pace", despite the lovely views, though folks staying at
the on-course guest house say all of that "typical Florida" foliage
"needs an improved grounds crew."

Kelly Plantation   ∇ 26 | 24 | 24 | 23 | $118
*307 Kelly Plantation Dr., Destin; 850-650-7600; 800-811-6757;
www.kellyplantation.com; 7099/5170; 74.2/70.9; 146/124*
■ "The service is unbelievable" rave golfing Adams and Eves biting
into the "apples on the first tee" at this "beautiful" Eden in a gated
community on Choctawhatchee Bay, where other "touches of
class" include iced towels for heated necks; the "fun-to-play" Fred
Couples layout with large greens and bold bunkering weaves
through woods and wetlands and leaves most players muttering
"what a course" as they stagger off No. 18.

Lost Key   ∇ 22 | 11 | 15 | 15 | $70
*625 Lost Key Dr., Pensacola; 850-492-1300; 888-256-7853;
www.lostkey.com; 6810/4936; 74.3/69.6; 144/121*
☑ "Condition is first rate" on this "excellent" barrier-island charmer
designed by Arnold Palmer, with "no major housing to spoil
its natural beauty"; still, while it's got "potential", architecturally
inclined aces argue that management has lost the key to success
here, as they're "running it out of a trailer on a gravel parking lot" –
"time to grow up" and get a real clubhouse.

Regatta Bay ⛳   ∇ 23 | 21 | 20 | 16 | $114
*465 Regatta Bay Blvd., Destin; 850-650-7800; www.regattabay.com;
6864/5092; 73.3/70.8; 148/119*
■ In an upmarket Emerald Coast community set among preserved
wetlands spitting distance from three state parks, this earth-friendly
daily fee is "better than your average Panhandler"; indeed, the
"superior" layout with views of Lake Regatta "will challenge every
player" with numerous forced carries and free-form bunkering.

Sandestin, Baytowne ⛳   20 | 20 | 23 | 18 | $105
*9300 Emerald Coast Pkwy., Destin; 850-267-6500; www.sandestin.com;
7046/5950; 73.4/68.5; 127/114*
■ "The beauty of the course is only overshadowed by the pristine
beaches" at this behemoth of a resort offering the "quintessential

vacation" packages with 1,000-plus accommodation choices, 15 tennis courts and over seven miles of beach tucked between the Gulf of Mexico and Choctawhatchee Bay; given scenic views and heavily bunkered, water-infused "holes with challenges from tee to great, true green", so what if it's "pricey"? – delighted duffers still squeal "I'll go back!"

Sandestin, Burnt Pines   ▽ 25 │ 23 │ 22 │ 19 │$145

9300 Emerald Coast Pkwy., Destin; 850-267-6500; www.sandestin.com; 7046/5950; 74.1/68.7; 135/114

■ "Bring your sand wedge" scream swingers stuck in all those strategic Rees Jones traps on this "wonderful", "lowlands layout" where fairways tumble through wetlands and "lots of pines"; with flat but natural terrain in "great condition" and "huge greens three or four clubs deep", it's "one of the favorites" for northwest Florida folks who might recommend a meal at the resort's top restaurant, Elephant Walk, after you play that second, cheaper round.

Sandestin, Links   21 │ 20 │ 21 │ 17 │$105

9300 Emerald Coast Pkwy., Destin; 850-267-8144; www.sandestin.com; 6710/4969; 72.8/69.2; 124/115

■ "The wind makes things very interesting" on this "nice" 25-year-old "links experience", so "be accurate" or your ball will meet up with "a little bit of everything": lakes, wetlands, towering pines and Choctawatchee Bay; the resort's original course boasts the Linkside Pub, where you can enjoy a brew 'n' burger while you watch the pros tee off on the big screen.

Sandestin, Raven   ▽ 23 │ 20 │ 23 │ 17 │$145

9300 Emerald Coast Pkwy., Destin; 850-267-8155; www.sandestin.com; 6910/5065; 73.8/68.4; 137/128

■ Reviewing ravens sure don't quoth 'nevermore' after a round on Robert Trent Jones Jr.'s "really fun yet difficult" layout sporting wide fairways, large asymmetrical bunkers and huge, undulating greens; eased into the wetlands, this dramatic test is "well kept" and "time-managed in a friendly way" by a host of headset-clad professionals, "so you can enjoy the round and not get caught by slow play."

Port St. Lucie

PGA GOLF CLUB, NORTH   26 │ 26 │ 25 │ 27 │$76

1916 Perfect Dr., Port St. Lucie; 561-467-1300; 800-800-4653; www.pgavillage.com; 7026/4993; 73.8/68.8; 133/114

■ "Go with the pros" urge enthusiasts because "the PGA knows how to run a golf facility"; the "lush" "North has a more Carolina feel to it", with "large, gentle greens, driveable par 4s and reachable par 5s" providing the Village's most "playable setup", which is accordingly "more crowded" than its siblings, though the fairways do clear out and the "prices drop when the snowbirds head north" for summer; given "first-class" practice facilities and "great teaching", swingers say "all courses should treat you this way."

PGA GOLF CLUB, PETE DYE   25 │ 26 │ 25 │ 26 │$59

1916 Perfect Dr., Port St. Lucie; 561-467-1300; 800-800-4653; www.pgavillage.com; 7150/5015; 74.5/68.7; 141/119

■ "You simply cannot beat the PGA Village for bang for your buck", or "bunker" for your buck either, as the "treacherous greens" on

Pete Dye's layout are guarded by "nothing but sand" "everywhere" fixing to "eat you up"; there's "no rough" on this "awesomely" "tough" track weaving through native wetlands, but there are "bugs, bugs and more bugs", so slather yourself in spray, and let the "very accommodating staff" help you to "lots of fun", despite dissenters who liken the "demented" design to "root canal work."

PGA GOLF CLUB, SOUTH   26 | 26 | 25 | 27 | $59

1916 Perfect Dr., Port St. Lucie; 561-467-1300; 800-800-4653; www.pgavillage.com; 7087/4933; 74.5/68.7; 141/119

■ If you're vacationing farther "south or in Orlando, it's worth the drive" to devour Florida's No. 1 Value on this "magnificent, difficult" "Tom Fazio layout" that winds Sunshine State–style through lush palmettos with "fast, undulating greens", multi-tiered bunkers and "the best finishing holes in the area"; it's "completely different" from and "less crowded" than the North, and along with the "great" 35-acre Learning Center and "extraordinary accommodations", you "won't be able to get enough" of it.

Sarasota

Legacy at Lakewood Ranch   26 | 20 | 20 | 19 | $100

8255 Legacy Blvd., Bradenton; 941-907-7920; www.lakewoodranch.com; 7067/5465; 73.7/71.4; 143/132

■ "Thank God Arnold came to bless the land" praise the flock forging across this "not sooo easy" Palmer layout with four-lane-highway fairways cut through forest, grasslands and wetlands; given "island greens", "plenty of pitfalls to catch wayward shots" and "still enough room for error", most muffers "just love playin' this course", though claustrophobes feel "crowded by houses."

Pelican Pointe ☺   ▽ 19 | 19 | 20 | 19 | $60

499 Derbyshire Dr., Venice; 941-496-4653; www.pelicanpointeflorida.com; 7192/4939; 75.1/68.9; 138/113

■ "A bit of water" surrounds this "quality course" that demands strategy and accuracy as it winds through nature preserves and lakes in a development not far from Venice's shark tooth–littered beach; pitching pelicans proclaim it "has it all", with "greens in great shape" and "excellent facilities", including a new, spiffy clubhouse, but wallet-wise waders "watch out" for "pricey in-season" fees and "the occasional gator" – "it is Florida, ya know."

River Club, The   ▽ 19 | 13 | 14 | 14 | $60

6600 River Club Blvd., Bradenton; 941-751-4211; 7026/5252; 74.5/70.4; 135/121

☑ Ball hitters burrow through "tunnel-like tees, over hazards and under overhanging trees", on "rolling fairways" to "undulating greens" at this "picturesque" "test" along the Braden River; its island green is "one of the best par 4s in the area", but grooming groupies gripe that it "had a chance to be great when it opened" in '88, but "it could be in much better condition" than it is today.

Riverwood   ▽ 24 | 22 | 20 | 23 | $90

4100 Riverwood Dr., Port Charlotte; 941-764-6661; 6938/4695; 73.8/68.0; 133/114

■ "This course can make you feel like Dorf if you're not careful" vent golf-film buffs imagining themselves as laughable as Tim

Conway's classic character, while the "members dressed in their Halloween costumes" during that spooky weekend's tournament really do look like "clowns putting"; the "terrific", "well-kept" treat is set among tall pines, lakes and marshes surrounded by some of the best boating and fishing in southwest Florida, so you're in for lots of "fun" during and after your round.

University Park Country Club ☼   24 | 21 | 23 | 21 | $50

7671 Park Blvd., University Park; 941-355-3888; 800-394-6325;
www.universitypark-fl.com
Course 1/Course 10: 7001/6000; 73.6/71.2; 138/124
Course 10/Course 19: 7247/6000; 74.4/71.7; 132/120
Course 19/Course 1: 7152/6000; 74.0/72.1; 134/123
■ "It keeps getting better" on this "immaculately maintained" 27-hole "must-play" in a "beautiful" live-on-the-links community just north of Sarasota: "the first nine is wonderful, the second tops it" but "the newest" is the "best" (though "greens being rebuilt" on Nos. 1–9 may turn the tables); "challenging without being daunting", it boasts a quartet of "the greatest par 3s around", "even if one of them is right up next to University Parkway with cars flying by", so "play this one now because if you don't, when it goes private" as planned in November 2003, "you will kick yourself."

Tampa

Bloomingdale 🏌   19 | 16 | 18 | 18 | $70

4113 Great Golfers Pl., Valrico; 813-685-4105; www.bgcgolf.com;
7165/5397; 74.4/72.1; 131/132
☑ Bite off "all you can handle from the back markers" at this "tough but fair" "neighborhood track" with "the fastest greens" in the Tampa area, and the swiftest hustlers – it's "home to a lot of good players who will take your cash" if you find the place "a bit difficult to navigate"; while the marsh areas are "pretty" amid the 100-year oaks and towering pines, the course has "slipped a little", with "few memorable holes", which are "not always in the best condition", and a "driving range that leaves much to be desired."

Fox Hollow   ▽ 24 | 22 | 22 | 17 | $85

10050 Robert Trent Jones Pkwy., New Port Richey; 727-376-6333;
800-943-1902; www.sandri.com; 7138/5203; 75.1/70.6; 137/127
☑ "Both Tampa's PGA and Senior PGA qualifying rounds take place" on this "nice" Robert Trent Jones Sr. stretch; with "rolling fairways and plenty of" marshland, forests and creeks, it "will give you everything you want", that is, dis doubters, if you're into "flat, uninteresting", "typical Florida development courses" "filled with retirees" – at least you "won't get mugged driving between holes", except by a management that makes you "dig deep in your pockets" to pay "high greens fees."

Lansbrook   19 | 16 | 17 | 18 | $62

4605 Village Center Dr., Palm Harbor; 727-784-7333;
6862/5333; 73.2/70.2; 131/124
☑ "In great shape for the amount of play it gets", this "long, tight course" with unusual, non-parallel fairways is "challenging" enough, say its "home" hackers; "you might have a more fair putt on a miniature golf course" sputter short-gamers shocked by the "mind-bending undulations in the greens", while a "clubhouse that

needs work" and an "apathetic staff" don't rate so well with
business travelers staying at nearby upscale hotels like Tampa's
Hyatt Regency Westshore.

Saddlebrook Resort, Palmer 🏌 19 | 22 | 20 | 15 | $130
5700 Saddlebrook Way, Wesley Chapel; 813-973-1111; 800-729-8383;
www.saddlebrookresort.com; 6469/5157; 71.9/70.0; 134/127
■ Jennifer Capriati's home base is one of the finest racquet resorts
in the world, so "watch for tennis balls in the fairways" at this
"short, target-style course" designed by The King and his partner,
Ed Seay, 20 miles north of Tampa, adjacent to a nature preserve
filled with cypresses, palms and pines; the "pace can be slow" in
this saddle, however, and the "pro shop staff is snooty."

Saddlebrook Resort, 19 | 23 | 22 | 16 | $130
Saddlebrook 🏌
5700 Saddlebrook Way, Wesley Chapel; 813-973-1111; 800-729-8383;
www.saddlebrookresort.com; 6564/4941; 72.0/70.6; 127/126
■ "If the woods and water don't eat your golf balls, the many
alligators will" warn herpetologically minded surveyors who
nevertheless embrace this "classic resort course with outstanding
amenities"; those who know their way around an expense account
form call this a "corporate paradise to do business" in, and though
there's "not a lot of challenge", it's a "slightly better layout than
its companion track."

TPC of Tampa Bay 🏌 23 | 23 | 22 | 17 | $112
5300 W. Lutz Lake Fern Rd., Lutz; 813-949-0090; www.tpc.com;
6898/5036; 73.4/69.1; 130/119
☑ "The Senior pros love it, and I think I know why" chime chipping
cheerleaders of this "daunting" but "always pleasing" host of the
Tour's Verizon Classic, where the mixture of "no-delay" play, "wind
and water", "fine conditioning", a "nice practice area" and a "high-
quality staff" makes for a "lovely" day of golf; nonetheless, short-
on-cash critics who "can't qualify for a second mortgage to pay
the greens fees" "would pass up" the "so-so course" "even if the
car breaks down in the parking lot."

Westin Innisbrook, 25 | 23 | 23 | 18 | $225
Copperhead 🏌
36750 US Hwy. 19 N., Palm Harbor; 727-942-2000; 800-456-2000;
www.westin-innisbrook.com; 7087/5537; 74.4/71.8; 140/130
■ "Once bitten, you'll come back again" to the (believe it or not)
"rolling" "hills of Florida" at this "expensive" but "excellent"
guests-only layout at a resort "just off the strip malls" of the Gulf; it's
"run by folks who love golf, and it shows" on the "long, demanding"
"Carolina-like" host of the PGA Tour's Tampa Bay Classic – it's "one
snake that can eat you alive", but "go ahead and enjoy it" anyway.

Westin Innisbrook, Island 🏌 23 | 23 | 24 | 17 | $225
36750 US Hwy. 19 N., Palm Harbor; 727-942-2000; 800-456-2000;
www.westin-innisbrook.com; 7063/5578; 74.1/73.0; 132/129
■ "Island means water, so bring two sleeves of balls" say swingers
swimming through this "difficult" guests-only design sporting
"elevation changes", abundant bunkering, "tight fairways" and
"water everywhere"; even landlubbers blubber that the "true
hidden gem" of Westin Innisbrook is "as good as Copperhead, and

that says a lot", but even given "terrific service", it's "a bit pricey" for conditions that "could use some maintenance."

WORLD WOODS, PINE BARRENS   29 | 23 | 22 | 25 | $120
17590 Ponce de Leon Blvd., Brooksville; 352-796-5500;
www.worldwoods.com; 6902/5301; 73.7/70.9; 140/132
■ "Fazio, Fazio, Fazio" chant chargers chewing on "challenges" at this "pure" "paradise" "in the middle of nowhere"; "fashioned after the infamous Pine Valley" private course in New Jersey and "set in all-natural surroundings" with "no homes" for miles, it's "an excellent mix of elevation changes, water, huge fairways, waste bunkers", "large, severely sloped greens" and "mega trees", with "unbelievable practice facilities" "worth the drive" an hour north from Tampa for that "golf-junkie" fix.

World Woods, Rolling Oaks   27 | 23 | 22 | 25 | $110
17590 Ponce de Leon Blvd., Brooksville; 352-796-5500;
www.worldwoods.com; 6985/5245; 73.5/70.7; 136/128
■ This "worthy" "contrast" to the "more famous Pine Barrens" "would be a terrific main course at many locations across the country"; with a "pastoral", "more traditional" layout of "rolling fairways" lined with moss-draped giant oaks, dogwoods, magnolias and azaleas, it's a "marvelous" Tom Fazio "gem" at a "great complex" offering a 36-hole "value that's very, very hard to beat" and where fine service is par for the course from "bagboys and starters who are quality individuals."

Georgia

★ **Best in State**
29 Reynolds Plantation, Great Waters, *Lake Oconee*
27 White Columns, *Atlanta*
25 Callaway Gardens, Mountain View, *Atlanta*
23 Chateau Elan, Woodlands, *Atlanta*
   Cobblestone, *Atlanta*

Atlanta

Bear's Best Atlanta ⛳   – | – | – | – | $95
5342 Aldeburgh Dr., Suwanee; 678-714-2582; 866-511-2378;
www.bearsbest.com; 6857/5076; 71.9/70; 138/127
On September 9, 2002, Jack Nicklaus himself launched the first ball at his new facility 35 minutes from downtown Atlanta; at this little brother to Las Vegas' Bear's Best, your forecaddie will help you tackle greatest-hits holes hand-selected from among the designer's repertoire, from No. 10 at St. Mellian in bonny olde Cornwall to the closing hole at Colorado's private Castle Pines Golf Club, home to the PGA Tour's International.

Brasstown Valley Resort ⛳   ▽ 20 | 22 | 22 | 21 | $75
6321 US Hwy. 76, Young Harris; 706-379-4613; 6957/5028; 73.9/69.2; 139/116
■ Brassy ball whackers boogie "off the beaten path" to this "challenging, well-kept" family resort course with a "hilly", "interesting" Blue Ridge layout, where "a lot of environmental areas" afford "great views" and the possibility of a soupy demise; it's "female-friendly" enough to have "very clean facilities for both sexes", and the lodge's 72-ft. fireplace warms chilly dew-sweepers.

Château Élan Course, Château Élan
23 | 24 | 22 | 18 | $77

6060 Golf Club Dr., Braselton; 770-932-0900; 800-233-9463; www.chateauelan.com; 7030/5092; 73.5/70.8; 136/124

■ It's "more of a haul than you think from Atlanta", but this "long, beautiful" "hidden gem in the backwoods" is "worth the drive (no pun intended)"; it's "fun to play and also a challenge", and there's no need to climb in the car afterward because the resort's "lodging is outstanding", the "restaurants are great", the spa is stellar and if your game is off, you can drown your sorrows at the on-premises winery – no wonder it's "a little pricey."

Château Élan Course, Woodlands
23 | 24 | 22 | 20 | $77

6060 Golf Club Dr., Braselton; 770-932-0900; 800-233-9463; www.chateauelan.com; 6735/4850; 72.6/68.5; 131/123

■ "Watch those rolls" because Chateau Elan's sister course is not only "narrow and woody", it's hilly as well, making for "scenic" play on "many interesting holes"; the resort's "impeccable service" includes clinics for women and juniors, so it's "excellent" for well-heeled families.

Cherokee Run
22 | 18 | 20 | 18 | $65

1595 Centennial Olympic Pkwy. NE, Conyers; 770-785-7904; www.cherokeerun.com; 7016/4948; 74.9/70.0; 142/123

■ Players who pony up at this "excellent all-around" Arnold Palmer Signature "right in the middle of an equestrian center" are hot to trot for the "real-treat zoysia grass fairways"; there are "no gimmicky tricks" from either the "outstanding layout" or the "friendly, helpful staff", and if encroaching McMansions are not your idea of "striking scenery", you'll be glad to discover "there is no housing on the course", for non-horses that is.

Cobblestone
23 | 18 | 18 | 24 | $51

4200 Nance Rd. NW, Acworth; 770-917-5151; www.cobblestonegolf.com; 6759/5400; 73.1/71.5; 140/129

☑ One of the "best values in the Atlanta area", this "quiet gem deserves more attention" for its "great scenery" and "elevation changes" that make for "real challenges from all sets of tees"; just try to pay no mind to "landing areas that are hard to decipher" and "goofy" "undulation in fairways that can give you some bad bounces" along with "the good ones."

Crooked Creek
22 | 23 | 20 | 18 | $89

3430 Hwy. 9 N., Alpharetta; 770-475-2300; www.crookedcreekgolf.com; 6917/4985; 73.4/70.0; 141/121

■ There's nothing crooked about this "wonderful course for players of all levels" in "the North Atlanta area"; golfers gung-ho on grooming gush over "excellent conditioning" of "wide fairways" and bowed, "potato-chip greens" on a "nice layout" begging for "every shot in the bag."

General at Barnsley Gardens
∇ 26 | 26 | 28 | 19 | $105

597 Barnsley Gardens Rd. NW, Adairsville; 770-773-7480; www.barnsleyresort.com; 7180/5450; 74.5/71.7; 141/127

■ Older Fazio brother Jim's "hidden treasure" in the north Georgia backwoods is "close enough to Atlanta to go for the day", but it's such a "beautiful course in [such] great shape" that you may want to hit this resort for the weekend and play a few rounds interspersed with fly fishing, trail riding and dining on produce from gardens first planted by the namesake antebellum cotton magnate; either way you'll "hate to tell anyone about it" because, despite a few "tricked-up holes", you'll want to keep this booty to yourself.

Georgia National   ▽ 24 | 19 | 19 | 21 | $65
1715 Lake Dow Rd., McDonough; 770-914-9994;
www.georgianational.com; 6907/5005; 74.1/70.5; 140/128
■ "One of Denis Griffiths' better designs", with water in play on many holes, this "very nice" parkland/woodland hybrid is a "good value", if you subtract the cost of the fuel it'll take to get "a long way from downtown"; maybe you can talk owner Economy Gas Company into a discount, and after your own day of hard driving, don't miss the action at the nearby Atlanta Motor Speedway.

Gold Creek   20 | 20 | 19 | 25 | $55
1 Gold Creek Ct., Dawsonville; 706-265-1950; 800-966-2441;
www.goldcreek.com; 6875/4750; 73.0/67.3; 130/111
■ "Three different nine-hole segments from which to choose is the drawing card" on this "visually intimidating but fun" track that's "long enough to use a driver on but manageable for the short hitter"; stake an "overnight/weekend" claim on the resort's "good" lodging in the foothills of the Georgia Mountains 45 minutes north of Atlanta, and if you don't strike it rich during your round, try your luck on a "side trip panning for gold" in nearby Dahlonega, the site of the country's first rush.

Golf Club At Bradshaw Farms ⌂   20 | 16 | 16 | 15 | $75
3030 Bradshaw Club Dr., Woodstock; 770-592-2222;
6936/4882; 73.7/68.8; 138/119
☑ Herds of "locals" low about "large elevation changes" that make for "extraordinary views" on a course "to conquer", followed by something probably harder than milk at the grill in the "great clubhouse made to look like an old barn and silos"; still, snobs turn up their noses at this "overpriced cow pasture" with "rude" service and greens that "seem to stay wet."

Heritage   20 | 16 | 17 | 13 | $90
4445 Britt Rd., Tucker; 770-493-4653;
www.theheritagegolfclub.com; 6903/5153; 73.6/68.8; 145/120
☑ "Get ready for a whippin'" on this "challenging, scenic" 27-holer in an "unexpected location near" Atlanta; though it caters to corporate club-wielders, its "fairly narrow fairways" are "not too crowded", possibly because short-gamers shy from "unreasonably undulated", "severe" greens that are "almost unputtable", or as on-course critics crack, it's "goofy golf at its finest."

Laurel Springs ⌂   21 | 21 | 20 | 17 | $90
6400 Golf Club Dr., Suwanee; 770-884-0064; www.laurelspringsclub.com;
6804/5720; 72.7/67.9; 138/126
☑ Fans feel that "this Nicklaus course is very impressive, from the beautiful clubhouse to a championship layout" that's "very pretty" and "playable for all handicaps"; "first-class pro shop and dining facilities" might be a clue-in that "they really want to be a private club", and even beaten ball-strikers who cry "Jack, don't kill us" will

"hate it" if it "reaches that potential"; snobbish swingers who consider it "uninspired" don't mind if its gates close to the public.

Nicklaus at Birch River   ▽ 18 │ 18 │ 21 │ 18 │ $75

639 Birch River Dr., Dahlonega; 706-867-1660; 6955/4992; 72.4/67.9; 134/118

■ "Want to play your very own course on a weekday?" – then head to this historic town at the base of the Blue Ridge and tee off on a "flat mountain course built in a valley"; it might "not be as pretty as the pictures in the ads", but it's still got a "fabulous layout", a "great clubhouse and a terrific driving range"; if you really have the place all to yourself and no one's looking, you won't have to "watch out for the fast greens" – just pick up that four-ft. come-backer and drop it in the hole.

Renaissance Pine Isle Resort 🔊   19 │ 19 │ 18 │ 17 │ $69

9000 Holiday Rd., Lake Lanier Islands; 770-945-8921; 6514/5099; 71.4/70.2; 131/126

■ "Bring plenty of balls (both kinds)" for "play in front of sun-drenched, well-lubricated fans" at this island "beauty" "on the water" "around a popular boating cove" at a conference-oriented resort; it's "tighter than a mouse's ear", so "walk single file, don't turn your head" and thank Mother Nature for "lake views that make up for" a Titleist that went to sleep with the fishes.

Southerness 🔊   19 │ 15 │ 16 │ 21 │ $53

4871 Flat Bridge Rd. SW, Stockbridge; 770-808-6000; www.southernessgolfclub.com; 6756/4916; 73.6/69.0; 136/119

☑ "If it were on the north side", this "nice little secret" with a "Scottish feel" and "great back nine" "would be packed", but "it's poorly located" beneath the "low-flying jets landing at Hartsfield" Airport; travelers on layover can tee off on "one of the best [tracks] for the money" near the city, even if it's "a bit rough at the edges."

St. Marlo   22 │ 19 │ 18 │ 17 │ $89

7755 St. Marlo Country Club Pkwy., Duluth; 770-495-7725; www.stmarlo.com; 6923/5071; 73.5/70.3; 138/119

☑ A cadre of "local" club-wielders compliment this "challenging track", a "favorite" for "well-maintained" "greens that roll fast and true and are as difficult as one will find"; perhaps the "expensive" course's "slow play" is caused by wanna-bes who "wish they had more jing in their pockets" as they ogle the "high-dollar houses that line the fairways and make golfers claustrophobic."

White Columns   27 │ 23 │ 21 │ 16 │ $120

300 White Columns Ct., Alpharetta; 770-343-9025; www.whitecolumnscountryclub.com; 7053/6015; 73.6/69.6; 135/116

■ "Southern hospitality comes alive" at the "nicest public course in the state", now turned semi-private at "pseudo-Pinehurst prices"; savvy swingers say "it will probably go members-only", so "play it soon" to enjoy "Kodak-moment holes" "set in the beautiful pines", but remember to "bring your wedge", since it seems Tom Fazio "could not see the value of saving some sand for the beaches."

Windermere   22 │ 19 │ 18 │ 18 │ $80

5000 Davis Love Dr., Cumming; 678-513-1000; www.discoverwindermere.com; 6902/4763; 73.6/68.8; 140/120

■ There are "so many options as to how to play this Davis Love III design, it makes your head hurt", but at least its Lake Lanier location is "very peaceful", "the longer holes are generally downhill, making them shorter than the yardage on the card" and the "super service" includes lessons from top teacher Bill Madonna; all in all, you're in for a "superb" round where the golf is "tough" but the cart girls are "schweet" and the livin' in homes along the fairways is easy.

Columbus

Callaway Gardens, Gardens View　　20 | 22 | 21 | 19 | $75

US Hwy. 27 S., Pine Mountain; 706-663-2281;
www.callawaygardens.com; 6392/5848; 70.9/73.4; 119/125
◪ The handful of hustlers who hail this "hidden gem" as "one of golf's best secrets" are hushed by disgruntled drivers declaring that "though the layout is interesting", the greens in "this garden must be replanted" and, despite the resort's unique butterfly house, "the facilities need a face-lift"; unimpressed urbanists argue "sadly, this course delivers exactly what you would expect for its being in middle-of-nowhere Georgia . . . not much."

Callaway Gardens, Lake View　　20 | 20 | 22 | 18 | $75

US Hwy. 27 S., Pine Mountain; 706-663-2281;
www.callawaygardens.com; 6051/5347; 68.6/71.1; 123/121
◪ "Short but scenic", this "fun course" serves up a "sporty layout in a great setting" that's "nice" and "tight" with plenty of "water" – just don't run afoul of the fowl, warns one errant ironist who accidentally "killed a goose here once"; there's dissension among the flock, however, with fans honking for "normally excellent conditions" and "outstanding service and amenities" while the flap among foes is it's "lousy."

Callaway Gardens, Mountain View　25 | 21 | 22 | 20 | $110

US Hwy. 27 S., Pine Mountain; 706-663-2281;
www.callawaygardens.com; 7057/5848; 73.9/74.3; 136/131
■ "They hold a PGA Tour event here", specifically the Buick Challenge, and "that speaks for" the "true test" of this "beautiful Southern" "classic"; "don't let the scenery take your mind off its difficulty" because you'll "need your best approach to hit the elevated, well-trapped greens", and pump up your muscles before you tee off, as "most holes have a long carry just to reach the fairway", making the "springtime Augusta wanna-be" "not a course for women" or, for that matter, "male golfers who are not in excellent shape."

Lake Oconee

Cuscowilla ⚐ ⏲　　　　▽ 27 | 20 | 21 | 20 | $150

640 Old Phoenix Rd., Eatonton; 706-484-0050; 800-458-5351;
www.cuscowilla.com; 6847/5348; 72.3/69.6; 130/123
■ It's a cool 80 miles from Atlanta, but if you have your "house built on the property", or at least spend a few nights in one of the resort villas, you can "roll out of bed and onto the first tee" of a "wickedly wonderful" Coore/Crenshaw design where the "great routing" and "difficult sandtraps" are "similar to Pinehurst" but "very different from other area courses"; "the caddie program is very nice", so take one along, ask for "all you want" from him or her and "enjoy a trip" that should prove "very memorable."

Reynolds Plantation ⛳   ∇ 26 | 22 | 27 | 22 | $200

100 Linger Longer Rd., Greensboro; 706-467-0600; 800-800-5250;
www.reynoldsplantation.com
Bluff/Cove: 7066/5440; 73.7/71.7; 137/128
Cove/Ridge: 7025/5386; 73.6/71.6; 136/126
Ridge/Bluff: 7015/5292; 73.5/70.7; 135/125

■ The Greensboro skies might "rain" on your parade across this
27-hole Tom Fazio "star", but don't worry because tale is told of
"the marshal bringing dry towels" on an "absolutely fantastic"
guests-only course with "service just as good" attached to a new
Ritz-Carlton; "don't let the lack of a clubhouse fool you" – some
discriminating swingers say the "rolling hills, ponds, creeks
and Lake Oconee" make "the Cove the best nine holes out of
all 81 fabulous ones at Reynolds", just "beware of the greens
with false fronts."

REYNOLDS PLANTATION,   29 | 24 | 24 | 21 | $215
GREAT WATERS ⛳

100 Linger Longer Rd., Greensboro; 706-467-0600; 800-800-5250;
www.reynoldsplantation.com; 7048/6022; 73.8/70.9; 135/117

■ If "this is a playable piece of heaven", as Atlanta golf disciples
testify, then the eternal hereafter "has a lot of water shots on the
back nine" and such a "spectacular layout" that "you might not
remember much of the round because you'll be too preoccupied
looking at the lake and the flowers", not to mention the "beautiful
clubhouse" and "excellent restaurant"; N.B. like that great golf
course in the sky, it's guests-only.

Reynolds Plantation,   ∇ 27 | 26 | 27 | 22 | $250
Oconee ⛳

100 Linger Longer Rd., Greensboro; 706-467-0600; 800-800-5250;
www.reynoldsplantation.com; 7029/5198; 73.8/70.0; 139/126

■ "Perhaps this is the best of the courses at Reynolds" hint happy
hackers who've fallen for the "challenging, beautifully landscaped"
guests-only layout where "every hole is carved from the hills and
woods, with waterfalls, creeks and Lake Oconee"; as if that wasn't
enough, there's "the epitome of service from your caddie cleaning
your clubs as you practice, to the forecaddies running ahead of
you, to the Ritz-Carlton Lodge as your 19th hole."

Reynolds Plantation,   ∇ 23 | 25 | 25 | 21 | $200
Plantation ⛳

100 Linger Longer Rd., Greensboro; 706-467-0600; 800-800-5250;
www.reynoldsplantation.com; 6698/5121; 71.7/68.9; 128/115

■ "Five star in every sense", with "unique holes" "in valleys
between hills with unobtrusive homes in the woods", this "well-
maintained" "fine alternative" may be "the easiest at Reynolds",
but it's still "as nice as the others"; one soggy swinger "enjoyed
it even in the pouring rain"; check into the resort to play it.

Lowcountry

Hampton Club, The   ∇ 22 | 19 | 18 | 19 | $79

100 Tabbystone, St. Simons Island; 912-634-0255; 800-342-0212;
www.hamptonclub.com; 6465/5233; 71.1/71.0; 135/121

■ "You should not feel bad about not playing the other courses on
St. Simons and Sea Island when you have the Hampton Club" insist

salty swingers who "love this" "fair" resort course in a "beautiful" marsh setting with a few floating holes and so much diversity it "plays like two separate nines"; call ahead to ask the "courteous" staff about pricing because the fees seem to change with the tides.

Osprey Cove   ▽ 25 | 19 | 18 | 23 | $85
123 Osprey Dr., St. Marys; 912-882-5555; www.ospreycove.com; 6791/5145; 72.9/69.7; 132/120
■ You could end up "behind Davis Love III" at this "pretty", "low-key" boating community course along the Atlantic, but it's "not very well known" to area outsiders, so its "well worth the drive up from Jacksonville" to escape the crowds and play an "outstanding" sleeper; "holes run adjacent to marshland close to the coast", which means you better hit long and straight if you ever want to hit into that famous Sea Island resident's foursome.

Sea Island, Plantation 杙   – | – | – | – | $175
100 Retreat Ave., St. Simons Island; 912-638-5118; 800-732-4752; www.seaisland.com; 6687/5194; 73.0/70.4; 133/122
In 1998, Rees Jones combined what used to be the Plantation and Retreat nines into one guest-only 18 lined with large oaks and flowers that give it a parkland feel, even though you can see the ocean from the fairways; its length may be a little tougher than you'd like on vacation, but if you're intimidated you can always stop by the spa for their Fairway Flexibility class before you tee it up.

Sea Island, Retreat 杙   – | – | – | – | $125
100 Retreat Ave., St. Simons Island; 912-638-5130; 800-732-4752; www.seaisland.com; 6715/5142; 73.9/74.5; 135/129
"Redone in 2000", this island layout "combines the old Retreat and Plantation nines" to form a "fantastic" guests-only course that "makes you think" on its "fast" greens, particularly on the 6th surrounded on three sides by water; "leave it to Davis Love, the king of southern Georgia" to design a track that's "beautiful in every way"; N.B. though the resort's upscale Cloister hotel is on Sea Island, the courses are on adjacent, larger St. Simons Island.

Sea Island, Seaside 杙   – | – | – | – | $215
100 Retreat Ave., St. Simons Island; 912-638-5118; 800-732-4752; www.seaisland.com; 6550/5048; 72.3/60.8; 137/120
The original nine at this resort and spa on the beautiful coastal island of St. Simons was built in the Roaring Twenties; in recent years Tom Fazio reshaped it into a championship-caliber 18-holer for guests only that stays true to its links-style origins, meandering along the coast and through tidal creeks and salt marshes dotted with mature oaks and cedars, all of which are visible from the many elevated tee boxes; after your round, you can rent a kayak to dive for balls amid the water fowl on those wetlands.

Hawaii

★ **Best in State**
28 Princeville, Prince, *Kauai*
    Kapalua, Plantation, *Maui*
    Challenge at Manele, *Lanai*
27 Mauna Kea Resort, *Big Island*
    Kauai Lagoons, Kiele, *Kauai*

Big Island

HUALALAI GOLF CLUB 26 │ 27 │ 27 │ 20 │ $165
100 Kaahumanu Dr., Kailua Kona; 808-325-8480;
www.hualalairesort.com; 7117/5374; 73.7/66.3; 131/116
■ "If there's golf in heaven, it looks like this", but you "can't just walk on" within these pearly gates; "you must be a Four Seasons guest" to play the "exclusive" "beauty", but what's so bad about one "pricey" night at the No. 1–rated resort in Zagat's *Top U.S. Hotels* when you can tee off into an "ocean view" on a "lava"-laced "stunner" "so empty you feel like it's your own private course" and a staff that "treats you like royalty" goes along with the fantasy?

Kona, Alii Mountain ⛳ 19 │ 17 │ 19 │ 21 │ $165
78-7000 Alii Dr., Kailua Kona; 808-322-2595; 6673/4945; 71.5/69.2; 133/125
☑ Perhaps "the steepest course in the islands" is this "wonderful" track that's "very well taken care of with great people everywhere" on staff; there "doesn't seem to be a level spot on the whole layout", and despite the "beautiful views of the Kohala coast", you'll really "hate those uphills" if you don't "take a cart"; needless to say, the Hawaii-style greens fees are as elevated as the landscape.

Kona, Ocean ⛳ 22 │ 17 │ 20 │ 22 │ $175
78-7000 Alii Dr., Kailua Kona; 808-322-2595; 6806/5573; 71.6/71.2; 129/121
■ "The former site of the LPGA Takafugi Classic" is "wide open and long", with a "few nice holes" and "fast greens"; "the wind can play a major role in club selection" and "make the course much more difficult" than you want, but "who cares when it's 85 degrees and you have a view of the ocean" from the course and your villa?

Makalei Hawaii ▽ 18 │ 10 │ 14 │ 18 │ $110
72-3890 Hawaii Belt Rd., Kailua Kona; 808-325-6625;
7041/5212; 73.5/69.4; 143/121
■ When they say "wild turkeys and peacocks roam the course", they don't mean chumps and braggarts on this "awesome" resort layout "high up on a volcano slope" "in the cool air" "3,000 feet above Kona", where even though "the long rough can make finding errant balls difficult", the "spectacular views" are worth going out there to knock down a few of those birdies.

Mauna Kea Resort ⛳ 27 │ 23 │ 24 │ 20 │ $195
62-100 Mauna Kea Beach Dr., Kamuela; 808-882-5404;
7114/5277; 73.6/70.2; 143/124
■ Trent Jones Sr.'s "grande dame of Hawaii golf" "has aged well" and "still shines on the Kohala Coast", delivering "everything you hope for" from a "thrilling" tropical "classic", with "unparalleled natural beauty", "long par 4s" and a "treacherous" "signature par 3 over the ocean that is breathtaking, and ball taking when the wind blows"; if you "feel beaten up after a round here", seek sympathy from the "friendly staff", or go to the swank resort hotel and commune with the koi coasting in the lobby pond.

Mauna Lani Resort, North ⛳ 26 │ 26 │ 25 │ 20 │ $185
68-1050 Makaiwa Pl., Kamuela; 808-885-6655; www.maunalani.com;
6993/5474; 73.2/71.4; 136/124
■ "Has anyone played here before?" – it's so "immaculate" that "divots are hard to find", but so are your "hooked or sliced balls"

'cause "endangered green turtles, humpbacks" and "Madam Pele eat them" on this "work of art" with "vistas from almost every hole", most notably the "incredible lava-island 15th"; all this and morning tai chi on the 18th fairway is "worth the freight", so "sell the farm if you have to" and jump a jet to this former Senior Skins Game host.

Mauna Lani Resort, South 🏌   26 | 25 | 25 | 20 | $185
68-1050 Makaiwa Pl., Kamuela; 808-885-6655; www.maunalani.com; 6938/5140; 72.8/69.6; 133/177
■ "The dramatic par 3s along the ocean allow you to fantasize that you're Tiger . . . until you end up in the drink" at this "beautiful" resort course where the "perfectly maintained fairways" weave "like green carpet around the lava and the ocean"; along with "elevation changes and windy holes", this makes it "tougher than its sister" though it's "not as famous", and chances are despite your daydreams or your super-glam bungalow digs, neither are you.

Waikoloa Beach Resort, Beach   22 | 21 | 21 | 19 | $150
1020 Keana Pl., Kamuela; 808-885-6060; 6566/5094; 71.5/69.4; 133/119
■ "Breaching whales are a distraction" on the "amazing" signature ocean hole at this 2002 LPGA Takefuji Classic host, a course "built through lava", which can be "nasty", so consider O.B. balls "a donation to the golf gods"; take the bunkers for punishment from the golf demons because "it's not sand in there", it's "crushed coral", which is "like playing out of a kitty litter box"; after the round, flag down a tram or boat to ferry you about the massive resort.

Waikoloa Beach Resort, Kings   23 | 21 | 21 | 19 | $150
1020 Keana Pl., Kamuela; 808-885-6060; www.waikoloagolf.com; 7074/5459; 73.9/71.0; 133/121
■ "Accuracy is the key, as almost anything off the fairway is in the lava rocks" at the Beach's links-style "sister", but of course, "if it's windy, it will not matter" whether you're "able to hit long and straight" or not, meaning "this Weiskopf/Moorish design is a real monster" in monsoon season; nevertheless, those who would be club-wielding kings claim slaying the "fun, relentless" and "visually stunning" dragon is "easy", as they pop another post-round pupu in their mouths at the Scottish-themed clubhouse grill.

Waimea   ▽ 18 | 12 | 16 | 22 | $65
47-5220 Mamamlahoa Hwy., Kamuela; 808-885-8053; 6210/5673; 71.7/71.3; 130/119
■ If you've had it with sun and ocean views, "head up into the foothills" to a "hidden gem" that's "very different from the other Big Island" tracks; "lots of wildlife" accompanies your "meander through cow pasture" and "rain forest" on an "interesting layout" that's "cooler than courses on the coast" but also "can be very wet"; at such "high elevation", "expect fog to roll in at 11 AM" and to tee off "into clouds", though hopefully you'll land on cloud nine.

Kauai

Kauai Lagoons, Kiele 🏌   27 | 25 | 25 | 21 | $170
3351 Hoolaulea Way, Lihue; 808-241-6000; 800-634-6400; www.kauailagoonsgolf.com; 7070/5417; 73.7/66.5; 137/123
■ "If you're not a good golfer, hope you're a good swimmer" at this "Jack Nicklaus masterpiece" "surrounded by a man-made lagoon

so large the builders had to factor in the curvature of the Earth"; it's "tough but gorgeous" and "extremely well maintained", with "great holes running along the ocean" and an "island green that's a real challenge", so bring your goggles and practice holding your breath.

Kauai Lagoons, Mokihana | 21 | 24 | 23 | 20 | $120 |

3351 Hoolaulea Way, Lihue; 808-241-6000; 800-634-6400; www.kauailagoonsgolf.com; 6960/5607; 73.1/71.8; 127/116

■ While it's "not nearly as pretty as its sister course", this "less expensive" links-style stretch is still "lush, and we're not referring to drinking", though it's "challenging" enough to make driving as difficult as it is under the influence; with "less traffic" than Kiele, it's "faster" to play, but slow down because the "airplanes landing left and right on almost every hole" make "persistant noise that can be quite distracting" – you may want that cocktail after all.

POIPU BAY 🏨 | 27 | 25 | 25 | 21 | $185 |

2250 Ainako St., Koloa; 808-742-8711; 800-858-6300; 7150/5241; 73.1/70.4; 134/122

■ Try this "if you want to play a course that Tiger plays", but though it's "properly designed" for it, it happens to be "wind-wind-windy", and those nasty trades can "add 10 strokes to your round"; so "bring your knock-down shot", "a steady putter, distance balls" and, of course, "your camera" because with a "backdrop of steep mountains and crashing waves", "each hole gets more beautiful" at a resort with many lodging options, including the Hyatt Regency.

Princeville, Makai | 23 | 22 | 22 | 21 | $125 |

5-3900 Kuhio Hwy., Princeville; 808-826-3580; 800-826-1108; www.princeville.com
Ocean/Lakes: 6886/5516; 73.2/69.2; 132/116
Ocean/Woods: 6875/5631; 72.9/70.4; 131/116
Woods/Lakes: 6901/5543; 72.5/69.6; 129/115

■ "If you're not a great golfer", any combo of these 27 "stunners" provides "relief from the Prince" with "a nice mix" of "beautifully laid-out ocean holes" in "the shadows of Bali Hai" at a gorgeous Hanalei Bay resort; "prepare to be" rendered "speechless" by the "rainbows on the greens" – so what's "a little drizzle"?

PRINCEVILLE, PRINCE | 28 | 27 | 26 | 22 | $125 |

5-3900 Kuhio Hwy., Princeville; 808-826-3580; 800-826-1108; www.princeville.com; 7309/5338; 75.3/72.0; 145/127

■ With "whales breaching in the ocean" and holes amid "trees, mountains and waterfalls", Hawaii's No. 1–rated Course feels like a cross between "church" and "the jungle"; track-wise Tarzans bellow "don't look for your ball out of bounds or you might be eaten by a large spider or ripped to shreds by razor-sharp leaves", and "bring ammo" because, with "forced carries and sloping fairways", this "paradise" is "sure to increase your handicap" – and mess up your hair, since "it rains sporadically, but only for five minutes."

Lanai

CHALLENGE AT MANELE 🏨 | 28 | 26 | 26 | 21 | $200 |

Manele Bay Hotel, Lanai City; 808-565-2222; 7039/5024; 73.3/68.8; 132/119

■ "If a course can be called romantic, this one is" say golf lovers who've fallen for the "dolphins frolicking" nearby this "luxury" resort "masterpiece" with several "scenic shots" "over crashing surf" making for a "drop-dead gorgeous" game (emphasis on the 'drop'); the "challenging wind" and "long carries" at the "aptly named" "beauty" can seduce even the world's biggest computer nerd, since "Bill Gates chose to marry" "on one of the many greens perched on the cliffs above the blue-green ocean."

EXPERIENCE AT KOELE 🏌 | 26 | 26 | 27 | 21 | $200 |

The Lodge at Koele, Lanai City; 808-565-4653; www.lanai-resorts.com; 7014/5425; 73.3/66.0; 141/123

■ Even weaklings "feel like Hercules" "hitting a ball into orbit" "on the drive-friendly signature" 17th that "drops 200 feet from the tee" to the green, which isn't the only "elevation change" on this "beautiful inland" course with "top-notch facilities" at a resort among the country's crème de la crème; "thick with pines", it's "mountain golf in heaven", allowing gamers "to play in Hawaii and also imagine they're in Vermont", if not on Mount Olympus.

Maui

Dunes at Maui Lani 🏌 | 22 | 21 | 21 | 23 | $95 |

1333 Mauilani Pkwy., Kahului; 808-873-7911; www.dunesatmauilani.com; 6841/4768; 73.5/67.9; 136/114

■ "The best combo of design, conditioning, value" and "access to the airport" on Maui is an "enjoyable" daily-fee rarity amid the resort jungle; it "looks like it should be flat but is amazingly hilly" and "breezy", so "be off the course by 1 PM to avoid being blown away", though range-aholics rave that you can't avoid being swept off your feet by "one of the best practice facilities in the state."

Kaanapali, North 🏌 | 19 | 19 | 20 | 16 | $150 |

2290 Kaanapali Pkwy., Lahaina; 808-661-3691; www.kaanapali-golf.com; 6994/5417; 72.8/71.1; 134/123

◪ "Tee off into an amazing sunset" and take advantage of "twilight rates for the best value" at this "beautifully landscaped" resort course connected to the big Kaanapali hotels; it's "not too long or punishing", so it's "easy to post a good score" even when the "fantastic views" dazzle you into duffing; pros who proclaim it "mediocre" might at least find solace in the fact that "not far away, a great beach" awaits, as well as the honky-tonk town of Lahaina.

Kaanapali, South 🏌 | 17 | 18 | 19 | 15 | $142 |

2290 Kaanapali Pkwy., Lahaina; 808-661-3691; www.kaanapali-golf.com; 6555/5485; 70.7/69.8; 127/120

◪ "Playing a bit harder than the North course", this sib is "a nice Hawaii golf experience" (and what isn't?); however, beyond a few "beautiful ocean holes", it's "less scenic", with "views obscured by hotels"; plus "the maintenance has declined recently" throughout the facility, making this "yesterday's course at today's prices" and a nonstarter "unless you're a real newbie or it's your second round of the day."

Kapalua, Bay 🏌 🏌 | 24 | 24 | 25 | 20 | $180 |

300 Kapalua Dr., Kapalua; 877-527-2582; www.kapaluamaui.com; 6600/5124; 71.7/69.6; 138/121

■ On "your typical Hawaiian track", "scenic holes make you not care where your ball goes", and the "exceptional" carry "across the Pacific with exposure to the trade winds" is par for the course on this Maui mama, "the original" layout at a "breathtaking", serene resort; as you "ramble" through a round "along the beautiful cliffs", ask yourself "where else can you go whale-watching and putt for bogey at the same time?" – answer: um, nowhere?

Kapalua, Plantation 🏌🏞   28 | 27 | 26 | 21 | $220
2000 Plantation Club Dr., Kapalua; 877-527-2582;
www.kapaluamaui.com; 7263/5627; 75.2/75.2; 142/129
■ "Bring your A-game" and "you'll feel like a pro" at this "home of the Mercedes Championship", a "not-to-be-missed" "mountainside treasure" where there are "only two holes without an ocean view" and the "conditions and service" are "plush-plush"; it's "not that pricey after 2 PM", so "polish up the big dog and let him eat" a late lunch and go for a "long" run, especially on "the 663-yard 18th, an unbelievable way to end an experience you'll remember forever."

Kapalua, Village 🏌🏞   23 | 23 | 26 | 19 | $180
2000 Village Rd., Kapalua; 877-527-2582; www.kapaluamaui.com;
6378/4896; 71.7/69.0; 134/116
◪ "If they could get the TV equipment onto it, they would have the tournament here" claim camera-happy native Villagers who insist that this "favorite of members and locals" is "the prettiest", "most interesting" and "least touted" of Kapalua's three courses; "a straight game is the only game" on a "nice variety of holes" "through beautiful mountains, valleys" and "pines", regardless of traditionalists tabbing it "too gimmicky on the front nine."

Makena, North   24 | 20 | 22 | 20 | $155
5415 Makena Alanui, Kihei; 808-879-3344; 800-321-6284;
www.makenagolf.com; 6914/5303; 72.1/70.9; 139/128
■ "There is paradise on earth", and if it ain't this, it "don't get better than this": "beautiful lava fields are interspersed with fairways" but "no homes or condos (yet)" on a "RTJ Jr. course that climbs onto the hills for fabulous views" of the Pacific, so you can "whale-watch while you triple bogey" at a "nice, relaxing pace"; it's "less crowded" and "not so windy", and some salacious swingers say it's "the most fun they've ever had golfing", and that's before "checking out the nude beach afterward" at Little Makena.

Makena, South   24 | 21 | 24 | 21 | $175
5415 Makena Alanui, Kihei; 808-879-3344; 800-321-6284;
www.makenagolf.com; 7017/5529; 72.6/71.1; 138/130
■ "You'll love it and want to do it again, and again and again and again and ...", well, you get the picture; this "peerless tropical golf experience" with "breathtaking ocean vistas" from its newly "replanted fairways and greens" is "more walkable" than its sibling, and if it's "not as scenic", that's "only by a smidge"; if you "don't want to leave even after playing both courses in the same day", you can delay the inevitable with some "great fish sandwiches" served by "friendly, accommodating attendants."

Wailea, Blue 🏞   23 | 22 | 23 | 20 | $140
100 Wailea Golf Club Dr., Wailea; 808-875-7450; 800-332-1614;
www.waileagolf.com; 6758/5291; 71.6/72.0; 130/117
◪ Take to this "impressive" track while "your non-playing spouse hits the spa", and enjoy "great sunsets" over "beautiful mansions

as you tee off" onto "elevated", "forgiving fairways"; though "the pro shop and restaurant are very nice", "the oldest of the courses" at this resort is "showing its age", "has no driving range" and "a small clubhouse", meaning it "needs to be updated."

Wailea, Emerald 🏌   25 | 24 | 23 | 21 | $150

100 Wailea Golf Club Dr., Wailea; 808-875-7450; 800-332-1614; www.waileagolf.com; 6825/5256; 71.7/69.6; 130/115

◪ It's "short" enough to be "women-friendly", but macho dudes say "men should wear grass skirts if they want to play from the forward tees" on this "first-class" resort course with "Molokini views from almost every hole", where you want to "stay out of the lava" and ignore the "terrible practice facilities"; fashion tip number two: it's on Maui's "desert side", so "wear white because it's hot."

Wailea, Gold 🏌   25 | 25 | 24 | 21 | $160

100 Wailea Golf Club Dr., Wailea; 808-875-7450; 800-332-1614; www.waileagolf.com; 7078/5317; 73.0/70.3; 139/121

■ There are "over 90 bunkers" at the "most difficult" and "nicest Wailea track", "home of the Senior Skins Game", so "bring a beach ball" and enjoy bouncing about in the sand on a "beautifully kept course" with "strategic holes" and "great greens" where the golden oldies play; "if you are lucky enough to be staying at one of the hotels" where the "facilities are world-class", "it's even better."

Oahu

Hawaii Prince 🏌   18 | 19 | 19 | 17 | $135

91-1200 Fort Weaver Rd., Ewa Beach; 808-944-4567; www.princeresortshawaii.com
A/B: 6759/5275; 70.2/70.4; 123/120
B/C: 6801/5205; 70.1/69.5; 125/117
C/A: 6746/5300; 70.1/69.9; 122/118

■ This typically Hawaiian 27-holer is "challenging" "when windy" and "beautiful with great landscaping" on "many water holes"; it's "generally flat", but "tough pin placements" keep things interesting for junkies strung out on Prince Resort's 99-hole special deal including hotel rooms and rounds on three islands; it must be a "good place to get a sunburn" because when was the last time you heard a golfer complain that a course "needs more trees"?

Kapolei 🏌   ▽ 22 | 18 | 19 | 19 | $150

91-701 Farrington Hwy., Kapolei; 808-674-2227;
7001/5490; 72.7/71.9; 134/124

■ "Plenty of water makes things interesting" at the "former home of the LPGA Cup Noodles Tournament", "one of Oahu's newest courses", which is "short", "easy and wide open" but "can get windy in the afternoon"; the "paspalum grass makes the greens very true", though "especially on short chips it can be hard to adjust to", unlike the first-class facilities, which are part of a "master-planned community" that features "great clubhouse food."

Koolau   22 | 19 | 17 | 20 | $125

45-550 Kionaole Rd., Kaneohe; 808-247-7088;
7310/5119; 76.4/72.9; 152/134

■ "Unless you own a Titleist factory", play from the front, "but take in the view from the tips" for a "spectacular" breather from tackling one of the "highest slope ratings in the nation" at this "tough s.o.b." "in the jungle on the side of several mountains" where it "rains 250 days a year"; "most holes require carries over gulches" with "long" "target" shots and absolutely "no bailouts" onto "forever wet" fairways and greens, so forget your "normal handicap", forget your "ruined golf shoes", aw heck, forget the "proper tees" – no matter what you do, "you'll still lose balls."

Ko Olina 🏨   26 | 24 | 24 | 22 | $145

92-1220 Aliinui Dr., Kapolei; 808-676-5309; www.koolina.com; 6867/5361; 72.3/71.8; 135/126

■ "Spam sushi at the halfway house" proves "they treat you well" at the JW Marriott Ihilani's "fantastic" track sporting mountain views, "some of the best par 3s anywhere" and "enough elevation changes to make things interesting", plus enough wind to make the short "drive from Honolulu the only drive you'll enjoy", unless you include your ride in the GPS-equipped cart, which veers near several waterfalls and even "right under one"; love birdies can tee off their marriage with a lagoon wedding at the resort's marina, and the spa is highly lauded.

Makaha 🏨   ▽ 22 | 14 | 14 | 22 | $90

84-626 Makaha Valley Rd., Waianae; 808-695-9544; 7077/5856; 73.2/73.9; 139/129

■ The "long drive from Honolulu limits the number of golfers" who are familiar with the "most underplayed, unknown course on Oahu" to those "with a lot of local knowledge"; that's too bad for all the vacationing mainlanders because the "great shotmaker's layout", formerly owned by the Sheraton, is "one of the best" on the island; *kamaainas* say "go there if you want a round to yourself" at a "good price for a resort" track, but you'd better hurry up before "it gets popular."

New Ewa Beach Golf Club   ▽ 18 | 14 | 14 | 17 | $65

91-050 Fort Weaver Rd., Ewa Beach; 808-689-8351; 6541/5230; 71.3/70.5; 125/121

🏧 Not far from the USS Arizona Memorial at Pearl Harbor is an "interesting" layout where "narrow starting holes open up to easier undulating fairways" and the two "very short", "drivable par 4s" make you feel like 'Wild Thing' John Daly; just steer clear of the "planes on their final approach into Honolulu International", the "problem paspalum grass" on the landing areas and the Budweiser.

Pearl Country Club 🏨   19 | 16 | 17 | 21 | $100

98-535 Kaonohi St., Aiea; 808-487-3802; www.pearlcc.com; 6787/5536; 72.0/72.1; 135/130

🏧 "Watch out for the mongoose on No. 10 that will steal your snack" advise once-bitten ball strikers; if that's not enough, this "good mix of holes" has "superb greens" that "can be deceptive", even if they "don't excite", plus it's "built on the side of a mountain, so if you slice or hook badly, watch out" – now, that bites.

Turtle Bay Resort, Arnold Palmer   24 | 17 | 18 | 18 | $155

57-049 Kuilima Dr., Kahuku; 808-293-8574; www.turtlebayresort.com; 7199/4851; 75.0/64.3; 141/121

■ "Site of a Senior PGA stop", this Oahu resort boasts "Palmer's best layout anywhere" according to Arnold aficionados wide-eyed over its "blind holes with surprises off the tees", "strategically placed bunkers" and "fairways you can putt on"; a "wicked wind" "makes it play very long", but you probably won't mind since it's so well maintained and has "views of the ocean" that render rounds "serene", and if the service is just "ok", at least "you're close to the hamburgers and ices on the North Shore."

Turtle Bay Resort, Greg Fazio　　20 | 17 | 20 | 20 |$155

57-049 Kuilima Dr., Kahuku; 808-293-8574; www.turtlebayresort.com; 6535/5518; 71.2/70.2; 131/116
■ It may be possible for "high-handicappers to have a good time" on this "friendly, wide-open layout that's easy on the eyes", but it presents "more of a challenge than it looks", with "bunkers and trade winds" leaving loopers with "a lot of 'what ifs'" – as in what if you just relaxed and enjoyed a "mature" "paradise away from the crowds" with "great views" and a "friendly, aloha-filled staff"?

Waikele 🖴　　　　　　　19 | 18 | 18 | 20 |$125

94-200 Paioa Pl., Waipahu; 808-676-9000; www.golfwaikele.com; 6663/5226; 71.7/70.1; 126/119
■ Ben Affleck is nowhere to be found among "the nice views of Pearl Harbor", Ko'olau and Waianea Mountains from the "fast greens" at this "interesting" resort course where the "challenging holes" include a signature par 4 that's "just short enough to reach in one" shot, though the guarding waterfall and lake "usually dictate otherwise"; "it can get very busy, so get tee times early" and have lunch afterward in a clubhouse backdropped by Diamond Head.

Idaho

Boise

Falcon Crest　　　　　　　– | – | – | – |$49

11102 S. Cloverdale Rd., Kuna; 208-362-8897; www.falconcrestgolf.com; 7005/5423; 72.5/68.9; 122/121
This championship layout near Boise is the first of three courses that will form an enormous golf complex including a shorter, easier spread for juniors and beginners and an open, walkable links; for now, Idaho iron workers can fire it up on this desert and parkland combination that has water on nine holes and views of the valley and mountains.

Coeur d'Alene

Coeur d'Alene Resort 🏌🖴⊙　27 | 27 | 27 | 20 |$180

900 Floating Green Dr.; 208-667-4653; 800-688-5253; www.cdaresort.com; 6309/5490; 79.9/70.3; 121/118
■ The "big-target", "floating par-3 hole" on the lake makes for "spectacular" but "not overly tough" play at this "beautiful" course with "mountain views"; it's "one of the most pristine resorts in the West", with "immaculate conditioning" and "hidden rakes" where the "forecaddies with range markers" deliver "unprecedented service", but the real secret to its popularity is that the "relatively short" fairways "make you appear to be a better golfer than you really are."

Illinois

★ **Best in State**
28 Eagle Ridge, The General, *Galena*
    Cog Hill, No. 4 (Dubsdread), *Chicago*
    Glen Club, The, *Chicago*
26 Kemper Lakes, *Chicago*
    Chalet Hills, *Chicago*

Chicago

Balmoral Woods   18 | 14 | 15 | 19 | $60
26732 S. Balmoral Woods Dr., Crete; 708-672-7448;
www.balmoralwoods.com; 6700/5400; 72.6/71.8; 128/118
☑ "Good routing" on "memorable holes" makes this "short, tight", "sporty" Tom Fazio co-design "enjoyable to play", "especially during the week", when low fees give "great value"; the "long drive from Chicago" takes you "so far south, you'll think you're in Tennessee", though it's northern enough that "no matter what the weatherman says, bring more clothing"; critics from all directions say "it's not that good except compared with nearby clunkers."

Big Run   21 | 13 | 15 | 21 | $67
17211 W. 135th St., Lockport; 815-838-1057; www.bigrungolf.com;
7025/5420; 74.4/71.9; 142/130
■ "Everyone talks about the length" of this "beautiful, hilly" track, but now that ladies' tees are installed, even "higher handicappers, short hitters and women" who used to complain can now have a go at it; the "600-yard par 5 and an uphill par-4 finish" are, indeed, "difficult", but putters counter that the "real test is the greens", not to mention the elevation changes; if you think you're a big runner, "go ahead and walk this course – we dare you."

Cantigny 🏌   26 | 25 | 23 | 20 | $80
27 W. 270 Mack Rd., Wheaton; 630-668-3323;
www.cantignygolf.com
Hillside/Lakeside: 6830/5183; 72.6/70.1; 131/119
Lakeside/Woodside: 6981/5425; 73.8/71.9; 138/127
Woodside/Hillside: 6939/5236; 73.4/70.3; 132/120
☑ Each combo is "in a perpetual state of beauty" on this 27-holer with an "excellent pro shop" on the late, great *Chicago Tribune* publisher's "spectacular" estate where "imaginative topiaries are scattered" and a Dick Tracy–shaped bunker catches wayward shots; don't hedge your bets, bluster backspinners who "beware the rough trimmed at four inches", while foes who find carved bushes nothing but silly rabbits want more "tough" tricks.

Chalet Hills 🏌   26 | 20 | 20 | 21 | $75
943 Rawson Bridge Rd., Cary; 847-639-0666; www.chaletgolf.com;
6890/4934; 73.4/68.1; 131/114
■ The "first four holes are a good warm-up", but "don't let them fool you" – you gotta "score early or you don't score at all" on this "very challenging course" where dew sweepers scoop up discount rates; with "tight, tight, tight" fairways girdled by "scenic hills, marshes and forest", it "isn't a monster in length but you'll need every club in the bag" say "middle-of-nowhere" suburban swingers who swear it's "sporty" and "interesting" and a "blast from the tips."

Cog Hill, No. 2 ⛳
23 | 22 | 21 | 22 | $49

12294 Archer Ave., Lemont; 630-257-5872; www.coghillgolf.com; 6577/5654; 69.4/72.3; 120/120

■ "For the dollar", this second Cog in a wheel of rural courses not far from Chicago is "favorite of all" for thrifty ball thumpers, even if "it lives in the shadow of Dubsdread"; dubbed "mini-Dubs", the former qualifying host of the U.S. Amateur is "almost as good" "without the hype", and varying layouts involving four "good additional holes" make it the "best-kept secret", "fun for mid- to high-handicappers" looking for a "tune-up before No. 4."

COG HILL, NO. 4
28 | 21 | 21 | 19 | $125
(DUBSDREAD) ⛳

12294 Archer Ave., Lemont; 630-257-5872; www.coghillgolf.com; 6940/5590; 75.4/70.6; 142/133

☑ The home of the Advil Western Open sparkles with "so much sand" that it's "like playing in the desert", which, combined with "tricky greens", makes it "a total challenge"; yet, while the "gem" of Cog Hill offers the "chance to play a PGA Tournament course at a reasonable price", "the conditions fall off after the tourney", leaving this diamond as rough as the help – "priests are nicer to sinners at confession than the rangers are to slow players" here.

GLEN CLUB, THE ⛳
28 | 27 | 25 | 18 | $150

2901 W. Lake Ave., Glenview; 847-724-7272; www.glenclub.com; 7149/5324; 74.5/71.5; 138/127

☑ Home to the Illinois Golf Hall of Fame, this North Shore "super all-around" "newcomer to the Chicagoland scene" "will be fabulous when it matures"; including an imposing clubhouse with guestrooms, its "country club feel" comes at "corresponding prices", which budget ball hitters believe are "too steep for the Fazio design"; forget about the hole in your pocket and fill the one in your stomach afterward by "hitting Little Louie's Red Hots for lunch in downtown Northbrook."

Golf Club of Illinois
19 | 18 | 17 | 17 | $55

1575 Edgewood Dr., Algonquin; 847-658-4400; www.golfclubofillinois.com; 6958/4896; 73.2/68.6; 132/115

■ There's "not a lot to get in your way but some dandy traps and waste areas" at this "links-style course" with a "600-plus yard" par 5 that "you need to play if you like quality for a small price"; it's "very good", "on the cusp of being great", but what stands in its way, argue aesthetes, are the "visually unappealing" "fairways that are too tight for the greens" and hemmed in by "too many homes."

Harborside International, Port
25 | 21 | 19 | 19 | $87

11001 S. Doty Ave.; 312-782-7837; www.harborsideinternational.com; 7164/5164; 75.1/70.8; 136/122

■ "Fifteen minutes from downtown" with "good views of Chicago" is "a real links course" "right out of the Scottish Highlands", where one minute "you can smell the moors" and the next "you may have to hold your nose if the wind shifts" because "it's built on a landfill" and "can be odiferous"; nothing else stinks at the 2002 SBC Senior Open host, however, including "the best practice facilities" and a "beautifully groomed" layout that "requires precise approaches to greens well guarded" by "knee-high tescue", which didn't stop Bill Clinton from acing the 6th hole – beers on Bubba!

Harborside International, Starboard 25 | 22 | 19 | 20 | $87
11001 S. Doty Ave.; 312-782-7837;
www.harborsideinternational.com; 7152/5106; 75.2/70.4; 137/122
■ "Line up your shots using the tallest building in the world as your
guide" at this Chicagolander that sits "close to Lake Michigan, so
there is a constant breeze" across the "bentgrass fairways, waste
and pot bunkers, and deep native rough"; "the greens are slick",
but have no fear, you can sight your putts off the "toxic fume vents"
that dot the former landfill where even grouches gush "if this is
what garbage dumps grow up to become, let's make more trash!"

Heritage Bluffs 25 | 17 | 18 | 26 | $44
24355 W. Bluff Rd., Channahon; 815-467-7888; www.channahonpark.org;
7106/4967; 73.9/68.6; 138/114
■ From the "rolling hills" at this "sweet" "affordable public golf"
course "you would never know you're in Illinois", and you may
feel like you've left the state "if you're driving from Chicago";
nevertheless, a "well-designed layout" with "enough difficulty to
keep you interested while allowing a few breather holes" "proves
that you don't need distance to create a challenge", despite "the
haul" down the Stevenson for which "you better fill up the gas
tank" and load your empty belly with a heart-smart meal at the
pleasant clubhouse eatery.

Kemper Lakes 26 | 24 | 22 | 17 | $135
Old McHenry Rd., Long Grove; 847-320-3450; www.kemperlakesgolf.com;
7217/5638; 75.9/73.9; 143/132
■ "Make a day of it because it is a long drive", "from downtown
Chicago" and from the tees on the many "marvelous" holes at
this "beautifully conditioned" former PGA, PGA Tour and Senior
PGA Tour host, which is so "challenging" that "high-handicappers"
can "feel like they've been tortured"; as the name suggests, there's
water, "water everywhere", and plenty of it is to drink, as the
"great amenities" include lots of wet stuff from the "friendliest
beverage cart personnel."

Naperbrook ∇ 19 | 15 | 16 | 21 | $50
22204 W. 111th St., Plainfield; 630-378-4215; www.napervilleparks.org;
6755/5381; 72.2/70.5; 125/118
■ The Naperville Park District is proud enough of its "groomed
fairways and greens" to publish the course-maintenance schedule
on its Web site, so you can avoid a visit when they're cleaning
house on this "flat", "links-style" muni "built on farmland"; it's
"suitably priced" for public pockets, but the "open, windy" layout
"can be pretty tough", so testy tracksters could have a cow when
the breeze kicks up and mooves their ball around.

Oak Brook – | – | – | – | $46
2606 York Rd., Oak Brook; 630-990-3032;
6151/5214; 70.7/71.1; 120/126
Penny-wise lady lofters say this "women-friendly" "little-known
secret" 25 miles from the Chicago Loop "can't be beat for the
price"; in "great condition" with "beautiful water holes", it sports
a full practice facility including a grass driving range and bunker
area, and if you think it's going to be easy just because it's a
bit short, then "good luck with the greens", which are "fast with
lots of slope."

Odyssey   ▽ 17 | 18 | 15 | 14 | $72

19110 Ridgeland Ave., Tinley Park; 708-429-7402;
www.odysseycountryclub.com; 7095/5564; 73.1/69.3; 131/116

◪ It may be "man-made to a fault", but it's "kind to women", and golfers of every ilk find "lots of variety" to "challenge" them on this "sporty, interesting course" that's "always in good shape" and only a half-hour drive from downtown Chicago; "you better like it because you'll be here for a while", as it can "play very slow", but maybe that's because partying par-seekers are too busy listening to the "rock stars practicing" "next door" at the Tweeter Center – so are the "pro shop personnel who act like thugs" really moonlighting roadies?

Orchard Valley   ▽ 25 | 21 | 19 | 20 | $96

2411 W. Illinois Ave., Aurora; 630-907-0500;
6745/5162; 72.8/70.3; 134/123

■ "The best course in the state" might not be a majority opinion but "my favorite public course in Illinois" doesn't seem such a stretch for this "top-condition" "short knockers' paradise that will keep you swinging tentatively all day"; "put the driver away", but take out your wallet because, despite twilight discounts, "it's getting a little pricey" for a muni, and the "staff is starting to get cocky", but "hey . . . it's Chicago", so you pay for a little attitude.

Pine Meadow ⚥   26 | 18 | 18 | 21 | $76

1 Pine Meadow Ln., Mundelein; 847-566-4653;
www.pinemeadowgc.com; 7141/5203; 74.6/70.9; 138/125

■ "The folks who own Cog Hill" run this "classic" "worthy of PGA talent", and it's just "what you'd expect" from late Chicagoland golf guru Joe Jemsek's outfit; the course "attracts better players who'll be challenged from the tips" by "lots of water, unbelievably deep rough" and "difficult greens"; the "peaceful, quiet" place is closed from November until mid-March, but when it's open, "it looks good even if you finish in the dark."

Plum Tree National 🏌   ▽ 22 | 17 | 18 | 26 | $65

19511 Lembcke Rd., Harvard; 815-943-7474;
www.plumtreegolf.com; 6648/5954; 71.8/74.9; 126/132

■ Set the alarm for a trip to the hills of McHenry County because "this is one of those sleepers you would ordinarily miss, but don't"; calling it a "poor man's country club" is another way of saying it's a "nice course" at a "good value" that "has the whole thing: decent tees, ample fairways, good length, difficult bunkers, water" and "thick, punishing rough", so consider this your wake-up call and go "play it."

Prairie Landing   24 | 23 | 20 | 17 | $90

2325 Longest Dr., West Chicago; 630-208-7600;
www.prairielanding.com; 6862/4859; 73.8/69.3; 131/119

■ "Grip it and rip it all day long" on the links at the Chicago area's "closest thing" to "transport cross-pond to the Motherland"; "they moved a lot of dirt to build" "ample landing areas", and "the rough is not terribly punishing", but "it can be a bear when the wind is up", and "the nice strategic split-fairway par 4" should keep prairie pros on their toes; "resort-style service" and amenities include a "cool" "three-hole practice course", "excellent food" and a landing strip for your private jet at DuPage Airport next door.

Ruffled Feathers ⛳
22 | 21 | 20 | 16 | $125

1 Pete Dye Dr., Lemont; 630-257-1000; www.americangolf.com;
6898/5273; 74.1/70.7; 140/123

✓ The foozling flock finds that "thinking is as important as swinging" when flapping its golf wings on this "nice Pete Dye layout" where "precision is needed" to make the "tight" shots on "some genuinely sporty holes with tough-to-read greens", particularly the "island 11th"; "full of adventure" of a suburban nature, it's so "shoehorned" "with homes" that it "feels like you're hitting out of someone's backyard" – maybe those "country club–like practice facilities" will help you keep from slicing into lawn ornaments.

Schaumburg
▽ 17 | 20 | 18 | 22 | $42

401 N. Roselle Rd., Schaumburg; 847-885-9000;
www.parkfun.com; 6542/4878; 70.7/67.5; 121/114

✓ A dozen years ago, the village of Schaumberg purchased a privately owned facility and "rescued it from years of disrepair"; now it's "a beautiful, well-maintained public course" with a "nice layout", a "friendly staff" and Chandler's Chop Shop restaurant; "pace of play can suffer due to the volume of golfers", but it's one of the "best park district courses out there."

Seven Bridges ⛳
23 | 20 | 21 | 16 | $100

1 Mulligan Dr., Woodridge; 630-964-7777;
www.sevenbridges.com; 7103/5262; 74.6/70.4; 135/121

✓ Before he jumped to Washington, "Michael Jordan was a regular" at this course "with two very different nines": while the "wonderful" back is "more enclosed" and "traditional", the front is "riddled with water" and "tricked up" with "mounds" that can make "good shots bounce from the middle of the fairway into the rough or worse, the drink; though "no driving range is a real negative", the "19th hole is enjoyable" for slamming and dunking.

Steeple Chase
20 | 17 | 16 | 20 | $74

200 N. La Vista Dr., Mundelein; 847-949-8900; 6827/4831; 73.1/68.1; 129/113

◼ Roundsmen riding this "fun test of skill" suggest "hit the long ball off the tee" to clear the hurdles amid swans, geese and turtles on a "beautiful" layout where "lots of variety" "calls for a different approach on each hole"; with a "super finish" and "reasonable greens fees", it's "a good value for your money", though your gallop might relax to a walk during "slow-play weekends."

Stonewall Orchard
▽ 28 | 14 | 16 | 19 | $72

25675 W. Hwy. 60, Grayslake; 847-740-4890;
www.stonewallorchard.com; 7074/5375; 74.1/71.2; 140/126

✓ "Bring your A-game, and it better be straight" say fans of all persuasions at this "challenging, scenic" daily fee that is "great if you can get there"; those on the other side of the fence feel the course "needs to mature some", but maybe the "rude staff" will be happier now that their spiffy new clubhouse, complete with a pro shop and the Sweetbriar Grill, is open.

TPC at Deere Run
– | – | – | – | $116

3100 Heather Knoll, Silvis; 309-796-6000; 1-877-872-3677;
www.tpc.com; 7138/5179; 75.1/70.1; 134/119

Tee it up where the big boys do it at this "real beautiful" host of the PGA Tour's John Deere Classic set on the "kick-butt undulations" of the Rock River foothills, where "very strong holes and great routing give you a sense of isolation" amid large oaks, beech, sycamores and rock outcroppings; "the course is in phenomenal condition, and the staff is very pleasant and helpful", making it a "must-play on the lists" of pros and amateurs alike.

Water's Edge ◷   23 │ 20 │ 20 │ 21 │ $63 │
7205 W. 115th St., Worth; 708-671-1032;
www.watersedgegolf.com; 6904/5332; 72.9/70.4; 131/122
☑ With a "nice layout" in "excellent shape", this muni is a "good value", if you've got time to spare; hookers happy with the "friendly, helpful staff" might not be referring to rangers who allow "hacks-aplenty" to cause "five-hour rounds" – the child players of the Hook a Kid on Golf program get a good jump on a faster game than that.

Galena

Eagle Ridge, North   25 │ 26 │ 24 │ 20 │ $130 │
444 Eagle Ridge Dr.; 815-777-2444; www.eagleridge.com;
6762/5609; 72.9/72.4; 133/128
☑ Hot-air balloonists float into this family-style "great golf getaway" where you can catch a ride in their sky-high baskets when you're not wrangling with the "very hilly" terrain on a "challenging and interesting layout with outstanding views" of the area around the Victorian gingerbread of Galena; it's "well worth the drive" to the northwest corner of the state, unless you're among the petulant Ping swingers who deem it "overpriced" and "nothing special."

Eagle Ridge, South   23 │ 25 │ 23 │ 21 │ $130 │
444 Eagle Ridge Dr.; 815-777-2444; www.eagleridge.com;
6762/5609; 72.9/72.4; 133/128
■ Some Southerly surveyors say "the best value for the experience at Eagle Ridge" is this "fantastic" track that provides "plenty of reasonable challenges", including "some real good par 3s"; it's rolling, so if you're walking, you have to be "sporty", and let's hope you're brainy too because you'll soak up facts at the nearby 19th-century mining town of Galena, where almost all the buildings are in the National Register of Historic Places.

EAGLE RIDGE, THE GENERAL 🏌   28 │ 26 │ 24 │ 18 │ $155 │
444 Eagle Ridge Dr.; 815-777-2444; www.eagleridge.com;
6820/5335; 73.8/66.7; 137/119
☑ "Bring your climbing shoes and extra clothing" to this resort course "in the middle of nowhere", and that's an order because you'll fire on "high hills and granite ridges" on a "brutally tough" battlefield with "breathtaking views" and a "truly spectacular back nine"; though it "has potential to be excellent", it's "overpriced" for the ordinary soldier's ration book, but you might want to splurge with a furlough at the inn overlooking Lake Galena anyway.

Peoria

Annbriar 🏌   ▽ 26 │ 23 │ 24 │ 25 │ $63 │
1524 Birdie Ln., Waterloo; 618-939-4653; 888-939-5191;
www.annbriar.com; 6841/4792; 72.8/66.4; 136/110
■ "One of the most beautiful, isolated courses in the entire St. Louis region" is this "incredible" "challenge" converted from

farmland; "in great shape", with over a thousand sprinklers keeping
the front and the "best back nine" around mighty green, it's the
"place for those 36-hole days" because the "friendly staff" at the
Smokehouse Restaurant "usually serves 25-cent peel-and-eat
shrimp" for a lunchtime break between rounds.

WeaverRidge Golf Club   ▽ 29 │ 23 │ 24 │ 21 │ $73

5100 N. Weaverridge Blvd.; 309-691-3344;
www.WeaverRidge.com; 7030/5046; 73.1/65.9; 136/115
■ If you think you won't play in Peoria, guess again because those
who deign to tee off here insist you "won't find a better designed
or maintained" facility in Illinois than this "must-play for serious
golfers" a "two-hour drive from Chicago"; it's "part of a huge
housing development, but you will hardly notice the homes because
the track is so lovely and challenging it requires all your attention."

St. Louis Area (see also Missouri)

Far Oaks ⛳   ▽ 26 │ 22 │ 20 │ 21 │ $63

419 Old Collinsville Rd., Caseyville; 618-628-2900;
7083/5196; 73.3/70.3; 141/113
■ "Setting the standard for ultimate value for public courses in the
St. Louis area" is this "excellent" muni that's in such "beautiful"
condition that it's "probably the nicest 18-holer around"; pack a
cooler 'cause "the lunch fare is just hot dogs and hamburgers", and
"call ahead to make sure there is no outing" hogging the joint.

Gateway National   ▽ 23 │ 20 │ 21 │ 24 │ $62

18 Golf Dr., Madison; 314-421-4653; www.gatewaynational.com;
6623/5187; 72.4/64.5; 133/109
■ "All-bentgrass fairways are a treat", particularly when they're
available so "inexpensively" at this "links-style" layout that's
"especially good if you have out-of-town guests" who want to get
a gander at the "terrific views of the skyline and the Arch"; good
driving is a double entendre on a track located so close to the
Raceway that, during Nascar events, "you can hear the cars run."

Rail, The   ▽ 21 │ 18 │ 18 │ 21 │ $38

1400 S. Club House Dr., Springfield; 217-525-0365;
www.railgolf.com; 6627/5406; 71.1/70.6; 120/116
☑ "Proving that good design reduces the need for distance", this
"well-laid out and maintained" Robert Trent Jones Sr. course is
"short but sporty", and "it's inexpensive and accessible" too,
even though it's an "LPGA stop"; just "don't expect much from the
ambiance side" because the "facilities are podunk at best."

Spencer T. Olin ⛳   23 │ 18 │ 20 │ 23 │ $55

4701 College Ave., Alton; 618-465-3111; www.spencertolingolf.com;
6941/5049; 73.8/68.5; 135/117
■ It's friendly to women on the forward tees, though macho drivers
"play the tips and enjoy" this "fun Palmer course", a "city park
track like few others, well-manicured with a variety of fauna and
flora" including "zoysia fairways" where you can "test most of your
skills"; the former "host of the USGA Public Links" is a "simple
municipal operation" with not a lot of amenities, but management
by The King's court is shipshape, so move "fast" "to avoid the
marshal", "or rue it."

Stonewolf   ▽ 22 | 23 | 18 | 18 | $63
1195 Stonewolf Trail, Fairview Heights; 618-624-4653;
www.stonewolfgolf.com; 6943/4849; 74.0/67.2; 141/126
☑ "Bring your fade" to this "typical Jack" Nicklaus daily fee
and carry along your shovel too, because there's "plenty of sand
around the greens and in the fairways", which are "very pretty",
with "a funneling effect that's somewhat forgiving"; the same can't
be said about an "unfriendly" staff that "generally acts as though
they couldn't care less if you ever come back."

Indiana

Carmel

Prairie View   ▽ 26 | 26 | 24 | 15 | $80
7000 Longest Dr.; 317-816-3100; www.prairieviewgc.com;
7073/5200; 74.3/70.2; 134/118
■ On the banks of the White River amid prairies lined in oaks and
sycamores, there is a "great but very hard layout" by Robert Trent
Jones Jr. with plenty of sand, water and wetlands to stir up trouble;
the "well-maintained", "fast greens" might account for the "stiff
fee" – try twilight hours for a better deal, or look on the Web for
contests to win free rounds.

Cincinnati Area (see also Ohio)

Belterra   – | – | – | – | $75
777 Belterra Dr., Florence; 812-417-7783;
www.belterracasino.com; 6910/5102; 73.3/69.2; 136/117
Tom Fazio designed this championship track that's part of a glitzy
casino resort with views of the Indiana ridges and the Ohio River;
"you need to hit the fairways", but if you do, the "layout is very
fair", though stubborn strikers insist the same can't be said about
the "excellent staff" because they might "not let you play in the
fog"; sit out the weather in the CenterStage Showroom grooving
to the likes of Trisha Yearwood or KC and the Sunshine Band.

Indianapolis

Brickyard Crossing   ▽ 26 | 18 | 19 | 15 | $90
4400 W. 16th St.; 317-484-6570; www.brickyardcrossing.com;
6996/5038; 74.5/68.3; 137/116
■ "Gentlemen and ladies, start your backswings" because this
Pete Dye redesign has "four holes located within the infield of
the Indianapolis Motor Speedway", which makes it "visually
intimidating", though daredevil drivers deem it "more playable than
it first appears"; "unique and enjoyable", it's "worth at least one"
spin, say pit-stop putters who pout it's "too bad you can't take the
golf carts on the race track"; N.B. of course you can't tee off into
careening vehicles, so check to make sure the Indy 500, Brickyard
400 or another car competition is not in progress before you visit.

Fort, The   ▽ 27 | 24 | 23 | 23 | $59
6002 N. Post Rd.; 317-543-9597; 7150/5000; 74.5/69.2; 139/123
■ "Bring your billy goat" to this "well-maintained", "surprisingly
hilly course in the flat part of Indiana" at historic Fort Harrison

Park; it "plays like a bear", especially from the back tees, so consider hitting "from the whites"; you can book a room in the Harrison House, where military VIPs once slept, and you can eat in the restored Garrison Restaurant, but note that the most "affordable" accommodations and dining here involve a tent, a sleeping bag, some sticks and a match.

Otter Creek   26 | 22 | 21 | 23 | $75

11522 E. 50 N., Columbus; 812-579-5227; www.ocgc.com
East/North: 7224/5581; 75.6/73.5; 137/128
North/West: 7258/5581; 75.6/73.5; 138/128
West/East: 7126/5403; 75.0/71.9; 137/123
■ You can keep up with the Joneses at this southern Indiana daily fee that provides a "classic" 27 holes of golf, the original 18 designed by Robert Trent Jones Sr. and an additional nine added by his son Rees who, like dad, took special care to work the features of the course into the natural rolling terrain, giving it an organic feel and making all three combos "must-plays."

Rock Hollow   ∇ 24 | 16 | 21 | 25 | $45

County Rd. 250 W., Peru; 765-473-6100; www.rockhollowgolf.com;
6944/4967; 74.0/69.1; 136/118
■ The "fairways and greens are always perfect" at this "amazing" daily-fee course owned by the "family of PGA Tour pro Chris Smith" and located in the clan's former quarry in "hard-to-find" "rural Indiana"; it's a "must-play", so make the trip, but pack your own lunch because, with a "trailer as a clubhouse", it's a "no-frills"/no grill facility, even though the brother of the 2002 Buick Classic winner keeps the greens fee accordingly reasonable for a snacks-only track.

Trophy Club, The   – | – | – | – | $60

3875 N. State Road 52, Lebanon; 765-482-7272;
www.thetrophyclubgolf.com; 7208/5050; 74.0/68.5; 125/117
The smattering of smitten swingers who've checked out this "must-play" outside Indianapolis "love it", though they warn "it's hard" thanks to links-style bentgrass fairways, plenty of bunkers, undulating greens, knee-high fescue and eight holes with water in play; what's considerably easier is rehashing the still-warm memories of your round over a cold one at Hogan Bar & Grill in the newly completed clubhouse.

South Bend

Blackthorn   ∇ 22 | 20 | 19 | 21 | $52

6100 Nimtz Pkwy.; 574-232-4653; www.blackthorngolf.com;
7136/5125; 75.2/71.0; 135/120
■ "Life doesn't get any better than playing here and then watching the Notre Dame football team lose on Saturday afternoon" insist students of swing at this "well-maintained, memorable" municipal "beauty" in the shadow of the university in South Bend; when they say it "has 19 holes", they're not referring to a cocktail lounge, or to the "fantastic" kitchen that serves a "Blarney Burger you'll dream about"; instead, they mean that the "great practice facilities" "start with a hole that doesn't count on your score but gives you a chance to warm up" – on top of that, all you need is a little "luck of the Irish."

Iowa

Burlington

Spirit Hollow   – | – | – | – | $60
5592 Clubhouse Dr.; 319-752-0004;
www.spirithollowgolfcourse.com; 7021/5053; 73.6/70.3; 129/116
Long and spread out, it's not as tough as the yardage might indicate, but there's a little bit of something here so that golfers of every bent won't leave with a hollow spirit: from Scottish-links mounding and bunkers to Myrtle Beach–style tree-trimmed fairways and raised tees, it's a soulful adventure near the banks of the Mississippi.

Cedar Rapids

Amana Colonies 🏨   ▽ 24 | 21 | 20 | 23 | $60
451 27th Ave., Amana; 319-622-6222; 800-383-3636;
www.amanagolfcourse.com; 6824/5228; 73.3/69.7; 136/115
■ "Flat lies are rare", but fat thighs might not be at this "very challenging" Iowan in a namesake tourist destination where the Germanic "food is to die for"; the skinny is it's "beautiful during the fall" when the foliage lights up an area settled by the pre–Civil War utopians, the Community of True Inspiration; you'll find inspiration on the fairways, but if your pre-round meal was a bit too inspired, "don't play on cart-path-only days" so you can ride your full belly right up to your ball.

Des Moines

Legacy, The   – | – | – | – | $45
400 Legacy Pkwy., Norwalk; 515-287-7885;
www.thelegacygolfclub.com; 7089/5340; 73.6/71.0; 132/123
There's plenty of room on these bentgrass fairways south of Des Moines, but the approaches require precision, and the undulating greens will test your putting stroke; in particular, watch out for several par 3s with long water carries, as H_2O is in play on 14 of the holes; a few reachable par 5s will tempt long hitters, though even the biggest sluggers can forget about scoring that eagle on the 611-yard finish.

Kansas

Kansas City

Alvamar Public   22 | 17 | 18 | 22 | $61
1800 Crossgate Dr., Lawrence; 785-842-1907; www.alvamar.com;
7092/4892; 75.5/68.8; 141/112
◩ If you aspire to sire a family of fanatics, start 'em young at the Junior Golf Camp where the little ones will get to work with the "very friendly and helpful staff" at this "long and challenging" Lawrence municipal parkland course that's got an "excellent layout", even though it's "not in as good shape as in previous years"; local club-wielders can sign up the whole clan to a family membership, and out-of-towners might want to book a room-golf deal with the Days Inn, which, while not the swankest of digs, offers "great value."

Deer Creek

21 | 23 | 19 | 17 | $80

7000 W. 133rd St., Overland Park; 913-681-3100;
www.americangolf.com; 6811/5126; 74.5/68.5; 137/113

◪ Choruses of swingers sing: over Deer Creek and "through the woods" (and, um, "across the street") to this "solid, sporty" track we go; Robert Trent Jones knows the way to give you a "tough day" on a layout that's "fun to play", oh!; nevertheless, "bunkers low on sand and greens that burn out easily" don't jingle anyone's bells on "one of KC's most expensive courses" where "even if you're walking, they charge for the cart", which, despite the tune, is not horse-driven.

Falcon Ridge

24 | 23 | 23 | 20 | $73

20200 Prairie Star Pkwy., Lenexa; 913-393-4653;
www.falconridgegolf.com; 6820/5160; 72.8/69.6; 130/119

■ "It's always an enjoyable round" at "one of Kansas City's best" facilities, where the "top-notch" staff "really caters to your needs" and the course is "exceptional"; "bring several sleeves" and plan to ride because they'd "charge for the cart even if you were walking", and given the "length from one green to the next tee" over "hills galore", you wouldn't want to peter out before you get yourself one of those crazy little women (or men) the town's so famous for.

Ironhorse

19 | 22 | 18 | 18 | $53

15400 Mission Rd., Leawood; 913-685-4653;
www.ironhorsegolf.com; 6889/4745; 73.8/69.7; 140/110

■ "Come early to utilize the unparalleled practice facilities and enjoy a burger before teeing off" to "challenge all aspects of your game" on this "wide-open" muni where the touring Nicklaus/Flick and Dave Peltz Shortgame schools make regular visits; it's "very affordable", but it's so "well designed" that it's "what you would expect from a much higher price range", and if it's "hard to walk", at least there is "outstanding scenery" amid the creek-laced woods along the way.

Prairie Highlands

∇ 23 | 15 | 20 | 21 | $48

14695 S. Inverness Dr., Olathe; 913-856-7235;
www.prairiehighlands.com; 7033/5122; 74.3/65.4; 132/114

■ Though this "brand-new course" "needs to grow in", it's already "taking shape" as a "beautiful challenge for any level golfer", with four sets of tees to choose from and 60 bunkers to avoid; since the owners first "sunk money into the course and not the facilities", "the clubhouse is a trailer right now", but when the new building is completed in spring 2003, there'll be a full-service grill and pro shop where you can sink some of your own money right back into the management's tapped pockets.

Sycamore Ridge

∇ 25 | 21 | 24 | 22 | $59

21731 Clubhouse Dr., Spring Hill; 913-592-5292;
www.sycamoreridgegolf.com; 7055/4877; 76.2/55.4; 150/118

■ "It's always a pleasure to play" this "fantastic" layout offering "exceptional value" even if it is "a bit pricier" than other munis and farther "out of the way" than most KC tracks; the "excellent staff" headed up by course designer and Senior Tour pro Jim Colbert is "friendly and down-to-earth", so they'll probably sympathize when you whine about a "difficult-to-walk" "back nine that's very challenging" both to your scorecard and to your feet.

Topeka

Colbert Hills 🏌️🏞 ▽ 29 | 23 | 23 | 23 | $80
5200 Colbert Hills Dr., Manhattan; 785-776-6475;
www.colberthills.com; 7525/4947; 77.5/69.4; 152/116
■ "Be prepared to be frustrated" at this "daunting" daily fee
boasting a "truly world-class" Jim Colbert design and "awe-
inspiring views of the surrounding prairie", the big sky and the
"unfinished clubhouse"; catch the Kansas State U. Wildcats
howling at "the wind" on their "great but difficult" home course.

Rolling Meadows ▽ 18 | 13 | 18 | 23 | $15
7550 Old Milford Rd., Junction City; 785-238-4303;
www.rollingmeadows.com; 6879/5515; 74.0/70.7; 134/116
☑ Like all "diamonds in the rough", this muni is "somewhat hard
to find, but you'll always want to go back" for more; test yourself
against water in play on no less than seven holes, and mine it for
its dirt-cheap $6 twilight rate when the sun is sinking on the rolling
meadows outside of Topeka.

Kentucky

Lexington

Marriott Griffin Gate Resort ▽ 21 | 24 | 25 | 19 | $59
1720 Newtown Pike; 859-288-6193; www.marriott.com;
6784/5053; 72.2/68.6; 133/122
■ It's a "little steamy in the summertime" at the "old" Kentucky
home of "one of Marriott's better courses", but since the Rees
Jones design is "excellently maintained", "never crowded" and
offers "good value" compared with other resort tracks, it's "still nice
to play"; skip on over to nearby "Keeneland for some great horse
racing", and you too might solve the riddle, what do golfers and
jockeys have in common? – answer: they both hit it and watch it run.

Wasioto Winds – | – | – | – | $37
1050 State Park Rd.; 606-337-1066; www.kystateparks.com;
7037/4058; 73.9/61.6; 137/112
Water comes into play on 14 of the 18 holes on this layout at Pine
Mountain State Park, so as the name indicates, it can get mighty
breezy; if you don't like the wet stuff, aim carefully on the bentgrass
links, which are fairly level despite the mountainous surroundings;
then again, you could always wait until all that water freezes over
and play at a reduced off-season rate while tooling around beneath
those all-weather golf cart covers.

Louisiana

Baton Rouge

Bluffs on Thompson Creek 26 | 22 | 20 | 19 | $62
Hwy. 965 at Freeland Rd., Saint Francisville; 225-634-5551;
www.thebluffs.com; 6000/4781; 69.7/75.1; 125/140
■ "It's absolutely worth the ride from New Orleans" to "one of
Louisiana's prettiest courses" with "great views along Thompson
Creek"; "in a state where elevation is generally near sea level" this

"solid design" includes "lots of height changes" and "severely sloped greens" for bayou ballers to "get off the beaten path" and onto a roller-coaster of a course out in the "middle of nowhere."

Lake Charles

Gray Plantation
▽ 26 | 23 | 24 | 27 | $45

6150 Graywood Pkwy.; 337-562-1663; 6946/5392; 73.6/71.9; 138/128

■ "Southern hospitality with unparalleled professionalism" charms the golf pants off northern swingers who make it down to Cajun country for a round on this "flat, new course" by Lake Charles; though it "needs to mature", it's "in good shape" already, according to environmentalists who enjoy the Audubon-certified spread's protected marshlands, from which water seeps onto 12 holes, where you'd best look out for gators.

New Orleans

Belle Terre
19 | 18 | 20 | 19 | $54

111 Fairway Dr., La Place; 985-652-5000; 6850/5409; 72.2/71.6; 130/122

■ "Play a Pete Dye course for how much?" drawl penny-wise putters "wowed" by fees that are mighty friendly for such "a location close to New Orleans"; this "outstanding experience" with "some neat", "swampy woodland" holes is "in its best shape in years", and boy is it ever "pleasing to the eye", so particularly at these prices, it's one Southern belle that's "worth a visit."

Golf Club of New Orleans at Eastover, Teeth of the Gator
▽ 19 | 14 | 14 | 16 | $105

5889 Eastover Dr.; 504-245-7347; www.eastovercc.com; 7005/5335; 73.3/71.7; 136/119

■ "Study the layout, be aggressive and know when to play smart" because there's "water in play on 80 percent" of this "windy course" 15 minutes from downtown; it may be euphemistic to call it "nice" when "all the gators present" "live up to its name" – just "bring a dozen balls" and try to "hit 'em straight" or you'll lose your sleeve between the teeth of some hungry reptiles.

Oak Harbour 🏌
20 | 16 | 17 | 22 | $79

201 Oak Harbor Blvd., Slidell; 504-646-0110; www.oakharborgolf.com; 6897/5305; 72.7/70; 132/118

■ "Wind blowing off the water" on 14 holes might be this "links-style" layout's "only defense against really low numbers"; indeed, the course is "a real bear" in a bluster, so focus on "tee selection and striking prowess", and "bring plenty of balls" because you'll probably be feeding this animal a whole heck of a lot of them.

Maine

Central Maine

Belgrade Lakes 🏌
▽ 28 | 20 | 23 | 23 | $100

West Rd. at Clubhouse Dr., Belgrade Lakes; 207-495-4653; www.belgradelakesgolf.com; 6572/4803; 71.6/64.1; 142/126

■ "Wow, what a view from the first tee" – "tucked away north of Augusta in a beautiful region of Alpine Lakes", Sugarloaf's "top-notch" neighbor boasts a "medium-length design with a combo of hazards to test golfers of all abilities"; it's only got a "small snack" stand, but it is "one of the rare public courses that offers [summer] caddies", who'll advise "staying on the fairway" because "the massive boulders that line them never kick the ball back into play."

Kebo Valley   ∇ 22 | 14 | 16 | 18 | $70

Eagle Lake Rd., Bar Harbor; 207-288-3000;
www.kebovalleyclub.com; 6131/5473; 69.0/68.0; 124/128
☑ It's got "character", "great history" and "a throwback layout", with "Acadia National Park's beautiful scenery" to "make you feel like you've been transported across the pond", plus a bonny "old clubhouse that matches perfectly its look and feel"; however, America's eighth oldest golf course also has "greens fees that are high for its overall value", considering there are "a few creative holes but a lot of boring ones too", and though it may feel like high tea in Britain, "the parking lot is the size of a cappuccino cup."

SUGARLOAF   28 | 20 | 21 | 20 | $99

Rte. 27, Carrabassett Valley; 207-237-2000; 800-843-5623;
www.sugarloaf.com; 6910/5289; 74.4/72.5; 151/131
☑ "Spellbinding" is how delirious drivers describe this "tough", "spectacular" "mountain challenge" where the views are "visually pleasing, unless you have vertigo"; "conditions vary depending on" the "severity of the past winter" and the resort's "ski income from the previous season", plus it's "expensive", "particularly given that it's deep in the middle of nowhere" with "so-so lodging, service and food", but somehow it's "still worth the trip and the money", even if you don't see "a moose crossing the fairways."

Southern Maine

Bethel Inn & Country Club   ∇ 17 | 18 | 18 | 19 | $50

1 Broad St., Bethel; 207-824-2175; 800-654-0125;
www.bethelinn.com; 6293/5280; 70.6/71.4; 130/129
■ As one proud parent of an A-game student boasts "my son had his first hole-in-one on the 3rd", where "you have to hit your tee shot over an old dam" at this "great little school course that'll challenge your ability"; valedictorians vouch for the resort's "inexpensive stay-and-plays", and with activities from canoeing to llama trekking, it's a "nice" class trip for non-golfers too.

Dunegrass 🏌   ∇ 24 | 21 | 19 | 19 | $80

200 Wild Dunes Way, Old Orchard Beach; 207-934-4513;
800-521-1029; www.dunegrass.com; 6656/5558; 68.8/64.9; 125/115
☑ This "Carolina Pines–style course" is "a novelty" "on the Maine coast", so it's "a challenge the first time", especially given greens where there's some "tricky putting"; though it's "on the pricey side" during the summer, it's a "great value before Memorial Day and after Labor Day", when you won't have to jostle the crowds to get a load of the state golf history exhibit beside the restaurant, courtesy of a management that otherwise is "not customer-friendly."

Ledges, The   – | – | – | – | $65

1 Ledges Dr., York; 207-351-3000; www.ledgesgolf.com;
6981/5028; 74.3/10.9; 144/126
"Wow!" – awed aces who make the "drive up from Boston" to this "beautiful course" along the coast find it's "well worth the

haul for "a super test with a variety of shots" onto "fairways with good roll" and "lush greens" in a setting that's "beautiful in fall."

Samoset Resort   25   23   23   20 $115
220 Warrenton St., Rockport; 207-594-2511; 800-341-1650;
www.samoset.com; 6548/5083; 70.8/70.2; 133/120
■ Downstaters declare there's "not a better, prettier, more relaxing round in New England" than at this "jewel of a links" with "fairway-like greens" set "along the rocky, picturesque shores of Penobscot Bay" at a newly restored vacation destination; if you "see a moose stroll across the track", it's probably just heading to "Marcel's, the resort's top-notch restaurant", where the "great service" is more consistent than the course's wind conditions, which "change every hour"; for a golf group immersion, book the reappointed, two-bedroom Flume Cottage perched on the rocks above the salty blue.

Maryland

★ **Best in State**
29 Bulle Rock, *Baltimore*
27 Links at Lighthouse Sound, *Ocean City*
    Whiskey Creek, *Frederick*
    Atlantic Golf At Queenstown, River, *Annapolis*
    Rum Pointe, *Ocean City*

Aberdeen

Beechtree   26   23   20   20 $85
612 S. Stepney Rd.; 410-297-9700; 877-233-2487;
www.beechtreegolf.com; 7023/5363; 74.9/70.4; 142/121
■ If the highway's backed up, don't despair because only "five minutes off I-95 there's a great place to kill four hours", this "gem" of "pure golfing fun" that plays neighbor to Bulle Rock "at less than half the price"; wait out the traffic amid "beautiful conditions", "generous driving areas" and "unforgiving" greens on "two very different nines": "the back is Carolina style" while the front "links" is so authentic you "expect to see 'Braveheart' William Wallace."

Annapolis

Atlantic Golf At South River   26   20   21   19 $72
3451 Solomons Island Rd., Edgewater; 410-798-5865;
800-767-4837; www.mdgolf.com; 6723/4935; 71.8/66.9; 133/115
☑ "Hit it straight" or have a "frustrating day" on this "interesting layout" where "a few challenging holes" offer slim chances to score but "a lot of opportunities to lose balls"; "the greens are excellent", and they have "eliminated their drainage problems" – now if they could just get a "lounge, a locker room" and a "better driving range", DC-area duffers' "biggest peeves" would be moot.

Baltimore

BULLE ROCK 🖈   29   27   28   19 $145
320 Blenheim Ln., Havre de Grace; 410-939-8465; 880-285-5375;
www.bullerock.com; 7375/5426; 76.4/71.1; 147/127
■ "Get your butt thoroughly kicked" on this rumored "future U.S. Open layout", a "fierce" "Pete Dye masterpiece" open to the

paying (and paying and paying) public; "a scan of the parking lot" shows that they're coming from "Maryland, Virginia, Delaware, Pennsylvania, New York, New Jersey", etc. to "swallow pride" in the "deep rough", on the "600-plus-yard par 5" and "spectacular finish"; it "costs you", but who's counting coins when they "treat you like an exclusive private club would" and everything from "the staff to the course to the facilities", including video-based instruction, "is impeccable."

Greystone   24 | 18 | 18 | 19 | $67

2115 White Hall Rd., White Hall; 410-887-1945;
www.baltimoregolfing.com; 6925/4800; 73.5/67.5; 139/112

◪ "It's hard to believe you're only 25 minutes from downtown Baltimore once you arrive at this beautiful, remote hilltop" where a "fantastic course" and its "outstanding clubhouse" are located; there's "always a good chance to get on with short notice", just "don't piss off the starter" or you'll get a glimpse of this muni's "country-club attitude."

Timbers at Troy, The   22 | 19 | 19 | 20 | $42

6100 Marshalee Dr., Elkridge; 410-313-4653;
www.timbersgolf.com; 6652/4926; 72.1/68.5; 134/115

◪ "High-handicappers may have some difficulty navigating through some of the tougher holes" on this "sporty layout" featuring quite a few "forced carries"; you get your frustration at an "excellent" value, however, "especially if you are a Howard County resident"; no matter where you live, you'll wanna "keep the driver in the car" and "wear boots if you're gonna walk" because "whoever designed this one never thought about where the water would drain after a rain."

Waverly Woods   24 | 20 | 18 | 18 | $66

2100 Warwick Way, Marriottsville; 410-313-9182;
www.waverlywoods.com; 7024/4800; 73.1/67.8; 132/115

◪ A "young course that plays like a golden oldie", this daily fee "in the woods" west of Baltimore is "worth every dime" you spend (especially if you "look for the coupon in the *Baltimore Sun*") because it's "challenging but fair" and in "fabulous shape" "with great scenery"; if the "head professional needs people skills", face it, you'd be a little testy too if you had to deal with these greens all the time – "sadistic" designer Arthur Hills "must have a thing for domes because on a hot, dry day" you can't "get a ball to stick on them."

Cumberland

Rocky Gap Lodge ⌂   ▽ 22 | 22 | 21 | 21 | $65

16701 Lakeview Rd. NE, Flintstone; 301-784-8500;
www.rockygapresort.com; 7006/5198; 74.3/69.4; 141/123

◪ The town of Flintstone in the Appalachian Mountains is home to the "only Jack Nicklaus Signature course in the state", and sure 'nuff, "it's a tough'en", with "a lot of elevation change", "ridiculously tall rough" and "two very distinct nines" to make fairway Freds shout 'yaba-daba-do'; a few "too many surprises" lead some ball-whacking Barneys to call it "tricked up", while the lake resort's "mediocre facilities and personnel" mean the brontosaurus burgers might not be up to par.

DC Metro Area (see also Virginia)

Swan Point Golf,   ▽ 28 | 21 | 22 | 22 | $79
Yacht and Country Club
11550 Swan Point Blvd., Issue; 301-259-0047;
www.swanpointgolf.com; 6761/5009; 73.2/69.3; 130/116
■ "Can't wait to play this course again" say smitten seaworthy slicers who "schlep down" in their yachts from Washington to dock free of charge at the Cuckold Creek marina and tee off on this "remote, often forgotten gem" where the "truly marvelous" "variety of holes" includes a par-5 island green and the "quirk" of "two par 3s in a row"; Beltway insiders might "wish it were nearby", but its "excellent facilities" are "worth the trip" by land or by sea.

University of   18 | 16 | 14 | 22 | $51
Maryland Golf Course
University of Maryland, College Park; 301-314-4653;
www.golf.umd.edu; 6713/6271; 71.6/69.8; 125/122
◪ Frat-boy foozlers get plenty of shots at this "cheap" university "challenge" in the shadow of "the football stadium", where you can pound the "drivable par 4" and drink up the "college environment" while enjoying a "great mix of holes"; even if they're "a little weak on conditioning", it's "one of the best values in the DC area", though, dude, "the 19th hole often seems too far away."

Easton

Atlantic Golf At   25 | 21 | 22 | 23 | $69
Queenstown Harbor, Lakes
310 Links Ln., Queenstown; 410-827-6611; 800-827-5257;
www.mdgolf.com; 6569/4666; 71.0/66.6; 124/111
■ Don't think of them as "lots of water" hazards, think of them as "beautiful bay views" on this "excellent course" that Annapolis albatrosses squawk is "more playable than its sister"; though it's "getting a little pricey", at least they seem to be using your dough on upkeep – "they do a great job" of keeping its "awesome shape."

Atlantic Golf At   27 | 20 | 22 | 21 | $89
Queenstown Harbor, River
310 Links Ln., Queenstown; 410-827-6611; 800-827-5257;
www.mdgolf.com; 7110/5026; 74.2/69.0; 138/123
■ It's a "long drive" both "in summer beach traffic" and on the "wooded and water-lined" fairways at this "demanding" "jewel", but Beltway insiders who make the "schlep from DC" to "get away from it all" are rewarded by the "feeling of escapism" that the Chester River, the Chesapeake Bay and "families of deer seen from the wooden cart bridges" afford; "play on twilight special during the summer" and you might even think it's "spectacular."

Hog Neck   24 | 17 | 18 | 23 | $55
10142 Old Cordova Rd., Easton; 410-882-6079; 800-280-1790;
www.hogneck.com; 7000/5500; 73.7/71.3; 131/125
■ Muni insiders tend to be as hush-hush as FBI agents about this "good" "alternative to Queenstown", so "shhh" on the "almost forgotten" "gem's" "windswept front nine" and "narrow, tree-lined" back, adjacent to a nine-hole par-32 executive track; its

"lovely" "eastern shore" location isn't far from the edifices of Washington, DC, and it's even closer to the Naval Academy at Annapolis, but it is still "one of the finest government-owned facilities around", though it certainly isn't the only one "run by grumpy old men."

Frederick

Little Bennett   22 | 17 | 18 | 22 | $46

25900 Prescott Rd., Clarksburg; 301-253-1515; 800-366-2012; 6706/4921; 72.9/68.2; 133/115

■ "Eighteen holes is a steal" at this "maturing new public course" where the "picturesque views of Sugarloaf Mountain", the "grass driving range" and the "excellent golfing" "compare to that of courses three times the price"; it's so "very hilly" that only "in-shape athletes can enjoy walking" the holes here, while oxymoronic aces add "the course has more blind shots than you have ever seen."

P.B. Dye Golf Club   22 | 22 | 22 | 17 | $89

9526 Doctor Perry Rd., Ijamsville; 301-607-4653; www.pbdyegolf.com; 7036/4900; 74.6/68.2; 141/130

☑ The peninsula "11th hole is not for the meek", and neither is the rest of the layout, with "tightly bunker-guarded", "super-fast greens" on this "wonderful, open and windy" course boasting "beautiful views" of Sugarloaf Mountain to the northwest of the nation's capital; "recent attempts to soften it up have not taken away its character" – it's still "tough in every aspect", though "P.B. Dye may have gone a little overboard with the railroad ties" and the "gimmicky" "blind shots"; check into a local B&B and keep your eyes open for post-round bargains among the antique shops of nearby Frederick.

Whiskey Creek   27 | 24 | 23 | 21 | $90

4804 Whiskey Ct., Ijamsville; 301-694-2900; 888-883-1174; www.whiskeycreekgolf.com; 7001/5296; 74.5/70.5; 137/121

■ Those 19th-century German immigrants never could have anticipated that the "remnants of their stone house" would end up "in the center of the landing area of a great finishing hole" on one of "the prettiest courses in Maryland"; co-designed by Ernie Els, it's "very hilly", but all those "good elevation changes" offer "majestic views" of the Catoctin Mountains for your troubles; though the "facilities are great", you might find that your cart's "GPS doesn't work well", particularly if the track's name inspires you to drink and drive.

Worthington Manor ⌂   24 | 20 | 21 | 22 | $79

8329 Fingerboard Rd.; 301-874-5400; 888-987-2582; www.worthingtonmanor.com; 7000/5206; 74.0/70.1; 143/116

■ It's got "everything a daily fee should" have: "unbelievable bentgrass fairways, zoysia-faced bunkers", "treacherous greens" and a "nice mixture of long and short par 4s"; that's why this "scenic" "challenge" "in the foothills of Maryland" is one of "the metropolitan DC area's best layouts", while a "friendly, helpful staff" and "decent facilities" lodged in the former manor house of the 19th-century namesake landowner help make it one of the region's "best values."

Ocean City

Bay Club, East
▽ 21 | 20 | 20 | 23 | $72 |

9122 Libertytown Rd., Berlin; 410-641-4081; 800-229-2582;
www.thebayclub.com; 7004/5231; 74.6/67.4; 134/115

■ When you tire of the mini-golf madness of the amusement strip,
get real on 7,000-plus "well-kept" yards of "good" links, including
an island green aptly dubbed the 'Paradise' hole; the crack staff
provides "excellent customer service", though it's still tough to
get them to turn down the Atlantic breezes on command.

Bay Club, West
▽ 20 | 18 | 18 | 21 | $72 |

9122 Libertytown Rd., Berlin; 410-641-4081; 800-229-2582;
www.thebayclub.com; 6956/5609; 73.1/71.3; 126/118

■ The same "great staff" that sets apart the East course caters to
clubbers at the West too; unlike its sister, this linkster comes in just
under 7K, so even though it serves up the wet stuff on eight holes,
including the floating 'Devil's Island', it's the easier of the two, and
its specialized lessons make it great for training your little Tiger.

Beach Club, Inner Links ⌂
▽ 19 | 18 | 17 | 19 | $75 |

9715 Deer Park Dr., Berlin; 410-641-4653; 800-435-9223;
www.beachclubgolflinks.com; 7020/5167; 73.0/69.0; 128/117

☑ It's "easy to get a tee time" at this "fun"-in-the-sun daily fee
where the "nice course" is complemented by a "great golf school";
however, the "cart-path-only" rule is a bit of a bummer and the
marshals seem reluctant to "control slow play"; when you finally
do get through with your round, visit the wild horses on nearby
Assateague and Chincoteague Islands.

Beach Club, Outer Links ⌂
▽ 21 | 21 | 20 | 23 | $75 |

9715 Deer Park Dr., Berlin; 410-641-4653; 800-435-9223;
www.beachclubgolflinks.com; 6548/5022; 71.7/68.6; 134/119

☑ The variation between this and its sister makes these "beautiful"
"beach" twins a blast to play in tandem, which is "nice for
vacationers", and for the local chapter of the Polar Bear Club,
since play here is particularly "great in winter", as long as you
don't mind teeing off with mittens on.

Eagle's Landing
25 | 18 | 18 | 23 | $45 |

12367 Eagles Nest Rd., Berlin; 410-213-7277; 800-283-3846;
www.eagleslandinggolf.com; 7003/4896; 73.6/67.9; 128/112

☑ Budget birdie hunters "never miss a chance to play" "golf as
it outta be" on this "real bargain", a "beautiful muni" where "links
and regular holes combine" as they weave "through the marsh";
the "tough risk/reward approaches" might "bite you", but the
"friendly staff" won't, even if you beg them to, since "services are
virtually nonexistent" on the "heavily used" track.

LINKS AT LIGHTHOUSE SOUND ⌂
27 | 27 | 26 | 19 | $135 |

12723 Saint Martins Neck Rd., Bishopville; 410-352-5767;
www.lighthousesound.com; 7031/4553; 73.3/67.1; 144/107

■ Lots of courses claim to be the "Pebble Beach of the Atlantic",
but this one might "live up to the moniker" because of its "amazing
location" with "Ocean City views" and a front nine that "plays
along the water"; of course it's windy, so you could end up with
"smashed" drives "that barely clear the hazards" or "hitting 3-wood

into the par 3s"; catch up by putting on the "perfect greens", eat at the "fabulous restaurant" and try not to mistake the "longest cart span on the East Coast" for the Chesapeake Bay Bridge-Tunnel.

Nutters Crossing ▽ 17 │ 14 │ 17 │ 19 │ $69

30287 Southampton Bridge Rd., Salisbury; 410-860-4653; 800-615-4657; www.nutterscrossing.com; 6033/4800; 67.1/66.5; 115/110
■ This daily fee "in and out of the trees" is "great for people who like to hack" but "good enough for the single-digit golfer to practice on"; it's "reasonably priced" and "easy to get on", with "rounds that rarely take more than four hours", plus you can "score well without hitting the ball solid", so really, "it's hard to complain."

Ocean City Golf & Yacht Club, Newport Bay ▽ 24 │ 17 │ 20 │ 19 │ $95

11401 Country Club Dr., Berlin; 410-641-1779; 800-442-3570; www.ocgolfandyacht.com; 6712/5230; 71.0/71.5; 126/119
☑ Really there are no yachts here, just "a shotmaker's course" on the mainland with "some nice bay views"; the entire back nine runs along the water, and even landlubbers blubber that it's "worth the time and money" to "play both" this and its sister, Seaside, followed by the obligatory lobster-and-corn dinner nearby.

Ocean City Golf & Yacht Club, Seaside ▽ 20 │ 15 │ 17 │ 18 │ $79

11401 Country Club Dr., Berlin; 410-641-1779; 800-442-3570; www.ocgolfandyacht.com; 6604/5720; 71.2/73.3; 120/124
☑ It's "easy to get a tee time" at Newport Bay's sib, but it's tough to avoid the marsh "challenging" you to feed the fishes, especially on the liquid-laden par 3s; nevertheless, the Ocean City boardwalk might offer a more exciting stroll than this, as seaside salts used to swinging when the surf's up call it a "fairly boring track" that's "similar to other local courses" and "the service – eh."

River Run 🏨 23 │ 18 │ 20 │ 19 │ $89

11605 Masters Ln., Berlin; 410-641-7200; 800-733-7786; www.riverrungolf.com; 6705/4818; 70.4/73.1; 128/117
■ "A true joy to play", this "serene" "Gary Player–designed" daily fee in a residential community "preserves the natural beauty" of the coastal surroundings on "two distinctly different" nines, a "links-style front" and a "more difficult back nine" "winding through marshes and woods over little hills"; the "wonderful people" who run it keep it in "great shape always", and though "it doesn't have ocean views", no one's looking anyway when they're concentrating on such "interesting holes."

Rum Pointe Seaside Golf Links 27 │ 23 │ 22 │ 21 │ $99

7000 Rum Pointe Ln., Berlin; 410-629-1414; 888-809-4653; www.rumpointe.com; 7001/5276; 72.6/70.3; 122/120
■ "The best course at the beach" "sits right on the water" with "magnificent views of Assawoman Bay" on "17 of 18" "fantastic links" holes; while designer Pete Dye was "tough but not unfair", Mother Nature is not so even-tempered, and the "winds come up unexpectedly" to "affect play" – rent an on-site apartment and stay for the weekend to get your shots in shape at the "second-to-none practice facilities" before motoring your GPS-equipped cart onto this "Ocean City must."

Massachusetts

★ **Best in State**
29 Crumpin-Fox Club, *Berkshires*
28 Pinehills, Jones Course, *Boston*
Country Club of New Seabury, Ocean, *Cape Cod*
26 Taconic, *Berkshires*
Farm Neck, *Martha's Vineyard*

Berkshires

Cranwell Resort   18 20 19 17 $95
55 Lee Rd., Lenox; 413-637-1364; 800-272-6935; www.cranwell.com;
6204/5104; 70.0/72.4; 125/129
☑ Check into the luxe Vanderbilt mansion or abolitionist Reverend
Henry Ward Beecher's cottage and soak in the history along with
"peak foliage season's" "wonderful sunset views" or the sweet
summer sounds of the Tanglewood Music Festival at this "lovely
Berkshires" resort and spa; the "beverage cart, pub and practice
facilities are great", and the course itself is "fun" and "moves pretty
quickly", though it's "not spectacular" enough for the "staff's
almost overwhelming sense of importance."

CRUMPIN-FOX CLUB 🕴   29 21 24 23 $69
Parmenter Rd., Bernardston; 413-648-9101; www.sandri.com;
7022/5432; 73.8/71.5; 141/131
■ "Almost every hole could be on a calendar" at state's No. 1–rated
Course, an "excellent" RTJ Jr. "champion" "epitomizing New
England golf" by "never letting up" its "challenge" while delivering
constant "diversity"; "the greens run fast and true", the Berkshires
"scenery can't be beat" and "if No. 8 doesn't test your nerves,
your first name must be Tiger"; calm yourself after your round
beside "the clubhouse's large fireplace", and try "the dinner
package to book a tee time in advance."

Ranch, The 🏞   ▽ 26 26 27 23 $100
100 Ranch Club Rd., Southwick; 413-569-9315;
www.theranchgolfclub.com; 7174/4983; 74.1/69.7; 140/122
■ "Why join a country club when you can play" on this "great new"
daily fee and enjoy a "beautiful, challenging layout" with "lots
of blind shots" and "fairways like carpets", plus "very cordial"
service and a "top-notch" clubhouse lodged in historic post-and-
beam barns?; "take your buddies or entertain for business", and
if you think "it doesn't get any better than this", guess again – as
it matures, the "young course should improve" even more.

Taconic 🕐   26 18 21 22 $140
19 Meacham St., Williamstown; 413-458-3997;
6640/5202; 72.5/70.2; 129/121
■ "View the plaque [on No. 14] commemorating Jack Nicklaus'
hole-in-one" "when he played in the U.S. Amateur" at this "truly
magnificent course" "in the heart of the Berkshires"; it's a "test
for good golfers but doesn't beat up high-handicappers", as long
as they "beware the slick, unpredictable greens"; its "idyllic"
town is "sleepy but getting busier" and the track "gets a great deal
of play", so "don't tell your friends about this gem" or they'll trail
you here, just like the "red fox that followed you for three holes."

Boston

Atlantic Country Club
23 | 19 | 18 | 20 | $55

450 Little Sandy Pond Rd., Plymouth; 508-759-6644;
www.atlanticcountryclub.com; 6928/5001; 74.3/68.9; 139/119

■ "Average golfers" give thanks for the "good value" available at this "well-maintained layout on hilly terrain" not far from where the Pilgrims landed on that rock; a "nice change of pace from the typical Boston-area golf course", it's "relatively easy" but still forces you to "use many clubs", and it "should get better every year as it grows" – just don't try to tee off December–March, as it's closed.

George Wright 🏌
19 | 9 | 12 | 23 | $29

420 West St., Hyde Park; 617-361-8313; 6440/5131; 69.5/70.3; 126/115

◪ You "can't find many Donald Ross courses for less money" than you'll pay at this "classic" muni "gem" "in the middle of the city"; under "new management", the "watering system" has been replaced and "the conditions only get better" while "the seedy neighborhood tends to keep down crowds", though it might also explain the preponderance of "Boston pols and cops playing there."

Juniper Hill, Lakeside
18 | 15 | 16 | 19 | $38

202 Brigham St., Northborough; 508-393-2444; www.juniperhillgc.com;
6282/4788; 70.9/68.5; 130/115

■ Savings-savvy swingers seeking "a real bargain for a tough round of golf" say this "great layout" (the younger one of two at this 1931 facility) is short on length but long on value; some penny-pinching pie-eyed putters go so far as to profess "an inner love for it", even if the weekend "required cart is a nuisance"; if you haven't played since the turn of the millennium, stop by to enjoy the expanded two-year-old clubhouse and the newly overhauled putting green, and stay in town for the annual fall Applefest.

Olde Scotland Links
▽ 23 | 11 | 18 | 22 | $41

690 Pine St., Bridgewater; 508-279-3344;
6790/4949; 72.6/68.4; 126/111

◪ "Forgiving off the tee" and "wide open with quite a few environmentally sensitive areas", this "very nice" "marshland" muni is "great for the weekend warrior", "but don't be complacent" because "nature" here means "plenty of heather in which to lose your ball" and "snapping turtles in the sandtraps"; it's "playable", "pretty" and "well maintained", though lexicon-loving lofters point out, "it's neither Scottish, nor a links, nor particularly olde."

PINEHILLS, JONES COURSE
28 | 27 | 26 | 21 | $95

54 Clubhouse Dr., Plymouth; 508-209-3000; www.pinehillsgolf.com;
7175/5380; 73.8/71.2; 135/125

■ "The holes look like paintings" on this "gorgeous" Rees Jones layout "reminiscent of the West Coast and Hawaii", though it's really located at the Boston area's "best new" facility; there are "no tricks" here – it's just "about placing your approach shots on huge greens" at the end of "wide-open fairways" after a spin through the "fantastic practice area" and before a meal at the "good restaurant"; given "beautiful views", three golf schools and a "helpful, friendly staff", starry-eyed sticksters stammer "can this really be a public club?"

Pinehills, Nicklaus Course
_ | _ | _ | _ | $95

54 Clubhouse Dr., Plymouth; 508-209-3000;
www.pinehillsgolf.com; 7243/5185; 74.3/69.4; 135/123
Opened May 2002, this sister to the Jones Course is a totally
different and unique experience but equally "fabulous" as it
slinks over glacier-carved elevation changes around large white
pines, accompanied by first-class amenities including a "great
practice facility right near the clubhouse"; it's all so lovely, no
wonder the Pilgrims landed nearby.

Poquoy Brook
24 | 20 | 19 | 22 | $43

20 Leonard St., Lakeville; 508-947-5261; www.poquoybrook.com;
6762/5415; 72.4/71.0; 128/114
■ The "long par 4s demand all the clubs in your bag" and "the
finishing holes are the hardest in Massachusetts" at this "solid"
"public entity" near all those ponds north of New Bedford; it's
"always in great shape", its "pro shop and service are good", but ya
gotta douse yourself in "insect spray or suffer" "these black little
gnats that drive you crazy."

River Bend
∇ 20 | 14 | 16 | 21 | $62

250 E. Center St., West Bridgewater; 508-580-3673;
www.riverbendgc.com; 6659/4915; 70.9/67.7; 127/120
☑ Your game better be in as "great shape" as this "fun" daily fee on
the Town River because "you'll use every club in the bag" on the
"many water holes" of its "wide-open front nine" and on the tighter
"tree-lined back"; however, whiny whackers still wail that the
greens can be "rock hard even after a day of rain" so that "wedges
from the fairway, with spin, don't hold here."

Shaker Hills 🏌
24 | 23 | 22 | 21 | $75

146 Shaker Rd., Harvard; 978-772-2227; 6850/4999; 72.3/67.9; 135/116
☑ It "doesn't have the reputation of other public courses, but it
should" say loose-lipped linksters pitching and telling about
this "well-managed", "woodsy" "old New England" track that's
particularly "scenic" "in the fall"; "several options off the tees",
"lots of elevation changes", "good facilities" and "fair" prices
are other inducements, but warning: "tight fairways" spell big
"trouble for hackers."

Waverly Oaks,
Championship Course 🏌
26 | 23 | 21 | 19 | $85

444 Long Pond Rd., Plymouth; 508-224-6016;
www.waverlyoaksgolfclub.com; 7114/4930; 73.5/68.5; 126/119
■ Putting pilgrims profess that there are "several memorable
holes" with "tremendous elevation changes" at this "simply
awesome" Plymouth daily fee that's frequently "forgiving off the
tee but demanding on the approach"; the "country-club setting"
includes a "great practice area" and carts with "GPS included" in
the price; you can walk it, but you'll be charged for the cost of a ride,
and the course is "sooo long" that "even after driving, you're beat."

Widow's Walk
20 | 15 | 18 | 22 | $42

250 The Driftway, Scituate; 781-544-7777; 6403/4562; 71.2/69.3; 129/115
■ "Built on a landfill", this "great" "environmental experiment" is
"short but diabolical", with "some of the narrowest fairways you'll
ever see" squeezed between wetlands protected by "bunkers

not for novices" and "mucho poison ivy"; the "panoramic ocean views" from its signature 17th are "incredible", but it "teaches patience in the worst way" – through "lost balls and high scores", so expect to "leave frustrated" unless you're "accurate off the tee" and can handle "bump-and-run approaches" on a "thinking man's" "target" muni that's "not for the faint of heart."

Cape Cod

Ballymeade 🏌   21 | 23 | 19 | 15 | $95
125 Falmouth Woods Rd., North Falmouth; 508-540-4005;
www.ballymeade.com; 6928/5001; 74.3/68.9; 139/119
☑ This "championship track" has "matured over the past several years" and been revamped by Joe Fazio and Chi Chi Rodriguez, so it's "in great shape"; "even with the changes", however, its "perplexing layout" is "a bit tricked up" "for the average golfer", so all those NFL, NHL and Major League stars who descend upon it for the Ocean Spray Celebrity Golf Classic to benefit the Special Olympics better "bring lots of balls", and the rest of you better bring lots of lira because "it's very expensive in the summer, like all Cape courses."

Bass River   17 | 15 | 15 | 17 | $50
62 High Bank Rd., South Yarmouth; 508-398-9079;
6129/5343; 68.5/69.9; 115/115
☑ "Ok", "nothing great" – this "fine old muni" remodeled by Donald Ross in 1914 may not inspire gushing adjectives, but it's "fun" and "easy" enough with "some interesting holes"; those who always expect masterpieces from the legendary architect gibe that he "must have been on a bender when he designed this one."

Bayberry Hills   20 | 18 | 17 | 20 | $69
635 W. Yarmouth Rd., West Yarmouth; 508-394-5597;
www.golfyarmouthcapecod.com; 7152/5323; 73.1/69.7; 127/119
☑ On the Lower Cape, this "very solid public course" owned by the town of Yarmouth is "comfortable" from the whites and blues, but can get "testy from the tips", so don't get too ambitious and it "will provide a decent round of enjoyment", particularly "if you live in the area"; "non-residents" resent "raised greens fees" for a track that's "not worth seeking out."

Brookside Club   ▽ 19 | 6 | 17 | 18 | $60
1 Brigadoone Rd., Bourne; 508-743-4653;
www.thebrooksideclub.com; 6300/5130; 71.1/69.6; 126/118
☑ "Bring a seeing eye dog" to help you score well on this "difficult test" "with more blind shots than most put together", and the pup will probably dig the "fun", "friendly atmosphere"; "conditions are good" on the course itself, but the facilities are still "under construction", so when you travel across the Bourne Bridge and hit the Cape, "don't drive by" it because "that's not a trailer park, it's the clubhouse."

Cape Cod Country Club   18 | 14 | 16 | 19 | $53
Theater Dr., North Falmouth; 508-563-9842;
www.capecodcountryclub.com; 6429/5348; 70.6/70.6; 120/119
■ "There are no frills here, just good golf" on a "fine, old course" with "long, straightforward" links-style holes and "wide greens"

with "room for error" "if the wind isn't howling"; "the people are great", which makes it even better "for beginners" and a "good value" for anyone, except snobs who find it "a bit too public" for their exclusive tastes.

Captains, Port　　　23 | 19 | 18 | 21 | $60
1000 Freemans Way, Brewster; 508-896-1716; 877-843-9081; www.captainsgolfcourse.com; 6724/5345; 70.6/70.4; 121/120
■ The folks captaining this Lower Cape Cod course "took the former 18, built 18 and blended them together" for "some excellent holes" in the pirate "mix" of both members of the fleet; however, even with "dramatic elevation changes carved through the pines" and a fairly "new clubhouse", mutinous mates declare this ship "just good" because you "have to travel to the driving range", "it's overpriced" for the area and the crew is "full of attitude."

Captains, Starboard　　　▽ 24 | 19 | 19 | 24 | $60
1000 Freemans Way, Brewster; 508-896-1716; 877-843-9081; www.captainsgolfcourse.com; 6776/5359; 70.9/70.9; 122/120
■ "A good track" "in great shape" with "a beautiful variety of holes", this sister to the Port sports "excellent conditions for a public facility"; "play is a bit slow, at least in the summer" when all those duffers come out to pay what locals consider too dear a price for their sunburns; well-heeled hackers can escape the après-round heat with a New French feast at the highly lauded nearby Chillingsworth restaurant.

Country Club of New Seabury, Dunes　　　22 | 26 | 24 | 19 | $150
95 Shore Dr. W., Mashpee; 508-539-8322; www.newseabury.com; 6340/5530; 71.0/67.5; 125/118
■ "Renovations in 2001" made this Cape resort course "more interesting and challenging" even though "the view is not as good as on the Ocean" course; since that track is "private for most of the year" and offers only limited access to non-members, why not hack up its sister? – she's "beautiful" and "fun to play" too; after your round, have a cocktail in the fine dining digs at the brand-new clubhouse before retiring to your cottage on-site.

COUNTRY CLUB OF NEW SEABURY, OCEAN ⊕　　　28 | 25 | 22 | 18 | $150
95 Shore Dr. W., Mashpee; 508-539-8322; www.newseabury.com; 7140/6469; 75.8/72.1; 133/127
■ No, that's not an unusually "large water hazard" – it's just "the ocean along the first six holes" at this "absolutely spectacular" "challenge"; "keep your head down" because the views of Nantucket and Martha's Vineyard "distract", and the "wind in your face makes it even more difficult"; with villas and beachy activities, the resort is "a great weekend destination for the whole family", but just off-season, as non-members can only get Tuesday–Thursday PM tee times mid-May–mid-October, and even if you do get on, you'll have to "apply for a greens fee loan" to afford it.

Cranberry Valley　　　23 | 16 | 16 | 21 | $65
183 Oak St., Harwich; 508-430-5234; 6296/5518; 70.4/71.5; 125/115
■ "Generous fairways" "carved through pines", "large well-bunkered greens" and "lots of elevation changes" make this an

"outstanding muni" for budget "vacationers" who feel "the need to play" and want to take advantage of "great twilight rates"; a "snobby" staff, "ok conditions" and a layout that critics call "run-of-the-mill" might not be "worth traveling for" but perhaps the weekend breakfast buffet in the new clubhouse is.

Dennis Pines
19 | 17 | 18 | 21 | $50

50 Golf Course Rd., East Dennis; 508-385-9826;
7029/5798; 74.0/72.3; 132/123

☑ "There isn't much room to spray the ball" at this "tight", "difficult municipal course" that's "more laid out for the low-handicapper", with "hilly", "narrow fairways" straight-jacketed in "pine trees left and right on seemingly every hole"; you can play here year-round, but the "people could be a lot nicer", the conditions can be "bad" and as for nasty vegetation, "did we mention the pines?"

Hyannis Golf Club
18 | 16 | 17 | 16 | $60

1840 Rte. 132, Hyannis; 508-362-2606; www.hyannisgc.com;
6750/5149; 69.9/69.7; 121/125

☑ "Close to the highway" smack dab in the middle of the Cape, this "decent", year-round daily fee "is working hard to improve and it's starting to show" on a "fair" but "tough track that's kept in condition"; it's "a little pricey", but the "locker rooms and dining areas are outstanding", that is, gripe grouchy gastronomes, if "you have a fondness for greasy hamburgers and fries."

New England 🏡
20 | 14 | 17 | 17 | $69

180 Paine St., Bellingham; 508-883-2300;
www.newenglandcountryclub.com; 6430/4908; 70.8/68.7; 130/121

■ This "well-conditioned", "good test of golf" by three-time U.S. Open champ Hale Irwin is one "local favorite" where "a cart is an advantage" because of the GPS systems, "the distance from the clubhouse" and the "length between holes"; there's "little room for error" on a "tight", "tree-lined layout" where play is made more difficult but less bothersome by the "ever-present beer cart", meaning you sure can get tipsy at the tips; N.B. ask about dine-and-drive packages.

Ocean Edge
21 | 23 | 23 | 17 | $80

832 Villages Dr., Brewster; 508-896-9000; www.oceanedge.com;
6660/5180; 72.6/69.6; 130/118

■ "Another Cape beauty", this "links"-style resort course is a "nice setting" for a "stay-and-play" weekend or an "off-site management meeting" replete with biking, tennis and swimming at the private beach on the glamorous grounds of the historical Nickerson estate; whether you're at work or play, "get the Bloody Mary with the shrimp in it", "watch out for the pot bunkers" and "keep the driver at home" or your ball will "be blown out to sea" leaving you enriching the cultural knowledge of your fellow flubbers, which is also known as "cursing at the wind in Gaelic."

Olde Barnstable Fairgrounds
23 | 18 | 18 | 22 | $55

1460 Rte. 149, Marstons Mills; 508-420-1141; 6479/5122; 70.7/69.2; 123/118

■ "A scenic course" with a "nice variety of terrain (for Cape Cod)", this municipal is "not too tough a test" so long as you "don't get overconfident – otherwise it might bite you"; it's a particularly "good value" for locals putting on "greens in great shape", but the "facilities could use a boost", and the "service folks need manners" to deal with outsiders.

Martha's Vineyard

Farm Neck   26 | 22 | 20 | 21 | $125
Farm Neck Way, Oak Bluffs; 508-693-3057;
6807/5004; 72.6/64.3; 133/121
⚑ Yet another contender for the title of "Pebble Beach of the East", this "superb" track open April–December on Martha's Vineyard is a "pleasure", though with non-members allowed to reserve only two days in advance, it's "gotten closer to private than public"; if you get on it, you'll be playing a "well-kept" course with "endless character", "beautiful views of the Atlantic" and "windy", "terrific risk/reward holes" that "can bring golfers to their knees", which may explain why it's been the site of so "many rounds by former President Clinton."

Worcester

Blackstone National   23 | 21 | 23 | 18 | $69
227 Putnam Hill Rd., Sutton; 508-865-2111;
www.blackstonegolfclub.com; 6909/5203; 73.5/70.0; 132/122
■ It's only a toddler, so this "beautiful Rees Jones" "championship layout" "needs to mature, but it will be wonderful in about five years"; "U.S. Open–like rough" and "funky holes" make it "a great experience" for everyone, including the experts coming through on the New England Pro Tour, and though "long distances from green to tee mean it's almost impossible to walk unless you run marathons", the separately owned Putnam House B&B is smack on the property, so it's not a hike to your room.

Butternut Farm   18 | 12 | 15 | 19 | $42
115 Wheeler Rd., Stow; 978-897-3400; www.butternutfarm.com;
6302/4778; 71.2/67.6; 130/119
■ Amid the "beautiful foliage" of "scenic New England" is this "deceptively challenging" daily fee where the "short, tight" holes "make you think more than most" longer stretches do; it's "not the place to go if you're looking for a fancy lounge, restaurant" or clubhouse, but if you want to play on a "very nice" track that's "well manicured" "for such heavy traffic", this is the place; just "bring a helmet" – "it's open season on some holes, and stray balls seem to come from everywhere."

Cyprian Keyes   23 | 24 | 22 | 19 | $55
284 E. Temple St., Boylston; 508-869-9900; www.cypriankeyes.com;
6871/5029; 72.7/69.2; 132/119
■ "You will have respect for the power of the wilderness" when you are restricted from chasing your "errant shots" into the "environmentalist's dream" of a "wetlands" where the endangered spotted salamander might just curse you if you don't bring your "shotmaker's" "A-game"; if you're a "high-handicapper", carry "a small bucket" of balls to this "tight", "quirky" "challenge" and try to "control your distance and accuracy off the tee" because it's not nice to fool (with) Mother Nature; P.S. the "best golf course burger in the state" ain't vegetarian, but the New England PGA Hall of Fame here appeals to every voracious golf fan.

Stow Acres, North
21 | 18 | 17 | 18 | $50

58 Randall Rd., Stow; 978-568-8690; www.stowacres.com;
6939/6011; 72.8/73.6; 130/130

"Don't let the easy first hole fool you" because this "long" "classic" is "the real deal", with "a great teaching facility, a nice clubhouse and a driving range right there", and "after they let the service and conditions slip" in the "last few years", it's "making a comeback" following "clearing and several new greens"; the fairways might be more wide open now, but the tee times aren't – "they book way too close together", so, "no joke", you're probably in for "a six-hour round."

Stow Acres, South
19 | 18 | 16 | 18 | $50

58 Randall Rd., Stow; 978-568-8690; www.stowacres.com;
6520/5642; 71.8/72.5; 120/120

The North's sister might be "more forgiving", but this "thinker's course" is "tougher than her reputation", with some "suspect" back "holes that remind you of goat hills"; nevertheless, ball hitters bleat that she's "not quite as well manicured", and there's "too much waiting" around for the "hackers" to clear her fairways – "it's not called Slow Acres for nothing."

Wachusett
▽ 19 | 18 | 16 | 22 | $35

187 Prospect St., West Boylston; 508-835-2264;
www.wachusettcc.com; 6567/6170; 71.7/70.0; 124/120

Donald Ross would be happy that "the charm and character" of his "wonderful" "old course with all his earmarks" and "a great variety of holes" has been kept in "good condition" at this club with "outstanding vistas" of the Wachusett Reservoir; "a pub that's a great place to relax" would also have pleased the late designer.

Michigan

★ **Best in State**
28 Arcadia Bluffs, *Traverse City*
27 Bay Harbor Resort, *Petosky*
   Treetops, Rick Smith Signature, *Traverse City*
26 Treetops, Robert Trent Jones Masterpiece, *Traverse City*
   Grand Traverse, The Bear, *Traverse City*

Bay City

Lakewood Shores, Blackshire
— | — | — | — | $62

7751 Cedar Lake Rd., Oscoda; 989-739-2075; 800-882-2493;
www.lakewoodshores.com; 6898/5740; 71.9/67.5; 125/109

On the eastern shore is a resort that offers golfers a whole lot of variety, starting with this imitation of New Jersey's famous Pine Valley with tree-lined fairways that have large waste areas dug out in strategic places; while it's not as difficult as its inspiration, it will keep you on your toes with hidden hazards, twisting creeks, false fronts and the aforementioned well-placed mimics.

Lakewood Shores, Gailes
— | — | — | — | $62

7751 Cedar Lake Rd., Oscoda; 989-739-2075; 800-882-2493;
www.lakewoodshores.com; 6954/6073; 75/72.2; 138/122

"Links in Michigan?" – "what a treat" this "terrific layout" is; "if you can't afford Whistling Straits, head to Oscoda for that pure feeling" you get from the windy shores of Lake Huron, where natural mounding, tall heather, fescue and deep sod-faced bunkers (including one hole with 18 little potties) add vérité; a number of the "really fast greens" are shared, which can be unnerving, though the "wonderful folks behind the counter" will soothe you.

Red Hawk
— | — | — | — | $75

350 Davison Rd., East Tawas; 989-362-0800; www.redhawkgolf.net; 6589/4933; 71.0/67.4; 130/117

The round "gets better every time you play" at this track where Arthur Hills carved a diversity of holes into valleys, ridges and wetlands on the eastern shore of Michigan; well-placed bunkers and hazards seduce you into taking risks that may or may not be rewarded, so make sure to give yourself a well-earned treat with a stop in the glass-and-cedar clubhouse that houses Falco Rosso, a fine Italian restaurant.

Detroit

Majestic at Lake Walden
∇ 26 | 19 | 19 | 19 | $69

9600 Crouse Rd., Hartland; 810-632-5235; 800-762-3280; www.majesticgolf.com; 7009/5081; 73.8/68.7; 132/111

■ "Bring extra balls" to play this "challenge" by Lake Walden, where No. 10 requires "a boat trip to the tee" and meadows and forests fuel a "picturesque" experience; clinical club-wielders note that "open heart surgery takes less time than playing 18 here" but readily concede that it "deserves a try, particularly if you like holes with no opposing links and exceptional scenery."

Orchards, The
— | — | — | — | $75

62900 Campground Rd., Washington; 586-786-7200; www.orchards.com; 7026/5158; 74.5/70.3; 136/123

As apples fall from its orchard trees, this "great" Robert Trent Jones Jr. design throws 93 bunkers up at you, many of them steep and nasty; this sure made things interesting at the 2002 U.S. Amateur, which was played over the wooded front nine and links-style back with a few adjacent fairways from which you can see downtown Detroit 30 miles away on a clear day.

Shepherd's Hollow
— | — | — | — | $85

9080 Big Lake Rd., Clarkston; 248-922-0300; www.shepherdshollow.com; 7236/4906; 76.0/69.7; 147/120

A flock of globe-trotting golfers "think they've found the best course and facilities on the planet" at this track with "excellent conditioning and a country-club feel"; five sets of tees "give many different looks" to each hole, a "few" of which are "gimmicky par 4s" that "detract from the experience" according to a critical herd of hackers.

Gaylord

Elk Ridge
∇ 25 | 23 | 24 | 22 | $75

9400 Rouse Rd., Atlanta; 517-785-2275; 800-626-4355; www.elkridgegolf.com; 7072/5261; 74.7/72.3; 143/130

■ Pork-loving putters "look out for the pig-shaped bunker" on No. 10 at this "must-play" "from the owner of the Honey Baked Ham" company; an "unbelievable find" that's "always in great shape" and "uncrowded" with golfing "groups" but loaded with wildlife (boars, perhaps?), it begs the question: "how does a course this good wind up in the middle of a one-light (blinking yellow at that) town?"; P.S. don't miss the "great sandwiches" loaded with the proprietor's specialty, natch.

Treetops, Rick Smith Signature   27 | 24 | 23 | 24 | $99
3962 Wilkinson Rd.; 989-732-6711; 888-873-3867; www.treetops.com; 6653/4604; 72.8/67.0; 140/123
■ "Elevated tees provide great looks onto creative bunkering and natural rough" at this resort course that exemplifies "spectacular northern Michigan golf"; though "playing from the tips can be way too much work" and "no fun in the sun" when the annual host of the PGA's Par 3 Shootout gets "baked", amenities such as a fine dining room can ease the burn.

Treetops,   26 | 26 | 25 | 24 | $99
Robert Trent Jones Masterpiece
3962 Wilkinson Rd.; 989-732-6711; 888-873-3867; www.treetops.com; 7060/4972; 75.5/70.5; 144/123
■ Designed by "one of the most well-known architects of our time", this "stunning" resort track "incorporates natural topographical features" into a "tough but beautiful" layout that palpitating putters "would play again in a heartbeat"; after surviving a rough round, wander over to the bar and slow your pulse with a bottle or two from the 300-strong "best selection of beer you've ever seen."

Treetops, Tom Fazio Premier   ▽ 29 | 25 | 27 | 24 | $99
3962 Wilkinson Rd.; 989-732-6711; 888-873-3867; www.treetops.com; 6836/5036; 73.6/70.0; 136/125
■ "Not as difficult as the Jones but just as gorgeous", this "great Fazio layout" has "lots of elevation drops and climbs" "that create dramatic vistas" over "fairways that are forgiving because they're bowl-shaped to keep the tee shots in"; you might want to think twice about visiting the "outrageous" multi-level putting practice area because it could lead you to "lose whatever confidence you have in your stroke."

Grand Rapids

St. Ives Resort, St. Ives   ▽ 28 | 27 | 26 | 25 | $75
9900 Saint Ives Dr., Stanwood; 231-972-4837; 800-972-4837; www.stivesgolf.com; 6702/4821; 73.3/68.7; 140/120
■ Michigan mashers say this Lake Mecosta "must-play" has "all the makings of a classic", with "awesome" water views, a "beautiful" woodlands layout and "the best six finishing holes you may ever see"; it's part of a resort sporting sister course Tullymore, the private Canadian Lakes track, two nine-holers and a notable pro shop, not to mention brand-new lodging and a wide selection of activities from basketball to trap shooting to keep non-golfers occupied.

St. Ives Resort, Tullymore ⊕   ▽ 29 | 19 | 23 | 26 | $85
11969 Tullymore Dr., Stanwood; 231-972-4837; 800-972-4837; www.stivesgolf.com; 7148/4668; 74.9/66.8; 148/115
■ St. Ives' new sister, this "absolutely gorgeous" resort course is destined to "become a household name" thanks to a "rare

combination of scenery and quality" on a "very tough" layout that's "all about hitting the target" over a links-style front nine and parkland back, designed by Jim Engh, who's considered by many swingers to be one of the best young architects in the sport, and who's tagged on a "great par-5 finishing hole"; once it "gets its clubhouse built, this facility will have it all."

Lansing

Forest Akers MSU, East ▽ 23 | 19 | 21 | 25 | $26

Harrison Rd., East Lansing; 517-355-1635; www.golfmsu.msu.edu; 6559/5111; 70.3/67.8; 114/110

■ Coed club-wielders clobber a few on the West's lesser-lauded, "lower-priced" yet nonetheless "absolutely gorgeous" sister course, where an already "phenomenal" value is increased with "continuing improvements" such as "a great practice range with targets to hit to along with a practice sand trap"; a university golf team member might be called a Spartan, but this "excellent" track is anything but.

Forest Akers MSU, West ▽ 29 | 24 | 22 | 26 | $41

Harrison Rd., East Lansing; 517-355-1635; www.golfmsu.msu.edu; 7003/5869; 74.4/69.2; 139/128

■ "They have changed the routing" and added a spiffy "new clubhouse" and "pro shop offering Michigan State University merchandise", and if this collegiate course was "great before all the changes, it's even better now"; "don't miss" this "favorite" "challenge for every level" of handicap, but "bring your A-game to score well" because, like a beloved professor, it's a "tough" but "never unfair" tester and will "keep you on your toes"; the immaculate spread is also a "beautiful example of greenkeeping", "as you would expect from an institution that started out as a school for agriculture."

Hawk Hollow 23 | 22 | 20 | 18 | $65

15101 Chandler Rd., Bath; 517-641-4295; 888-411-4295; www.hawkhollow.com
10/19: 6693/4962; 72.8/69.7; 134/120
1/10: 6974/5078; 72.1/69.7; 133/120
19/1: 6487/4934; 71.7/69.7; 129/120

☑ "You could play all the time" if you lived in one of the couple of houses along the fairways of this "pretty" daily-fee course with "a northern resort feel"; its ample landing areas and large, bentgrass greens make it "great for any handicap", though disappointed duffers declare "the new nine is a little weak", and even though the 19th hole has a view of the finish, boozy foozlers say "the clubhouse is worthless."

Pohlcat ▽ 23 | 19 | 19 | 19 | $75

6595 E. Airport Rd., Mount Pleasant; 517-773-4221; 800-292-8891; www.pohlcat.net; 6810/5140; 74.2/70.8; 139/124

☑ "Long hitters (like the course's namesake designer, Dan Pohl) are rewarded" at this "enjoyable" course with a "good layout" interlaced by the Chippewa River; the bunker-and-water-guarded signature 17th prompts surly swingers to sneer "one great hole, 17 average ones", but a catered post-outing cookout at the new clubhouse might make them forgive and forget.

Timber Ridge   ▽ 25 | 24 | 23 | 24 | $50
16339 Park Lake Rd., East Lansing; 517-339-8000;
www.golftimberridge.com; 6497/6128; 72.4/69.8; 140/136
■ "Hit it straight or make double" warn wallet-wise woodsmen
wooed by the "good price" at this "well-maintained target track";
if you like trees, this "little slice of paradise" just may be "the
prettiest course you've ever played", and after a brush-clearing
"redesign that helped its ratings", it's more than ever an "all-
around great" golf experience.

Muskegon

Double JJ Resort Ranch,   ▽ 23 | 18 | 23 | 19 | $75
Thoroughbred
6886 Water Rd., Rothbury; 231-894-4444; www.doublejj.com;
6900/4851; 74.4/69.5; 147/126
🗹 Double-eagle dudes swing high up in the saddle at this cowboy
course on a weekender's resort ranch in central Michigan with
accommodations ranging from adult-only saloonvilles to kid-
friendly cowtowns; "all kinds of interesting holes make you pay
attention", but "the hardest, No. 2", makes you pay period; some
thoroughbreds throw up their hands at the "few goofy holes",
whinnying "it could be great" but hasn't yet won the race.

Petoskey

BAY HARBOR RESORT 🏌   27 | 29 | 27 | 20 | $199
3600 Village Harbor Dr., Bay Harbor; 231-439-4029; 800-462-6963;
www.boyne.com
Links/Preserve: 6816/4087; 73.7/69.4; 143/113
Preserve/Quarry: 6726/3881; 72.5/69.1; 145/112
Quarry/Links: 6780/4126; 72.2/69.3; 145/113
■ There are enough "windswept vistas" "to fill a photo album", so
after a round you might want to "borrow a cart to go back and snap
shots" at this Lake Michigan resort's trio of nines, which features
some holes "high above Traverse Bay"; the "spectacular" Links
gets the most enthusiastic response, the Quarry has "great risk/
reward shots" and "a few gimmicky holes", and the Preserve is,
relatively speaking, "the weak sister", with only one water view;
the answer to the question "is any golf worth $200?" just might be,
if it's this "spectacular" to look at and also has a "fantastic pro shop
and locker room", yes.

Boyne Highlands, Arthur Hills 🏌   – | – | – | – | $129
600 Highland Rd., Harbor Springs; 231-526-3029; 800-462-6963;
www.boyne.com; 7312/4811; 76.4/68.5; 144/117
It's spanking new, so it "needs a few years to mature", but this
"good complement to the other Boyne courses" gives "great golf"
already; designed by the namesake architect and laid down in 2001,
it sports his signature massive bunkers plus lots of liquid in play, and
maybe those "couple of funky holes" will mellow with age.

Boyne Highlands, Donald Ross 🏌 ▽ 24 | 26 | 23 | 22 | $99
600 Highland Rd., Harbor Springs; 231-526-3029; 800-462-6963;
www.boyne.com; 6814/4929; 75.5/68.5; 136/119
■ "Recreating some of Donald Ross' more famous holes" is the
"outstanding concept" behind "one of the most memorable and

frustrating rounds" you'll ever encounter; "testing your game on a few of the toughest links that the man designed" is especially "great if you have not seen his others", but for those who've 'been there, done that', the hodgepodge of replica tees may "never really create a feel for itself"; the resort, on the other hand, demands distinction with the largest hot tub in the Midwest.

Boyne Highlands, Heather 🏌️   ▽ 25 | 23 | 23 | 19 |$129|
600 Highland Rd., Harbor Springs; 231-526-3029; 800-462-6963; www.boyne.com; 6890/4794; 74.0/67.8; 136/111
🏁 There "nothing tricked up", "and there's no need for it" in the "classic design" of this "pretty" course from Robert Trent Jones Sr.; while it's "still the best of the Highlands", it's also "heavily played", and "the cost is up there"; nonetheless, it's so addictive, don't be surprised if you "wind up going an additional nine with the kids handling the bags" – if you're pooped after your round and a half, take a load off at the spa.

Boyne Highlands, Moor 🏌️   ▽ 20 | 24 | 23 | 21 | $79|
600 Highland Rd., Harbor Springs; 231-526-3029; 800-462-6963; www.boyne.com; 6809/5061; 74.6/72.0; 135/122
🏁 It's "plain vanilla" to thrill-seekers, and it's "a bit short" to big-hitting birdie chasers (though their caddies don't seem to mind), but there's "a little less traffic than the Heather" at this soupy sister, so it's an "enjoyable" alternative when you don't want to wait in line; "given the choice", however, serious swingers "never play it."

Traverse City

ARCADIA BLUFFS 🏌️   28 | 26 | 24 | 22 |$160|
14710 Northwood Hwy., Arcadia; 231-889-3001; 800-494-8666; www.arcadiabluffs.com; 7404/5529; 75.1/69.2; 143/122
■ "A stunning meeting of rugged, heathered dunesland and inland water" will make you wonder if you're "playing into a stiff wind off the Irish Sea or Lake Michigan" at this "incredible" "A+" daily fee with "no surrounding homes to spoil the atmosphere"; the "must-play" is so "challenging" to both your skills and your wallet, it may be "the Pebble Beach of the region", though its "beauty takes most of the edge off."

Black Lake   – | – | – | – |$116|
2800 Maxon Rd., Onaway; 989-733-4653; www.blacklakegolf.com; 7046/5058; 74.3/69.9; 140/125
Rees Jones designed this beaut at the UAW's Walter and May Reuther Family Education Center on the tip of the Lower Peninsula, where auto workers and everyone else can choose from among nine tees for a comfortable takeoff; since practice makes perfect, discounted union brothers and sisters brush up their short games on the extensive facilities, including a nine-hole par-3 course, with pointers from Debbie Massey, the former British Open winner who's now on staff.

Dunmaglas 🏞️   ▽ 24 | 14 | 18 | 17 | $95|
09031 Boyne City Rd., Charlevoix; 231-547-1022; www.dunmaglas.com; 6897/6105; 70.1/69.8; 139/123
■ If you're parked in a city to the south, this "heck of a challenge" is "out of the way", but it's a "tough", "terrific" track with "scenic"

views of Lakes Michigan and Charlevoix, and if you buy a lot on the property, you've got "a nice overall setup" for a retreat; locals labeled it "Doom-a-dozen" after the balls they'd lose on its few "gimmicky" holes, but a 2002 redo may prove its alias anachronistic.

Grand Traverse, The Bear 🏠

26 | 26 | 24 | 16 | $135

100 Grand Traverse Blvd., Acme; 231-938-1620; 800-236-1577; www.grandtraverseresort.com; 7065/5281; 76.8/73.1; 146/137

☑ "Carved out of a cherry orchard" by the paws of the Golden Bear himself, this "beautiful" course is part of a resort that houses a huge new spa and fitness center, two other 18s as well as the Jim McLean Golf School, which might come in handy to those who find Nicklaus' "target golf" layout "brutally difficult"; dissenting duffers who declare "there are much better for the money" sniff "just because Jack's name is on it doesn't mean it has to cost a fortune."

High Pointe

▽ 21 | 16 | 18 | 20 | $69

5555 Arnold Rd., Williamsburg; 231-267-9900; www.highpointegolf.com; 6890/4974; 73.3/68.7; 136/120

☑ "The front and back nines are like two different courses" at this "excellent" dual-personality daily fee where "groups of turkeys follow you from hole to hole" – no, not those you'd like to play for a $10 Nassau but rather the wild fowl; ask about banquet facilities and inexpensive package deals you can gobble-gobble up.

LochenHeath Golf ⏱

– | – | – | – | $105

7951 Turnberry Circle, Williamsburg; 231-938-9800; www.lochenheath.com; 7062/5044; 75.6/70.4; 144/128

Get here quick before it goes private and you miss the stunning East Grand Traverse Bay views from this brand-new semi-private residential course; featuring dramatic bunkering, well-contoured greens and plenty of wind, it's a true test of your golfing abilities.

Natural at Beaver Creek Resort

▽ 26 | 21 | 24 | 22 | $57

5004 W. Otsego Lake Dr., Gaylord; 989-732-1785; 877-646-7529; www.thenatural.org; 6350/4830; 69.3/67.8; 129/118

■ "Good deals (especially in spring and fall)" lead bargain-hunters to seek out this "challenging", "well-maintained" resort course with lots of wildlife and "difficult shots over marshland"; naturals finessing the finish say the 18th is the "ultimate risk/reward hole" where "going for the green means either making it or winding up in big trouble"; to wind up near big game, visit the elk preserve nearby.

Shanty Creek, Cedar River

– | – | – | – | $145

5780 Shanty Creek Rd., Bellaire; 616-533-6076; 800-678-4111; www.shantycreek.com; 6989/5315; 73.6/70.5; 144/128

Lauded among the Midwest's best, this sister to The Legend and its Michigan PGA Championship co-host is a Tom Weiskopf design that winds through dramatic land and water features, finishing in a 604-yard par 5; large greens and five tees to choose from cater to all levels of play, and if you're as happy with a pole in hand as you are with a club, go catch a trout afterward in its namesake river.

Shanty Creek, The Legend

▽ 28 | 24 | 23 | 19 | $145

5780 Shanty Creek Rd., Bellaire; 616-533-6076; www.shantycreek.com; 6764/4953; 73.6/69.6; 137/124

■ "Aptly named", the "superb Arnold Palmer design" on Lake Bellaire at this golf-and-ski resort is among the "best courses in

Michigan", with a "good mixture of difficult/moderate holes" that "flow very nicely" up and down "stunning elevation changes" affording "beautiful forested views"; it's so "excellent" that swingin' Sams will want to "play it again", as time goes by.

Minnesota

Brainerd

Grand View Lodge, Deacon's Lodge

▽ 28 | 25 | 22 | 20 | $98

Breezy Point, 9348 Arnold Palmer Dr., Pequot Lakes; 218-562-6262; 888-437-4637; www.deaconslodge.com; 6950/4766; 73.1/68.4; 134/120

■ "Arnie has designed a great course" at a grand old Gull Lake resort where a slew of package deals are on offer for affordable family vacations; that's a good thing because "you must play a few times to understand proper landing areas" on The King's layout, where even a "couple of questionable holes" don't keep giddy grippers from "giving it top marks"; book a cabin overlooking the practice facilities and roll out of bed onto the range.

Grand View Lodge, Preserve

– | – | – | – | $85

23521 Nokomis Ave., Nisswa; 800-432-3788; 218-568-4944; www.grandviewlodge.com; 6620/4918; 71.6/69.1; 135/119

The third of the Grand View triplets likes the water, dishing up 40 acres of wetlands you'll have to keep high and dry of; she's also one for roller coasters, as elevation changes make for a number of careening tee shots onto bentgrass fairways; you might not look forward to watching your ball zoom downward into water, but you'll probably want to see your kids do so on the indoor pool's slide.

Grand View Lodge, Pines Course

– | – | – | – | $85

23611 Nokomis Ave., Nisswa; 218-963-0001; 888-437-4637; www.grandviewlodge.com
Lakes/ Woods: 6874/5134; 74.1/70.7; 143/128
Marsh/Lakes: 6837/5112; 74.2/71.0; 145/131
Woods/Marsh: 6883/5210; 74.3/71.5; 145/128

In the heart of the Minnesota lakes region, this 27-hole sister course to Deacon's Lodge provides a great golf challenge among rolling hills and thick forests at a beautiful resort with first-class amenities, including an award-winning pro shop and a large practice area, which you'll need because no matter which combination of nines you choose, they're all tough from the tips.

Minneapolis

Baker National

▽ 19 | 18 | 16 | 21 | $32

2935 Parkview Dr., Medina; 763-473-0800; www.bakernational.com; 6762/5395; 73.9/72.5; 135/128

■ "You could pay double and get a worse challenge and layout" than the one anchored by the red barn within Baker Park Reserve, where "very intriguing holes" offer "different challenges from the various tees"; given the added bonus of the environmental education you get from signage along the Audubon-certified track, "is there a better golf value in the Twin Cities?"

Chaska Town
28 | 22 | 19 | 24 | $52

3000 Town Course Dr., Chaska; 952-443-3748;
www.chaskatowncourse.com; 6817/4853; 73.8/69.8; 142/116

■ "Once Mother Nature kicks in", the "prairie wildflowers" and "knee-high grass" make for a "beautiful" herbaceous "challenge" at this "links-style" "favorite" in the same town as the fabled (and very private) Hazeltine National; "if you're not a Chaska resident", it's almost as "difficult" to get on as the aforementioned bastion of exclusivity, but the municipality's regular Joes tee off here on "great par 3s requiring shots over water or marsh", "par 4s needing well-positioned tee shots" and an "18th that begs for some course knowledge."

Dacotah Ridge
– | – | – | – | $56

31042 County Hwy. 2, Morton; 507-644-5050; 800-946-2274;
www.dacotahridge.com; 7109/5055; 73.9/68.9; 134/121

Not many surveyors have made it out to this "golf oasis in the middle of nowhere" in southwest Minnesota where Rees Jones does his best to dunk you on half the holes in the Wabasha Creek and a good-looking lake; the maestro takes advantage of the natural elevation changes on a well-defined layout with contoured greens that allow for a variety of pin locations, and those fickle prairie winds complete the challenge; it's a haul back to any city, so try a stay-and-play at the Jackpot Junction Casino Hotel.

Edinburgh U.S.A. 🏃
23 | 24 | 21 | 21 | $46

8700 Edinbrook Crossing, Brooklyn Park; 763-424-7060;
www.edinburghusa.com; 6850/5255; 73.1/71.4; 141/128

■ "Man, I love this course" swoon swingers sweet on the "top-notch", "links-style" urban muni that has "six par 3s, par 4s and par 5s each", with "huge" "undulating greens, tight fairways and long rough nestled between tall trees"; all that, a "demanding signature 17th" island hole and a "nice clubhouse" at an "excellent value" is why locals stick with it even though "non-residents get stuck pretty good"; N.B. like lots of layouts in these parts, it's closed in winter, though MacTavish's Grill in the clubhouse is open year-round.

Les Bolstad University of Minnesota Golf Course
▽ 19 | 15 | 18 | 25 | $28

2275 Larpenteur Ave. W., St. Paul; 612-627-4000;
www.uofmgolf.com; 6108/5550; 69.5/72.2; 141/123

■ The University of Minnesota's Golden Gophers burrow into the holes at their home course, where discounts are available not only to juniors but to freshmen, sophomores and seniors as well; while it's sort of short and not that difficult, the classic parkland layout is so inexpensive that penny-wise putters can play it on a public university professor's salary.

Rush Creek 🏃
23 | 25 | 23 | 17 | $80

7801 Troy Lane Hwy. 101, Maple Grove; 763-494-8844;
www.rushcreek.com; 7020/5317; 74.2/71.1; 137/127

◪ "Always in perfect shape" and "looking like you can get a great score", this Twin Cities teaser "sucks you in from the outside", but like most rushes, it "eats you up" in the end with perhaps the "hardest 18th in Minnesota"; meanwhile, it's chowing down on your wallet, with "gimmicky holes" "geared to the 0-20 handicapper with deep pockets" and an addictive personality that compels him or her to travel "far away from downtown" to "try it again and again."

Stonebrooke   ▽ 18 │ 16 │ 18 │ 18 │ $47
2693 County Rd. 79, Shakopee; 952-496-3171; 800-263-3189;
www.stonebrooke.com; 6475/4830; 71.7/68.5; 136/120

☑ The "greens are in great shape" and there are "some very interesting holes" at this tree-laden daily fee, so much so that "some are hard to play the first time because they don't make any sense", like the "gimmicky 8th where you take a boat across the lake to fetch your ball", which "slows play to a grinding halt" (though it's nicer to be on the water than in it); like most Minnesota spreads, it's closed from December to April, when you'd have to ride in an icebreaker to get to that crazy green.

Wilds Golf Club, The   24 │ 23 │ 24 │ 18 │ $99
3151 Wilds Ridge Ct. NW, Prior Lake; 952-445-3500;
www.golfthewilds.com; 7025/5095; 74.7/70.2; 140/126

■ As if there isn't enough chill in the Minnesota air already, this "very good" muni in a planned community southwest of downtown gets golfers hoping for cold weather, as a fall/spring special lets you "pay the temperature" to play on "fairways cut tight and greens that are fast and true", where "easy bogeys and tough pars" are the "earmark of a good design"; "one of the last Weiskopf/ Morrish courses", it's "a fitting finale" to a wild collaboration.

Willinger's   ▽ 24 │ 19 │ 19 │ 21 │ $42
6900 Canby Trail, Northfield; 952-652-2500;
www.willingersgc.com; 6711/5166; 73.4/71.7; 148/133

■ Beer-guzzlin' ball swatters swear it's best "not to be hungover when" you visit this challenging daily fee because it's "a 45-minute drive [south on Hwy 35] from the Twin Cities", and it "demands that you play smart golf" and "think about every shot" to avoid the "lurking trouble" of "bunkers, water and O.B."; even teetotalers should plan to tack on "six shots over their handicap."

Mississippi

Gulfport

Bridges at Casino Magic 🏌   ▽ 21 │ 20 │ 19 │ 15 │ $88
711 Casino Magic Dr., Bay Saint Louis; 228-467-9257;
www.casinomagic.com; 6841/5108; 73.5/70.1; 138/124

■ "If you like water, lots and lots of water", this "nice" daily fee has the "tough forced carries" for you; Arnold Palmer "did the best he could with a swamp beside Bay St. Louis", but "if the wind is up, it could be a two-sleeve day", so roll yours to your elbows and get busy on a "target track" "in great shape" with "NY-style service"– just remember to slather repellant on your arms to "avoid the gnats", and if you're playing for cash, save some for the slots.

Grand Casino Gulfport,   ▽ 29 │ 29 │ 28 │ 21 │ $85
Grand Bear
12040 Grand Way Blvd., Saucier; 228-604-7100; 800-283-9121;
www.grandcasinos.com; 7204/4802; 73.8/63.5; 126/98

■ "Don't take a driver off the first tee or the only person who will find your ball is named Robin Hood" at this "awesome" Jack Nicklaus design set amid the DeSoto National Forest; it's "in the middle of nowhere, but it's grand once you get there", as a band of merry men and women "cater" to you with luxuries like laminated yardage books and "bottled water in the carts", "nice tee areas" and "great" conditioning that'll "take the edge off losing your money in the casino"; N.B. if you're not a local, you have to "stay at the Grand to get on" it.

Oaks, The   ▽ 23 | 17 | 21 | 22 | $68

24384 Club House Dr., Pass Christian; 228-452-0909;
www.theoaksgolfclub.com; 6900/4700; 72.5/66.4; 131/107
■ "Another beautiful layout through the Mississippi woodlands", this "tight but not long" bit of "excellent" golf "fun" at a gated community "right off the highway" along the Gulf Coast offers a "good mix of playable and demanding holes" on "Bermuda grass that is kept in nice shape"; "host to a Nike Tour event" in 1999 and the Buy.com Tour in 2000, it's got its fair share of experience in delivering "Southern hospitality."

Jackson

Canebrake   – | – | – | – | $50

1 Cane Dr., Hattiesburg; 601-271-2010; 888-875-5595;
www.canebrakegolf.com; 7003/5129; 73.3/69.5; 130/117
With 56 bunkers and four lakes, including a monstrous 12-acre ball swallower, this semi-private course near Jackson designed by former PGA Tour professional Jerry Pate offers a daunting test to high and low handicaps alike; club-breakers will appreciate the double-ended driving range, chipping and putting area and multiple practice bunkers as well as great stay-and-play deals at a number of area hotels so they can hang around for the weekend and brush up on their strokes.

Dancing Rabbit, Azaleas 🏌   ▽ 28 | 24 | 22 | 24 | $96

1 Choctaw Trail, Philadelphia; 601-663-0011; 888-372-2248;
www.dancingrabbitgolf.com; 7128/4609; 74.4/68.6; 135/115
■ "Especially when you're a dew sweeper", the experience "is almost without peer" sigh early birdies watching the sun come up over this resort track named for the spring-blooming flowers made famous by The Masters tournament, which leads swinger to make the inevitable "closest-thing-to-Augusta" comparison; while the course itself might be "outstanding", the adjacent hotel and casino are "ordinary", so if you are fortunate enough to score that morning tee time, you might consider booking one of the eight guestrooms in the clubhouse instead.

Dancing Rabbit, Oaks 🏌   – | – | – | – | $80

1 Choctaw Trail, Philadelphia; 601-663-0011; 888-372-2248;
www.dancingrabbitgolf.com; 7076/5097; 74.6/69.0; 139/123
"Don't be fooled by the location" – the Mississippi Band of the Choctaw Indians knows how to do golf right: get Tom Fazio to design this and its "equal sister" for a "great pair" of layouts, build a clubhouse with a veranda overlooking the course and a halfway house for noshing at the 10th tee, hire forecaddies and caddies and work with Audubon International to make the whole thing environmentally friendly; in other words, they offer an overall experience that's "as good as you will find anywhere."

Timberton | ▽ 26 | 21 | 19 | 22 | $70 |
22 Clubhouse Dr., Hattiesburg; 601-584-4653; www.timberton-golf.com
Creekside/Lakeview: 6740/5430; 73.4/69.7; 135/129
Lakeview/Valley: 6735/5487; 72.7/69.5; 131/127
Valley/Creekside: 7003/5439; 73.4/70.5; 145/132
■ Down-home duffers "don't care which" of these "terrific" nines "you tee off on"; "you'll enjoy" them all for "elevation changes", "undulating greens" and a "shot variety" on generous fairways and protected putting surfaces "cut out of Loblolly pine forest"; though Lakeview might be the easiest, it's also the most scenic.

Missouri

Kansas City

Tiffany Greens | ▽ 26 | 26 | 22 | 18 | $69 |
10111 N. Helena Ave.; 816-880-9600; www.tiffanygreensgolf.com; 6977/5391; 73.5/70.6; 133/121
■ "Wonderful in all respects", the state's No. 1–rated Course and Facilities include a "great clubhouse and pro shop" doling out "the best free tees in the world", plus a "fabulous practice" area; the "generous fairways and undulating greens" at the "tremendous" home of the Senior PGA Tour TD Waterhouse Championship are "convenient to the airport for a quick round" before you fly.

Lake of the Ozarks

Osage National | ▽ 25 | 21 | 19 | 17 | $65 |
Osage Hills Rd., Lake Ozark; 573-365-1100; www.osagenational.com
Links/Mountain: 7165/5076; 74.7/69.9; 139/121
Mountain/River: 7150/5016; 75.6/69.3; 145/119
River/Links: 7103/5026; 74.6/69.1; 141/120
☑ "If you're on this side of the lake", it's "worth playing" the "pretty holes" at this "good Palmer" 27; it's "beautiful" say locals who rate it among their "favorites", with hill-loving hackers hollering that "the Mountain nine is the best part" while water rats root for the River; too bad "poor service" means "tees are not properly marked" and the course can be "in average to below-average shape."

Tan-Tar-A, The Oaks | 23 | 20 | 22 | 18 | $79 |
State Rd. KK, Osage Beach; 573-348-8521; 800-826-8272; www.tan-tar-a.com; 6432/3931; 72.1/62.5; 134/103
☑ "The Oaks loves women", giving them "the advantage over men" on a "tough" resort layout where it seems you can't "drive on the fairway with a cart or your driver"; honeymooners hacking up "well-maintained" greens overlooking the Lake of the Ozarks "enjoy it", if they can get on it – it's "hard to get a tee time in the summer", but when you do, no matter your gender, "bring extra balls."

Springfield

Branson Creek | – | – | – | – | $90 |
144 Maple St., Hollister; 417-339-4653; www.bransoncreekgolf.com; 7036/5032; 73.0/68.6; 133/113
"Beautifully laid out and maintained", this Tom Fazio resort track is a challenging par 71 that weaves through the dips and heights

of the Ozarks, with elevated tee boxes for lovely mountain views and five sets of tees so any golfer can find an appropriate test; there's "no out of bounds", so "errant shots can leave a few interesting lies among the rocks and weeds", but whatever your trouble, "the free gourmet coffee" before your round should help "make up for it."

St. Louis (see also Illinois)

Innsbrook Resort   21 | 19 | 17 | 20 | $50
1 Innsbrook Estates Dr., Innsbrook; 636-928-3366;
www.innsbrook-resort.com; 6465/5035; 70.0/67.7; 130/120
☑ Hop on a plane, land in St. Louis, take a 45-minute drive out to Lake Aspen, and while your wimpy colleagues work their way around the massive business resort's putt-putt track, you can go a round on the "hilly" real course where the "water features are well placed" on a "tight front nine and an open back"; "some holes are very beautiful", but prepare for "conditioning that's not consistent."

Missouri Bluffs   26 | 23 | 22 | 17 | $85
18 Research Park Circle, Saint Charles; 636-939-6494;
www.mobluffs.com; 7047/5197; 74.4/69.2; 140/115
■ With a "great design by Fazio and superior management by Walters Golf", no wonder "one of St. Louis' nicest" is "set to go private"; in the meantime, it's "in prime shape" and open to the public, so go for a "great experience" involving "dramatic elevation changes, tall trees and no houses" while you still can because it's no bluff that, pretty soon, the only non-members allowed to "hike through these hills" will be "deer, turkeys and an occasional snake."

Pevely Farms 🏌   24 | 22 | 21 | 22 | $69
400 Lewis Rd., Eureka; 636-938-7000; 7115/5250; 74.6/70.7; 138/115
☑ "A beautiful course" "on the bluffs over the Mermac River" where "you can see for miles", this "surprising jewel in a very rural setting" "plays long" and is "always in good shape"; the "clubhouse and restaurant are worth the drive" "pretty far from St. Louis", but "housing construction will surely reduce" the facility's "rustic, serene" "charm", which is already lost on macho medalists who think it's got "too many flat, vanilla holes."

Quail Creek   20 | 13 | 15 | 18 | $58
6022 Wells Rd.; 314-487-1988; www.quailcreekgolf.com;
6984/5244; 73.6/70.0; 141/118
☑ "Water, sand, hills, doglegs – every deterrent imaginable" makes this "one of the toughest courses in the area"; despite "inconsistent greens", it's possible to have "pleasant rounds here" on "some really nice holes", but the biggest hazard on a track that "plays very long" might be "no restrooms other than the clubhouse."

Montana

Big Fork

Eagle Bend, Championship 🏌   – | – | – | – | $57
279 Eagle Bend Dr., Bigfork; 406-837-7310; 800-255-5641;
www.eaglebendgolf.com; 6724/5397; 71.4/70.1; 128/123
If you're lucky, the eagles will bend your way at this top-flight 27-holer in a golfing and yachting community on Flathead Lake; in

1995, Jack Nicklaus added nine to the original 18 holes, and the whole big bird is a "fun course" now featuring some serious carries and doglegs on soft fairways to excellent greens with gorgeous views of the lake, the Swan Mountains and Glacier National Park.

Butte

Old Works   ▽ 27 | 23 | 23 | 25 | $40

1205 Pizzini Way, Anaconda; 406-563-5989; 888-229-4833;
www.oldworks.org; 7705/5348; 76.0/70.3; 133/124
■ "Awwwesome, baaabyyy" shout shagadelic shotmakers working out on this "out of the way" Nicklaus design that makes "ingenious use" of a former Superfund site, blending the old smoke stack and buildings of a copper smelting plant into a "picturesque course" that stretches to an astounding 7,700 yards; after your round, take a breather at nearby Glacier or Yellowstone National Parks, or visit historic Anaconda and its surrounding ghost towns.

Nebraska

Lincoln

Wilderness Ridge   – | – | – | – | $65

1800 Wilderness Woods Pl.; 402-421-2525;
www.wildernessridgegolf.com; 7107/5965; 74.9/68.9; 133/118
"If you're anything above an eight handicap, don't even think about the black tees" at this sprawling, environmentally friendly track that sits on the edge of a wilderness preserve where 22 lakes puddle and four waterfalls plummet along a mile-and-a-half of streams winding through "generous fairways and large greens"; a stunning stone-and-log clubhouse, a great driving range and GPS on the carts add a huge helping of civilization to this wilderness.

Woodland Hills   – | – | – | – | $35

6000 Woodland Hills Dr., Eagle; 402-475-4653;
www.woodlandhillsgolf.com; 6592/4945; 72.6/70.3; 132/122
"Shhh . . ." whisper secretive wood-wielders, as this "very good course" is "never busy", and they don't want word to get out that it's "less than you would expect to pay" for "beautiful bentgrass fairways" "full of trees and water" and carts with GPS to "give you exact measurement to the pin as well as a map of each green"; if others knew how "great" it was, this "favorite" might be swamped.

North Platte

Heritage Hills   – | – | – | – | $27

6000 Clubhouse Dr., McCook; 308-345-5032; 888-740-2488;
6800/5800; 73.7/74.8; 130/130
This muni "oasis" in "middle-of-nowhere" southwest Nebraska serves up an open and relatively tame front nine to get your juices flowing for a testy back that weaves through rugged canyons and gullies with scenic views of the hardscrabble countryside; it's got a "great pace of play", so you can fly through to a softer landing at the Heritage Hills restaurant where the food and drink will enhance the memory of your round or help you forget the pain; try it on a "Play the West" package with four neighboring courses.

Wild Horse ⏱   – | – | – | – | $35
40950 Road 768, Gothenburg; 308-537-7700; 6805/4668; 73.0/71.7; 125/123
Wild horses couldn't drag dollar-wise drivers away from what
they claim is "the absolute best value in Nebraska"; it's worth
galloping, trotting, cantering or "driving out of your way to play"
the "spectacular" spread, but you don't have to – it's right by the
highway ramp, so you can just "get off I-80"; if you do, you'll find
"minimal facilities" but a "wonderful course" that's so "fun" and
in such "great condition" that you might consider leaving "the wife
home so you can play 36" or, better still, lose the husband and check
out the special women's clinic.

Omaha

Player's Club At Deer Creek   – | – | – | – | $62
12101 Deer Creek Dr.; 402-963-9950;
www.playersclubomaha.com; 7088/5277; 74.1/65.1; 140/116
In rolling bentgrass fairways, multi-tiered greens, deep bunkers
and water on 10 of 18 holes, Arnold Palmer has scrawled his long
and challenging signature across farmland in northwest Omaha;
generous landing areas, large greens and multiple tee boxes allow
hackers of any ability to have an enjoyable day, while players of
any appetite will find a fine meal under the vaulted ceiling next to
the large stone fireplace in the clubhouse.

Quarry Oaks   ▽ 28 | 25 | 24 | 25 | $53
16600 Quarry Oaks Dr., Ashland; 402-944-6000; 888-944-6001;
www.quarryoaks.com; 7077/5378; 73.2/70.7; 135/131
■ "In a state that's supposedly flat from one end to the other, the
elevation changes are never expected" on the "rolling hills" of
Nebraska's "most beautiful course", which "winds in and out of
old oaks so dense you feel you are alone, with the exception of
the occasional turkey wandering across the green"; "only five
minutes from Mahoney State Park between Lincoln and Omaha",
it offers "incredible views of the Platte River on the back nine",
when you get the rare chance to peek through the trees.

Nevada

★ **Best in State**
29 Shadow Creek, *Las Vegas*
28 Edgewood Tahoe, *Reno*
   Reflection Bay, *Las Vegas*
   Primm Valley, Lakes, *Las Vegas*
27 Primm Valley, Desert, *Las Vegas*

Las Vegas

Angel Park, Mountain 🏁   19 | 19 | 18 | 16 | $165
100 S. Rampart Rd.; 702-254-4653; 888-629-3929;
www.angelpark.com; 6722/5150; 72.4/69.9; 128/119
■ "Regardless of how you play, you've got beautiful scenery" at
this "straightforward" muni with views of the Spring and Red Rock
Mountains and the city skyline; it's "a tad breezy", and a tad
"expensive if you're from out of town", but it still offers "good value
by Las Vegas standards", considering it's "convenient to the Strip"
with "great service and facilities", including the "plus of a putting

course"; however, like so much else in Sin City, it's "not as deserty as you may think" and "it's not a slice of heaven."

Angel Park, Palm 🔙 19 | 20 | 18 | 18 |$165
100 S. Rampart Rd.; 702-254-4653; 888-629-3929;
www.angelpark.com; 6525/4570; 70.9/66.2; 129/111
☑ "If you don't like wind, schedule your tee time for early morning" at the "much easier" but "still beautiful" – and, some sensitive types say, "nicer" – sister of the Mountain course; on the other hand, you may want a little "afternoon" breeze to spice up this "straightforward", "wide-open" layout or you may find yourself reciting the mantra of Vegas' eternal overstimulation – "ho-hum."

Bali Hai 🏌 🔙 23 | 22 | 24 | 10 |$295
5160 Las Vegas Blvd. S.; 702-450-8000; 888-397-2499;
www.waltersgolf.com; 7002/5535; 73.0/71.5; 130/121
☑ "Get ready to mortgage your house" to make good on the "hefty tag" of "an enjoyable round" "complete with a helpful caddie" and "a recommended forecaddie" on "a very walkable", "immaculate" course "right on the Strip"; the "service is excellent" indeed, as is the Wolfgang Puck chow, but the course is "squeezed onto a parcel of land" where "too many planes overhead" as well as "the Interstate and power lines on top of you" undermine the palm-tree-and-lava theme – "you'd have to be hallucinating to think you were in the South Pacific."

Bear's Best Las Vegas 🏌 🔙 ▽ 27 | 26 | 26 | 20 |$235
11111 W. Flamingo Rd.; 702-804-8500; www.bearsbest.com;
7194/5043; 74.0/68.7; 147/116
■ "A spectacular course in great shape", this new Nicklaus design is more "meticulously groomed" than the average Bear cub and only "will get better with age"; already, the "superb clubhouse" is as good as it gets, while the "mandatory forecaddie makes it all the more fun" – you just better have a "great evening at the blackjack table" if you want to pay off that greens fee.

Desert Pines 🏌 17 | 19 | 18 | 17 |$175
3415 E. Bonanza Rd.; 702-388-4400; www.waltersgolf.com;
6810/5873; 70.4/69.4; 122/116
■ "Pine trees in the desert, what a concept" – who else could come up with the idea for a "nice Southern course" that's "handy to downtown" Vegas but Pete Dye, who has built a "tight", "short", "narrow" track "in top condition" not far from the Strip; it's a "great deal if you play after 11 AM", though the "friendly staff" might remind you you're not on the Atlantic but in the parched Southwest, so you should "bring a canteen and a mule" – "maybe once the trees mature it will be more realistic" and less sweltering.

DragonRidge 🔙 ⏲ 26 | 18 | 21 | 17 |$195
552 S. Stephanie St., Henderson; 702-614-4444;
www.dragonridgegolfclub.com; 7039/5040; 72.9/68.3; 143/118
■ There are "views of Vegas from every hole" at this "outstanding" millennial daily fee, host of the 2002 Wendy's Three-Tour Challenge; "in great condition", it "just awaits a new clubhouse" so it can "compete with the best facilities in the area"; don't get so distracted by the neon blinking on the Strip in the background that you forget to "watch for rattlesnakes."

Las Vegas Paiute Resort, Snow Mountain

26 | 24 | 23 | 20 | $165

10325 Nu Wav Kaiv Blvd.; 702-658-1400; 800-711-2833; www.lvpaiutegolf.com; 7146/5341; 73.9/70.4; 125/117

■ The "Indian gods have blessed this" golfing "oasis" amid "miles of [seemingly] nothing" on the Paiute reservation "a bit of a drive from the Strip"; when you spend your vacation banging on slots, the "great, tough" Pete Dye track is so "quiet and peaceful with the mountains in the background" that it's almost "eerie", but it is "one of the best values in an overpriced market", even if the "unrelenting" "desert winds make you think" you've "angered one of those dieties."

Las Vegas Paiute Resort, Sun Mountain

25 | 23 | 22 | 19 | $165

10325 Nu Wav Kaiv Blvd.; 702-658-1400; 800-711-2833; www.lvpaiutegolf.com; 7112/5465; 73.3/71.0; 130/123

■ If you like the idea of a "milder Pete Dye", this is the "perfect course" for you; "it's amazing what water and dollars can do in the middle of a desert", mainly lay down "fun-to-play" "fairways that are plusher than the carpets in most homes"; where "mesmerizing views" refer to both "the natural beauty of the land" and the "good beer-cart girls", it "will make for an excellent getaway once the resort is built" to surround it.

Las Vegas Paiute Resort, Wolf

21 | 23 | 23 | 20 | $195

10325 Nu Wav Kaiv Blvd.; 702-658-1400; 800-711-2833; www.lvpaiutegolf.com; 7604/5130; 76.3/n/a; 149/n/a

■ "Can Las Vegas be any prettier" than this "splendid" Dye course with a "lush" layout, "colorful flowers" and "views of snow-capped mountains"?; "wide fairways", "an island green" and an "unbelievable clubhouse" make it "well worth the ride into the desert" howl packs of putters, and "who cares" if it's "a little pricey" when you can make it up at the blackjack table later?

Legacy, The

18 | 19 | 17 | 15 | $125

130 Par Excellence Dr., Henderson; 702-897-2187; 888-629-3929; www.thelegacygc.com; 7233/5340; 74.5/71; 137/120

☑ "Interesting variety between the front and back", "immaculate" conditioning, "tee boxes in the shapes of card suits on No. 10" and a "great driving range and clubhouse" make this "decent" daily fee a "good backup if you're in a pinch"; but "the wind that blows here can only be rivaled by that found in some of the guestrooms on the Strip", and it's lined in houses with "lots of glass", so you'd better shoot straight, especially on the "three holes that get tight", or you might have to drag the window repairman away from the nudie revue.

Oasis Golf Club, Oasis

25 | 18 | 20 | 22 | $135

100 Palmer Ln., Mesquite; 702-346-7820; www.theoasisgolfclub.com; 6729/4513; 71.7/64.9; 133/109

■ "Elevated tees offer nice views of the surrounding area", which happens to be composed of "stunning" desert canyons at this Palmer-designed semi-private track just over an hour outside of Las Vegas, where the "dramatic elevation changes" are "thrilling"; you "need to be straight off the tee" on the "excellent" layout or (say it ain't so) the thrill is gone, and so is your ball.

Primm Valley, Desert 🏌️ 27 | 25 | 26 | 24 | $195
31900 S. Las Vegas Blvd., Primm; 702-679-5510; 800-386-7837;
www.mgmgrand.com; 7131/5397; 74.2/72.1; 135/124
■ The "facilities are country-club level while the service makes
you feel as if you should tip everyone" at this fairly young but
"maturing" "first-rate" "challenge" "a bit of a hike from the Strip"
in a town with lots of outlet shopping and a monster roller coaster
to keep non-golfers occupied; a "real contrast to the surrounding
arid wasteland", it's a "wonderfully conditioned" "treat for the
eyes" that comes at a discount to vacationers staying at any
MGM Grand Mirage hotel.

PRIMM VALLEY, LAKES 🏌️ 28 | 24 | 27 | 23 | $195
31900 S. Las Vegas Blvd., Primm; 702-679-5510; 800-386-7837;
www.mgmgrand.com; 6945/5019; 74.0/69.1; 134/118
■ "Don't let the drive scare you away" – "if you have to leave
the casinos" on the Strip, commit to a "real schlep" and get in on
the MGM Grand Mirage's "great stay-and-play package deals" at
this "beautifully set-up" "masterpiece" of a sister to the Desert
course; "the wind can really howl" here, so hold onto your toupee,
and afterward "hop" back on the roulette wheel and win a few
spins so when they call this the "poor man's Shadow Creek",
they're not thinking of you.

REFLECTION BAY 🏌️ 28 | 27 | 25 | 17 | $250
75 Montelago Blvd., Henderson; 702-740-4653;
www.lakelasvegas.com; 7261/5166; 74.8/70.7; 138/128
☑ "Awesome says it all" about the "great finishing hole" and other
"real challenges" of this "good Jack Nicklaus" design laid down
amid the "stunning surroundings" of the Lake Las Vegas Resort; it's
"always in perfect condition" in that "very Vegas, manufactured"
way, but "it may be cheaper to fly to Scottsdale and play better
courses", unless you score a reduced rate by rooming at the
adjacent Hyatt Regency, or at the Ritz-Carlton when it opens at
the start of 2003.

Revere at Anthem, The 🏌️ 24 | 19 | 19 | 18 | $185
2600 Evergreen Oaks Dr., Henderson; 702-259-4653; 877-273-8373;
www.revereatanthem.com; 7143/5305; 73.6/73.5; 139/122
■ Oh, listen my friend, and you shall hear of a golf course "built
in the hills above the city" called Revere; it's "very challenging",
with "wonderful views of Nevada", and if that means it's got
"topography" only a "billy goat" could love, take heart in the fact
that "every drive is downhill", so the 7,000-yarder "plays short",
though the "narrow fairways" give that cruising ball "the chance
to smash a window or two."

Rio Secco 26 | 25 | 26 | 15 | $250
2851 Grand Hills Dr., Henderson; 702-889-2400; 888-867-3226;
www.playrio.com; 7332/5684; 75.7/70.7; 142/127
■ "Back tees = death" at this "very difficult" daily fee in the
"foothills of Las Vegas" where Rees Jones plays the grim reaper
with some "neat holes" weaving "through canyons"; if the course
doesn't get you, the wildlife might, as "Tiger sightings" are possible
on Woods' coach's home course, but the scariest thing of all may be
playing without "an expense account" because you don't want to
see what the greens fee can do to a credit card – "gulp."

Royal Links 🏌
20 ｜ 22 ｜ 20 ｜ 11 ｜ $250 ｜

5995 Vegas Valley Dr.; 702-450-8123; 888-427-6682;
www.waltersgolf.com; 7029/5142; 73.7/69.8; 135/115

■ "Each hole is designed to" mimic famous "British Open holes", a "cute idea" that makes this "very well-done" daily fee a "novelty" that's "hokey but fun", especially if you "take a caddie who can explain the relevance of various" design features; despite the castle-like clubhouse, "it's hard to recreate the [Highlands] in the desert", so you probably "won't feel like you've been to Scotland", though you could almost buy a ticket there for the "obscene price" of play here.

SHADOW CREEK
29 ｜ 29 ｜ 28 ｜ 16 ｜ $500 ｜

3 Shadow Creek Dr., North Las Vegas; 702-791-7161; 888-778-3387;
www.shadowcreek.com; 7239/6701

■ If "any round of golf is worth $500", the MGM Mirage's "sinfully good" spread "comes close" – a "truly magical experience" that feels like "playing Pine Valley, only in the desert", "it matches the hype" surrounding it with "lush foliage, running brooks, peacocks", caddies, a "driving range that's nicer than most courses", "Kobe beef in the clubhouse", limousine transport to and fro and "wait-till-you-see-'em 17th and 18th" holes"; flubbing it at this "high rollers' paradise" is "better than losing your money at the tables"; N.B. the formerly private course is awaiting USGA ratings and slopes.

Siena 🏌
▽ 21 ｜ 19 ｜ 20 ｜ 22 ｜ $160 ｜

10575 Siena Monte Ave.; 702-838-4196; 888-689-6469;
www.sienagolfclub.com; 6816/4978; 71.5/68.0; 129/112

■ If you need proof that this is "one of the best values in Vegas", you should know that "lots of local retirees play" this "tough layout" with views of the city skyline and "great risk/reward shots"; it's "new" and "needs time to mature", but it's already in "great shape", and the "facilities are fantastic now that the clubhouse is open."

TPC at The Canyons 🏌
24 ｜ 24 ｜ 23 ｜ 16 ｜ $240 ｜

9851 Canyon Run Dr.; 702-256-2000; www.tpc.com;
7063/5039; 73/67; 131/109

■ Barring "pitons and snakebit vaccine", "bring a lot of balls" for "forced carries to blind landing areas over the canyons" at this "tough, tough, tough" host of the PGA Tour's Invensys Classic; "from the clubhouse to the pro shop and practice facility, everything is so well thought out that you can experience how the pros feel", but of course, they're getting paid and you're paying, so if the rattlers don't get you, the "ridiculous price might make you keel over" – "play twice" and the "reduced second round" will "take the bite out of the fees."

Wolf Creek 🏌
– ｜ – ｜ – ｜ – ｜ $200 ｜

401 Paradise Pkwy., Mesquite; 702-346-3800; 866-252-4653;
www.playthewolf.com; 6994/4169; 75.4/61.0; 154/106

It's "as close as you can get to those impossible golf-hole cartoons and still have a real course" howl Wolverines and Ironmen hacking up this "spectacular" technicolor "stunner" spilling lusciously across the cliffs of the high desert outside Las Vegas at the Paradise Canyon Resort; "beautiful" and shockingly "difficult", it's "like nothing you've ever played before", in your superhero fantasies or in your everyday life.

Reno

EDGEWOOD TAHOE 🕴 28 | 23 | 21 | 17 | $200
180 Lake Pkwy., Lake Tahoe; 775-588-3566; www.edgewood-tahoe.com;
7445/5567; 75.7/71.3; 139/136
■ "Everything goes left to right" at this "slicer's paradise", a
"magnificent" resort course in "pristine condition" with "one of
the most beautiful holes anywhere" on the 16th; for "Lake Tahoe
and mountain views beyond compare", the track's "elevation
makes a difference" to all those famous flubbers who fall in line
here during the Celebrity Golf Championship (in 2002 benefiting the
Uniformed Firefighter Scholarship Fund) and who "don't pass up
the chance to have dinner at sunset in the clubhouse."

Incline Village, Championship ▽ 24 | 17 | 20 | 21 | $125
955 Fairway Blvd., Incline Village; 775-832-1143; 866-925-4653;
www.golfincline.com; 6931/5245; 72.2/70.1; 133/131
☑ "The Spyglass of the Sierras" just may be this "immaculately
groomed, pure, old-style course" by Robert Trent Jones Sr. with
"sweeping views" of the mountains and lake; it's 6,500 feet up, and
"you'll need the elevation for the 600-plus-yard par-5" 4th hole on
the "very tough" layout; the "driving range requires a total redo and
the restaurant and pro shop could use some TLC", but you can get
some yourself at the Hyatt Regency at Lake Tahoe and other area
accommodations offering stay-and-play deals.

Lake Ridge ▽ 21 | 16 | 17 | 18 | $93
1200 Razorback Rd.; 775-825-2200; 800-815-6966;
www.lakeridgegolf.com; 6715/5159; 71.8/68.5; 130/121
■ "The holes are varied and interesting" at this "honest test" with
"more than a few forced carries over water", making for a "very
friendly" experience for scuba-diving drivers; "lending distinction"
is the "famous par 3" "where it's a challenge to land" on the island
green, though it might be an even bigger struggle to avoid "the
rattlesnakes in the tunnel" you ride through to get to the first tee.

New Hampshire

Colebrook

Balsams Panorama 26 | 25 | 25 | 23 | $60
R.R. 1; 603-255-4961; 800-255-0600; www.thebalsams.com;
6804/5069; 72.8/67.8; 130/115
■ Rumor has it "Donald Ross lived on-site while this track was
under construction", and you can see why with "stunning"
"mountain views" that span "three states" and are especially
"breathtaking in the fall"; the resort classic is "well kept" and
"tough as a $2 T-bone", which is ironic, since "the food here is
so good, you're almost too full to play golf"; if you do, "remember,
the ball breaks toward Vermont."

Keene

Bretwood, North ▽ 23 | 16 | 17 | 26 | $35
E. Surry Rd.; 603-352-7626; 6976/5140; 73.3/70.0; 139/121
■ There are "many memorable holes", including "an island green
that you can hit" on this "fun" but "deceptively difficult" course

that's "well groomed but not fussy", with "varied terrain" and "excellent practice facilities"; there seem to be "no rangers" in sight, so on a "typical summer weekend" when it's "crowded", a "round takes five-and-a-half hours", but there's "pretty good grub" to nosh on while you wait, if you can find someone to sell you a sandwich at the "seldom-staffed concessions at the turn."

Shattuck　　　　　▽ 27 | 15 | 15 | 25 | $49
50 Dublin Rd., Jaffrey; 603-532-4300; 6764/4632; 74.1/73.1; 145/139
■ "A test for your manhood" or womanhood "carved into the side of the Monadnock Mountains", this "picturesque but ultra-demanding target" track requires *cajones* of male and female golfers alike, since all players must navigate "over lagoons, swamps and marshlands" onto fairways so "narrow" they're "almost impossible to hit" unless you're a mucho macho straight shooter – needless to say, "bring lots of balls."

Manchester

Souhegan Woods　　　　　▽ 17 | 17 | 17 | 20 | $46
65 Thortons Ferry Rd. II, Amherst; 603-673-0200;
6507/5286; 70.4/70.6; 122/123
■ "Lots of traps" are set in these woods, so "be prepared" to land in "fairway and greenside bunkers", but don't panic because "you can putt out of practically every one" at this "nice, comfortable layout" "for the average player" and the average income: with "good overall conditions", decent "variety" and a "great pro shop", you get real "bang for your buck" and, unfortunately, bite for your buck – play it "if you can stand the black flies."

New Jersey

★ **Best in State**
27 Hominy Hill, *Freehold*
　　Pine Hill, *Cape May*
　　Crystal Springs, Ballyowen, *New York City Area*
26 Sand Barrens, *Cape May*
　　Hawk Pointe, *New York City Area*

Atlantic City

Blue Heron Pines, East　　　　　25 | 22 | 21 | 19 | $125
550 W. Country Club Dr., Cologne; 609-965-4653; 888-478-2746;
www.blueheronpines.com; 7221/5165; 74.8/69.0; 135/120
■ "A great place to play before a night in AC", this "gorgeous" track "away from the grunge" of the shore has "a links vibe" that makes it "wonderful" to "take a motorized handcart and enjoy the walk", just "watch out for the bunkers – they're everywhere"; it's "very penal if you don't find the fairway", but a variety of "tee boxes allows you to accept whatever test you wish" because, after all, you wouldn't be headed for the casinos if you weren't a gambler.

Blue Heron Pines, West　　　　　24 | 22 | 22 | 18 | $125
550 W. Country Club Dr., Cologne; 609-965-4653; 888-478-2746;
www.blueheronpines.com; 6810/5053; 72.9/69.2; 132/119
☑ "Excellent teaching facilities" help make this "well-maintained, scenic" spread "one of the best public plays in the state"; still, it's

"a notch below" its sibling because it's "very flat", "every par 4 looks the same" and it's "filled with knuckleheads" who, along with the "frequent planes flying overhead, detract from the experience"; "try to catch one of their specials" "during the week", or the "too-darn-expensive" prices might have you gasping "these New Jersey shore courses must think they're in Beverly Hills."

Harbor Pines 🏌 23 | 21 | 20 | 18 | $120
500 Saint Andrews Dr., Egg Harbor Township; 609-927-0006; www.harborpines.com; 6827/5099; 72.3/68.8; 129/118
■ "Get away from the beach awhile" on this "well-plotted layout" with "superb conditioning", "lots of water" and "a good diversity of holes" for "beginners and high-handicappers" about 25 minutes as the seagull flies from Frantic City; to avoid "high summer prices", tee off "after 2 PM for a bargain", and don't skip "post-round cocktails on the deck overlooking" the fairways, a "highlight" at a "vanilla" course where the only thing hard is the liquor.

Sea Oaks 23 | 19 | 20 | 19 | $105
99 Golf View Dr., Little Egg Harbor Township; 609-296-2656; www.seaoaksgolf.com; 6950/5150; 72.4/73.8; 129/129
☑ "Beautiful to look at" and "a joy to play", with "great risk/reward" shots and "pretty big greens", this newish course "needs another year or so, but it will soon be" "top of the list" for seaside swingers; regardless of the "black flies" and "pins sometimes set on false fronts and halfway down ledges", golfers gush "if I were a gopher, I would make my home here" it's so "nice" – humans themselves can linger now that the clubhouse is complete.

SEAVIEW MARRIOTT, BAY 🏌 22 | 25 | 24 | 18 | $129
401 S. New York Rd., Absecon; 609-748-7680; 800-932-8000; www.seaviewgolf.com; 6247/5017; 70.7/68.4; 122/114
☑ Play is "100 percent dependent on wind" at this "beautiful, historic" host of both the ShopRite LPGA Classic and Sam Snead's 1942 PGA Championship clincher; the "views of the marshes are pretty" despite the "biting flies" they harbor, "the practice facilities are excellent", "the resort is a top-notch" octogenarian and, though Donald Ross' classic course "could use a bit of a manicure", it is "very convenient to AC", which is a boon, since "you may have to hit blackjack to cover the greens fee" on summer weekends.

Seaview Marriott, Pines 🏌 24 | 25 | 24 | 19 | $129
401 S. New York Rd., Absecon; 609-748-7680; 800-932-8000; www.seaviewgolf.com; 6371/5276; 71.7/69.8; 128/119
☑ "You rarely see another golfer on the tree-lined" fairways of this "classic Pine Barrens beauty", but you do encounter swarms of "murderous bugs", so "bring spray" and be prepared for "straight", "long par 3s" on a course that's "tougher than its sister"; the "gentleman's club" of a Marriott "hotel is very, very, very old", but the "nice facilities" include a Faldo Golf Institute for an pre-round brushup and an Elizabeth Arden Salon for a post-play rubdown.

Twisted Dune 23 | 9 | 15 | 19 | $99
2101 Ocean Heights Ave., Egg Harbor Township; 609-653-8019; 7384/5381; 79.8/71.8; 132/124
☑ "Wear a hat on a warm day, because there's only one tree" and "they encourage walking" on this new "true links course" where

"little fanfare and posturing" provide a "wonderful, memorable and different" twist on the usual pretentious offerings; "lots of risk/ reward holes" and some of "the best greens you'll ever putt on" make for a "stunning" "adventure" "you'll want to return" to, particularly at "spring and fall rates."

Cape May

Cape May National
20 | 15 | 15 | 17 | $85

Rte. 9 & Florence Ave.; 609-898-1005; 800-227-9874; www.cmngc.com; 6905/4711; 72.9/68.8; 136/115

■ Cape May bed-and-breakfasters brave "biting flies" to play this "beautiful" but "not terribly challenging" daily fee that "cleverly incorporates a shore-terrain" "protected nature reserve" into a "nice layout" with "a spectacular finish"; however, "maintenance isn't what you'd expect for the price you pay in season", so "somebody should get on the ball, buy some grass seed" and try to keep all those fine feathered waders from eating it.

Pine Hill 🏄 ⏱
27 | 22 | 22 | 19 | $130

500 W. Branch Ave., Pine Hill; 856-435-3100; 877-450-8866; www.golfpinehill.com; 6969/4922; 74.2/68.3; 140/121

■ If you "don't know some big shot", this "great Fazio layout" is as "close" as you're gonna get to "playing Pine Valley next door"; "the only truly hilly course in South Jersey", it's "tough even from the whites", with "steep lies and elevations" affording "wonderful Philadelphia views"; it's "young, but it will mature like wine", and in the meantime, the "great staff" will pour you a glass of the stuff at the "excellent restaurant" in the "beautiful clubhouse", if you've got the jack – the fee is "a bit expensive for the average Joe."

Sand Barrens
26 | 22 | 21 | 22 | $115

1765 Rte. 9 N., Swainton; 609-465-3555; 800-465-3122; www.sandbarrensgolf.com
North/South: 6969/4946; 72.7/68.0; 133/120
South/West: 6895/4971; 71.7/68.3; 130/119
West/North: 7092/4951; 73.2/67.9; 135/119

■ "While the family is at the beach, spend your time playing in the sand" at this "tremendous" 27-hole shore "favorite" where "the fairways are like carpets and the greens are unsurpassed"; "it lives up to its name" with "relentless" traps so deep they "need a tow rope to pull you out", and maybe the "GPS on the carts" to find you first; if you're stranded in that waste bunker long enough, you might be hungry for a meal afterward at one of the many fabulous Cape May restaurants nearby.

Freehold

Eagle Ridge
21 | 21 | 20 | 19 | $78

2 Augusta Blvd., Lakewood; 732-901-4900; www.eagleridgegolf.com; 6900/4800; 72.4/68.3; 132/125

■ With so many "surprising" "elevation changes for a South Jersey course", you "must use a cart" at this "flat-out" (but not outright flat) "fun" daily fee that's "very good for women" and those who like a little post-round partying, since it has an "excellent restaurant and watering hole"; the "links layout" has "raised tee boxes", "slick greens", "long par 3s" and superb conditioning, and the biggest hazard might be "the passing wheelchairs from the retirement community surrounding the course."

HOMINY HILL
`27` `16` `15` `26` `$60`

92 Mercer Rd., Colts Neck; 732-462-9223;
www.monmouthcountyparks.com; 7049/5793; 74.2/73.6; 131/129

☑ It's "the Augusta of NJ", it's "Monmouth County's answer to Bethpage", it's "the jewel in the muni crown of Jersey" – it's "grip-it-and-rip-it heaven", "living up to its billing" with "a lot of doglegs", "deceptive bunkering, large greens and good-size landing areas"; it's a "classic RT Jones Sr. layout" at a "great price for locals", but even if you're "out-of-county", it's "worth the effort", the "attitude", the "tough tee times" and "rates that are too high."

Howell Park
`23` `14` `16` `25` `$43`

225 Southard Ave., Farmingdale; 732-938-4771;
www.monmouthcountyparks.com; 6916/5725; 73.4/73.0; 128/127

☑ You could argue whether this "often overlooked" layout is "second only to" or "the equal of if not superior to" Hominy, but either way it's certainly "another gem in Monmouth County" that, like its cousin, is "fabulously challenging", with "interesting holes"; even if the "conditioning is inconsistent" and the "tricked-up greens make it harder than it should be", it's "worth the patience to get on" it, and the "friendly staff" will help ease the wait.

NYC Metro Area (see also New York)

Beaver Brook
`18` `16` `16` `17` `$85`

25 Country Club Dr., Annandale; 908-735-4200;
www.beaverbrookcc.com; 6601/5384; 71.7/71.7; 125/122

☑ "There are deer everywhere and bear tracks in the bunkers" at this "tight", "hilly" animal kingdom about an hour west of the NYC's urban jungle; it's "easy to get to and to get a tee time on", and it's "usually well maintained", with "fun par 5s and well-sculpted greens", but birdie lovers bitten by "bugs", "crowds", "slow play" and "poor service" say "the Beaver isn't much more than a rodent these days."

Bowling Green
`20` `13` `16` `20` `$67`

53 School House Rd., Milton; 973-697-8688;
www.bowlinggreengolf.com; 6771/5051; 72.4/69.4; 131/127

■ With so many balls run afoul of the "tight, pine-lined" fairways, it "sounds like a pinball machine in the woods" around this "great [Geoffrey] Cornish layout" offering "value for walkers"; it's "difficult beyond the slope rating", with "some long, uphill par 3s" and an "18th that's one of the best par 5s in the state", but there's a "nice 19th hole", so "all but scratch-level golfers" can lick their wounds.

CRYSTAL SPRINGS, BALLYOWEN 斜
`27` `23` `24` `19` `$125`

105-137 Wheatsworth Rd., Hamburg; 973-827-5996;
www.crystalgolfresort.com; 7032/4903; 73.1/67.7; 127/109

■ "While the bagpipes emit gutteral yet soothing sounds", the "sheep graze" and "the golden gorse glows as the sun sets on a glorious day of golf", you "finish off that pint of bitter" at the 19th hole and feel "like you're in *Brigadoon*", not just over an hour out of NYC; all this plus "immaculate conditions", "true, fast greens better than at most private clubs" and the resort's "beautiful amenities" makes the "high-end" linkster "highly recommended", though someone should tell the "obnoxious" staff that the "wind is dangerous for kilt-wearers."

Crystal Springs, Black Bear 🔛
20 | 19 | 20 | 18 | $78

138 State Rte. 23 N., Hamburg; 973-209-2226;
www.crystalgolfresort.com; 6673/4756; 72.2/67.7; 130/116

◩ Given "beautiful mountain vistas", some "exciting elevated tee shots" and "park-like fairways", Crystal Springs' "most basic", "best-value" layout "can be enjoyable for higher-handicappers", particularly if they "bring their foot wedges to get out of the trees", enroll at the David Glenz Golf Academy and giddayup to avoid the "obsessive marshals"; better ball lofters believe the least "boring" things about it are the "good burgers at the turn", while offspring of "beat-up" duffers won't find the adjacent Mountain Creek Adventure Park too tedious either.

Crystal Springs, Crystal Springs Course 🔛
21 | 20 | 20 | 16 | $90

123 Crystal Springs Rd., Hamburg; 973-827-7144;
www.crystalgolfresort.com; 6816/5091; 74.1/70.5; 137/123

◩ "You'll either love or hate" this design by Robert von Hagge, who's akin to "Pete Dye on acid"; if you love it, it'll be for the "meticulous maintenance" and the "memorable" par-3 "island green" 10th "built in a quarry" you can "ping-pong your ball off"; if you hate it, it'll be because it's so "penal" and "goony-golf" "gimmicky" that "the only things missing are a windmill and a clown's mouth", but try telling that to those "packs of businessmen entertaining clients."

Crystal Springs, Wild Turkey 🔛
24 | 19 | 22 | 20 | $90

123 Crystal Springs Rd., Hamburg; 973-827-1444;
www.crystalgolfresort.com; 7100/5015; 74.8/69.0; 131/118

◩ Certainly no turkey and only mildly wild, this 2001 chick will "grow into a strong course" "once the trees, etc. mature" thanks to an "interesting distribution of long and mid-length par 4s", "demanding par 5s" and an "über par 3 over a lake and rock outcropping"; nevertheless, "wide fairways" and "large greens" make for "lots of birdie opportunities", but "bring suntan lotion" lest you roast, and "don't valet it" or you'll have to wrangle young turks "with a penchant to chat and ignore you."

Farmstead ⏱
19 | 15 | 16 | 19 | $61

88 Lawrence Rd., Lafayette; 973-383-1666;
www.farmsteadgolf.com
Clubview/Lakeview: 6680/5094; 71.9/68.1; 129/116
Lakeview/Valleyview: 6161/4713; 66.6/67.1; 118/116
Valleyview/Clubview: 6221/4929; 70.1/68.1; 124/117

◩ "Lots of wildlife comes out of the woods at dusk" on this "nature lover's delight" of a "sporty" 27-holer in the rolling hills of western Jersey, so watch out for "cow chips" and the "duck" you-know-what, even though "better maintenance recently takes it out of the farm league"; the "Lakeview nine is nice if you have a scuba kit", but long-timers say the "new", "short" Valleyview, with "four par 3s and no driving range", "is the least interesting", so "insist on the Club/Lake" combo, and don't miss out on "the best part of the day, having cocktails in the barn/bar" combo.

Flanders Valley, Red/Gold
| 22 | 13 | 14 | 24 | $49 |

Pleasant Hill Rd., Flanders; 973-584-5382;
www.parks.morris.nj.us.com; 6770/5540; 72.6/72.0; 126/123

■ "Take a hike" on the "beautiful", "hilly Gold", the concluding half of this "great all-around, all-purpose" "challenge" that's so "immaculately maintained", "you'd never know" it's a muni; the Red "front is flat and not as pretty", but "don't avoid" the "gem" because "its rep on the back" is deserved; if you live in Morris County or you're a senior, "it's a bargain", but if you don't, "come Monday after 1 PM" or any day May–August after 6 PM for a rock-bottom rate, say neighbors who pout "I wish Union County could do it this way."

Flanders Valley, White/Blue
| 22 | 12 | 14 | 25 | $49 |

Pleasant Hill Rd., Flanders; 973-584-5382;
6765/5534; 72.7/71.6; 126/122

✍ "They're buying houses in Morris County just so they can" "snag a tee time" and get the "awesome locals' deal" at this "spectacular" "combo of scenic and challenging holes" that's "easier to walk" than its sister spread; "all munis should strive to be like" it, rave excessive fans who claim it's as "efficiently" "run as a Fortune 500 company" – that is, critics crabby over "check-in time" crank, if the staffers at those conglomerates all had "white hair and never worked computers."

Great Gorge ⌂
| 21 | 17 | 19 | 18 | $89 |

State Rte. 517, McAfee; 973-827-5757; www.play27.com
Lake/Quarry: 6819/5390; 69.4/66.6; 125/119
Quarry/Rail: 6826/5539; 68.8/66.8; 120/115
Rail/Lake: 6921/5555; 69.4/67.2; 121/117

■ 'Swingers' has had a new meaning "on the grounds of the old Playboy Club" ever since Sussex County's "straightforward", "scenic" 27-hole "grandaddy" an hour out of NYC was "created under the skilled hand" of George Fazio back in the '70s; though, unlike that of the Bunnies, its condition is "sometimes spotty", there's still plenty to "feast your eyes upon", particularly the "pretty spectacular first tee on the Lake"; "each nine has its own personality", but the "Quarry is especially fun", as one Hef wanna-be who claims to have "made love on its 4th fairway" can attest.

Hawk Pointe ⌂
| 26 | 15 | 19 | 18 | $105 |

294 Rte. 31 S., Washington; 908-689-1870; 877-322-4295;
www.hawkpointegolf.com; 6374/4789; 73.4/58.0; 137/119

✍ "Just off the beaten path of the metropolitan crowd", this millennial "modern-style course tempts" locals "to go for it all on wide landing areas or to play position" on "lush fairways and greens" with "lots of fescue"; it's "expensive" considering the "clubhouse is not yet built" and there are "three or so" "funky holes" that "don't really fit an overall" design that only members are allowed to walk, but cough up the dough and play it anyway before it goes private as planned in the next year or so.

High Bridge Hills
| 21 | 10 | 15 | 21 | $65 |

203 Cregar Rd., High Bridge; 908-638-5055;
www.highbridgehills.com; 6189/4928; 70.2/75.2; 123/128

■ "Bring a weed whacker" to hack your way out of the "ridiculously high, thick fescue" "at this old farm" turned "picturesque" muni with a "very linky feel"; despite the "Scottish-style gorse", it's a "great find" with a "nice practice facility" at a "solid value", but while the "grass eats balls", you might go hungry, since dining in "the clubhouse is one step above the food in the beer cart."

Knoll Country Club, West ☉ 　　19 | 17 | 17 | 19 | $66

Knoll & Green Bank Rds., Parsippany; 973-263-7110;
www.knollcountryclub.com; 6735/5840; 72.2/74.4; 128/128

◪ A "hidden gem" with "old-style" "charm", this "1929 layout" is "carved" through "big, fully grown trees" with "large, undulating greens" "you'll never tire of", including "one of the prettiest finishing holes anywhere"; it "needs some TLC", as "it's heavily played" by an upscale "crowd that's less amusing" than the "casual players" on the East course, the "shooting gallery"/"dog track" that serves as its "polar opposite sister."

New Jersey National 　　21 | 17 | 18 | 14 | $110

579 Allen Rd., Basking Ridge; 908-781-9400;
www.newjerseynational.com; 7056/5019; 73.7/68.8; 137/121

◪ "If you enjoy mountain golf", note that "almost no hole is flat" on this "overall good course" that "uses topography and relatively small landing areas to challenge golfers"; while the "facilities are excellent", "glass-like greens", "variable" maintenance, "too many cart-path-only days" and a "staff that treats you as if it's your honor to be there" peeve players who've paid the "high tag"; as for the encroaching "ultra-posh housing", says one "ritzy" neighbor, "darling, get over it."

River Vale ⌸ 　　18 | 14 | 14 | 13 | $93

660 Rivervale Rd., River Vale; 201-391-2300;
www.rivervalecc.com; 6470/5293; 71.4/70.7; 128/123

◪ The "beautiful rolling layout proves tougher than it looks" at this "great traditional" track with "narrow greens" on a "mature design" created by Donald Ross in 1928; drivers drone *domo arigato* to the Asian owners for the clubhouse's "great Japanese food", but bargain ball strikers believe it's a "touch expensive" considering it's "cart-path-only" and "can get slow", while the "driving range is a demolition zone."

Sunset Valley 　　21 | 12 | 14 | 23 | $48

47 W. Sunset Rd., Pompton Plains; 973-835-1515;
6483/6039; 71.4/71.0; 129/122

■ "The dance floors can be pretty slick", so get your feet firmly planted at this "fantastic public course nestled in the hills of Morris County", where you can cut a rug on the carpet-like "fairways and greens" of a "hilly, tough" layout; it's got a "grumpy staff", "horrible food service" and "no clubhouse, locker room or driving range", but twinkle-toed tracksters still "can't wait to get back", "if they can get a tee time."

Trenton

Architects 　　25 | 13 | 20 | 19 | $90

700 Strykers Rd., Phillipsburg; 908-213-3080;
www.thearchitectsgolfclub.com; 6863/5233; 73.3/71.0; 130/123

■ "The only way for mere mortals to play the 13th at Augusta" is to come to this west Jersey daily fee where "each hole" recreates a "design of a noted golf architect"; though it's "only two years old", it's "nicely grown in" and "looks like it's been around for years", except that the temporary "clubhouse and pro shop are pretty meager" and the "dining room is one step ahead of the food cart" – perhaps when the permanent facilities do open, they'll feature meals copped from the menus of 18 famous restaurants to complete the faux experience?

Knob Hill　19　12　16　14　$78
360 Rte. 33, Manalapan; 732-792-7722;
6500/5000; 72.2/69.5; 130/120
✍ "From your opening tee shot to the uphill climb to the 18th, this course challenges every part of your game", as "water in some interesting places" and deep "woods" mean that "errant tee shots will guarantee you penalty strokes"; check out the newly completed clubhouse – just don't bring the Kodak because the "surrounding homes are ugly with a capital U."

Pine Barrens　26　21　21　19　$115
540 S. Hope Chapel Rd., Jackson; 732-408-1154; 877-746-3227;
www.pinebarrensgolf.com; 7118/5209; 73.5/72.5; 132/126
■ "With a couple more years of maturity", this 1999 "target" track "cut into the lush fauna" off the Garden State "will fit right in there with the terrific upscale South Jersey courses"; even now, it's an "outstanding challenge" with "a joy" of a back side sporting a par-3 "beautiful monster" of "pure intimidation" "over a quarry pit", a "600-plus-yard par 5" at the finish and "more sand than the shore"; it "comes close but is not quite" the "poor man's Pine Valley" it bills itself to be – "facilities that leave a little to be desired" are a bit too barren for that.

New Mexico

Albuquerque

Paa-Ko Ridge　▽ 29　23　25　27　$69
1 Club House Dr., Sandia Park; 505-281-6000; 866-898-5987;
www.paakoridge.com; 7562/5702; 75.2/71.8; 138/134
✍ On the high desert of the Sania Mountains lies "the most pristine golf course imaginable", with "magnificent views" and a "country-club atmosphere" at a "steal" of a price; it's a "treat to play", with "tough rough", "sloped greens" and "difficult tee boxes", but the "terrain is too hard to walk" and there are "no carts on the fairways", which means "in high season" your round becomes "a six-hour death march" – relax with a stay on a package deal at the Marriott in Albuquerque 20 minutes away, and "play on a spring or fall" morning, when "first off in the dew is heaven."

Piñon Hills　▽ 26　18　21　29　$29
2101 Sunrise Pkwy., Farmington; 505-327-9673;
www.farmington.nm.us; 7249/5522; 73.3/71.1; 130/126
■ "Incredible sunsets on the glowing red rocks" are a must-see at this "must-play" on the mesas of the Four Corners area "a long way from anywhere", but close enough to Farmington for "gorgeous city views"; hyperbolic hookers call it "the world's absolute greatest value" for dirt-cheap play on a "well-run", "first-class" muni layout that just might rate the title "Troon on a shoestring."

UNIVERSITY OF NEW MEXICO CHAMPIONSHIP GOLF COURSE
26 | 18 | 19 | 26 | $43

3601 University Blvd. SE; 505-277-4546; www.unm.edu/~golf;
7272/5451; 74.3/71.0; 134/129

■ "When they say 'elevated', they mean elevated" of the greens at this "excellent" collegian with "many blind shots" but also lots of "scenic views of the downtown skyline" around "twists and turns", where the "maintenance crew does a super job" keeping "wonderful conditions"; "take a cart" and "watch out for geese", since "overflights" doesn't just refer to the "Air Force Base located nearby" but those honking migrants who land "on the fairways."

Las Cruces

Inn of the Mountain Gods ⌂
▽ 23 | 21 | 19 | 20 | $70

Carrizo Canyon Rd., Mescalero; 505-257-5141; 800-446-2963;
www.innofthemountaingods.com; 6478/5478; 70.1/70.2; 128/128

■ Golfing gossips swear that 10-time PGA Tour winner "Fuzzy Zoeller said this was the best mountain course he ever played"; "the highest regulation" track in southern New Mexico, it sits in what is "truly the gods' country" at a tribally owned, family-friendly resort on the Mescalero Apache reservation nestled in the White and Sacramento ranges, where "you can have a great time" on "holes front and back", especially the "incredible" par-3 9th.

New York

★ **Best in State**
29 Bethpage State Park, Black, *Long Island*
27 Seven Oaks, *Finger Lakes*
    Leatherstocking, *Albany*
26 Links at Hiawatha Landing, *Finger Lakes*
    Bethpage State Park, Red, *Long Island*
25 Montauk Downs State Park, *Long Island*
    Grossinger, Big G, *Catskills*
    Concord Resort, Monster, *Catskills*
    Branton Woods, *Hudson Valley*
    Long Island National, *Long Island*

Adirondacks

Lake Placid Resort, Links
21 | 19 | 19 | 20 | $65

1 Olympic Dr., Lake Placid; 518-523-2556; 800-874-1980;
www.lakeplacidresort.com; 7006/5133; 74.0/72.1; 131/111

◪ "The fainthearted need not apply" croon Lake Placid loopsters whooping like loons over the "daunting length" of this "stunning beauty", a "nicely designed" and "well-maintained" "test made difficult by long rough and undulating greens"; though the "gem" at a resort built for summer family frolicking "features beautiful vistas and is among the Adirondack's standouts", its "young staff" needs a few more seasons to mature.

Lake Placid Resort, Mountain
▽ 20 | 21 | 19 | 20 | $44

1 Olympic Dr., Lake Placid; 518-523-2556; 800-874-1980;
www.lakeplacidresort.com; 6156/4995; 70.8/72.0; 126/120

■ Mountain goats playing on this "good overall" "but not great" centenarian bleat that it's "not as nice as the Links" at the same resort; nevertheless, "in an area where there is not much of a choice", "you can't beat the breathtaking views" from its "beautiful location"; "the weather is spotty and the season is short", so "play it in July", and then take a dip after at the lakeside beach.

Sagamore, The   23 | 23 | 23 | 18 | $108
Frank Cameron Rd., Bolton Landing; 518-644-9400;
www.thesagamore.com; 6392/5177; 72.0/73.0; 133/122
☑ "Your ball can almost roll off the mountain" at this "classic", "old Donald Ross course" at a "true Adirondack legend" of a resort; needless to say, there are "stunning views", particularly from the "first tee", and the "bright, fresh air adds to the experience"; insiders say "play this year" – it's recently been "beautifully" spruced up, and it "hasn't been in this shape in over two decades."

Whiteface Club   ▽ 18 | 18 | 19 | 20 | $39
Whiteface Inn Rd., Lake Placid; 518-523-2551; 800-422-6757;
www.whitefaceclub.com; 6345/5635; 70.5/69.2; 122/119
☑ Starting holes "in a thick grove of trees" "demand accuracy and management" at this "historic" resort course "not far from the shores of Lake Placid"; after that, "you play on lush meadows where the only consideration is a stray fox running across the fairway", plus those nasty "black flies in springtime"; critical cottagers would rather "chat with author, keeper of local lore and pro J. Peter Martin", because he's a "bigger gem" than a track "in bad shape" with "slow greens."

Albany

Leatherstocking   27 | 23 | 24 | 21 | $80
60 Lake St., Cooperstown; 607-547-5275; 1-800-348-6222;
www.leatherstockinggolf.com; 6416/5178; 70.8/70.2; 135/122
■ "If you go to Cooperstown for the Baseball Hall of Fame, don't forget your clubs", because this is "among the most interesting courses in New York State", with "difficult approaches", "lots of bunkers" and "one of the best finishing holes ever" along Lake Otsego; if you wanna play even an iota as well as LPGA star Laura Diaz, you can knock a few balls with her father, Ron Philo, who's head instructor on a staff that's "always polite and helpful."

Saratoga National 斗   24 | 22 | 20 | 19 | $125
458 Union Ave., Saratoga Springs; 518-583-4653;
www.golfsaratoga.com; 7265/4954; 74.5/70.0; 143/125
☑ "Long and tough, but not murderous", this "stellar" stretch "serenely carved through tall oaks" has golfers gambling on "the three-plus-hour drive from New York City just to play it again"; "you might as well go when you're up in August for the ponies", since "you need to win at the races to afford it", and low-rollers are droll about a "snobby" staff that "thinks it's [working at] Pebble Beach."

Catskills

Concord Resort, International ⌂   19 | 16 | 16 | 17 | $55
209 Chalet Rd., Kiamesha Lake; 845-794-4000; 888-448-9686;
www.concordresort.com; 6600/5700; 72.1/69.4; 127/116
☑ Lesser known than its notoriously difficult sister, this Catskiller is "one of the gems of old-style layouts"; it's "off the beaten path"

and "could use some more attention", but it offers "tremendous value" to "anyone who likes a nice, quiet round"; thrill-seekers sneer "why bother when the Monster is next door" taunting you?

Concord Resort, Monster 🏌   25 | 17 | 17 | 18 | $95

209 Chalet Rd., Kiamesha Lake; 845-794-4000; 888-448-9686;
www.concordresort.com; 7650/5200; 76.9/70.6; 137/125
☑ Lurking in a "ghost town" of a resort that's undergoing rehab is "zee biggie"; "sadistic in length and compounded by small, fast greens", it "earns its name", as "even its par 3s will wear you out", though veterans feel it's "not what it used to be, maybe because" the main "facilities are nonexistent" until 2004.

Grossinger, Big G   25 | 15 | 17 | 21 | $85

127 Grossinger Rd., Liberty; 845-292-9000; 888-448-9698;
6907/5730; 73.7/73.5; 129/127
☑ "The colors in October will help you forget how badly you're playing" at this Catskills "classic" punctuated by "big bunkers" and "breathtaking vistas"; its "traditional" layout is "a bit boring" for postmodern putters, but it's "a good place for kids to learn", so sign junior up for specialized lessons, but don't expect too many other amenities, as they "all seem to be gone."

Nevele Grande   20 | 16 | 18 | 20 | $69

1 Nevele Rd, Ellenville; 800-647-6000; www.nevele.com
Blue/Red: 6823/5145; 72.7/72.8; 130/129
Red/White: 6532/4600; 71.4/71.1; 128/126
White/Blue: 6573/4600; 71.8/71.1; 126/126
☑ No, those aren't matzo balls flying on the "White nine's beautiful 7th" at this "serviceable and scenic" 27-hole "target" track attached to a grand old resort where Milton Berle and Red Buttons once wowed 'em in the Stardust Room; as for the other two-thirds, "Blue is the nicest nine, Red is the worst", but all of it is "in good shape" because it's "not overplayed" – "too bad the hotel is a dump" drone Borscht Belt ball launchers who feel the "definite lack of amenities" isn't kosher.

Windham   20 | 18 | 21 | 21 | $52

36 South St., Windham; 518-734-9910;
www.windhamcountryclub.com; 6088/4876; 70.4/69.2; 120/112
■ "The mountain setting alone makes the trip worthwhile" to this "charming course" where a "short, tight" layout with "small greens" "demands" that you "use a lot of irons off the tee"; start with Sunday brunch at the club restaurant, Weatherby's, and afterward, if "you find yourself stuck behind vacationers who don't play much and are taking forever" on those "two or three quirky holes", at least you can take solace in the fact that the track is "kept well in summer."

Finger Lakes

Bristol Harbour 🏌   21 | 20 | 19 | 20 | $55

5500 Seneca Point Rd., Canandaigua; 585-396-2460; 800-288-8248;
www.bristolharbour.com; 6732/5482; 72.6/73.0; 124/126
☑ With a "wide front" "overlooking beautiful Canandaigua Lake" and a "great back" "carved through mountainside forest", this "tight" track is "particularly nice in the fall", when "the changing

leaves" give you something to look at during "slow weekend rounds"; sample local wines as part of an accommodations package and order a bottle afterward at the clubhouse, where "the killer view makes you forget all those sandtraps you were in", "poorly maintained" as they are by a staff with a "bad attitude."

Chenango Valley State Park   ▽ 20 | 13 | 14 | 24 | $23
153 State Park Rd., Chenango Forks; 607-648-9804;
6271/5246; 70.6/69.5; 124/116
■ Happy hookers hail this "uncrowded" woodland state track as "the best value in New York" for a "well-kept" 18 of "moderate difficulty", with "beautiful" scenery that's "fun for the mid- to high-handicapper"; "it's extremely good for a muni" boast alumni of area schools who "drive the three hours each way from Manhattan every year to play our old college course."

Conklin Players Club   – | – | – | – | $42
1520 Conklin Rd., Conklin; 607-775-3042;
www.conklinplayers.com; 6772/4699; 72.5/67.8; 127/116
"The best course you never heard of" just might be this "fantastic layout where no two holes are the same" but all are "worth the trip" to suburban Binghamton say the few fortunate club-wielders konked out by the "challenge" of the water-laden, "mountainside" "find"; "cheap", "playable" and "beautifully maintained", it's also "hilly, so don't walk it."

En-Joie Golf Course   – | – | – | – | $32
722 W. Main St., Endicott; 607-785-1661; 888-436-5643;
www.enjoiegolf.com; 7034/5477; 74.4/71.7; 130/123
"Where else can you play a PGA tournament course for less than $50?" ask the handful who have found the En-Joie-able host of the B.C. Open; "never mind that the staff can be brusque and play favorites even if you have a tee time" – its signature 432-yard par-4 15th, one of the hardest holes on Tour, is worth suffering the attitude.

Greystone   ▽ 29 | 24 | 26 | 25 | $41
1400 Atlantic Ave., Walworth; 315-524-0022; 800-810-2325;
www.234golf.com; 6529/5277; 70.2/70.7; 121/122
■ Savvy upstate linksters agree this Scottish-style course "in the Rochester suburbs" is an "awesome" "layout that's well groomed", with "great finishers" on each side and "very fast greens"; "multiple tees accommodate all levels of play", but even if you're suffering a chronic triple bogey, "you feel like a member every time", since the "friendly starter encourages good-natured ribbing" and "the cart girls are so sweet."

Links at Hiawatha Landing 🏞   26 | 20 | 23 | 25 | $62
2350 Marshland Rd., Apalachin; 607-687-6952;
www.hiawathalinks.com; 7104/5101; 73.5/68.4; 131/113
■ By the shores of Gitche Gumee, aka "on the banks of the Susquehanna" not far from Binghamton, this "amazing star" of a bonny "links challenge" "demands both length and accuracy"; the swinging tribe sings "never be in the heather", "bring a lot of extra balls if you're over a four handicap", play on "more enjoyable weekdays", don't expect much from the "small clubhouse and pro shop", "watch out for bugs in summer" and if you do all that, "you'll love this place."

Seven Oaks
27 | 19 | 21 | 25 | $54

13 Colgate University, Hamilton; 315-824-1432; sevenoaks.colgate.edu; 6915/5315; 73.0/72.0; 127/128

■ There are Raiders invading this "storybook setting", home to Colgate University's golf club, where "an RTJ Sr. masterpiece" is laid out "with a creek wandering throughout" "the middle of cow country" in the historic town of Hamilton; if that weren't reason enough to visit your kid at school", there's also "a cozy clubhouse, a good restaurant and a nice pro shop", all "at a reasonable cost" – "alumni only wish they'd held up as well as the course has."

Hudson Valley

Branton Woods
25 | 21 | 22 | 20 | $115

178 Stormville Rd., Hopewell Junction; 845-223-1600; www.brantonwoodsgolf.com; 7100/4057; 73.3/67.8; 129/114

■ Open in 2001, this "outstanding" newcomer has "immediately moved to the top rank of high-end courses" with "excellent service" at good "weekday values", particularly at 'super twilight' time; in a "lovely" setting "far from developments", the "bucolic track meanders through deep woods and valleys", giving players "many options" on an "interesting variety of holes", and though it does "need time to mature", you can "dig the hot dogs on nine" in "tranquillity" while you "watch the rough grow."

GARRISON ⊕
19 | 14 | 16 | 18 | $80

2015 Rte. 9, Garrison; 845-424-4747; 6470/5041; 72.1/69.9; 134/124

■ "Knockout", "panoramic" "views of the Hudson River, West Point and Bear Mountain" highlight this "narrow", "demanding" old-style track toughened by "twisted, sloping" fairways and "glass-like greens" with occasionally "evil pin placements", all of which "wreak havoc on your game"; nevertheless, it's "a good place to play on a summer Friday after work" say Metro-North commuters who applaud "new ownership that's made all the difference" in course conditions, even if the clubhouse hasn't ceased to "give new meaning to the term 'rustic.'"

Links at Union Vale
24 | 20 | 22 | 23 | $57

153 N. Parliman Rd., Lagrangeville; 845-223-1000; www.thelinksatunionvale.com; 7002/5198; 73.0/72.0; 132/126

■ "The staff is nicer to me than my family" whisper inner children playing at this "little bit of Ireland tucked into Dutchess County", but "please don't tell anyone" because "not many know about it yet", and ball-whacking brats don't want to share the "large, double-tiered greens, sloping fairways and blind pin locations"; if "the clubhouse is a little bare", "the course needs maturing" and "a few holes are plain unfair", "for the money", it's nevertheless a "must for serious golfers."

McCann Memorial
21 | 16 | 15 | 24 | $37

155 Wilbur Blvd., Poughkeepsie; 845-471-3917; 6524/5354; 71.5/71.1; 122/114

☑ "A jewel set in an unlikely place", the "best public value in the Hudson Valley" has "a little bit of everything: sand, water and doglegs", plus "it's always in excellent shape"; "what else could you want besides a day under par?" – how about more chop-chop from the rangers "to speed up the six-hour rounds"?

Tennanah Lake Golf & Tennis ∇ 19 | 15 | 17 | 22 | $51

100 Belle Rd., Roscoe; 607-498-5502; 888-561-3935;
www.tennanah.com; 6546/5154; 72.1/75.9; 128/133

◪ "A little far from Manhattan but worth the drive" and "a steal"
to boot, this "little gem" at a sporty resort on a lake "off the main
drag" is "interesting" but "not difficult"; it's "beautiful to play in
the fall", when the "awesome country views" come in technicolor
and there are "no lines, so just tee it up and go", even though you
might think the place "could use some sprucing up."

Town of Wallkill Golf Club 19 | 16 | 17 | 22 | $47

40 Sands Rd., Middletown; 845-361-1022;
6437/5125; 72.5/70.7; 125/118

■ "Holy doglegs", Batman! – "you're not going to hit driver too
often" at this "unheralded, tight, tree-lined" muni two hours via
Batmobile up the Hudson from Gotham; it's "a short course with
a premium on accuracy and very unforgiving of wayward shots",
so Girl and Boy Wonders who resist the temptation to "grip it and
rip it" can "beat their long-hitting buddies"; where the "fall foliage
is spectacular" and "wildlife abounds", "beautiful conditions,
scenic holes and friendly service" add up to "excellent value"
worth leaving your Batcave for.

Long Island

BETHPAGE STATE PARK, BLACK 29 | 21 | 19 | 29 | $39

99 Quaker Meeting House Rd., Farmingdale; 516-249-0700;
www.nysparks.state.ny.us; 7295/6281; 76.6/71.4; 148/134

■ "Heaven for the skilled golfer, hell for the duffer", NY's No. 1–
rated Course was the "heroic and penal" host of the 2002 U.S. Open;
the "mother of all public" tracks, it's "the country's best value", but
it's "harder to get on than Augusta National"; still, with "long,
long, long" "ribbon fairways", "lightning-fast greens" and "multi-
tentacled bunkers" "that force you to think constantly", "they could
charge $150 and it would sell out" to fans who "sleep in their
cars for two nights" to give it a "chunk of their rumps"; N.B. for
non-golfing kin of all those obsessives, an hour's drive will
get you west to NYC and east to the beachy Hamptons.

BETHPAGE STATE PARK, BLUE 22 | 20 | 17 | 27 | $29

99 Quaker Meeting House Rd., Farmingdale; 516-249-0700;
www.nysparks.state.ny.us; 6684/6213; 71.7/75.0; 124/129

■ "Another gem in the Bethpage crown", this "walk in the woods"
sporting "one of the toughest front nines on Long Island" is
certainly "not for babies"; "as with all of the state park's courses,
play is slow and tee times difficult to acquire", but it's "normally
in supreme condition" and "not a bad alternative to the Black",
since "you can't always date the pretty sister."

BETHPAGE STATE PARK, GREEN 21 | 19 | 17 | 27 | $29

99 Quaker Meeting House Rd., Farmingdale; 516-249-0700;
www.nysparks.state.ny.us; 6267/5903; 69.5/73.0; 121/126

■ The original layout at this storied complex, "the Green meanie is
no easy 18" – it's "short, but not too short, challenging, but not too
challenging", with "small greens that demand accurate approach
shots"; it's "an incredible value", but par for the course, "it can be
crowded with long waits."

BETHPAGE STATE PARK, RED   26 | 19 | 17 | 28 | $29
99 Quaker Meeting House Rd., Farmingdale; 516-249-0700;
www.nysparks.state.ny.us; 6756/6198; 72.5/75.1; 127/130
◪ With "emphasis on accurate iron play" around a "large array"
of "picturesque doglegs" newly "preened" for the Open spillover,
this "chip off the old Black" is "the Bethpage course for mortals";
make sure to warm up before you tee off, lest the "impossible par-
4" first hole "makes you see red."

HARBOR LINKS   21 | 17 | 18 | 18 | $101
1 Fairway Dr., Port Washington; 516-767-4807;
www.harborlinks.com; 6927/5465; 73.2/69.1; 128/121
◪ It "looks quirky from afar, but when you step to the tee", this
"links-style course" "feels like Scotland instead of a former
landfill", despite remaining "a bit aromatic"; "stay out of the
fescue, or you might never find your ball", though you will locate
the clubhouse – "in temporary trailers that just don't work"; "if
you're not a town resident", you must pay top dollar to play.

Island's End   20 | 15 | 17 | 21 | $47
R.R. 25, Greenport; 631-477-0777; 6639/5039; 71.4/68.4; 121/116
◪ "Pebble Beach has little on" the "spectacular" par-3 6th hole,
"one of the world's tops", at this "windy", "pretty" stretch "situated
right on Long Island Sound"; pros yawn "aside from that, it's not
the most exciting" track, though the "many ducks" that gather here
appear to quack to the contrary.

LONG ISLAND NATIONAL 🏌   25 | 20 | 21 | 16 | $125
1793 Northville Tpke., Riverhead; 631-727-4664;
www.americangolf.com; 6838/5006; 69.6/69.4; 117/116
◪ "A stone's throw from a weekend at the Hamptons", Robert Trent
Jones Jr.'s "fun links-style track" is what players "imagine Ireland
to be"; a "humbling test when the wind blows", it's "expensive,
tight" and "kind of gimmicky, with shared and split fairways" – "not
the best combination" for your weekend duffer who'll probably find
himself in "rough up to his butt."

MONTAUK DOWNS STATE PARK   25 | 17 | 17 | 26 | $36
50 S. Fairview Ave., Montauk; 631-668-1100;
6762/5797; 73.3/74.2; 135/132
■ "Shinnecock Hills for the poor unwashed", Robert Trent Jones
Sr.'s "wonderful slice of Scottish golf on the tip of Long Island" has
a handful of heretics hailing it "the best public course in America";
it's "well worth the 100-mile trip" from the city, so "forget about
Bethpage Black and drive here" for "a windswept, rollicking
delight" that "leaves each hole etched in your memory."

Oyster Bay Town Golf Course   22 | 17 | 16 | 20 | $67
Southwoods Rd., Woodbury; 516-364-1180;
6376/5109; 71.5/70.4; 131/126
■ "You're likely to contribute your share of balls to the heavily
wooded outskirts of the narrow fairways" at this "meticulously
maintained public course" that attracts "Mets, New York Islander
hockey players and John McEnroe"; it's "short but sweet", "with
a lot of interesting holes", so "leave your driver at home", bring
your putter and don't forget to sink a few at the "gem" of a 19th,
where sports stars sigh "what a view from the patio!"

Rock Hill 🏌

18 | 15 | 15 | 17 | $66

105 Clancy Rd., Manorville; 631-878-2250; www.rockhillgolf.com;
7050/5390; 73.6/70.7; 136/120

☑ Get "two courses in one" on the "tight, hilly" "front nine carved through the forest" and "easier" "open, flat back" at this "solid" spread sporting "greens even better than at some private clubs", now that it's "kept up much better than it was in past years"; it's "easy to reach from Westhampton", so summering duffers swarm the place, making for "very slow" rounds on a track that city snobs sniff is "not as nice as locals think it is."

Smithtown Landing ⏲

19 | 15 | 16 | 20 | $33

495 Landing Ave., Smithtown; 631-979-6534;
www.smithtownlanding.com; 6114/5263; 69.4/70.1; 129/126

☑ Though it's pretty darned cheap for anyone, you "need to be a town resident for [particularly] good value" at this "nice track with some tight fairways, plenty of trees", "lots of hillside lies" and "a view of the Nissequogue River"; though it's home to Mike Hebron, "one of the best pros in the country", thrill-seekers say its "uninspiring design" makes for "uneventful" golf and it "could use an infusion of capital to improve conditions."

Swan Lake

20 | 14 | 16 | 18 | $40

388 River Rd., Manorville; 631-369-1818; www.usegolf.com;
7011/5245; 72.5/69.0; 121/112

☑ "Pay close attention to the pin location or you'll be three-putting" caution short-gamers swallowed by "lightning-fast", "swimming pool"–sized greens at this "good alternative to pricey Hamptons" "newbies"; it's "not bad" farther away from the holes either, though "they put all their money into maintaining the course rather than the clubhouse", and there is "no driving range" to speak of.

NYC Metro Area (see also New Jersey)

Blue Hill

19 | 14 | 15 | 20 | $39

285 Blue Hill Rd., Pearl River; 845-735-2094
Lakeside/Pines: 6489/5464; 70.6/69.8; 124/119
Pines/Woodland: 6372/5111; 70.6/69.8; 124/119
Woodland/Lakeside: 6357/5077; 70.6/69.8; 124/119

☑ "Fun to play, easy to pay" for, this "terrific little" parkland muni "is a great one to get the rust off after a long winter" putting into your cocoa mug, if you can get on it – "tee times are nearly impossible for non-residents", but Rockland County club-wielders clamor onto "all three nines", seeking out those "nice, individual holes" that are "kept in immaculate condition considering the amount" of "beginners" hacking things up; if you're hungry or rusty, note "there should be more food and beverages" on offer, and "the lack of a range hurts."

CENTENNIAL GOLF CLUB 🏌

23 | 23 | 22 | 16 | $125

185 Simpson Rd., Carmel; 845-225-5700; 877-783-5700;
www.centennialgolf.com
Fairways/Meadows: 7050/5208; 73.6/70.7; 135/122
Lakes/Fairways: 7133/5208; 74.0/70.4; 137/126
Lakes/Meadows: 7125/5208; 73.8/70.3; 135/126

☑ Hillside hackers say "go in the fall when the leaves are changing" for the "awesome vistas" at this 27-holer "the golf gods dropped out of the sky and onto a mountainside" "in the NYC metro area", and tee off at "twilight, when specials offer great value" on otherwise "pricey" play; dissenting duffers dis "dumbfounding routing" and "high traffic" on a "truly ordinary public-access track clothed in a high-end facility."

MANSION RIDGE ⛳   24   22   22   15 $135
1292 Orange Tpke., Monroe; 845-782-7888; 6889/4785; 73.5/67.9; 138/121
◪ Jack Nicklaus' Signature is scrawled in "brutal par 5s, strategic par 4s and testy par 3s" with "great mountain views" "through the rolling woods" of Orange County; unlike the club course at neighboring old money–meets–new money Tuxedo Park, it's open to the public, but you still "have to own a mansion to afford the greens" fee, and penny-pinching putters pout "its practically non-existent clubhouse and pro shop, plus the irons-only, off-mats driving range, make it a top tri-state rip-off."

Spook Rock   22   14   14   21 $55
233 Spook Rock Rd., Suffern; 845-357-3085; 6894/4953; 73.1/68.1; 127/120
◪ "A perfect layout for mid-handicappers" with "great bunkering on every hole", this parklander is "a solid course close to NYC"; it's "hard to get on and a little expensive" if you're not a "local", but that hasn't spooked "all the hackers" away, so "bring reading material to kill the time" during "six-hour weekend rounds."

North Carolina

★ **Best in State**
29 Pinehurst Resort, No. 2, *Pinehurst*
28 Tanglewood Park, Championship, *Winston-Salem*
   Pine Needles Lodge, *Pinehurst*
   Carolina National, *Myrtle Beach Area*
27 Pinehurst Resort, No. 4, *Pinehurst*
26 Mid Pines Inn, *Pinehurst*
   Pinehurst Resort No. 8, *Pinehurst*
   Duke University Golf Club, *Raleigh-Durham*
25 Pinehurst Resort, No. 7, *Pinehurst*
   Legacy, *Pinehurst*

Asheville

Linville Golf Club   ▽ 26   20   19   21 $82
83 Roseboro Rd., Linville; 828-733-4363; www.eseeolalodge.com; 6914/5086; 73.3/69.3; 139/117
■ On-course historians swear that this Donald Ross "classic" is "unspoiled from the days it was built, without machines, when the power brokers met to tee it up in the North Carolina mountains"; it's still got the same "great views" and remains "super-fun", but the aging "greens are slower than they've ever been" say modern mavericks staying at the Esseeola Lodge, which is the only way you can get on the track unless you're a member or a guest of one.

Mt. Mitchell   – – – – $75
7590 Hwy. 80 S., Burnsville; 828-675-5454; www.burnsville.com/mmgc; 6495/5455; 71.3/70.9; 141/131
It's in the shadow of the highest point east of the Rockies, not atop it, so this peak performer is "in the mountains but not mountainous";

set amid the Pisgah National Forest, it's a "scenic" "hidden gem" that's "always in top condition", making it a "must-play" for Carolina club-wielders.

Charlotte

Birkdale   21 | 21 | 20 | 16 | $67
16500 Birkdale Commons Pkwy., Huntersville; 704-895-8038; www.birkdale.com; 7013/5175; 74.1/69.3; 138/123
◪ It's "sneaky long" say iron enthusiasts, but this Arnold Palmer layout is still a "very fair" "pleasure to play", particularly on a package deal with a neighboring hotel; at an "upscale club" nine miles north of downtown Charlotte near Lake Norman, it's got "great conditioning", a "don't-miss practice putting green" and a clubhouse porch just ripe for a post-round julep, though none of that impresses nature lovers who imagine "it was much nicer before they removed all the trees and replaced them with power lines" "buzzing overhead."

Highland Creek ⌂   23 | 19 | 18 | 19 | $63
7001 Highland Creek Pkwy.; 704-875-9000; www.charlottegolf.com; 7043/5080; 74.2/70.1; 138/127
■ If tipsters don't "find their ball landing in the [namesake] creek", they'll probably follow it into rough where they "may never hack it out" at this "difficult", "oh-so-scenic" parklander that's "quite playable from the whites but can be challenging from the blues on back", with a "very good finish" on a "fun risk/reward par 5" skirting a pond; plus, it's "in better shape" than some of its more exclusive neighbors.

Rocky River at Concord   ▽ 21 | 16 | 19 | 18 | $59
6900 Speedway Blvd., Concord; 704-455-1200; www.rockyrivergolf.com; 6970/4754; 73.5/68.4; 137/119
◪ "On a par with many of the better private courses", this "outstanding municipal" facility features a "wonderful layout" and "holes that are varied in style, each with their own character"; "vroom! vroom!" voice vociferous detractors, referring to the noise "of the Lowe's Motor Speedway in the background – too bad it's not the sound of the carts in front of you" moving out of your way, "since the pace of play is maybe the slowest in town, thanks to the number of blind tee shots"; a more appropriate place to park it is on the veranda of the 19th hole overlooking the finish.

Greensboro

Grandover Resort, East ⌂   ▽ 26 | 27 | 24 | 24 | $75
1000 Club Rd.; 336-294-1800; www.grandover.com; 7100/5500; 74.3/71.7; 140/121
■ "Bring plenty of balls to this picture-perfect course" say the few lucky lofters who've made it to these thinking-golfer's links, where brains and accuracy are your weapons against water on 10 holes, deep pot bunkers and large, undulating greens; folks at the Ken Venturi Golf Academy can help wishy-washy wallopers, as decisions abound on the proper club to use at the tee and how much yardage to bite off on the par 4s and par 5s – after your round you can relax your mind because the resort spa has the rest all figured out for you.

Grandover Resort, West ⛳　▽ 25 | 27 | 23 | 23 | $88
1000 Club Rd.; 336-294-1800; www.grandover.com;
6800/5050; 72.5/69.2; 136/116

■ "An extremely playable course for all handicaps, but still tough"
say a Grandoverjoyed group of golfers of this "pleasant surprise"
at a "pretty facility" in a "farm-like locale" "in a beautiful spot right
off I-85", 16 miles from the Piedmont Triad International Airport; it
may be "expensive for the area", but it's "not as difficult" as the
East, "you will get immaculate conditioning and a very friendly
staff" for your money, and if you can't sink your balls in the holes
on the course, maybe you can do so in the resort's billiards room.

Myrtle Beach Area
(see also South Carolina)

Angels Trace, North ⛳　▽ 21 | 18 | 20 | 22 | $78
1215 Angels Club Dr. S., Sunset Beach; 910-579-2277; 800-718-5733;
www.golfangelstrace.com; 6640/4524; 72.7/66.7; 137/111

☑ "I've played this course several times with a local, and I've been
treated like one" say out-of-towners who approve of the angelic
staff at this "nice, expertly kept" woodlander; though it's "without
many surprises, most still find it a challenge", except for those
devilish drivers who confess "with so much to choose from in North
Carolina" (including resorts with the type of amenities not offered
here), "it's hard to rate this perfectly nice track particularly high."

Angels Trace, South　　▽ 18 | 17 | 19 | 22 | $78
1215 Angels Club Dr. S., Sunset Beach; 910-579-2277; 800-718-5733;
www.golfangelstrace.com; 6866/4811; 74.1/68.9; 139/121

☑ "Low- and medium-handicappers will find plenty of good scoring
opportunities" on the North's "woodsy" sister at this Grand Strand
north facility located just over the border from South Carolina; it's
got "very nice views, it's always in good shape" and its layout is
"fairly straightforward", as are the "gators", so "watch out if you
venture into the ponds" from the 7th to 10th holes, lest those angels
leave no trace of you.

Bald Head Island ⛳　　▽ 21 | 21 | 19 | 19 | $100
704 E. Moore St., Southport; 910-457-5000; 800-888-3707;
www.baldheadisland.com; 6855/4810; 74.3/70.1; 139/117

☑ It's "hard to get to" blubber landlubbers, as "you must take
a ferry" to play this "terrific beach course that winds through
maritime forest", finishing with "three holes that are great in the
wind"; seasick slicers say "it isn't worth the rip-off price" of the
passage over, though if you ask the "gators sunning near some of
the tees" on the "unique" island preserve, they might point out it's
the "only choice" in a "secluded yet warm and gorgeous place to
relax"; N.B. if you're too queasy for a quick return trip, rental
properties include free access to the course.

Calabash Golf Links ⛳　　▽ 19 | 16 | 18 | 20 | $65
820 Thomasboro Rd. SW, Calabash; 910-575-5000; 800-841-5971;
www.calabashgolf.com; 6612/4907; 71.2/68.4; 129/112

■ Just across the border from the monsters of Myrtle Beach is
this "golfer-friendly course" that's "easy to get on, fun to play",
"fairly open and usually in pretty good condition", with water on
10 holes; critics capable of crushing the mid-length layout say it's

"great if you get a discount", but otherwise "look elsewhere", and try to tee off before you pig out on the fishing town's namesake style of seafood, which is fried and all-you-can-eat.

CAROLINA NATIONAL ⛳ 28 | 23 | 21 | 23 | $95
1643 Goley Hewett Rd. SE, Bolivia; 888-200-6455; www.carolinanatl.com
Egret/Heron: 6944/4631; 73.4/63.5; 136/116
Heron/Ibis: 7017/4759; 74.2/66.6; 145/114
Ibis/Egret: 6961/4048; 74.0/67.1; 147/111
■ "Boom-Boom's three nines are very, very cool" – "thanks, Freddie" say cuckoo-for-Couples club-wielders of his "very picturesque", "inventive layout on a beautiful piece of land along the marsh coast" "where the best holes are on the water"; it "tests all skill levels" "with lots of sand and hazards to challenge even the lowest handicappers but with bailout areas for the hackers."

Ocean Ridge Plantation, Lion's Paw ▽ 19 | 22 | 21 | 20 | $77
351 Ocean Ridge Pkwy., Sunset Beach; 910-287-1703;
www.panthersrun.com; 7003/5363; 75.0/70.3; 137/129
■ "This big cat was a joy" purr pleased players slinking across these links where the feline gets its paw wet on 17 holes; "in terrific condition" with "some nice par 3s", it's packed with both wild and well-manicured aesthetics on mounded fairways and well-protected, sloping greens, and you can bring home a lion's share of top-shelf merchandise from the excellent pro shop.

Ocean Ridge Plantation, Panther's Run ▽ 22 | 24 | 23 | 21 | $87
351 Ocean Ridge Pkwy., Sunset Beach; 910-287-1703;
www.panthersrun.com; 7089/5023; 75.2/70.0; 148/123
■ "This is a keeper" say big-game hunters who "always return to try to tame" this "amazing" track with danger lurking in "some tricky holes" running along the edge of a marshland preserve; it's "somewhat of a hidden gem with immaculate fairways", and some feline aficionados call it "the best of the three at Ocean Ridge", even though "the greens could be faster."

Ocean Ridge Plantation, Tiger's Eye ▽ 27 | 28 | 26 | 24 | $112
351 Ocean Ridge Pkwy., Sunset Beach; 910-287-1703;
www.panthersrun.com; 7014/4502; 73.5/66.6; 144/108
■ "It's as good as any course in North Carolina not located in Pinehurst" say men and women with the will to survive the island par 3 and other "attractive holes" at this "excellent" "treat" "in superb condition"; the newest of the three at "an outstanding complex", "it has a separate clubhouse" with a "very good pro shop" giving "unmatched service" and "a great deck to watch players come into the 9th and 18th."

Pearl Golf Links, East ⛳ 24 | 21 | 20 | 24 | $80
1300 Pearl Blvd. SW, Sunset Beach; 910-579-8132; 888-947-3275;
www.thepearlgolf.com; 6793/5125; 73.5/69.2; 134/117
☑ "It's all golf in the Carolina woods" – "no developments here" say pleased pals of this Pearl, "an excellent layout" "in good condition" with "tough rough" and "great-looking finishers along the Calabash River"; nevertheless, one lackluster lofter laments

"they redid all the greens a few years ago and made every one with the same big, obnoxious crown."

Pearl Golf Links, West 🏌
▽ 24 | 21 | 19 | 24 | $80

1300 Pearl Blvd. SW, Sunset Beach; 910-579-8132; 888-947-3275; www.thepearlgolf.com; 7006/5188; 74.9/69.0; 131/121

■ "A nice mixture" that "varies" between open stretches with "plenty of tricks" and water holes "forces you to use most of the clubs in your bag" at this "picturesque" spread; in other words, the "well-maintained" sister to the East course is "worth the money" you shell out to pry par from it.

Porter's Neck Plantation 🏌
▽ 22 | 22 | 22 | 22 | $70

8403 Vintage Club Circle, Wilmington; 910-686-1177; 800-947-8177; www.porters-neck.com; 7112/5145; 75.3/70.3; 136/121

■ "Tom Fazio at his best" smile satisfied swingers of "one of the favorites" "around Wilmington", a port town brimming with delicious seafood; hungry hookers hail the "consistent course" because "each hole lays nicely into the topography and not a single one is tricked up", resulting in some "very challenging golf" that's "reasonably priced", given its "excellent condition" and "private-club ambiance."

Rivers Edge 🏌
▽ 25 | 20 | 21 | 23 | $120

2000 Arnold Palmer Dr., Shallotte; 877-748-3718; 877-748-3718; www.river18.com; 6909/4700; 74.7/68.2; 149/119

■ Even though it's across the state border, "be sure to include this amazing place on any trip to Myrtle Beach" exclaim enthusiasts of Palmer's super-size sloper where "every hole is picturesque", with "dramatic views of the marshes and the Shallotte River", especially the "stunning par-5 9th"; "talk about challenging": its "penal golf will age a group of pretty decent players about 10 years."

Sea Trail, Dan Maples 🏌
▽ 20 | 21 | 20 | 22 | $85

75 Clubhouse Rd. SW, Sunset Beach; 910-287-1150; 800-546-5748; www.seatrail.com; 6797/5090; 70.6/69.0; 131/115

■ While "all of Sea Trail is fair and playable", this links set among tall Carolina pines and twisted oaks featuring 10 holes with water seems "the easiest of the bunch"; "complete with replays, there's a lot of good golf", and the resort sports pristine barrier island beaches for lolling about between rounds, but with all of that fresh fish flipping on plates in nearby Wilmington, "plan to eat off-site."

Sea Trail, Rees Jones 🏌
▽ 23 | 23 | 22 | 24 | $100

75 Clubhouse Rd. SW, Sunset Beach; 910-287-1150; 800-546-5748; www.seatrail.com; 6761/4912; 72.4/68.5; 132/115

■ "Great rooms" make this resort "the place to have an outing", and this target-style links layout is "the best of its three courses" rave those jonesin' for a Rees-designed round; highlighted by wide fairways, large mounds, pot bunkers and water lurking on 11 holes, it was planted (with the architect's approval) a few years ago with native grasses and wildflowers to create a more natural look.

Sea Trail, Willard Byrd 🏌
▽ 19 | 19 | 20 | 21 | $85

75 Clubhouse Rd. SW, Sunset Beach; 910-287-1150; 800-546-5748; www.seatrail.com; 6750/4697; 72.1/67.9; 128/111

☑ "On a three-play pass", the Sea Trail tracks are "an outstanding value", and fans who flock here find that this triplet, built around man-made lakes and constricting trees with undulating greens and the designer's signature decorative sand and waste bunkers, is certainly not for the birds; dissatisfied swingers, on the other hand, squawk that it's "very tired"; if you're pooped post-round, schedule yourself a relaxing massage at the resort's activity center.

St. James Plantation, Gauntlet 🏌

∇ 19 | 22 | 22 | 20 | $99

3640 Players Club Dr. SE, Southport; 910-253-3008; 800-247-4806; 7004/5048; 76.2/70.5; 151/131

☑ "P.B. Dye's designs can be quirky to the point of bizarre", but this layout is "fun to play and a good test" attest advocates who throw down the gauntlet for the "beautiful setting" in a gated community along the Intracoastal; a couple of complainers counter it's "too tricked up" and the groundskeepers need to pull a few more tricks out of their bag, since it's "not in the greatest shape."

St. James Plantation, Members Club 🏌 ⏱

– | – | – | – | $99

3640 Players Club Dr. SE, Southport; 910-253-9500; 800-474-9227; www.stjamesplantation.com; 6887/5948; 73.5/69.8; 138/122

"If you had to pick one, a perfect course to play for the rest of your days" just might be this "excellent layout with super greens" say a few Members-for-life wanna-bes who "highly recommend" it for a "very enjoyable" round; a handful of dissenters who dis it as "nothing special without much strategy or interest" "go other places in the Myrtle Beach area for more fun."

St. James Plantation, Players Club 🏌 ⏱

– | – | – | – | $99

3640 Players Club Dr. SE, Southport; 910-457-0049; 800-999-6664; www.stjamesplantation.com; 6940/4902; 74.6/69.6; 149/121

"The best layout of the three here", according to pleased players, is this relatively flat scenic track in "excellent condition", with green complexes open in front; it's laden with wetlands you'd better lay up short of, or you'll be deep in the drink; "if you're a righty and hit a draw, this is your course."

Outer Banks

Currituck Club

∇ 26 | 22 | 22 | 18 | $145

1 Currituck Clubhouse Dr., Corolla; 252-453-9400; 888-453-9400; www.thecurrituckgolfclub.com; 6885/4766; 74.0/68.5; 136/120

■ Contented coastal-links lovers "would play this one every day for the rest of their lives" if they resided close enough to the historic site of what once was a hunt club for 19th-century steel and railroad magnates; Rees Jones' design is "lots of fun and very challenging when the wind is up", it "stays in good condition off-season" and it's always got "great views" of the shoreline; budget ball whackers lacking repellent lament it's "overpriced" when "the only memory at the end of the round is of the vampire bug bites."

Nags Head

∇ 20 | 15 | 19 | 18 | $105

5615 S. Seachase Dr., Nags Head; 252-441-8073; 800-851-9404; www.nagsheadgolflinks.com; 6126/4415; 68.8/64.7; 130/117

☑ "The breeze off Roanoke Sound can put your tee shot onto a neighboring veranda", so "count on shooting twice your handicap on a windy day" and watch out for folks dozing in their porch swings on this "scenic and tight" "little gem" of a links "where you'll use most every club in the bag"; though "the staff couldn't be nicer", naysayers nag that the course is "overpriced" and under-length.

Pinehurst

Carolina Club, The ⛳　　21 | 15 | 18 | 20 | $84

277 Ave. of the Carolina; 910-949-2811; 888-725-6372;
ww.thecarolina.com; 6928/4828; 73.2/68.6; 142/117

☑ "Some of the most challenging greens you'll ever see" are laid out "fast and undulating" amid protected wetlands on this "exquisitely maintained" Palmer design; since "long carries" make it "difficult for ladies", the "superb staff" just might throw women a few "range balls", but they can't seem to do anything about "choppy" "blind shots with more risk than reward" or all those airborne pests in what eight-iron entomologists dub the "flying bug and mosquito capital of Pinehurst" – when the clubhouse is finally completed, there'll be an indoors to escape the critters.

Hyland Hills Resort　　▽ 17 | 15 | 15 | 25 | $49

115 Fairway Ave., Southern Pines; 910-692-3752; 888-315-2296;
www.hylandhillsgolfclub.com; 6782/4677; 70.2/68.2; 122/116

☑ Just about the "best bang for your buck in" the center of the North Carolina golf universe, this is a "pure experience without fancy extras" offering an "average loop for the mid- to high-handicappers", "where putting is at a premium on the biggest greens you'll ever see"; it's even more of a deal with a package at the adjacent, eponymous inn, but that doesn't stop those who can afford a finer tee-off from tsking that "too much play" by penny-wise pairings is turning this into "one big goat track."

Legacy ⛳　　25 | 22 | 21 | 23 | $109

12615 Hwy. 15-501 S., Aberdeen; 910-944-8825; 800-344-8825;
www.legacypinehurst.com; 7018/4948; 73.2/68.3; 132/120

■ "Get here when you're in Southern Pines" because this is "the place to play if you don't want to spend the big money at Pinehurst"; a secluded, "interesting" course cut out of the woods by the Nicklaus group with no encroaching houses or developments, it's "scenic, hilly and demanding", with "challenging greens" but "no tricks" – "ladies seem to like it" in particular.

Little River Farm　　▽ 21 | 13 | 18 | 22 | $83

500 Little River Farm Blvd., Carthage; 910-949-4600; 888-766-6538;
www.littleriver.com; 6909/5092; 73.6/69.4; 132/118

☑ Carved through forests and meadows with some nearly 200-ft. elevation changes, this "very difficult design" is one of "the best layouts for the money in the area", particularly for North Carolina golfers, who can download coupons off the Web; it's a "great" links-style round if you "bring your A-game", "keep the horseflies off you" and "watch out for rocks embedded in the fairways."

Mid Pines Inn 🏌 ⏱　　26 | 25 | 25 | 24 | $160

1010 Midland Rd., Southern Pines; 910-692-2114;
www.pineneedles-midpines.com; 6515/4907; 71.4/68.2; 127/120

■ "Killer breaks on awesome greens" with "lots of three-putt opportunities" highlight a "classic", "minimalist" "Donald Ross gem" that's "the essence of his work at Pinehurst"; this means you're in for "a visually marvelous outing" that's "not long but with plenty of trouble if you're not hitting it straight" and capped by "a spectacular finish" where "the view of the hotel is one of the best in golf"; plus, when you stay at "the stately inn, you're greeted by a wonderful staff, the beds are comfortable, the food is as good as it gets – what else needs to be said?"

Pinehurst Resort, No. 1 🏌   22 26 25 20 $150
700 Morganton Rd.; 910-295-8141; 800-795-4653; www.pinehurst.com; 6128/5297; 69.4/70.5; 116/117
■ The least punishing of Pinehurst's guests-only posse, this "old" "confidence-builder" is a "lovely" "warm-up to its more famous, difficult" siblings; a "short, tight" "shotmaker's as opposed to driver's course", it's "a good test of keeping the ball in play"; enroll the kids in the Summer Program for a host of activities to occupy them while you putt.

PINEHURST RESORT, NO. 2 🏌   29 28 27 20 $325
700 Morganton Rd.; 910-295-8141; 800-795-4653; www.pinehurst.com; 6741/5035; 72.8/69.6; 131/124
■ "If you have the dough, you must go" to "genius" Donald Ross' guests-only "mecca" for golfers, the state's No. 1–rated course and former and future (in 2005) U.S. Open host, where "the humpback greens are like none you've ever seen", the "facilities are amazing and the staff is friendly"; "pay for the caddies, who make the round better" – you can't walk the "sublime" "gem" without them.

Pinehurst Resort, No. 3 🏌   20 25 25 19 $150
700 Morganton Rd.; 910-295-8141; 800-795-4653; www.pinehurst.com; 5682/5232; 67.2/69.9; 115/117
▨ Beware the "narrow fairways" and "leave the driver in the bag at this short, hilly target test with maddening greens"; if "local members love it" for "an enjoyable round", resort guests whose moves "aren't good enough to match" the "quick" dance floors huff "if you can play any other at Pinehurst, do so."

PINEHURST RESORT, NO. 4 🏌   27 28 26 21 $225
700 Morganton Rd.; 910-295-8141; 800-795-4653; www.pinehurst.com; 7117/5217; 74.5/70.6; 136/123
■ Possibly "the most frustrating fun you'll ever have east of Pebble Beach", guests-only Pinehurst's esteemed "close second to No. 2" is "more difficult since [Tom] Fazio's redesign of the classic Ross layout"; "if the added traps don't get you, the hard, domed greens will", but you'll still feel like you've "died and gone to golf heaven."

PINEHURST RESORT, NO. 5 🏌   21 26 27 21 $150
700 Morganton Rd.; 910-295-8141; 800-795-4653; www.pinehurst.com; 6848/5248; 73.4/70.1; 137/119
■ Giving "great golf but even better Southern hospitality", this "busy" guests-only course "surrounded by homes" is "very playable", with "some special holes like the Cathedral 15th and "par 5s reachable from back tees"; "elevation changes, doglegs and hills" "encourage players to work their ball in every direction", so "make this the start of a wonderful resort weekend" including tennis, sailing and shopping, and finish by soaking your tired bones at the "spectacular new spa."

Pinehurst Resort, No. 6 🏌   23 ‖ 23 ‖ 23 ‖ 19 ‖ $150 ‖
Hwy. 5; 910-295-8141; 800-795-4653; www.pinehurst.com;
7157/5430; 74.2/71.4; 135/124

🔲 This guests-only "sleeper" "gets little recognition alongside" its sisters, perhaps because it's "away from the main clubhouse" and "not a gathering place for after-round libations"; whatever the reason, it "has a different feel than the others", "with a couple of spectacular holes" and "fairly wide-open" fairways; status-seekers say "Pinehurst's weakest" is still "a decent filler of downtime."

Pinehurst Resort, No. 7 🏌   25 ‖ 24 ‖ 25 ‖ 20 ‖ $215 ‖
Hwy. 5; 910-295-8141; 800-795-4653; www.pinehurst.com;
7125/4996; 74.4/69.7; 140/125

■ In a "quaint town where golfing rules supreme" lies "one of the prettiest woodlanders in the U.S., with great vistas" and an "immaculate" guests-only "super-duper layout" "that makes use of all your clubs"; "don't play the tips unless you like pain", and "if there's no wind, bring bug spray", as the little critters like it here too.

Pinehurst Resort, No. 8 🏌   26 ‖ 27 ‖ 26 ‖ 21 ‖ $225 ‖
700 Morganton Rd.; 910-295-8141; 800-795-4653; www.pinehurst.com;
7092/5177; 74.0/68.9; 135/112

■ "[Tom] Fazio really knew what he was doing in using every bit of landscape to create challenges" on Pinehurst's guests-only centennial course; the "wonderfully sweeping holes" are "far apart, so you enjoy a peaceful round of nature" on a "truly superb layout" that is "a short drive from the main Pinehurst clubhouse and courses, and thus is much less crowded"; fanatics "go so far as to say that this is the next No. 2."

PINE NEEDLES LODGE 🏌   28 ‖ 25 ‖ 25 ‖ 21 ‖ $175 ‖
1005 Midland Rd., Southern Pines; 910-692-7111; 800-747-7272;
www.rossresorts.com; 6727/5039; 72.2/68.4; 131/118

■ Two-time host of the U.S. Women's Open, this "rustic" round is "a stellar, hilly, well-conditioned Ross design where you can play forever, never get bored" and always "feel first-class", which is "great even if you're a man, though it caters to ladies" with "great winter camps" by golf legend Peggy Kirk Bell; the "mounded greens are a bear to hold, but rarely do you have this much fun getting challenged"; check into the lodge and stay the weekend.

Pinewild, Holly 🏌   ▽ 24 ‖ 25 ‖ 21 ‖ 23 ‖ $115 ‖
801 Linden Rd.; 910-295-5145; 800-523-1499; www.pinewildcc.com;
7024/5475; 73.4/71.4; 131/126

■ "It doesn't have the pedigree of some of its neighbors, but it also doesn't have their stiff price tags", so this "great course is a great bargain" say wallet-watchers wild about the daily fee at a gated residential country club a few minutes from Pinehurst; the "terrific" traditional track is "extremely well maintained", with "exceptional facilities, including a three-hole practice course", even though straight shooters who find it "tricked up" "like Magnolia a lot more."

Pinewild, Magnolia 🏌   ▽ 26 ‖ 25 ‖ 22 ‖ 23 ‖ $125 ‖
801 Linden Rd.; 910-295-5145; 800-523-1499; www.pinewildcc.com;
7276/5362; 75.0/71.1; 135/121

■ On its "wonderful" "wind through the woods", the "outstanding" "first Pinewild course" blooms with "nice aesthetics"; it's "not easy, but it's fair", and the "good range" and par-3 Azalea track help hackers warm to the "super test"; one reviewer pines for less cocky cart codgers, complaining "the arrogant rangers ruined the experience."

Pit Golf Links, The | 20 | 17 | 19 | 20 | $89 |
Hwy. 5; 910-944-1600; 800-574-4653; www.danmaples.com/pit; 6600/4759; 72.3/68.4; 139/121
☑ "General consensus has always been either you love this course or you hate it"; set in an "old mine pit" with "many blind shots", it's "strange but somehow appealing, if a little too tricked up", a "fun experience if you're hitting it straight" but "arduous" if you're not; critics call it "borderline unfair" . . . no, make that plain "unfair" . . . ok, it's "very unfair."

Talamore | 23 | 20 | 19 | 22 | $120 |
48 Talamore Dr., Southern Pines; 910-692-5884; 800-552-6292; www.talamore.com; 6840/4993; 71.0/71.0; 142/125
■ "Llamas as caddie carts is a unique experience" indeed during the winter at what "should be a must in the Pinehurst area" say shotmaking sherpas who want to tally more acclaim for this "excellent" Rees Jones layout "with gently rolling terrain" that's always "in good shape"; after "one of the toughest opening holes anywhere", it's "a pleasant walk in the park" with "just the right amount of challenge to keep you interested."

Tobacco Road | 23 | 20 | 21 | 18 | $95 |
442 Tobacco Rd., Sanford; 919-775-1940; www.tobaccoroadgolf.com; 6554/5094; 73.2/66.1; 150/115
☑ It's "golf on steroids" at this "unforgettable", "fantastic course" with many "hidden greens and fairways", "quirky holes", "untamed woods" and "well-placed water hazards"; musclemen call the Mike Strantz creation "one of the most interesting rides you'll ever have", but "punished" putters pout it's a "crazy circus" where the "only thing missing is the clowns."

Woodlake Country Club, Maples ▽ 22 | 19 | 18 | 21 | $69 |
150 Woodlake Blvd., Vass; 910-245-4686; 888-843-5253; www.woodlakecc.com; 6791/5303; 73.2/71.6; 134/130
■ "It is very nice to play golf" on such a "good variety of holes" at this "great course" where the four openers are surrounded by water and several other fairways feature doglegs; the heavily wooded track on a man-made lake has a sister course, the Palmer, with nine wooded and nine links holes.

Raleigh-Durham

Duke University Golf Club | 26 | 26 | 23 | 24 | $80 |
Duke University, Rte. 751 & Science Dr., Durham; 919-681-2288; www.dukegolfclub.org; 7045/5505; 73.9/71.2; 137/124
■ "Oh, baby, what a track!" sigh students of swing studying the "dandy holes" at this "lovable layout the Joneses made" "on a wonderful piece of land" "nestled inside Duke Forest"; originally designed by RTJ Sr., with a "terrific redo by Rees", the "excellent, mature" host of the 2001 NCAA Championships "exemplifies the Southern hospitality and guile" that "spoil" alum and others checked in to the Washington Duke Inn with views of the course.

Winston-Salem

TANGLEWOOD PARK, CHAMPIONSHIP ©

| 28 | 22 | 20 | 28 | $58 |

4061 Clemmons Rd., Clemmons; 336-778-6300; www.tanglewoodpark.org;
7022/6504; 74.5/70.9; 140/127

■ "What a steal of a deal at this fantastic course", the Tar Heel State's top-ranked Value; "you keep saying to yourself, 'this can't be a public track', but it is" – in fact, it's "one of the best municipals in the country", "demanding" and "well-kept", with a "great history" as host to the 1974 PGA Championship as well as the 15th and final RJR Championship in 2002; "hint: practice your sand play before coming here" and "prepare to spend time at the beach" because this "classic" layout boasts "bunkers galore."

North Dakota

Bismarck

Hawktree

| – | – | – | – | $45 |

3400 Burnt Creek Loop; 701-355-0995; 888-465-4295; www.hawktree.com;
7085/4868; 74.6/63.9; 135/107

"How'd they get that many elevation changes in a flat state like North Dakota?" wonder wowed ball hawks on this links "treat" where "the staff goes out of their way to help" you, but you should "beware" of the wicked "wind" and its accomplices: eight holes with Burnt Creek and three others with small lakes in play; flatly speaking, if you "cannot believe they found this land" with all these hills, "you'll have to make the trip" here and see for yourself.

Williston

Links of North Dakota

| – | – | – | – | $45 |

Hwy. 1804 E.; 701-568-2600; www.redmike.com;
7092/5249; 73.5/69.5; 126/114

If Smokey's on rubber and he's over your shoulder, don't feed the bear; just pull your rig into the RV park next to the clubhouse at this "wonderful, scenic" course on Lake Sakakawea and relax over a round of "great links golf without the overseas travel"; conditioning on its wide rolling fairways and large, multi-tiered greens "has dropped over the past two years, but it was sold" in winter 2002, and the local band of citizens "feels it will be back to the shape that made it" soon – is that a big ten-four, good buddy?

Ohio

Akron

Windmill Lakes

| 24 | 20 | 22 | 25 | $51 |

6544 State Rte. 14, Ravenna; 330-297-0440; www.windmill-lakes-golf.com;
6936/5368; 73.8/70.4; 128/115

■ Despite nice ratings, Akron advocates tilt at windmills griping that this "straightforward, no-gimmicks" woodlander "doesn't get the credit it deserves" for "toughness" at "great value"; it's "nothing fancy, just long and tight and well maintained", and though its clubhouse has a "rustic muni feel", it sports a "tremendous pro shop" with "tons of equipment and apparel, most not burdened with the club's logo."

Cincinnati (see also Indiana)

Shaker Run ♨   26 | 25 | 24 | 21 | $69
4361 Greentree Rd., Lebanon; 513-727-0007; www.shakerrungolf.com
Lakeside/Meadows: 6991/5046; 73.7/68.4; 136/118
Meadows/Woodlands: 7092/5161; 74.1/69.6; 134/119
Woodlands/Lakeside: 6963/5075; 74.0/68.8; 138/121
☑ "The new Meadows nine delights" area dawn-patrollers who "demand you go out and play each combination", including Arthur Hills' original 18 on this "country club–quality course" at a formerly private facility with a "very nice pro shop"; you should "prepare to be humbled" because it's "big-time golf" on a number of "intimidating" holes like "the beautiful and challenging Lakeside finish that carries over the water", which almost makes up for the "very ordinary" Woodlands.

Vineyard   – | – | – | – | $29
600 Nordyke Rd.; 513-474-3007; 6789/4747; 72.8/67.9; 132/114
The Cincinnati grapevine has it that "a country-club experience and excellent conditions for under $30" are par for the course at this tight, tree-trimmed muni with lightning-fast greens where water (not wine) awaits on five holes; given all this plus khaki-clad greeters who carry your bags from your car and an impressive winter Sunday brunch at the Sweetwine Lodge, of course it's "difficult to get a prime tee time."

Cleveland

Avalon Lakes   ∇ 26 | 21 | 19 | 19 | $135
1 American Way NE, Warren; 330-856-8800; www.avalonlakes.com; 7551/4904; 76.9/68.5; 143/119
■ Water-loving masochists whoop "wow, what a course" "for this area"; the "must-play" diabolical Pete Dye woodlander brings the drink into play on 12 holes, so save money for extra balls with the twilight discount; 19th-holers should slum it at the on-course grill and steer clear of Opus 21, the upscale "restaurant/bar on property, which is owned by a different company and doesn't really cater to the golfing crowd."

Fowler's Mill   24 | 20 | 20 | 22 | $67
13095 Rockhaven Rd., Chesterland; 440-729-7569;
www.americangolf.com
Lake/Maple: 6595/5828; 72.1/73.6; 128/123
Maple/River: 6385/5712; 70.7/73.0; 125/125
River/Lake: 7002/5950; 74.7/73.9; 136/122
■ Only the class dunce can't "see why par is a good score" on this "required course for students of golf architecture, a relatively early Pete Dye" where "experiments in railroad ties and split fairways" make for an "outstanding challenge"; the "beautiful Lake" nine's No. 4 is "one of the state's best holes", with or without the "prominent geese droppings", so "bring your splatter guard" and ignore the fowls fouling up the joint – it's still "one of the most picturesque", "well-maintained" and "well-designed" tracks near Cleveland.

Reserve at Thunder Hill, The   24 | 17 | 17 | 18 | $62

7050 Griswold Rd., Madison; 440-298-3474;
www.reserveatthunderhill.com; 7223/5524; 78.0/68.5; 151/127
◾ "Bring your fishing pole and a dozen X-out" balls to sink into the
drink at this "former fish hatchery" with "lakes everywhere they
should be and many places they shouldn't"; "the hardest, most
penal and unforgiving course they've ever encountered" leads
linksmen "playing poorly" to thunder it's "a long day" that gets
"quite annoying after awhile."

Sawmill Creek   22 | 23 | 21 | 21 | $79

2401 Cleveland Rd. W., Huron; 419-433-3789; 800-729-6455;
www.sawmillcreek.com; 6702/5124; 72.3/69.4; 128/115
◾ "You can figure on a boost-your-handicap day if the wind blows"
at "Ohio's version of Pebble Beach", "a well-maintained resort
course, challenging but fun, with excellent holes near Lake Erie";
a marina, three restaurants, shops and indoor/outdoor pools, plus
Sheldon Marsh nature preserve and Cedar Point amusement park
nearby make the resort "a good place just to get away for a couple
of days", even if spoilsports sputter that the golf facilities are "too
expensive and too busy, with an arrogant staff."

StoneWater ⌂   27 | 22 | 20 | 18 | $90

1 Club Dr., Highland Heights; 440-461-4653; www.stonewatergolf.com;
7002/5500; 74.8/72.6; 138/132
◾ A "great practice facility" and a "phenomenal" "new clubhouse
round out the package" at this "beautiful", "stiff challenge for low-
to middle-handicappers"; nevertheless, stone-faced ball strikers
insist that the "wonderful" links-style layout "has been destroyed
by home development covering every inch of the place", and
a "staff with an attitude" doesn't make up for the loss or the
high "summer charges."

Columbus

Bent Tree   18 | 18 | 19 | 15 | $58

350 Bent Tree Rd., Sunbury; 740-965-5140; www.americangolf.com;
6642/5110; 72.3/69.2; 122/113
◾ "One of the first upscale public courses to open in Central Ohio's"
"farmland" just north of Columbus, this "scenic challenge" "with
a country-club feel" is still "popular for outings", though it's so
"demanding at times", it "could overpower short hitters" in the
group; aesthetes argue that "a lack of trees and rather plain terrain
take away from the experience", and "conditions have suffered
recently, especially in the bunkers."

Cooks Creek 🕐   25 | 18 | 18 | 20 | $60

16405 US Hwy. 23, Ashville; 740-983-3636; www.cookscreek.com;
7071/5095; 73.7/68.2; 131/120
◾ "Save for Longaberger, this is by far the most scenic course in
the area" announce Ashvillers agog over the "sweeping changes
in vista" at this "tough test that uses all your clubs amid beautiful
rolling hills and trees" and "lots of water"; "fair but fun" and fast
as can be, with 18 clocking in at an "awesome" "two hours", it's "a
great day for all who play" it, at least in the sunshine – with "poor
drainage in its lowland position next to the Scioto River", it "holds
rain like a sink."

Eaglesticks   24 | 20 | 20 | 23 | $41

2655 Maysville Pike, Zanesville; 740-454-4900; 800-782-4493;
www.eaglesticks.com; 6508/4233; 70.1/63.7; 120/96

☑ "Avoid the tall grass and you'll have a fabulous experience" at
this "excellent test for hackers"; "a lot of golf on a small plot of
land", it's a "short but fun" "target course with very fast greens"
that disgruntled drivers dis as "overhyped and overrated", with
"several holes crammed in" and "many delays and backups"
leading to "rounds that easily take five hours."

Granville   24 | 16 | 20 | 23 | $51

555 Newark Rd., Granville; 740-587-0843; www.granvillegolf.com;
6559/5197; 71.3/69.6; 128/123

☑ Many golfin' Granvilleans continue to call this "a fabulous Donald
Ross" "fave for good players", with "fast, difficult-to-read greens",
"thick rough" and "various slopes that make the approaches to
elevated greens difficult"; a handful of historians harrumph that
"Michael Hurdzan's recent redo" to "accommodate housing" "does
not seem to fit."

Longaberger   28 | 29 | 29 | 21 | $115

1 Long Dr., Nashport; 740-763-1100; www.longaberger.com;
7243/4985; 75.2/68.9; 138/122

■ Its "immaculate" Course, "fantastic Service" and "outstanding"
Facilities all rate No. 1 in the state, so clearly this "must-play" is
"unmatched in Ohio"; where "everything is first-class", everyone
wants to play and it sells out lickety-split for March 30–November 2
rounds, so book in February through a Longaberger home products
sales representative, try your luck calling in March or attempt to
fill a cancellation in season because any way you can get on it,
the "wonderful 12-minute tee-time spacing" is "worth" the hassle
and the money; N.B. the planned Tom Weiskopf course may
double the offerings.

Royal American Links   20 | 20 | 18 | 18 | $45

3300 Miller Paul Rd., Galena; 740-965-1215; www.americangolf.com;
6859/5172; 72.5/69.2; 127/117

■ "Get a map or hire a guide to find" this "pleasant but demanding"
"links-style layout" "located in a farm field in middle-of-nothing"
central Ohio; getting there might be a royal pain, but the "windy"
course itself is "nicely routed", "playing firm, fast" and "tighter
than it looks"; mid-mashie monarchs proclaim it "well priced"
for "some memorable holes", plus a "wonderful castle-style
clubhouse" where "banquet facilities that are better than most"
will have you and your court feasting like kings.

Dayton

Heatherwoode   ▽ 20 | 21 | 20 | 18 | $52

88 Heatherwoode Blvd., Springboro; 937-748-3222; 800-231-4049;
www.heatherwoodegolf.com; 6730/5069; 72.9/69.8; 138/127

☑ "The 'Woode is the place to play" shout Dayton duffers, who
enjoy a "challenging layout" featuring "fast greens" and 14 water
holes (15 if you include the spacious clubhouse and bar) in "great
condition" at a decent price; pointing out "some quirky spots"
where "the designer ran out of land", critics crab "there are too
many better courses in the area to choose from."

Yankee Trace

| 24 | 23 | 19 | 19 | $60 |

*10000 Yankee St., Centerville; 937-438-4653; www.yankeetrace.org;
7139/5204; 74.1/70.6; 136/121*

■ Yankee yipsters yap that the honor of hosting a Buy.com Tour event is "properly deserved" by this "very challenging" track that "demands both shotmaking skills and the ability to play in the wind" as well as around water on half the holes; "always in tip-top shape", it's a "nice muni" with "a private-club feel", and "the three-hole practice loop is a good touch", as is the restaurant, where the Sunday brunch layout rivals the course itself.

Toledo

Maumee Bay Resort

| ▽ 24 | 22 | 21 | 23 | $44 |

*1750 Park Rd. #2, Oregon; 419-836-9009; www.maumeebayresort.com;
6941/5221; 73.3/70.5; 129/118*

■ "It's way good" say wowed whackers of this "tough", "well-designed links course at a nice state park facility" "along the shores of Lake Erie" where there's "always a stiff breeze"; "one of Arthur Hills' best", it combines "high rough and rolling hills" with that wind for "a great test" – be sure to "bring lots of balls."

Oklahoma

Durant

Chickasaw Pointe

| – | – | – | – | $60 |

*Hwy. 70 E., Kingston; 580-564-2581; 877-242-8040;
www.oklahomaparks.com; 7085/5285; 74.5/72.2; 125/126*

"Similar to Karsten Creek but better priced", this "winner from the Oklahoma Parks Department" along with a private owner boasts a "well-groomed" "excellent design" that's the most "challenging" in the state system, it's hilly, wooded and watery, with 15 holes along Lake Texoma, where you can bet that "wind is a big factor."

Oklahoma City

Jimmie Austin University of Oklahoma Golf Course

| ▽ 24 | 22 | 19 | 23 | $40 |

*1 Par Dr., Norman; 405-325-6716; www.ou.edu/admin/jaougc;
7197/5310; 74.9/71.6; 134/119*

■ "A great redo by Bob Cupp in the mid-'90s" turned this "nicely varied", "well-kept" collegian into a "long, brutal" "beauty" "with small greens" so well guarded, you'd "better bring a shovel, as you'll dig out of the sand plenty"; chicks and ducks and geese better scurry, 'cause it's "beastly when the wind" comes sweepin' down the plain, and some Sooners would sooner swing a few on "the best practice facilities they've seen at a public course", even though "the clubhouse needs a remodel" – perhaps some fringe on top?

Stillwater

Karsten Creek

| ▽ 28 | 24 | 22 | 16 | $225 |

1800 S. Memorial Dr.; 405-743-1658; 7095/4906; 74.8/70.1; 142/127

■ The OSU Cowboys are home on the range at this host of the 2003 NCAA Men's Championship, an expense-account-er that would be "great in any state"; "quite challenging and at times extreme", with "super finishing holes" in "unbelievably good condition", it's "priced to keep the public off", but if you do cough up the cash, explore the clubhouse, "which captures the outdoor atmosphere and Okie State U. golfing lore quite well."

Tulsa

Forest Ridge   ▽ 25 | 23 | 24 | 21 | $75

7501 E. Kenosha St., Broken Arrow; 918-357-2443; www.forestridge.com; 7069/5341; 74.8/73.3; 137/132

■ There may be broken clubs in Broken Arrow after frustrated flubbers get through with this "super but very tight" and "tough little track" "with dense stands of trees just off the fairway" in a planned community right outside of Tulsa; locals say it's "the best we have that everyone can play", and it's perfect chased by a big meal at Café Savannah's in the clubhouse, where the menu is longer than the layout – just "bring two extra sleeves of balls", and try not to throw your irons.

Oregon

★ **Best in State**
30 Bandon Dunes, Bandon Dunes Course, *Coos Bay*
29 Bandon Dunes, Pacific Dunes, *Coos Bay*
27 Sunriver Resort, Crosswater, *Bend*
     Pumpkin Ridge, Ghost Creek, *Portland*
     Running Y Ranch Resort, *Klamath Falls*

Bend

Black Butte Ranch, Big Meadow   23 | 20 | 21 | 21 | $65

13457 Hawksbeard Rd., Black Butte; 541-595-1500; 800-452-7455; www.blackbutteranch.com; 6850/5716; 72.0/70.5; 127/115

■ "Snow-capped mountains are on view" at this "great" layout that some ranch hands say is "the better of the two BBs", with "a welcome new clubhouse", which, along with the entire resort, survived the recent Cache Mountain wildfire relatively unscathed; a few surveyors in a blacker mood say "being picturesque and nicely groomed doesn't make up for a five-and-a-half hour round."

Black Butte Ranch, Glaze Meadow   22 | 18 | 20 | 20 | $65

13457 Hawksbeard Rd., Black Butte; 541-595-1500; 800-452-7455; www.blackbutteranch.com; 6574/5616; 71.5/72.1; 128/120

☑ "You feel like you're on top of the world" at this "wonderfully" scenic, "beautifully kept" track at a resort with biking, hiking and fishing amid the Ponderosas not far from the Santiam Pass summit; still, some golfers glaze over at "its weird design" that they rate "not as good as Big Meadow", with "the worst opening hole in Oregon" – perhaps they should tell that to a "staff that has a tendency to act as if they're working at Augusta National."

Eagle Crest, Resort   ▽ 19 | 18 | 19 | 16 | $55

1522 Cline Falls Rd., Redmond; 541-923-4653; 877-818-0286; www.eagle-crest.com; 6673/5395; 71.5/69.8; 128/120

☑ "The wildflowers make this nicely kept course great to look at" say aesthetes weighing in on the "scenic resort" track at the foot of the Cascades; the dogleg right par-5 2nd, where you tee off 80 feet above the Deschutes River canyon floor, is "everyone's favorite", but "some others are quite good too"; dissenters say it's "not nearly as nice as the Ridge", its slightly more pricey sister.

Eagle Crest, Ridge   ▽ 22 | 19 | 21 | 19 | $65

1522 Cline Falls Rd., Redmond; 541-923-4653; 877-818-0286; www.eagle-crest.com; 6927/4792; 73/66.1; 131/115

■ More hilly and highly acclaimed than the Resort, this "pleasant" alternative is designed to be challenging but playable for all levels, with no forced carries, four water holes and plenty of canyon and mountain views; stop into the "nice pro shop" before leaving, or stick around to play the 18-hole par-63 course to fine-tune your iron game.

Lost Tracks   ▽ 18 | 17 | 19 | 20 | $58

60205 Sunset View Dr.; 541-385-1818; 7003/5287; 71.8/69.7; 124/127

☑ "Bring your bag tag to add" to the enormous "collection in the railroad dining car" that serves as a bridge to the island-green 16th at this "cute track" "for the money", where you'll wind up "leaving the driver" at home and "working on your slice" because there are "doglegs everywhere"; its "best-looking cart gals" will appeal to dogs of another kind.

Sunriver Resort, Crosswater ⛳   27 | 25 | 23 | 22 | $155

1 Center Dr., Sunriver; 541-593-1221; 800-547-3922; www.sunriver-resort.com; 7683/5359; 76.9/69.8; 150/125

■ "Beautiful to the eye and teasing to the club", this "amazing" resort's guests-only spread is "appropriately named" – the "long carries over wetlands" are "very tough", so "bring your A-game or lots of balls" and "don't make the mistake of playing from the tips" when "there's a variety of tee boxes to help you choose your challenge"; the "wonderful" "drive from the airport" is "through the national forest", but this "great destination" in "excellent condition" is the "climax" of the trip.

Sunriver Resort, North Woodlands ⛳   ▽ 19 | 16 | 18 | 19 | $125

1 Center Dr., Sunriver; 541-593-1221; 800-547-3922; www.sunriver-resort.com; 7012/5287; 72.8/69.8; 128/127

■ "I would play it again in a heartbeat" swoon swingers sweating this "gorgeous, tough" meadow-laced layout "set among the pines and junipers offering excellent views of the Cascade Mountains" and hotels set on "a variety of terrains"; the "very well-operated facility" is carts-only, but you might be able to hoof it on the rare slow day here.

Sunriver Resort, South Meadows ⛳   ▽ 19 | 20 | 22 | 19 | $125

1 Center Dr., Sunriver; 541-593-1221; 800-547-3922; www.sunriver-resort.com; 6880/5446; 73.0/70.2; 131/127

■ Its course rating may not be all that, but insiders know that in 2001, the "resort spent an enormous amount" to turn this "really fun" woodlander into "a first-rate facility" equal to its "spectacular views" of Mt. Bachelor, Three Sisters and Broken Top Mountains, and indeed, "it's immaculate" now; "sometimes play can slow down, but you're there to relax anyway, so enjoy it."

Coos Bay

BANDON DUNES, BANDON DUNES COURSE 🏌

30 | 27 | 27 | 26 | $175

Round Lake Dr., Bandon; 541-347-4380; 888-345-6008;
www.bandondunesgolf.com; 6732/5125; 74.6/72.1; 145/128

■ "Words cannot describe" the "orgasmic" "sublimity" of
Scottish designer David Kidd's "world-class" links, rated No. 1 in
this *Survey*; as if "sprung up from the dunes", it's the game as it
"was meant to be played": "no carts, no buildings, nothing but golf",
"with birds and whales" and a "Ballybunion" feel; "stay at the
lodge" because the "food is excellent", and be prepared to "test all
your skills" where "wind and length are your biggest obstacles,
but the elevated greens with huge, deep-pot bunkers get in the
way too" – "oh, yeah, and then there's the ocean . . ."

BANDON DUNES, PACIFIC DUNES 🏌

29 | 26 | 27 | 26 | $175

Round Lake Dr., Bandon; 541-347-4380; 888-345-6008;
www.bandondunesgolf.com; 6623/5107; 72.9/71.1; 133/131

■ It's "Heaven on Earth II" at this "magnificent" "addition to an
already spectacular destination"; "looking more like Northern
Ireland than Northern Ireland" itself, it features "great ocean
views" and "natural bunkering" on "challenging holes that vary in
direction, allowing the wind to have its way with you"; "golf
nuts" sigh "if I had a million dollars, I'd buy a house in Bandon and let
my whim decide which course I'd play that day" because there
are possibly "no two finer on earth."

Eugene

Sandpines Golf Links

▽ 25 | 12 | 15 | 25 | $55

1201 35th St., Florence; 541-997-1940; www.sandpines.com;
7252/5346; 76.3/72.7; 131/129

☑ "Who needs fancy facilities" when there's this "unbelievable
course for the money" that's "close in caliber to Bandon" claim
ardent admirers; "it can be difficult when the gales blow" in the
afternoon, so "play in the morning", or wrestle the gusts for
"especially" good "twilight rates", and try to ignore the few
sandbaggers who say "everyone gushes over it, but I don't get it."

Tokatee Golf Club

25 | 18 | 19 | 26 | $37

54947 McKenzie Hwy., Blue River; 541-822-3220; 800-452-6376;
www.tokatee.com; 6807/5018; 72.4/67.8; 127/109

■ "Some holes recall Spyglass . . . really" at this "old-school"
"gem", a "perfect mountain course" "next to a trout-fishing river"
"with unbelievable views on great holes" between "firs, water and
nice sand" "you must think your way around"; "they can be a little
Gestapo-like with marshaling, but better that than sitting around."

Klamath Falls

Running Y Ranch Resort

▽ 27 | 24 | 23 | 25 | $75

5790 Coopers Hawk Rd.; 541-850-5580; 888-850-0261; www.runningy.com;
7133/4842; 73.0/66.3; 125/120

■ "Oregon's most enjoyable course for all handicap ranges" rave
roused Running Y Ranchers rooting for this Palmer-designed "user-

friendly" 18 in "a beautiful setting" that begins amid restored wetlands ("wear bug repellent"), then meanders into woodlands and Payne Canyon; its "very good resort amenities" include a spa, restaurant and lots of family activities like trail riding and canoeing.

Portland

Heron Lakes, Great Blue　　　22 │ 11 │ 13 │ 24 │ $39
3500 N. Victory Blvd.; 503-289-1818; www.heronlakesgolf.com; 6916/5825; 73.6/69.8; 132/120

■ "Where else can you get your butt kicked by Robert Trent Jones Jr. for under $40" than this "best-kept secret in Oregon" with a "mild front nine" and a "very hard" back fueled by "sloped, fairly quick greens"?; on the downside, it's "too busy most of the time", both with golfers and "untold thousands of Canada geese", so "prepare to wipe your shoes" because no one else is gonna do it for you, i.e. it "doesn't have many amenities", and "it may be time for a new clubhouse, but don't let that stop you."

Heron Lakes, Greenback　　▽ 17 │ 11 │ 13 │ 25 │ $37
3500 N. Victory Blvd.; 503-289-1818; www.heronlakesgolf.com; 6608/5240; 71.6/69.4; 123/113

◪ "Bring hip-waders" to this "fun" liquidy track because while its "easier" than its sibling, it "doesn't drain as well"; it's also "less memorable" and more "crowded", but it does offer a nice old-style experience "for the money" doled out by duffers, and it's usually a "good course to post a low score on"; get the weather report before you play it, though, because it "can be a challenge when the wind kicks up" and those "huge greens" start to act like they're moving.

Langdon Farms　　　　　　19 │ 20 │ 20 │ 16 │ $84
24377 NE Airport Rd., Aurora; 503-678-3262; www.langdonfarms.com; 6931/5246; 73.3/64.8; 125/108

◪ Fans among the farmhands fuss over this "real treat with a links-style layout" and "barn-style clubhouse"; it's "nice if you can get over the noise of the I-5 right next to you", but demanding drivers dis a "company-outing setup" that's "contrived to seem Scottish, but is not – aren't there laws against degrading the land like this?"

Oregon Golf Association　　▽ 21 │ 18 │ 18 │ 22 │ $51
Members Course at Tukwila
2850 Hazlenut Dr., Woodburn; 503-981-6105; 6650/5498; 71.7/71.8; 131/129

■ "The views from the second-story patio overlooking the joined 9th and 18th greens are best experienced with a very tall glass of Northwest microbrew" note beer-bellied ball swipers on this "nicely built modern track" carved out of an orchard by the Oregon Golf Association, with "discounted rates for members"; given "challenging holes" and good drainage that "can handle the wet winters", it's "totally worth the 30-mile drive from Portland."

Persimmon ⊕　　　　　　▽ 17 │ 22 │ 19 │ 16 │ $65
500 SE Butler Rd., Gresham; 503-667-7500; www.persimmongolf.com; 6445/5444; 71.0/71.3; 126/127

■ "Only mountain goats will walk it" wail flat-footed foozlers weighing in on this "well-maintained", forested and "quite hilly" course with "some tremendous views of Mt. Hood, Mt. St. Helens" and Mt. Adams to compensate for an "oddly routed" layout with "not enough level lies to be highly playable"; nonetheless, its 30-minute proximity to downtown Portland and impressive facilities make it fruitful for corporate gatherings.

Pumpkin Ridge, Ghost Creek   27 | 27 | 24 | 21 | $120

12930 NW Old Pumpkin Ridge Rd., North Plains; 503-647-9977; 888-594-4653; www.pumpkinridge.com; 6839/5111; 73.8/70.0; 139/128

■ "Some of the holes are a little scary, but so is my game" howl hackers haunted by this "championship" track "with beautiful sloped fairways and a nice natural woodsy setting" in which lurk "some of the state's fastest greens and brutal thick rough", plus "said creek that swallows balls when it snakes out of nowhere"; "it's the kind of course that makes you think", so "now you know why the USGA selected it for the 2006 U.S. Senior Open."

Reserve Vineyards, Cupp   ▽ 22 | 27 | 22 | 18 | $85

4805 SW 229th Ave., Aloha; 503-649-8191; www.reservegolf.com; 6852/5198; 72.6/69.6; 132/115

■ Its sibling "the Fought gets a lot of well-deserved praise, but some should be reserved for this course" too say Cuppers up on the "quirkily routed", rolling Portland-area links layout with "very few bunkers", "most of which aren't in play", but lots of water hazards, difficult greens and "an unusual par 37/35 layout"; "don't get discouraged because you can really tear up the back nine", and if you're worried its "expensive" fees will rip up your wallet, look for one of the "constantly promoted specials."

Reserve Vineyards, Fought   ▽ 25 | 28 | 24 | 21 | $85

4805 SW 229th Ave., Aloha; 503-649-8191; www.reservegolf.com; 7172/5189; 74.3/70.3; 134/121

■ The Cupp's sister is "its opposite" in many ways due to a longer, flatter, "more conventional route" and "bunkers everywhere"; "with some great holes that really push you" and "a number of high risk/reward approaches that make for a memorable round", "you'll feel like a pro playing it, until you look at your scorecard"; the annual Fred Meyer Challenge is hosted here, but its participants always "make the course look much easier than it is."

Pennsylvania

★ **Best in State**
26 Nemacolin Woodlands, Mystic Rock, *Pittsburgh*
   Hartefeld National, *Philadelphia*
   Wyncote, *Philadelphia*
24 Center Valley, *Allentown*
23 Toftrees Resort, *State College*

Allentown

Center Valley Club   24 | 18 | 20 | 18 | $72

3300 Center Valley Pkwy., Center Valley; 610-791-5580; www.centervalleyclubgolf.com; 6916/4925; 73.7/68.6; 138/116

☑ "Bring your A-game or enough balls to get you around" this Lehigh Valley daily fee, because "oh that rough" can make you suffer whether you're on the "links front nine" you'd "swear was in Scotland if there were more dogs" or the "parkland American"-style back; speaking of suffering, unless you're a "mountain goat", "don't attempt to walk" the "regular mini-tour stop" that's "sneaky-close to NYC" with "nice" "after-prime rates" to make up for the fact that it "needs better dining facilities."

Olde Homestead
23 | 19 | 20 | 21 | $55

6598 Rte. 309, New Tripoli; 610-298-4653; 6800/4953; 73.2/68.2; 137/116

■ "It never takes more than four-and-a-half hours to play" this "relaxing" "gem hidden away in the northern Lehigh Valley", where "higher elevations" afford "beautiful views" of the Blue Mountains and the fairways are "fairly wide open" but the going gets "tough when the wind picks up"; "recent renovations" "changed two holes on the front nine, making the course better", while "the best public practice facilities in the area" are as "nice" as ever.

Whitetail
23 | 19 | 21 | 21 | $50

2679 Klein Rd., Bath; 610-837-9626; www.whitetailgolfclub.com; 6432/5152; 70.6/65.3; 128/113

■ "Scenic No. 8 overlooks four lakes, making it memorable" to "low double-digit handicappers easily playing from the tips" on this "relatively short", "beautiful" layout stretching "over the hills and through the woods"; the "most friendly staff" in the "nice pro shop" might tell you not to be fooled by the track's lack of length – "you will be tested with sloped fairways and beautiful greens", and you might be bamboozled by the "couple of gimmicky par 3s."

Gettysburg

Bridges, The
22 | 22 | 19 | 19 | $60

6729 York Rd., Abbottstown; 717-624-9551; 800-942-2444; 6713/5134; 72.5/70.1; 133/117

■ It's "a gem of course", this Gettysburg area daily fee that you "must play to appreciate", with "well-kept" bentgrass greens and fairways, four sets of tees that make it accessible to all levels of play and a historic brick clubhouse with lodging, a fine restaurant and an extensive pro shop; it's "well worth the money", but if you find it "a little pricey" for these parts, you'll "like the early-bird special."

Carroll Valley,
Carroll Valley Course
▽ 21 | 15 | 17 | 19 | $54

121 Sanders Rd., Fairfield; 717-642-8211; 800-548-8504; www.carrollvalley.com; 6633/5005; 71.2/67.6; 120/114

▨ "Excellent off-season rates" make for a "decent getaway" at this Catoctin Mountains resort 10 minutes from Gettysburg offering play-stay-and-partay packages; "another course that's kept in good shape", it's "fun and a bit challenging when the wind is up" on the lakes that lace it, but the "staff appears stuck-up", meaning "service could be better."

Carroll Valley, Mountain View
▽ 20 | 16 | 16 | 16 | $46

121 Sanders Rd., Fairfield; 717-642-8211; 800-548-8504; www.carrollvalley.com; 6343/5024; 70.2/68.2; 122/113

▨ Happy hoofers hoot "thank goodness for a walkable layout" where strolling is "allowed on weekend mornings" at a "decent" track that's "worth playing if you're in the area"; you might just make it over to these parts if you and your family are lured by the ample resort activities, including cooking classes with the award-winning chef, even if the entire experience is "well overpriced."

Links at Gettysburg, The   – | – | – | – | $80

601 Mason-Dixon Rd.; 717-359-8000; 888-793-9498;
www.thelinksatgettysburg.com; 7031/4861; 73.9/68.8; 128/116

There's not one but "12 signature holes" on this "awesome" daily-fee course near the site of Abraham Lincoln's famous address to the nation in central Pennsylvania; not only is the place steeped in history, the course itself is "very scenic", with waterfalls and other forms of H_2O on 15 fairways surrounded by stunning red-rock cliffs; though it's "expensive for the area", it's "worth the cost to play it just once", since "you'll never be disappointed, even when you're scoring poorly."

Penn National, Founders   ▽ 25 | 22 | 23 | 22 | $44

3720 Club House Dr., Fayetteville; 717-352-3000; www.penngolf.com;
6958/5367; 73.9/71.4; 139/123

■ A speedy swinger can "walk on as a single and be off in about a half hour" at this "fantastic, classic old course", a longish resort track with tree-bordered, "super fairways", "very good greens" and a lake that comes into play; even if you can't cash in on the discounts for seniors, juniors and off-peak putters, it's "pricey but worth it" to go a round here and then sleep in a bed where Robert E. Lee once laid his own head at the historic White Rock Manor House on the premises.

Penn National, Iron Forge   ▽ 26 | 22 | 22 | 19 | $49

3720 Club House Dr., Fayetteville; 717-352-3000; www.penngolf.com;
7009/5246; 73.8/70.3; 133/120

■ Ball-launching bards sing of this "phoenix risen from the ashes of modern golf architecture"; it's on the long side and "very difficult", though there's a positive to all the punishment you receive – "with the high scores, you get your money's worth per stroke", plus the course is a mere 18 miles from the Civil War battlefields of Gettysburg, so you can forge ahead on an educational family weekend after your round.

Harrisburg

Country Club of Hershey, South 🏨   22 | 21 | 22 | 19 | $65

600 W. Derry Rd., Hershey; 717-534-3450; 6332/4979; 71.0/68.6; 129/119

■ As "sweet" and "satisfying" as the local product, this "short but demanding" track requires you to use "all your clubs" and your willpower, because "the smell of chocolate abounds" around the "picturesque setting" where non-golfers have the "added benefit of a certain nearby amusement park" – bring the kids and you're in for some kisses.

Heritage Hills   ▽ 19 | 21 | 17 | 17 | $60

2700 Mount Rose Ave., York; 717-755-4653; 800-942-2444; www.hhgr.com;
6628/5145; 71.1/69.9; 122/112

■ "You will hit every club in your bag" because it's "quite hilly" on this "decent course" with "very strong 9th and 18th holes" and a landmark 100-year-old oak standing on its "well-maintained" layout; though it "could be a little better priced" for western Pennsylvania, the "very helpful and friendly staff" "treats you well", so even "on the hottest day of the year", you'll probably "enjoy it", particularly if you're checked into the luxury duplex suite overlooking the fairways.

Lancaster

Pilgrim's Oak
22 | 15 | 20 | 24 | $57

1107 Pilgrim's Pathway, Peach Bottom; 717-548-3011;
www.pilgrimsoak.com; 6766/5004; 73.4/70.7; 143/129
■ Golfers give thanks for this "fun-to-play" "links-style course that tests your accuracy off the tee"; a little wampum goes a long way here, since it's considered by spendthrifts to be "the best for the price in eastern Pennsylvania", and with the "friendly staff" helping to make it an overall "pleasant experience", the Amish country course is certainly no turkey.

Philadelphia

Downingtown Country Club
20 | 18 | 17 | 18 | $65

85 Country Club Dr., Downingtown; 610-269-2000;
www.golfdowningtown.com; 6619/5092; 72.3/69.4; 129/119
☑ "Most people walk" this "tight, rebuilt" daily fee that's "nicely maintained", where "they make up for its shortness with thick rough and fast greens"; don't "underestimate its difficulty", and other than the "excellent restaurant", don't overestimate the club's facilities – there's "no driving range" here, even though the "inattentive caddies" could use a bit more practice themselves.

Golf Course at Glen Mills
– | – | – | – | $90

221 Glen Mills Rd., Glen Mills; 610-558-2142; www.glenmillsgolf.com;
6636/4800; 71.0/62.0; 131/114
"One of the best-kept secrets in southeastern Pennsylvania", this "intimidating" layout on a "spectacular site" near the Delaware River has a "great mix of challenging holes", with "some long and wide open" and others "narrow with hazards"; all, however, are "beautifully manicured" by a staff drawn from the Glen Mills School, a home for troubled youths who train at the course for careers in turf management and golf house operation, so check into a local B&B and hit a few for a good cause.

Hartefeld National
26 | 24 | 23 | 18 | $110

1 Hartefeld Dr., Avondale; 610-268-8800; 800-240-7373;
www.hartefeld.com; 6969/5065; 73.2/69.8; 131/123
■ "Almost demonic from the tips" and "punishing of poor tee shots", this "beautifully groomed" "championship caliber course" done up in "thick rough and waist-high fescue" eats "all skill levels" alive, and it also devours wallets – money-wise masochists would "play here every week if it were more reasonable"; though "recent home development takes away from the country atmosphere" and the "amazing view from the grill", there's always "the smell of the neighboring mushroom farm" for rural realness.

Hickory Valley, Ambassador
17 | 12 | 14 | 20 | $40

1921 Ludwig Rd., Gilbertsville; 610-754-9862; 6448/5058; 70.3/69.0; 116/116
☑ "A fine public course" "for the average golfer", this 6,400-yard suburban shorty still presents a "good challenge", and it's a "deal for the money", that is if you're not looking to warm up or chow down; it "lacks a decent post-round eating facility", the "driving range is poor" and, as one workaday whacker whines, the "putting green is about the size of my office" – but "at least they have one", and it sure beats being behind that desk.

Hickory Valley, Presidential   22 13 15 19 $55
1921 Ludwig Rd., Gilbertsville; 610-754-9862; 6676/5271; 72.8/71.8; 133/128
■ "Much better and more challenging than its sibling", this "great layout" serves up "well laid-out, visually appealing holes", including the 5th, for which the walls of an old stone barn double as the tee box; despite the "very attentive staff", City of Brotherly Lovers insist that "local knowledge is the key to a good round" here, probably because the "dining facilities are lacking", so if golf gets your gut grumbling, look for anyone in an Eagles jersey and ask 'em where to get a good cheesesteak.

Turtle Creek   20 10 15 19 $50
303 W. Ridge Pike, Limerick; 610-489-5133; www.turtlecreekgolf.com; 6702/5131; 72.1/68.6; 127/115
■ There once was a man from Nantucket, who loved this "fun and different" Limerick daily fee because it was, and still is, of "medium difficulty" and "in great shape", with some "very tough holes", including "outstanding par 5s"; the "clubhouse trailer", "staff and services are not quite up to [any] par", but "where else can you tee it up and walk for less the $30 during the week" on a course "owned by an area turf farmer" who "keeps the greens just that – green"?

Wyncote   26 20 20 20 $88
50 Wyncote Dr., Oxford; 610-932-8900; www.wyncote.com; 7012/5454; 74.0/71.6; 130/126
■ It's such a "tough ride from Center City Philly" "to the boonies" that you might actually think you've come as far as Loch Lomond to play this "Scottish links course"; the "par 3s are unforgiving", the "rough is treacherous", the "quick-running greens are like putting in your bathtub" and, of course, it's so "open" that it's "very hard when the wind is blowing"; "good shots [still] get rewarded", perhaps with a hearty meal and some hooch, since they finally got their liquor license and a "restaurant in need of some work" recently redid its menu.

Pittsburgh

Chestnut Ridge, Tom's Run   ▽ 26 24 22 22 $60
1762 Old William Penn Hwy., Blairsville; 724-459-7188; www.chestnutridgeinn.com; 6812/5363; 73.0/71.0; 135/126
■ "Country club–like conditions" make this "one of the best public courses in the greater Pittsburgh area"; "picture-perfect through the first six holes", "the front nine is terrific", and the "excellent design and construction" throughout make for an "interesting layout" that's "demanding but eminently playable", while the fare at the resort is eminently edible, despite the fact that accommodations don't get more luxurious than the Comfort Inn.

Deer Run   ▽ 22 20 18 19 $50
287 Monier Rd., Gibsonia; 724-265-4800; deerrungolfclub.com; 7066/5255; 74.2/70.9; 135/127
■ This "very good, varied layout is kept in excellent condition", but you better make sure to spend a little time at the putting green and the chipping and bunker practice areas because it's tougher than chugging a warm six-pack of Iron City ale; recover with a night in a neighboring B&B, like Sun and Cricket, where they'll lodge not only you but your horse.

Hidden Valley Resort ⌂
▽ 22 | 18 | 19 | 20 | $40

1 Craighead Dr., Hidden Valley; 814-443-6454; 800-458-0175;
www.hiddenvalleyresort.com; 6589/5027; 73.1/70.3; 142/127

■ "You get what you pay for" at this challenging carts-only resort course that offers up a "good value for your money" thanks to a rolling, woodland layout with five sets of tee boxes amid the "great scenery" of the Laurel Highlands, where skiers slush in winter; convenient to a host of state parks and preserves and earth-friendly itself, it's a natural choice for back-to-the-land linksters.

Nemacolin Woodlands, Mystic Rock ⌂
26 | 26 | 25 | 16 | $150

1001 Lafayette Dr., Farmington; 724-329-8555; 800-422-2736;
www.nemacolin.com; 6832/6300; 75.0/71.5; 146/140

■ That mystic jeweler "Pete Dye has done it again" declare duffers dazzled by this "difficult but fun" "unfound diamond" in a "beautiful setting", where "huge boulders accentuate the course", creating "scenic vistas" amid "lush conditions"; the resort's "world-class spa and food" "make for a great visit", and a rockin' place to pop the question.

Nemacolin Woodlands, Woodlands Links
▽ 22 | 24 | 25 | 16 | $84

1001 Lafayette Dr., Farmington; 724-329-8555; 800-422-2736;
www.nemacolin.com; 6814/4835; 73.0/67.3; 131/115

■ Though it's "a nice resort course" with an "excellent layout by former owner Willard Rockwell", this woodsy track comes off "pretty bland after Mystic Rock"; since its sister is closed off-season, however, it's your only winter option at Nemacolin, when it's "a great value" and you can warm up while you walk it, so stop pouting, put on your parka and play.

Olde Stonewall
▽ 25 | 21 | 23 | 16 | $135

1495 Mercer Rd., Ellwood City; 724-752-4653; 6944/5051; 73.2/69.7; 140/123

■ To drive or not to drive, that is the question on this "cheap, beautiful course" where the bards of ball-hitting belly up to the bar at Shakespeare's Pub in the "unique but very classy castle clubhouse" after an "awesome" round featuring "spectacular views" and the namesake architectural feature; holes "Nos. 11–16 are "as good a stretch as you'll find in the state", and the "superb staff" isn't bad either.

Quicksilver
21 | 22 | 19 | 20 | $65

2000 Quicksilver Rd., Midway; 724-796-1594; www.quicksilvergolf.com;
7120/5067; 75.7/68.6; 145/115

☑ "Bring your putting skills" to this long, "hidden gem" where "the fastest greens ever" are of "championship" quality; "several blind tee shots make local knowledge important" say Pitts players pitching for a "seriously excellent value" only 15 minutes from downtown, where the "clubhouse is nice" and "the staff is polite", but perhaps not attentive enough to a track that's "starting to slip."

Seven Springs Mountain ⌂
▽ 22 | 18 | 20 | 21 | $72

R.R. 1, Champion; 814-352-7777; 800-452-2223; www.7springs.com;
6424/4934; 71.7/68.3; 132/111

■ Leave your walking shoes and swim fins at home, because this champion in Champion is carts-only and has water on just two holes; from the first tee atop Laurel Mountain there's an impressive view that encompasses Pennsylvania, Maryland and West Virginia, and when you're not driving, chipping or putting, you can go in for a little alpine sliding, biking, hiking or horseback riding at the off-season ski resort.

Poconos

Hideaway Hills 🏨
23 | 13 | 18 | 20 | $57

Carney Rd., Kresgeville; 610-681-6000; www.hideawaygolf.com; 6933/5047; 72.7/68.4; 127/116

■ "The only straight shot is on the first hole" at this "beautiful but little known" resort "gem with terrific mountain views" and "fantastic elevation changes" that make it "like a ride"; the course itself is "well maintained", but the "pro shop and dining facilities are below-average", which is a shame because, since it's "in the middle of nowhere", you'll probably want to "make it a weekend and play it twice."

Mount Airy Lodge 🏨
20 | 11 | 14 | 16 | $55

Woodland Dr., Mount Pocono; 570-839-8811; 800-441-4410; www.mountairyresort.com; 7123/5771; 74.3/73.3; 140/120

☑ When perky putters pipe about a "great bang for the buck" they're not just referring to the action amid the "love tubs and mirrors" in this "ancient" honeymoon hot spot; though a "resort that has fallen on hard times" reminds geographically challenged chippers of "the Catskills in 1940", a course with "breathtaking autumn" vistas may still be "the most scenic in the Poconos", if you can see around "all the blind shots"; "bring bug spray" 'cause the critters like those "great big greens."

Shawnee Inn
19 | 18 | 19 | 18 | $98

1 River Rd., Shawnee-On-Delaware; 570-424-4000; 800-742-9633; www.shawneeinn.com
Blue/Red: 6200/5600; 70.4/72.5; 126/123
Blue/White: 6250/5298; 70.2/71.1; 128/121
Red/White: 6086/5424; 69.4/71.4; 130/121

■ "If you want to try an [Arthur] Tillinghast course, this is one you can get onto", and it's also "his first"; where Jackie Gleason learned the game and Arnold Palmer met his future wife, the 1906 "classic Poconos resort" track today is a "hacker's delight" that's "flat compared with others in the area", with "wide-open fairways" for "easy scoring", "pretty views" and "two hits over the Delaware"; it's "manicured" and, despite the hot historical action it's seen, so "peaceful you could be in North Carolina", but you're riverside in Pennsylvania, so "bring the Off" because it's "very buggy."

Tamiment Resort ☉
∇ 17 | 15 | 15 | 17 | $52

Bushkill Falls Rd., Tamiment; 570-588-6652; 800-233-8105; www.tamiment.com; 6599/5598; 71.4/71.9; 127/124

■ "You'll get good use out of your fairway woods" as you clobber the ball for a shot that goes "very long and up, up, up, especially on the 17th" hole at this sprawling historical Poconos resort; the Robert Trent Jones Sr. track is "nothing spectacular" and "play is slow", but what's the rush, anyway? – the "friendly staff" "makes you feel special, only adding to the pure enjoyment" of playing a leisurely round within such "beautiful" mountain surroundings.

State College

Toftrees Resort   23 | 23 | 22 | 21 | $79

*1 Country Club Ln.; 814-238-7600; 800-458-3602; www.toftrees.com;
7026/5514; 74.3/72.2; 138/125*

■ "Everything is first-class" say collegiate club-wielders at this
Penn State–area track offering a "very challenging" "bang for the
buck" that won't cost you a semester's tuition; though the "greens
could be a little faster", tailgating Nittany Lions fans checked
into the resort for homecoming weekend say it's "very nice" to
"combine with football."

Puerto Rico

Dorado

Dorado Del Mar Country Club   ▽ 21 | 21 | 21 | 19 | $90

200 Dorado Del Mar; 787-796-3070; 6937/5283; 75.2/71.9; 138/125

■ Led by a "super head pro who cares about your enjoyment", the
"quite friendly staff" on this "tight", "well-kept" course includes
"rangers who do their job" by keeping things clicking when it
"gets too crowded"; "super views", "a great hole by the ocean"
and a "fine finishing par 5" help make it a "much better value
than nearby" tracks.

Hyatt Dorado Beach, East 🏨   23 | 22 | 20 | 17 | $181

*Hwy. 693; 787-796-8961; www.doradobeach.hyatt.com;
6985/5883; 72.5/74.2; 132/126*

■ "The wonderful sound of the coqui frog" and the "tranquil setting
calm even the most frustrated golfer" on this "tough" oceanside
resorter boasting "plenty of sun", "beautiful views and unusual
holes", including possibly "the best par 5 in the Caribbean"; it's
so "well kept", "they even irrigate the rough", but beyond the
groundskeepers, the "Hyatt needs to teach some service to its crew
if it wants to compete at the top."

Hyatt Dorado Beach, West 🏨   22 | 22 | 18 | 18 | $151

*Hwy. 693; 787-796-8961; www.doradobeach.hyatt.com;
6913/5883; 74.5/75.2; 132/132*

☒ If you get lucky, you'll meet [local PGA Tour legend] Chi Chi
Rodriguez" relaxing with a round on the "great fairways and
greens" of this "really nice" layout that beachcombers searching
the dunes for their balls call "challenging"; citing "maintenance
problems that can hamper the quality of play", club-wielding critics
complain that "it offers your typical Caribbean-style golf – not a
very good course on a beautiful piece of land that overlooks the
ocean . . . oh, well."

Hyatt Regency Cerromar Beach, North 🏨   18 | 19 | 20 | 18 | $110

*Hwy. 693; 787-796-8915; www.cerromarbeach.hyatt.com;
6841/5547; 72.2/71.1; 125/121*

☒ Island swingers set their ball sail on this seaside spread with a
"creative", "wide-open" RTJ Sr. design "made difficult by wind"
and 95 bunkers; aesthetes say the "disappointing" track "needs
fixing up", but they do speak well of the "wonderful" staff at the
Hyatt, who will shuttle you over to Dorado Beach if you want.

Hyatt Regency Cerromar Beach, South ⛳ | 20 | 19 | 20 | 18 | $110 |

Hwy. 693; 787-796-8915; www.cerromarbeach.hyatt.com;
7130/5680; 76.4/72.6; 138/142

☑ While it's "harder", "longer and better kept than the North", with "fast greens" and more water, this "good design" can also be windy; package-minded poobahs insist they "wouldn't pay full price", though they might enjoy an après-round drink at the poolside bar you can swim up to.

Las Croabas

Wyndham El Conquistador | 21 | 23 | 20 | 18 | $185 |

Rd. 987, K.M. 3.4; 787-863-6784; 800-468-8365; www.wyndham.com;
6662/4939; 72.5/70.9; 131/130

☑ "Watch for iguanas" at this "tough" track "sculpted into the plush green hills" at a self-contained resort overlooking the sea "close to the rain forest, which should indicate how much rain falls during a round"; indeed, though it's "paradise" "when dry", critics crank "the groundskeepers don't stop it from becoming a muddy mess."

San Juan

Westin Rio Mar, Ocean | 21 | 23 | 22 | 17 | $185 |

Rio Grande County, Palmer; 787-888-6000; 888-627-8556;
www.riomar.com; 6782/5450; 73.8/72.6; 132/126

☑ Even though some lazy lofters could "spend the whole day resting in the facilities reading a book and relaxing" at the gorgeous Westin Rio Mar, "the idea is to go out and play" this "wide-open track" with "a good variety of holes" and "lots of wildlife"; quibblers who find a course with "only one" "beautiful, tough par 3" "bordering" the blue call it "overpriced" – "excuse me, where was that ocean?"

Westin Rio Mar, River | 22 | 21 | 22 | 18 | $185 |

Westin Rio Mar Country Club, Palmer; 787-888-6000; 888-627-8556;
www.riomar.com; 6945/5169; 74.5/69.8; 135/120

☑ "Bring your camera to snap pictures of iguanas" on Greg Norman's "beautiful" course, where a river separates the front and back nine; since some consider it the "island's best 18" "if you're looking for a challenge", expect it to be "tighter than the Ocean", with "forced carries" and "several par 4s where target golf is a must"; while conventioneers find it "typical resort fare" that's "not worth the price", they appreciate the "wonderful hospitality."

South Carolina

★ **Best in State**
29 Kiawah Island, Ocean, *Charleston*
28 Barefoot Resort, Fazio, *Myrtle Beach*
   Caledonia Golf & Fish Club, *Pawleys Island*
   Harbour Town Golf Links, *Hilton Head*
26 Tidewater, *Myrtle Beach*
   Heritage Club, *Pawleys Island*
   Dunes Golf & Beach Club, *Myrtle Beach*
   Barefoot Resort, Love, *Myrtle Beach*
25 Wild Dunes Resort, Links, *Charleston*
   Barefoot Resort, Dye, *Myrtle Beach*

Charleston

Charleston National 🏌   ▽ 21 │ 17 │ 18 │ 22 │ $80
3375 Hwy. 17 N., Mount Pleasant; 843-884-7799;
www.charlestonnationalgolf.com; 7084/5086; 74.0/69.6; 142/114
■ "Lotta marsh, lotta hazards" and lotta "long carries" amount to
lotta "difficulty" on this "deceptive" Rees Jones design that's been
"tough in the wind" ever since "Hurricane Hugo took care of most
of the trees"; though it's "overshadowed" by other area courses,
locals insist "people don't know how good a track they're missing"
at such a "reasonable price."

Crowfield   ▽ 24 │ 21 │ 20 │ 27 │ $54
300 Hamlet Circle, Goose Creek; 843-764-4618; 800-707-6421;
7003/5682; 73.7/67.3; 134/121
■ "Dirt cheap, and worth twice the price" crow the lucky few
who've located this "nice layout with matching staff" that boasts
views of the historic Crowfield Plantation houses; though some
swingers sigh "it's been softened up from its opening format", most
tracksters testify this "true shotmaker's" course "can be very
humbling – you'll know what a mogul is when you're through."

Dunes West 🏌   ▽ 19 │ 23 │ 21 │ 20 │ $85
3535 Wando Plantation Way, Mount Pleasant; 843-856-9000;
www.golfduneswest.com; 6871/5278; 73.5/69.2; 138/118
☑ A "well-run facility" with a "nice country-club feel" and "friendly
staff" has some lofters loving this "lush, pretty" links set amid
moss-draped oaks and bermuda dunes; but anti-housing hackers
huff that, while the "fast greens" "have potential", it's "just another
development with closely cut grass advertised as a golf course."

Kiawah Island, Cougar Point   22 │ 20 │ 22 │ 19 │ $149
12 Kiawah Beach Dr., Kiawah Island; 843-768-2727; 800-576-1570;
www.kiawahgolf.com; 6887/4776; 73.0/67.6; 134/118
☑ "Thank God they redid it" because, "with the prices they charge,
you have a right to expect the course to be in better shape than
your local 18", and now this "solid", "narrow", "enjoyable" track
at a beachy family resort is so "pristine", it's "like playing off the
carpet" in your living room, that is if your wall-to-wall sports "fun
par 3s" and "holes over salt marshes"; a few cats carp that the
pro shop doubling as a clubhouse "is too rustic."

Kiawah Island, Oak Point   17 │ 15 │ 18 │ 18 │ $90
12 Kiawah Beach Dr., Kiawah Island; 843-768-2727; 800-576-1570;
www.kiawahgolf.com; 6759/4956; 73.8/69.8; 140/121
☑ A few funereal foozlers feel this "track is being improved
each month", and it's "enjoyable to read the headstones in the
cemetery after a good slice on No. 1"; rating it "nothing like the
others", with a "poor design" and what looks like "a double-wide
for a clubhouse", a macabre majority mocks it as "Choke Point",
whimpering "the Kiawah package forced a dog upon us."

KIAWAH ISLAND, OCEAN 🏌   29 │ 25 │ 25 │ 21 │ $245
12 Kiawah Beach Dr., Kiawah Island; 843-768-2727; 800-576-1570;
www.kiawahgolf.com; 7296/5327; 78.0/72.9; 152/133
■ "Imagine yourself playing in the Ryder Cup" here, and you'll
"know why [Mark] Calcavecchia cried" on South Carolina's No. 1

Course, possibly "the toughest, most visually spectacular links in the U.S."; "hackers, bring plenty of ammo", "pray before", "hope the wind doesn't blow", "don't keep score" and "you'll love every minute of the torture" – "if you tee off into a sunset on 18, you'll never want to leave" this "golf heaven" and hell; N.B. the "killer" is even more "memorable" now following a Dye redesign for the 2003 World Cup.

Kiawah Island, Osprey Point | 24 | 24 | 23 | 21 | $179 |
12 Kiawah Beach Dr., Kiawah Island; 843-768-2727; 800-576-1570; www.kiawahgolf.com; 6871/5023; 72.9/69.6; 137/120

■ Birdies of a feather flock to the Fazio-fashioned "wide fairways" amid "stunning scenery" at "probably the most playable of all Kiawah courses", though luckily "tee times are spread out so it doesn't appear crowded"; it's "excellent in all facets" and "lots of fun" where "water everywhere" means "gators everywhere", except in the "lovely" dining room, which is "excellent" for non-reptilian types "après golf."

Kiawah Island, Turtle Point ⅋ | 23 | 24 | 23 | 21 | $145 |
12 Kiawah Beach Dr., Kiawah Island; 843-768-2727; 800-576-1570; www.kiawahgolf.com; 7054/5210; 74.2/71.5; 141/126

■ "If you're not ready for the Ocean course, try this little beauty", a "wonderful early Nicklaus design" that's "recently been renovated" and is "now much tougher and in great condition"; "beware afternoon winds" on the "three fantastic ocean holes", and try not to "hit too many homes along the fairways", but definitely don't avoid the "beautiful new clubhouse" because, if you do, you'll miss "some of the best food at the resort."

Links at Stono Ferry | ▽ 19 | 18 | 19 | 26 | $50 |
5365 Forest Oaks Dr., Hollywood; 843-763-1817; 6606/4928; 71.9/69.2; 136/119

■ "Cheap for the area", this "mid-level" track offers "a place to play with friends and family that doesn't require competitive dressing" or cut-throat golf; "the par 3s on the back are [especially] enjoyable", and though it's "not the prettiest", it's still "a nice layout", "with lots of ocean" waves lapping at its edges.

RiverTowne ⅋ ⏲ | – | – | – | – | $125 |
1700 Rivertowne Country Club Dr., Mount Pleasant; 843-216-3777; 877-216-3777; www.rivertownecountryclub.com; 7200/5089; 74.5/71.5; 145/121

"For being one year old", this "nicely designed", "outstanding new course" by Arnold Palmer "is in terrific shape" say the handful of pioneering putters of the Charleston track; it winds among marshlands and live oaks, with 13 holes along the Wando River and Horlbeck Creek, and between rounds you can take in the charms of its picturesque Southern city on a stay-and-play deal at any number of area accommodations.

Wild Dunes Resort, Harbor ⅋ ⅋ | 24 | 22 | 22 | 20 | $119 |
5757 Palm Blvd., Isle Of Palms; 843-886-2180; 800-845-8880; www.wilddunes.com; 6446/4774; 70.9/68.1; 124/117

☑ "Everyone talks up the Links", but this "narrower, shorter" "target track" with a "very small clubhouse" nonetheless "holds its own", offering "better value" for "picturesque" play "throughout the resort and along the Intracoastal"; like most siblings who "suffer an inferiority complex next to their better-looking sister", this "nice" gal gets nasty sometimes, with "wind that can wreak havoc with your ball" and "bugs that can be unruly."

Wild Dunes Resort, Links   25 22 21 19 $185
5757 Palm Blvd., Isle Of Palms; 843-886-2180; 800-845-8880; www.wilddunes.com; 6722/4849; 72.7/69.1; 131/121
■ "Before he got lazy", Tom Fazio fashioned "two of the finest finishing holes" "along the ocean with spectacular views" at the "heavenly" 17th and 18th on this "tight, tough" "test of your shotmaking abilities" whose "playability for most handicaps" and "location just outside Charleston" make it "one of the U.S.'s best links" "for vacationers"; holes 1 through 16 "are forgettable" fuss frugal foozlers, who find these fairways "overpriced."

Hilton Head

Country Club of Hilton Head ☺   23 24 21 20 $97
70 Skull Creek Dr., Hilton Head Island; 843-681-4653; www.hiltonheadclub.com; 6919/5373; 73.6/71.3; 132/123
■ Country-clubbers crow that this doglegged, former U.S. Open qualifier host is "challenging and nice", with "great service and practice areas", though the "conditions can get spotty at times"; food for thought: the restaurant is for club members only, who may or may not reside in those "beautiful homes bordering the fairways."

Daufuskie Island, Bloody Point   – – – – $85
1 Seabrook Dr., Hilton Head Island; 843-341-4810; 800-648-6778; www.daufuskieresort.com; 6900/5220; 73.2/69.7; 135/126
Contrary to its name, Melrose's sister won't bloody your rep as a golfer – it sits on the site of a nasty 1715 English vs. Indians skirmish; along the Mungen River and puddle-jumping Daufuskie's coastal marshes and lagoons for water on 10 holes, it still emphasizes playability for linksters of all levels; a couple of clever, short par 4s highlight a nice mix, where brains are at least as useful as brawn.

Daufuskie Island, Melrose   – – – – $85
1 Seabrook Dr., Hilton Head Island; 843-341-4810; 800-648-6778; www.daufuskieresort.com; 7081/5575; 74.2/72.3; 138/126
Take a ferry over to this resort on a small island a mile off Hilton Head, where the highlight of the Golden Bear's Signature track is the closing trio of holes along the Atlantic, with a finisher that has beachfront all along the right side; besides the golf, there are three swimming pools, plenty of water-sport activities, tennis courts, an equestrian center and four restaurants, so you won't have to swim back to the mainland to fulfill any of your needs.

Golden Bear Club At Indigo Run   21 21 21 18 $99
72 Golden Bear Way, Hilton Head Island; 843-689-2200; www.goldenbear-indigorun.com; 7014/6184; 73.7/70.1; 132/122
◪ Those who call this "solid" plantation 18 golden believe it's "lovely", though they're divided as to whether it's "one of Jack's friendliest layouts" or "very challenging"; everyone "loves the GPS on the carts", but bearish beaters say "there are better in the area", calling it "a boring design in bad shape", with "some strange" holes making for "very slow" play, regardless of "overzealous marshals."

HARBOUR TOWN GOLF LINKS   28 | 24 | 23 | 16 | $250

11 Lighthouse Ln., Hilton Head Island; 843-363-4485; 800-955-8337; www.seapines.com; 6973/5208; 75.2/70.7; 146/124

◪ It's "harder than it appears on TV", kids, so screw up your "courage" and "be wise choosing the correct side" of the "tight" fairways "for placement" onto the "tiny greens" at the newly tweaked "famous" home of the former WorldCom Classic (now dubbed The Heritage), where "the second-best finishing hole next to Pebble's", with the Calibogue Sound "lighthouse in the distance, is worth the trouble of the previous 17"; hackers harbor a grudge against the "overpriced" course in non-PGA season, arguing "goat pastures are better-kept 10 months of the year" – drown your disgruntlement with a family spree at the shops by the beacon.

Hilton Head National ⌂   22 | 21 | 22 | 23 | $85

60 Hilton Head National Dr., Bluffton; 843-842-5900; 888-955-1234; www.scratch-golf.com
National/Player: 6660/4563; 72.8/66.2; 135/106
Player/Weed: 6655/4682; 72.7/66.0; 135/111
Weed/National: 6718/4631; 72.7/66.0; 131/108

◪ It's "fairly simple" say accurate aces: "because of marshes" lining the fairways, "you must drive the ball straight" on these three "enjoyable" woodland nines "just off Hilton Head" that serve up some "solid stuff", though "by no means is all of it classic"; "some holes make you feel like you're at Augusta National", but "goofy ones abound", leading lots of lofters to lament that it is "middle-of-the-road."

Old Carolina   ▽ 21 | 18 | 19 | 25 | $68

91 Old Carolina Dr., Bluffton; 843-785-6363; 888-785-7274; www.oldcarolinagolf.com; 6805/4725; 73.1/67.0; 145/121

■ Despite the barn on-premises, this "nice, little track" is no longer for horses; this linkster on a former equestrian farm "plays a little tight" and "difficult when the wind is blowing" your ball toward "water everywhere" on 17 holes; though it's "in very fine shape", it "needs some maturing", but so do the juniors teeing off here at a reduced rate.

Old South   20 | 18 | 20 | 22 | $92

50 Buckingham Plantation Dr., Bluffton; 843-785-5353; 800-287-8997; www.oldsouthgolf.com; 6722/4776; 73.3/68.2; 141/116

■ Offering "target golf in a beautiful setting" and a "nice blend of length and accuracy with tricky greens to test the best putters", this "excellent, fun" facility is "well worth the drive off Hilton Head Island to play"; just "bring the bug spray" and "hit the fairways to keep dry", as the course winds its way from oak forest to open pasture to tidal salt marsh.

Oyster Reef   22 | 21 | 20 | 19 | $115

155 High Bluff Rd., Hilton Head Island; 843-681-7717; 800-234-6318; www.americangolf.com; 7005/5288; 71.2/70.1; 123/118

■ There's no reefer madness here, just "great par 3s", one of which, No. 6, has a Port Royal Sound "vista worth remembering"; in fact, this parkland/woodland spread is so "beautiful and challenging", it "feels like a country club", but it offers its "good variety of play at a reasonable rate" – just remember, with "lots of gators" around, "accuracy off the tee is necessary."

Palmetto Dunes, Arthur Hills   24 | 23 | 22 | 20 | $148
2 Lemington Rd., Hilton Head Island; 843-785-1140; 800-827-3006;
www.palmettodunesresort.com; 6651/4999; 71.4/68.5; 127/118
■ "What a spectacular experience" say swingers on this "lush, beautiful" woodlander that "gently lulls you in over the first eight holes before it begins to tighten the noose" with "lots of water hazards", "going for the throat on Nos. 16 and 17", with "back-to-back par 4s where accuracy is at a premium", and "spitting you out onto a par-5" finish; hardcore hookers harrumph "pity the fun only starts on the 12th" hole – perhaps those luxury villa beds are too soft for them too.

Palmetto Dunes, George Fazio   23 | 21 | 21 | 20 | $105
2 Carnoustie Rd., Hilton Head Island; 843-785-1130; 800-827-3006;
www.palmettodunesresort.com; 6873/5273; 73.9/70.8; 135/127
☑ By George, Tom's uncle's got it on this "good resort test" with "tight fairways, water" on 10 holes, "long par 4s" and "bunkers, bunkers and more bunkers" to "drive the mid- to high-handicapper bonkers" with "obstacle-course" play; fans feel "the only drawback is having to go to the Jones course for the practice range" – that, plus a "not very interesting" layout with "lots of similar holes", sniff crabby critics.

Palmetto Dunes,   24 | 23 | 23 | 21 | $125
Robert Trent Jones
7 Trent Jones Ln., Hilton Head Island; 843-785-1136;
www.palmettodunesresort.com; 7005/5035; 74.3/64.9; 138/109
■ Everyone is "looking forward to" this "magnificent" Robert Trent Jones Sr. design newly updated by former protégé Roger Rulewich; "open", "beautiful and forgiving", it's said to be "Bill Clinton's favorite on the island" (natch) and "a nice place for the higher handicap because the landing areas are so wide, though there's plenty of trouble to get into if you care to", with water on half the holes; look for more movement to the fairways, elevation changes for more ocean views and the incorporation of the area's only "short course", with a set of tees designed just for juniors.

Palmetto Hall, Arthur Hills 🏌   24 | 21 | 22 | 20 | $95
108 Fort Howell Dr., Hilton Head Island; 843-689-4100;
6918/4956; 74.0/68.6; 140/119
■ "Why not schedule a Tour event here?" beg boosters of this "demanding but fair" shotmaker's woodlander where the staff makes sure things are "well maintained", with "exceptional pace of play"; if you like to "use every club in the bag" and "bring extra balls", "it has everything you're looking for", though Art lovers lament that Hills "has done better" than this "nothing-awful, nothing-great" track.

Palmetto Hall, Robert Cupp   20 | 19 | 19 | 18 | $95
108 Fort Howell Dr., Hilton Head Island; 843-689-4100;
7079/5220; 75.2/71.1; 144/126
☑ Is the Cupp half full or half empty? – depends on who you ask about this computer-generated design: fans call it "different in a good way", with "fair play" amid "geometrically formed bunkers that make for interesting sight lines", while foes lured into the "dark side" of the math here say "weird shapes are one thing, but bad strategy and layout is another – go somewhere else."

Sea Pines Resort, Ocean
21 | 20 | 20 | 17 | $90

100 N. Sea Pines Dr., Hilton Head Island; 843-842-8484; 800-732-7463;
www.seapines.com; 6172/5325; 69.7/71.1; 125/124

☑ "Enjoyment is everywhere", but so are the reptiles, so "watch out for alligators" in "water left and water right" at what select slicers celebrate as an "exquisite" exercise with a "scenic and difficult back nine"; swift swingers swipe at the rangers on Harbour Town's "mediocre" "stepchild" for "having no interest in speeding up play", thus causing "the longest rounds ever."

Myrtle Beach (see also North Carolina)

Arrowhead ⌂
22 | 20 | 22 | 21 | $98

1201 Burcale Rd.; 843-236-3243; 800-236-3243; www.arrowheadcc.com
Cypress/Lakes: 6666/4802; 71.6/71.2; 139/116
Lakes/Waterway: 6612/4688; 71.6/70.7; 138/118
Waterway/Cypress: 6644/4624; 71.6/70.9; 141/121

■ "Watch out for the water" or your ball will head like an arrow right over the "beautiful" holes and into the Intracoastal at this "not spectacular but consistently good" "warm-up to tougher Myrtle Beach courses"; "all three nines are challenging and in great shape", with "super par 5s" "for a good price", and the "excellent service" includes starters who "always space out the play so your round doesn't last all day."

Barefoot Resort, Dye
25 | 22 | 23 | 21 | $150

4980 Barefoot Resort Bridge Rd., North Myrtle Beach; 843-399-7680;
877-237-3767; www.barefootgolf.com; 7343/5021; 75.3/69.1; 149/116

☑ "Typical Dye-abolical trappings" abound, say Dye-hards, at this "gorgeous" track with "lots of sand", i.e. it's "very difficult", but "the more you play, the more you like it", so much so that you may "want to take the grass home with you" from a sporty resort where a host of athletic activities are on hand; rating it "too short from members' tees", with "not enough interesting holes" for "not that much fun" at "too high a price", maligners mark it merely "mediocre."

BAREFOOT RESORT, FAZIO
28 | 24 | 24 | 23 | $130

4980 Barefoot Resort Bridge Rd., North Myrtle Beach; 843-399-7680;
877-237-3767; www.barefootgolf.com; 6834/4820; 73.7/68.0; 139/115

■ Tip-toeing to the tee off, testers who tout "Barefoot's most scenic" as "one of the finest courses I have ever set foot on", with shoe or without, "fully understand why the Canadian Tour has made this a stop, as there's every type of hazard imaginable and the conditions are top-shelf"; "with very difficult, very firm greens", the fab Fazio Lowcountry spread is so "tough on the score", it just might burn the cleats clear off your soles.

Barefoot Resort, Love
26 | 23 | 23 | 20 | $130

4980 Barefoot Resort Bridge Rd., North Myrtle Beach; 843-399-7680;
877-237-3767; www.barefootgolf.com; 7047/5346; 75.1/70.9; 138/118

■ It's largely a Love-in at this "Donald Ross–style beauty", which is "reminiscent of Pinehurst No. 2 around the greens" that, like all Casanovas, are "super-fast", "in fantastic shape" and "hard to hold"; the "wide fairways" on a "delightfully different design" simulating an old plantation "demand the length of [Tour pro and architect] Davis III himself from the back tees", but savvy slicers swear "you can bank your shots off the walls" of the "fake ruins."

Barefoot Resort, Norman   23 | 20 | 24 | 22 | $130

4980 Barefoot Resort Bridge Rd., North Myrtle Beach; 843-399-7680;
877-237-3767; www.barefootgolf.com; 7035/4953; 73.9/68.6; 136/112

☑ "Best greens I've ever putted on" say "lightning" speed freaks at
this "challenge" with "great par 3s on the back" and "three greens
along the Intracoastal"; Shark attackers say "with the exception of
a few holes" and, unfortunately, "too much housing", the "pretty
flat" track "isn't memorable" "compared to other Barefooters" –
the Great White must have "just phoned this one in"; the same can't
be said for Greg Norman's Australian Grill nearby.

Belle Terre 🖼   19 | 19 | 18 | 18 | $94

4073 Hwy. 501; 843-236-8888; 800-957-9786; www.belleterre.com;
7013/5049; 74.0/69.6; 134/120

☑ "A lot of sand and many long carries with open areas that make
wind a huge factor" create a "challenge" on this "almost links-
style" Rees Jones design; but while fans find it's a "great value,
since they always run specials", other ballers bitch "with so
many choices" in the area, "why go to" this "dog track"?

Blackmoor 🖼   21 | 20 | 19 | 20 | $98

6100 Longwood Dr., Murrells Inlet; 843-650-5555; 866-952-5555;
www.blackmoor.com; 6619/4807; 71.1/67.9; 126/115

☑ Blackmoor backers believe that this "beautifully maintained",
"nifty" woodlander by Gary Player is "super", and with juniors
playing free with an adult, it's "a real bargain" for families; those
claiming 'Moor is less argue there's "not enough room" for the
"overrated", "kind-of-everyday" layout that, as befits a former rice
plantation, "does not drain well."

Dunes Golf & Beach Club   26 | 22 | 22 | 21 | $155

9000 N. Ocean Blvd.; 843-449-5914; 866-386-3722;
www.dunesgolfandbeachclub.com; 7165/5390; 75.4/72.3; 141/132

☑ Supporters call this "stately" former site of the Senior PGA Tour
Championship "a classic must-play" where "each hole seems
better than the next", though you have to "stay at [one of a select
group of] hotels to get access" to it; modernists moan that "the
grand old lady of Myrtle Beach is beginning to show her age", and
the "surly staff" is "arrogant" enough to just "rest on its laurels."

Glen Dornoch Waterway 🖼   25 | 23 | 23 | 24 | $125

Hwy. 17 N., Little River; 843-249-2541; 800-717-8784;
www.glendornoch.com; 6850/5002; 73.2/69.8; 141/129

☑ "Wow" marvel masochists, "the last three holes are murder –
you'll love 'em", particularly when you're scoping other duffers at
"the shared green on 9 and 18" while you laze in a "rocking chair"
on the clubhouse's "great porch" "sipping Tanqueray-and-tonic";
fans feel the "outstanding layout" "along the Intracoastal" is "one
of Myrtle's best five", though slicers axe "too much protected
marsh", "too many gimmicks" and "too-short holes" that make it
"undeserving of association with the real Dornoch" in Scotland.

Grande Dunes   – | – | – | – | $160

8700 Golf Village Ln.; 843-449-7070; 888-886-8877;
www.grandedunes.com; 7618/5353; 77.3/71.2; 142/123

Perhaps "the best new course on the strip" at Myrtle Beach is this
2001 design that's "young", sure, "but already in great shape",

while "time will only improve" its "picturesque, challenging" layout; located right on the Intracoastal Waterway, the precocious monster with water on seven holes has already hosted the South Carolina Open, a PGA of America sectional event.

Heather Glen ⌂   24 │ 21 │ 22 │ 23 │ $91

Hwy. 17 N., Little River; 843-249-9000; 800-868-4536;
www.heatherglen.com
Blue/Red: 6783/5101; 72.4/69.3; 130/117
Red/White: 6771/5053; 72.4/69.3; 127/117
White/Blue: 6822/5082; 72.4/69.3; 130/117

■ It's "always fun" to visit "Scotland in South Carolina" at this "superb" 27-holer giving "great links golf in a beautiful setting" "any way you play it"; "the three nines are all so challenging", they "make you want to come back and redeem yourself after posting that big number", but before you tee off again, "grab a pint, sit in a rocker on the porch and watch the groups behind you suffer"; when you're finished gloating, take in a seafood supper along the Grand Strand.

Legends, Heathland ⌂   23 │ 25 │ 22 │ 21 │ $96

Hwy. 501; 843-236-9318; 800-377-2315; www.legendsgolf.com;
6785/5115; 72.3/71.0; 127/121

■ Folks stoked for Tom Doak's design croak "don't get caught in the pot bunkers" and "watch out for the pampas grass" at this "great links experience reminiscent" of spreads across the pond "when the wind blows"; a "superbly maintained" "warm-up", it's "not as hard as the other Legends" layouts, but "what service! – "they do everything for you", and they won't even let you use your own feet on the carts-only course.

Legends, Moorland ⌂   22 │ 25 │ 22 │ 20 │ $96

Hwy. 501; 843-236-9318; 800-377-2315; www.legendsgolf.com;
6799/4905; 73.1/72.8; 128/118

◪ Brains and brawn come together on this "crazy and challenging" stadium-style stretch where "Pete Dye on steroids" meets a "thinking man's game at its best", whoop wallopers who warn "watch out for Hell's Half Acre", the "sadomasochistic" bunker on the 14th; vocal dissenters decry it as "goofy golf without the windmill", with "the feel of a tourist trap and a pretty girl at the first tee to take your picture . . . for a price."

Legends, Parkland ⌂   23 │ 26 │ 22 │ 21 │ $96

Hwy. 501; 843-236-9318; 800-377-2315; www.legendsgolf.com;
7170/5518; 74.9/71.0; 137/125

■ "A real challenge from the tips (or the green tees, for that matter)", this traditional tree-lined spree boasts "huge bunkers" and a "beautiful back nine" with plenty of "tests for your putting skills" – if you're "tired of flat, boring greens", "you'll be desperate for them after this"; South Carolina's Top-ranked Facilities include swanky resort digs and a 30-acre lighted practice area.

Long Bay Club   22 │ 20 │ 21 │ 19 │ $112

350 Foxtail Dr., Longs; 843-399-2222; 800-344-5590; www.mbn.com;
7021/5598; 74.3/72.1; 137/127

◪ "Long is the key word" at this aptly named "fair but challenging test", "an early Nicklaus" creation with a "memorable" 10th hole, where you should "let them take the photo of you", preferably before you knock your ball into the horseshoe bunker; detractors who deem it "disappointing for a Signature course" tsk that the track is "a little tattered" from "too much play" "over the ages."

Myrtle Beach National, Kings North
23 | 21 | 21 | 19 | $147

4900 National Dr.; 843-448-2308; 800-344-5590; www.mbn.com; 7017/4816; 72.6/67.4; 136/113

◪ A royal "risk/reward" round rouses loyalists of this "stunning" track with "an island par 3, wide fairways", "extremely deep bunkers" and a "beautiful clubhouse"; "pure fun" is the rule for queens-for-a-day at the "very women-friendly" course, even though insurgents storm its "gimmicky" gates with cries of "don't believe the hype", while coin-juggling jesters joke "I would give my first-born, but they only take an arm and a leg" – clothed, that is, as one subject sighs "they lost my shoes when I checked in."

Myrtle Beach National, South Creek
20 | 23 | 22 | 18 | $84

4900 National Dr.; 843-448-2308; 800-344-5590; www.mbn.com; 6416/4723; 70.5/66.5; 123/109

◪ "Everything here is top-shelf, from the clubhouse to the course conditions" following 1999 renovations on all MBN properties, and clans of "average golfers" clamor for the "nice", "fair" track where "rounds are fast" and "not extremely difficult" and junior can play free with mom or pop (or any adult, for that matter); sour swingers sigh that "too many homes" are sending it south.

Pine Lakes International 🏊
19 | 21 | 26 | 20 | $110

5603 Woodside Ave.; 843-449-6459; 800-446-6817; www.pinelakes.com; 6700/5162; 72.0/70.5; 130/121

■ With inspiration from "to-die-for gumbo", "clam chowder in winter and mimosas in summer", it's easy to understand how "*Sports Illustrated* was born one night over dinner" at this "historic layout" that "best captures the experience" of the Grand Strand; the "Myrtle Beach granddaddy" has "kept to a very high standard", with "recent renovations creating a much more challenging back nine, making it a new must-play" all over again, where "attentive folks in skirts" "treat you like royalty."

Possum Trot
18 | 16 | 17 | 20 | $50

1170 Possum Trot Rd., North Myrtle Beach; 843-272-5341; 800-626-8768; www.possumtrot.com; 6966/5160; 73.0/69.6; 127/111

■ "Lovely and friendly, both golf- and people-wise", this "not too difficult", "old" "Myrtle Beach favorite" sure ain't playing dead, with "consistently fine conditions", "a lot of trees and water" and a "great practice facility"; it's "good for seniors", so trot on over with granny and gramps in tow.

Tidewater 🏊
26 | 20 | 21 | 20 | $160

1400 Tidewater Dr., North Myrtle Beach; 843-249-3829; 800-446-5363; 7138/4665; 74.9/67.5; 140/127

◪ "For a long time, you will remember" this "fantastic layout with views of the Atlantic, the Intracoastal and Cherry Grove Inlet" "balanced by tough wooded holes" – indeed, it's "beautifully integrated with the environment", but unfortunately that includes "too many houses"; still, duffers drowning in debt declare this Tidewater "a little on the high side" price-wise, "but worth it" for a "world-class" course with "old-world service."

TPC of Myrtle Beach   24 | 25 | 24 | 18 | $165

1199 TPC Blvd., Murrells Inlet; 843-357-3399; 888-742-8721; www.tpc.com;
6950/5118; 74.0/70.3; 145/125

☑ "You feel like a PGA Tour player the minute you drive through the gates" to this host of the 2000 Senior Tour Championship where "everything clicks", from "first-rate conditioning" to a "challenging, fair" layout to the "best services money can buy" and, finally, to the "nice clubhouse rocking chairs" where you can "down a cool one after a round" of "forced carries"; citing "undeveloped root structure", grass groupies grouse, the "youngster" "needs to mature" to live "up to the TPC name."

Wachesaw Plantation East   20 | 18 | 19 | 18 | $119

911 Riverwood Dr., Murrells Inlet; 843-357-2090; 888-922-0027;
www.wachesaweast.com; 6833/4995; 73.6/68.8; 132/117

☑ Whatcha get at Wachesaw depends on who you talk to: fans call the former LPGA Classic host a "fantastic test" on "an excellent layout", while detractors bark it's a "boring" "dog track" that's "not in good condition", despite the fact that it's "always under repair"; it's even hard to locate the pup's hair – say bitten boozers, "after that, I needed a cold one, but all I could find was the staff dining room."

Wild Wing Plantation, Avocet 🏌   23 | 24 | 24 | 22 | $122

Hwy. 501 N.; 843-347-9464; 800-736-9464; www.wildwing.com;
7127/5298; 74.2/70.4; 128/118

■ This "beauty" is "the best of the bunch" at a "great complex" that's "golf's answer to the mini-mall", with "everything you want under one roof" including "friendly" "beer-cart girls everywhere" adding to the "fun"; "all the courses are immaculately kept", but this "excellent layout" with "generous fairways, rolling mounds" and "tremendous greens" in a "no-houses setting" is hoopla'd by hustlers as "one of the top five in Myrtle."

Wild Wing Plantation, Falcon 🏌   23 | 24 | 23 | 21 | $120

Hwy. 501 N.; 843-347-9464; 800-736-9464; www.wildwing.com;
7082/5190; 74.4/70.4; 134/118

☑ "It's easy to play, but hard to score" say birdie-hunters on this "really nice", "very challenging" modern-meets-traditional Rees Jones design, part of a "nice" resort where the staff "knows how to do it right"; "mounding all around gives you a sense of isolation" to help you ignore the "herd mentality" of the vacationing flocks of flubbers, as well as the "small concrete plant that's visible from a few holes."

Wild Wing Plantation, Hummingbird 🏌   21 | 24 | 22 | 21 | $83

Hwy. 501 N.; 843-347-9464; 800-736-9464; www.wildwing.com;
6853/5168; 73.6/69.5; 135/123

☑ "Watch out for the water hazards" in play on 15 holes at this "tough" but "nice layout" by Willard 'Humming' Byrd, where love grass and other native species grow around "good greens"; "incredible service" "sans snobbery" sweetens the nectar of this "excellent value", despite the fact that the resort's popularity has a minority buzzing off what they call "factory golf."

Wild Wing Plantation,   23 | 25 | 22 | 21 | $99
Wood Stork 🏌
Hwy. 501 N.; 843-347-9464; 800-736-9464; www.wildwing.com; 7044/5409; 74.1/70.7; 130/121

🏌 Though you'd think the water on two-thirds of the holes at this traditional parklander would attract the namesake fowl, one bird-watcher whines "I didn't see one"; nevertheless, fine dining at Wishbones overlooking the fairways helps make it "a beautiful experience" at a "nice complex" where all the "courses would be the pinnacle" if the view weren't "kept from being absolutely perfect" by a bit of local industry and "too many golfers."

Witch, The 🏌   20 | 17 | 19 | 19 | $90
1900 Hwy. 544, Conway; 843-448-1300; www.mysticalgolf.com; 6702/4812; 71.2/69.0; 133/109

🏌 She mesmerizes you into "the quietest, most soothing round you'll ever play" say swingers spellbound by this "truly unique" and "challenging" dark lady of the "wetlands"; "play early in the morning, when the mist sits on the swamp" shrouding her eerie clubhouse, and you "can hear the gators chewing on the stumps that used to be tree trunks", and you'll probably agree that her "unique sights and sounds" make her worthy of her name, even though witch hunters might roast her as "average."

Wizard, The   20 | 18 | 19 | 18 | $90
4601 W. Leeshire Blvd.; 843-236-9393; www.mysticalgolf.com; 6720/4972; 70.4/71.2; 119/121

■ If you're off to see The Wizard, it's because, because, because, because, because ... of "several interesting holes requiring you to think about club selection", "with enough easy ones to keep you interested after getting frustrated with bad shots on the harder ones"; the clubhouse conjures confusion: "it's supposed to look like Camelot", amateur architects argue, "but I expected to see dead French legionnaires propped up on the roof, à la *Beau Geste*."

Pawleys Island

CALEDONIA GOLF & FISH CLUB   28 | 24 | 25 | 23 | $150
369 Caledonia Dr.; 843-237-3675; 800-483-6800; www.fishclub.com; 6526/4957; 70.9/68.2; 132/113

🏌 "It's the nicest 17-holer I've ever played" razz rounders making "a joke" out of the "dinky" 118-yard 9th, which, compared with the "great" 18th, is "a sad finish if you have to start on the back" at "perhaps the most beautiful course near Myrtle Beach"; it's set amid a game reserve up a "magnolia-lined driveway leading to a plantation-style clubhouse that evokes images of Augusta", and "best of all is a terrific wrap-around porch to unwind with a few cold ones."

Heritage Club 🏌   26 | 24 | 23 | 22 | $105
478 Heritage Dr.; 843-237-3424; 800-377-2315; www.legendsgolf.com; 6985/5315; 74.1/71.0; 142/125

🏌 "Spectacular antebellum live oaks, Spanish moss", "water and gators galore" "eating golf balls" "add to the charm" of the "Old

South atmosphere" at this "mature", "scenic plantation" with "both
punishing and potential birdie holes", where "long" describes
the "solid layout" as well as the "Guiness and Harp" pours in
the "great clubhouse"; "conditioning has been an issue for a
few years", lament local loopers, but "if they get that right, it will
rival Harbour Town."

Litchfield Country Club   18 | 17 | 19 | 19 | $106

Hwy.17; 843-237-3411; www.mbn.com; 6295/5308; 70.9/71.2; 124/122

☑ This serene veteran stirs some controversy: loyal linksters praise
it as "a nice oldster, well-cared for and fair for all skill levels", with
"charming facilities and a pristine layout" that's "simply beautiful in
the spring when the flowers are in bloom"; the discontented dunk
it, droning "the historical markers are more interesting than the
course", declaring it's "difficult to understand how it can exist side-
by-side with tracks that far outshine it."

Pawleys Plantation 🏠 🕐   23 | 22 | 19 | 20 | $125

70 Tanglewood Dr.; 843-237-1736; 800-367-9959;
www.pawleysplantation.com; 7026/4979; 75.3/70.1; 146/126

☑ "The par 3s are unforgettable, and the back nine is extremely
strong" at this "stunner that plays along a saltwater marsh" amid
"wonderful live oaks" "in a beautiful area on the coast"; however,
with "forced carries" over "lots of water", soggy duffers "can have
a lousy day" here, and the "holier-than-thou attitude" of a resort
staff that's "snooty from the parking lot through the pro shop"
doesn't help soften the blow.

Tradition Club, The   23 | 21 | 21 | 21 | $90

1027 Willbrook Blvd.; 843-237-5041; 877-599-0888;
www.traditiongolfclub.com; 6875/4106; 72.6/63.9; 132/104

■ It's drive 'n' dive on more than half the holes at this liquid-laced,
Lowcountry woodlander, an "excellent" design with "a lot of
variety", so make good use beforehand of the extensive practice
facilities; membership has its privileges here – walking (on water?)
is the sole province of the dues payers.

True Blue 🕐   22 | 20 | 21 | 18 | $130

900 Blue Stem Dr.; 843-235-0900; 888-483-6800; www.truebluegolf1.com;
7090/4920; 73.8/69.5; 139/115

☑ "The more rugged of the Mike Strantz courses" in the area, this
"picturesque" "brute" will make "you think you're in Arizona with
all the sand"; leather-hide lofters say the "excellent layout" "is fun
if you like it tough" and "don't get caught in the bunkers", but it's
"too tricked up" for True boo-ers, who argue "any resemblance
between the front nine and a golf course is simply coincidental."

Tennessee

Chattanooga

Bear Trace At   ▽ 26 | 20 | 24 | 24 | $59
Cumberland Mountain

407 Wild Plum Ln., Crossville; 931-707-1640; 888-800-2327;
www.beartrace.com; 6900/5066; 72.0/70.0; 129/120

■ "In the mountains of Tennessee", this lair of the Golden Bear is
where Nicklaus "does what he set out to do – provide all levels

with a purely enjoyable experience", "with various tee boxes so you avoid getting beaten up"; with a "very friendly staff" and a "can't-be-beat" price tag, this "well-maintained" track is the state's No. 1 Value, so bargain-hunters say if "the whole Trace collection is like this, make sure you play 'em all."

Knoxville

Stonehenge ⛳   ▽ 26 | 19 | 19 | 19 | $79
222 Fairfield Blvd., Fairfield Glade; 931-484-3731;
www.stonehengegolf.com; 6549/5043; 71.8/69.6; 135/124
■ Druidic drivers deem this "tough but beautiful" woodlander named for its stone walls "a Cumberland Plateau must-stop"; those who've tapped into its secrets say "it should be better-known", since it's "maintained to perfection" and blessed with a "truly memorable back nine"; P.S. the grill room "lunch is great" too.

Memphis

Bear Trace At Chickasaw   – | – | – | – | $42
9555 State Rte. 100 W., Henderson; 888-944-2327; www.beartrace.com;
7118/5270; 73.4/71.9; 134/123
Along the route of the Golden Bear there's this "wonderful course that's friendly to walkers and to anyone whose game is past the duffer stage"; club-wielding cubs amble along several split fairways framed by wide oaks and towering pines past natural wetlands and streams on many holes; rouse from your den for "an early tee time" and enjoy breakfast afterward in the log cabin clubhouse, but don't expect a lot of good practice beforehand because you've probably "seen better driving ranges."

Nashville

Bear Trace At Ross Creek Landing   – | – | – | – | $59
110 Airport Rd., Clifton; 931-676-3174; www.beartrace.com;
7200/5500; 74.8/72.1; 135/126
Smarter than your average Bear, Nicklaus' "long challenge" runs along the Tennessee River, with *mucho agua* in play, a drivable par 4 and a cache of risk/reward holes; the "excellent staff" at the star newbie is one among the many reasons track tracers "wish it were closer" to the city, though its full-service bar and grill does mean that they don't have to pack their own pic-a-nic baskets.

Hermitage, General's Retreat   ▽ 19 | 18 | 21 | 21 | $39
3939 Old Hickory Blvd., Old Hickory; 615-847-4001;
www.hermitagegolf.com; 6773/5437; 72.3/70.8; 129/120
☑ No one's retreating from the "incredible Southern hospitality", "beautiful fairways" and "greens very smooth and true to the putter" at this "excellent value" "convenient to Nashville"; the "challenging" parklander generally makes hooking hermits happy, though a few feel "the conditioning isn't up to par."

Hermitage, President's Reserve   ▽ 24 | 18 | 21 | 21 | $48
3939 Old Hickory Blvd., Old Hickory; 615-847-4001;
www.hermitagegolf.com; 7157/5138; 74.2/69; 134/115
■ Clearly "the cat's meow of the two" Hermitage courses, this "great track" trails through protected wetlands and along the banks

of the Cumberland River; penny-wise Presidential putters proclaim it "the best value in the high-end category in Nashville."

Springhouse 🏞   18 | 21 | 21 | 12 | $74 |
18 Springhouse Ln.; 615-871-7759; www.springhousegolf.com; 7007/5126; 74.0/70.2; 133/118

☑ "Located along the Cumberland River", this host of the Senior PGA Tour's BellSouth Classic is a crazy "combo of links-style and Pete Dye–type holes", with "perfect lies on the zoysia fairways" and "great practice facilities"; however, detractors dis its "average conditioning", and you'd better take "a caddie your first few times around" lest all those "punitive" "blind shots" "sneak" up on you.

Texas

★ **Best in State**
29 Cowboys, *Dallas*
28 Barton Creek, Fazio Canyons, *Austin*
   Falls Resort & Club, The, *Houston*
   La Cantera, Palmer, *San Antonio*
27 Barton Creek, Fazio Foothills, *Austin*
   Woodlands Resort, TPC, *Houston*
   Four Seasons at Las Colinas, TPC, *Dallas*
   La Cantera, Resort, *San Antonio*
26 Four Seasons/Las Colinas, Cottonwood Valley, *Dallas*
   Horseshoe Bay Resort, Ram Rock, *Austin*

Austin

Barton Creek, Crenshaw Cliffside   22 | 25 | 23 | 18 | $99 |
8212 Barton Club Dr.; 512-329-4001; 800-336-6158; www.bartoncreek.com; 6678/4843; 71.0/67.2; 124/110

☑ Contented cliffside club-wielders call this "very open" Hill Country course "fun", with "a number of unique holes" where "the action is on greens" that are "huge and have devilishly subtle (and not-so-subtle) breaks"; though its Kids' Club and award-winning pro shop are high on the list of the resort's "first-class facilities", foes creak that "grainy greens and little imagination make this the poor stepchild at Barton Creek, so insist on playing one of the Fazio designs instead."

BARTON CREEK, FAZIO CANYONS   28 | 24 | 24 | 21 | $159 |
8212 Barton Club Dr.; 512-329-4001; 800-336-6158; www.bartoncreek.com; 7161/5078; 74.0/70.0; 135/124

■ "One of the best courses in Texas", this "beautiful" track a couple of miles from the main clubhouse is "highly recommended" for "excellent" "playability" on a "superbly conditioned", "awesome design" "with breathtaking scenery and lots of wildlife"; though canyon crawlers "can't wait to go back" for another round, when they drain their sleeves, they skip the "small pro shop" here and head straight for "the larger selection" at Crenshaw Cliffside.

Barton Creek, Fazio Foothills   27 | 26 | 24 | 21 | $159 |
8212 Barton Club Dr.; 512-329-4001; 800-336-6158; www.bartoncreek.com; 6956/5207; 74.0/69.4; 135/120

☑ "Always in tip-top shape", this "fabulous layout with many special holes" and "some blind shots to hidden greens" is "lovely, hard" and sports "great views" of caves and waterfalls; "a little attitude in the pro shop downgrades the service" a bit, "but overall, it's a great golfing experience" that you might follow up with an equally splashy spree at the spa.

Barton Creek, Palmer Lakeside　　24　24　22　20　$99
8212 Barton Club Dr.; 512-329-4001; 800-336-6158; www.bartoncreek.com; 6668/5107; 71.0/71.0; 124/124

■ "Worth the half-hour drive" from Barton Creek, this "excellent, challenging design" with "spectacular lake views" is "as good as the Fazio courses", with "several outstanding holes" in "fabulous condition"; it's "not long, but there's more than enough sand, water and ravines to tax any talent level while remaining very playable", and "the staff provides a comfortable atmosphere" for a waterside nip or two after an "enjoyable round."

Circle C　　20　20　17　20　$65
7401 Hwy. 45; 512-288-4297; 6859/5236; 72.2/69.9; 122/120

◪ Host of a 2002 Canadian PGA Tour event (go figure), this "well-designed Hill Country course", about as far south from the Great White North as one can get in these States, is "challenging if played from the back tees", which "require precise shotmaking and full attention"; however, though she "has the potential", the old gal's been "inconsistently maintained" and is "a bit run-down."

Forest Creek Golf Club　　▽ 22　17　20　19　$60
99 Twin Ridge Pkwy., Round Rock; 512-388-2874; www.forestcreek.com; 7147/5394; 73.8/71.9; 136/124

■ "Tight fairways and plenty of lateral hazards make for a long day if you're wayward off the tee" at this "lush" "Austin-area favorite" that "requires thinking" and accuracy on those "can-be-trouble shorter par 4s"; "extremely well-priced" and just a half-hour's drive from downtown's hip 6th Street, it's "good for group outings."

Horseshoe Bay Resort, Applerock ⌂　　▽ 26　26　24　21　$115
1 Horseshoe Bay Blvd., Horseshoe Bay; 830-598-2561; 800-252-9363; www.horseshoebaytexas.com; 6999/5509; 73.9/71.6; 134/117

■ "Wonderful use of water and stonework" on rolling fairways with "nice elevation changes" amid "beautiful surroundings" overlooking Lake LBJ makes this "very nice" Robert Trent Jones Sr. "the fave of the three" guest-only tracks at the "good" Hill Country resort, where amenities include exotic bird habitats, a 100-ft. man-made waterfall and an elaborate, night-lit putting course.

Horseshoe Bay Resort, Ram Rock ⌂　　26　25　23　20　$115
1 Horseshoe Bay Blvd., Horseshoe Bay; 830-598-2561; 800-252-9363; www.horseshoebaytexas.com; 6946/5306; 73.9/71.4; 137/121

■ "Stay on the fairway" or you'll get rammed by the rock–"hardest of the resort's three"; with 62 deep bunkers and water in play on 10 holes including "classics" like the signature par-3 island green, it may be "too difficult for many players", but this guests-only course that's hosted the Texas State Amateur and Southern Texas PGA Championship also sports "beautiful vistas" that all golfers can admire; says one critic of its conditioning, it "has the potential if they would make the investment" to keep it "well maintained."

Horseshoe Bay Resort, Slick Rock ⛳

▽ 22 | 25 | 22 | 20 | $115

1 Horseshoe Bay Blvd., Horseshoe Bay; 830-598-2561; 800-252-9363; www.horseshoebaytexas.com; 6834/5832; 72.6/70.2; 125/115

■ "After playing Ram Rock, this is a breeze" say vacationing city-slickers taking it easy on this "excellent" guests-only course where multiple sets of tee boxes make the "fun" "fair for all handicaps", despite the chance to slip into the drink on 11 holes; after a round, grab a burger at the clubhouse grill and gossip about the resort's planned Nicklaus track, Saddlerock.

Dallas

Buffalo Creek

23 | 15 | 16 | 19 | $85

624 Country Club Dr., Rockwall; 972-771-4003; www.americangolf.com; 7018/5209; 73.8/67.0; 133/113

☑ "Bring your A-game if the wind is up" say the hacking herds "challenged" by this "excellent", "enjoyable layout over nice, rolling terrain", which is "beautiful", though "you've got to travel awhile to get to" it from downtown Dallas; some nickle-counting "average golfers" feel "penalized by hazards a good player won't notice" and by "too-high weekend fees" for which they'd "expect a better clubhouse" and less "inconsistent conditions."

Chase Oaks, Blackjack ⛳

▽ 19 | 19 | 19 | 21 | $70

7201 Chase Oaks Dr., Plano; 972-517-7777; www.chaseoaks.com; 6773/5123; 72.1/72.7; 129/128

☑ It used to be blackjack on this track, with players dealing hands ranging from "nice, well-bunkered and tough in wind" to "average" and "in so-so shape"; but after a "recent upgrade" featuring all new greens, repositioned trees and revamped rough, "an excellent layout" is in the cards for a golfer-friendly, "solid value."

Cliffs Resort, The ⛳

24 | 20 | 21 | 23 | $80

160 Cliffs Dr., Graford; 940-779-4040; 888-843-2543; www.thecliffsresort.com; 6808/4876; 73.9/68.4; 143/124

■ "A little local knowledge goes a long, long way" at this "difficult-to-get-to" Hill Country course where "blind shots, swirling winds, tough holes and huge elevation changes" are "impossible for the first-time player, but wonderful the second round"; like Texas itself, it's a long stretch, so "don't even think about walking" such a "tough track for short hitters", and "watch out for snakes if you miss the fairway" – just stay in your cart and enjoy the resort's "pretty setting" on the cliffs above Possum Kingdom Lake.

COWBOYS

29 | 26 | 27 | 20 | $125

1600 Fairway Dr., Grapevine; 817-481-7277; www.cowboysgolfclub.com; 7017/4702; 74.2/68.9; 140/114

■ Golf and football have teamed up at the Lone Star state's No. 1–rated Course, where the "unbelievable 18 holes" and "outstanding facilities" are NFL-themed; "especially recommended for good players" who can carry the ball over "tree-lined, hilly" fairways to "challenging greens", it's a "better-than-excellent value", with promotional fees that "include food and beverages" quarterbacked by a "great" staff; all this plus the Cowboys' Super Bowl trophies on display and "good-quality merchandise in the shop" has cheerleaders chanting "even a 49ers fan can find it exciting."

Four Seasons at Las Colinas, Cottonwood Valley ♙
26 | 26 | 26 | 20 | $157

4150 N. MacArthur Blvd., Irving; 972-717-2500;
www.thesportsclubfourseasons.com; 6927/5320; 73.4/70.0; 133/118

☑ To "really understand what a tournament player has to deal with", check into the Four Seasons or "find a member" to gain access to the co-host of the PGA Tour's Verizon Byron Nelson Classic; citing "several very good holes", club-wielders who cotton to this "solid challenge" say it's got "more character" and is "more forgiving but still just as beautiful" as its sister, though geography buffs argue it offers "nothing memorable except for the Texas-shaped green, Oklahoma-shaped bunker" and Gulf of Mexico-like water hazard on the first hole.

FOUR SEASONS AT LAS COLINAS, TPC ♙
27 | 28 | 27 | 19 | $157

4150 N. MacArthur Blvd., Irving; 972-717-2500;
www.thesportsclubfourseasons.com; 7009/6004; 73.5/68.9; 135/122

☑ "Wonderful course, impeccable service, fabulous facilities – and you pay for it" say hordes of cash-happy hookers on this "beautiful, tricky, long" and "continually improving" guests-only traditionalist that "plays as good as it looks on TV"; oh, "blah, blah, blah" – you're shelling out shillings "largely" for the "fantasy factor" fret fussbudgets who frown upon "unmemorable par 4s" where it's "a thousand degrees in the shade", concluding "if they didn't play a Tour event here, they couldn't get $75."

Iron Horse
▽ 19 | 15 | 18 | 20 | $52

6200 Skylark Circle, N. Richland Hills; 817-485-6666;
www.ironhorsetx.com; 6580/5083; 71.8/69.6; 130/119

☑ It's "tricked up" claim "long hitters frustrated" on this "tight", "short course that requires precision" and not a lot of power hitting; a "very good municipal" parklander offering "solid value", it "can get crowded", so "get there early" to beat the rush and see for yourself whether or not, as detractors dryly note, it's "always too wet."

Ridgeview Ranch
21 | 15 | 14 | 20 | $36

2701 Ridgeview Dr., Plano; 972-390-1039; www.americangolf.com;
7025/5335; 74.1/70.4; 130/117

☑ One of the "best values in Metroplex" is this forgiving, "fun course with better-than-average conditions", where the "good variety" includes "No. 11, the toughest hole" when you're swinging "against prevailing winds"; its "greens are its best feature", but their condition "can be poor", as "the course backs up" "with tournament activity" and "bunched-together tee times", exhausting the grass and resulting in "five-hour weekend rounds."

Tangle Ridge
▽ 24 | 21 | 19 | 21 | $62

818 Tangle Ridge Dr., Grand Prairie; 972-299-6837; www.tangleridge.com;
6835/5187; 72.2/70.2; 129/117

☑ They're not all tangled up at the blues on this "tight", "well-kept" and "windy" muni, featuring "some good risk/reward holes" and "frequent elevation changes"; it's "always challenging" but "enjoyable for all skill levels", though loopers looking for luxury lament "pretty much nonexistent service" at a track that's "living on past reputation."

Texas Star
25 │ 23 │ 22 │ 23 │ $77

1400 Texas Star Pkwy., Euless; 817-685-7888; 888-839-7827;
www.texasstargolf.com; 6936/4962; 73.6/69.7; 135/129

■ "Talk about a fun course that you'll tell others about" – "we took
in a second round and made our plane just in time" raves one
teed-up traveler taking off from this municipal star of a "shotmaker's delight",
where "just the names of holes like 'Double Barrel', 'Long Arrow'
and 'Cannon's Run' are great" and oh-so-Texas; with "lots of blind
shots traveling up and down the rolling hills", it's "a hell of a test"
"created out of the original environment."

Tour 18 Dallas 🏌
23 │ 23 │ 22 │ 18 │ $95

8718 Amen Corner, Flower Mound; 817-430-2000; 800-946-5310;
www.tour18golf.com; 7033/5493; 74.3/66.3; 138/119

▣ "Play the tough ones you've only read about", or at least try their
"excellent replicas" at this "unique" copycat whose "dimensions
are very faithful to the original famous championship holes";
amateurs aching for authenticity call the mimic "a gimmick that
can't replace the real thing", but even though dubious duffers might
"never be able to buy into the idea that they're playing at Augusta
National", "lots of tournaments and groups" glut the schedule here,
so it's best to "call first and be flexible with your plans."

Tribute
▽ 27 │ 24 │ 21 │ 21 │ $105

1000 Boyd Rd., The Colony; 972-370-5465; www.thetexasgolftrail.com;
7002/5352; 73.2/65.6; 128/111

■ "They nailed the Scottish golf experience" at this Lone Star
linkster "situated on the shores of Lake Lewisville", where the
"excellent replicas" of "fabled British Open holes" are "much
cheaper than a trip overseas and as enjoyable"; the "wonderful
clubhouse" boasts a "great pub" and "well-appointed rooms
upstairs, making early-morning tee times more practical" and
après-round ales appealing; as "at St. Andrews", "watch out if it's
windy", and "don't look for lost balls in the native grasses" 'cause
"other things live there", and they're certainly not Scotsmen.

Westin Stonebriar, Fazio
– │ – │ – │ – │ $115

1549 Legacy Dr., Frisco; 972-668-8748; www.stonebriar.com;
7021/5208; 73.8/71.0; 133/121

At a conference-oriented Westin hotel attached to an upscale,
private country club, this well-regarded millennial links course by
Tom Fazio forces carries over water hazards and wetlands and
bends the dog's leg on several holes; you've gotta check in to play
it, but you won't be disappointed by your room, and you can treat
yourself to a spa treatment and a meal at the Legacy Grill.

Houston

BlackHorse, North
24 │ 24 │ 23 │ 19 │ $75

12205 Fry Rd., Cypress; 281-304-1747; www.blackhorsegolfclub.com;
7301/5077; 75.0/69.1; 130/115

■ "When I'm there I feel like a player" exclaim enthusiasts of this
"tough" track that's "a little out of the way but worth the drive from
Houston" for the "terrific holes along the creek south of Fry Road"
sporting "probably the best views in the area"; though thirsty three-
putters are "disappointed" by a "beverage cart" that plays hard

to get, lady lofters don't have any trouble attracting "great service" from "a staff that loves women."

BlackHorse, South   24 | 24 | 24 | 21 | $75

12205 Fry Rd., Cypress; 281-304-1747; www.blackhorsegolfclub.com; 7171/4843; 74.7/68.5; 138/123

☑ It "brings golfers to their knees" whinny whackers walking this "very nice" parklander known for "many memorable holes" "in and across the quarry"; thoroughbreds snort that it's "a little contrived", stamping their hooves at "rates that are too high" for a track you can't gallop across because it "takes too long to play."

Cypresswood, Tradition   25 | 18 | 18 | 18 | $75

21602 Cypresswood Dr., Spring; 281-821-6300; www.cypresswood.com; 7220/5255; 74.4/68.9; 134/122

■ "Unlike almost any course in Texas", this "absolute beauty" is "tucked inside a heavily wooded area" with "no sign of man or buildings", except those at the "nice clubhouse, snack bar and practice facilities"; "one of the longest and least crowded publics in the area", it's a "great course, tough but fair", so "if you really want to test your game, this will do it."

FALLS RESORT & CLUB, THE   28 | 18 | 18 | 22 | $65

1750 N. Falls Dr., New Ulm; 979-992-3123; www.thefallsresort.com; 6765/5348; 72.5/70.0; 135/123

■ "The prettiest course in the Houston area" just might be this "hidden jewel" where "deer and other wild game populate the woods along the fairways"; fans who've fallen for it feel it's "worth the drive" to the resort at the edge of Hill Country to take a few swings on a layout that "looks easy but plays much harder", with undulating greens, "a nice mix of holes" and "enough challenges to keep your interest for a full round."

Greatwood 🏌   19 | 18 | 18 | 18 | $55

6767 Greatwood Pkwy., Sugar Land; 281-343-9999; www.greatwoodgolfclub.com; 6829/5290; 72.3/70.0; 138/125

☑ Swingers sweet on this "very well-kept track" near Sugar Land "love every minute" of "a good round at a good price" on what they swear is "one of Houston's better" layouts; grumpy golfers grumble that this not-so-great woodlander is "the Enron of courses" – "overrated, overpriced and unfair", adding that it "was more fun when there were fewer houses lining the fairways."

Meadowbrook Farms   24 | 23 | 24 | 16 | $85

9595 S. Fry Rd., Katy; 281-693-4653; 7100/5000; 74.2/64.1; 137/108

■ "Greg Norman design – 'nuff said" about the "straightforward", "tour-quality course" with "no tricks, just demanding, solid golf" over "variable terrain, changing from tree-lined to marsh to prairie"; a sappling yet, it "needs to mature", but the "impeccable" staff is already well developed – they "really know what customer service is about" say pampered players who get why it's "pricey."

Memorial Park   21 | 13 | 13 | 25 | $42

1001 E. Memorial Loop; 713-862-4033; www.ci.houston.tx.us/municipalgolf/memorial; 7164/5494; 73.0/67.7; 122/114

■ "Many of golf's legends have walked" this "storied track, once home to the PGA Tour's Houston Open", but they probably weren't sporting the regulars' attire – "blue jeans and sneakers are in abundance" at the "great traditional layout" "brought back from decay by a multimillion-dollar renovation in the mid-'90s"; "it's hard to believe you're in the middle of the city" and "very hard to secure a tee time" on a layout "worthy of consideration as one of the tops in Houston, including all the private clubs", while "Beck's Prime, the great upper-end hamburger restaurant attached to the clubhouse", only furthers its status.

Old Orchard
22 | 16 | 19 | 21 | $65

13134 FM 1464, Richmond; 281-277-3300; www.oldorchardgolf.com
Barn/Range: 6927/5166; 73.6/96.4; 127/114
Range/Stables: 6687/5010; 71.7/68.1; 124/111
Stables/Barn: 6888/5035; 73.5/69.0; 130/113

☑ "Time your backswing to the chain-gang tunes" at this "old-school" course "a thin river away from the state prison" ("which makes for some interesting views"); "hitting the woods well" lately? – "you will be here, whether you want to or not", as those "long, lush par 5s" are set on "an old pecan orchard" thick with "giant", "100-year-old trees"; the "stable" of the site's former quarter horse ranch "gives it a nice atmosphere", and the "super barbecue" served by "friendly staff" completes an "adventure" where the only thing "needed is a beverage cart" – and a cake with a file baked into it.

Tour 18 Houston ⛳
23 | 20 | 22 | 16 | $110

3102 FM 1960 E., Humble; 281-540-0404; 800-856-8687;
www.tour18golf.com; 6782/5380; 72.7/65.9; 129/117

☑ This "tourist curiosity" may be in Humble, but it doesn't behave that way – as the "very friendly and helpful staff" might tell you, its 18 "uncanny likenesses" to PGA Tour faves offer a "blast" of a "chance to play" "some of the greatest holes in golf"; pshaw pipe putting pros who pout "unless they speed up the greens, it ain't even close to realistic", and with starstruck swingers coughing up fees as "stunning" as those at the "private clubs" it simulates, "it's reminiscent of that Yogi Berra comment – the place is so crowded, no one goes there anymore."

Windrose
▽ 21 | 18 | 20 | 22 | $68

6235 Pinelakes Blvd., Spring; 281-370-8900; www.windrosegolfclub.com;
7203/5355; 73.0/69.3; 128/117

☑ "They advertise 'the fastest greens in the Houston area'", and pedal-to-the-metal putters think "they're right about that", since "you can find concrete that's slower"; though par 3s guarded by water lend variety to other "wide-open" spots, bored baggers believe "a lot of holes seem to run together" on a course that's "gone downhill in the last two years after being one of the best values in town."

Woodlands Resort, TPC
27 | 24 | 22 | 19 | $125

2301 N. Millbend Dr., The Woodlands; 281-367-1100; 800-433-2624;
www.thewoodlands.com; 7018/5326; 73.7/72.1; 136/128

■ "The island-green 13th and the 17th and 18th holes are terrific" on this "class" act with a "devilish layout" for shotmakers who can work around "trees and water"; a "championship atmosphere" plus fairways and greens "clean enough to eat off" has Lone Star Staters rating it "one of Texas' best experiences" at a "great value compared with other TPCs" – "hopefully they will keep it in such pristine condition despite losing" hosting privileges to the PGA Tour Shell Houston Open; N.B. its sister course, The Pines, is closed for a face-lift until late in 2002.

San Antonio

Canyon Springs 🏞   ▽ 24 | 23 | 22 | 23 | $100
24400 Canyon Golf Rd.; 210-497-1770; www.canyonspringscc.com;
7077/5234; 72.8/70.0; 130/115
■ "A lot of attention was paid to blending the course through the natural terrain" at this "very demanding", "beautiful layout in Texas Hill Country", highlighted by "the spectacular waterfall on 18"; "stretches of considerable distance between some holes are definitely not for walkers", unless they're in as "excellent condition" as the track itself, but the "friendly pro shop staff" makes for "real Texas hospitality in the clubhouse", where you can rest your feet.

Hyatt Hill Country Golf Club   21 | 26 | 25 | 18 | $135
9800 Hyatt Resort Dr.; 210-520-4040; 888-901-4653;
www.sanantonio.hyatt.com; 6913/4781; 73.9/67.8; 136/114
☑ "Superior service" from "wonderful people" "makes the day very pleasant" at this "relaxing track" for families staying "at one of Texas' best golf resorts"; a "good course is made great by the Hyatt Hotel", which "kids love", while parents adore it for the new Wildflower spa; if you're not checking in, San Antonio locals drawl, it's "a nice layout but hardly merits a special trip."

La Cantera, Palmer   28 | 26 | 25 | 17 | $130
16641 La Cantera Pkwy.; 210-558-4653; 800-446-5387;
www.lacanteragolfclub.com; 6926/5066; 74.2/65.3; 142/116
■ "If Texas had a Pebble Beach, this would be it" because the Spanish colonial–style Westin's "new Palmer course" is "nothing less than outstanding" – "beautiful views" are "worth the fee alone", though the "excellent staff and pro shop" don't hurt either; "blind shots, uneven lies" and "extremely tough [play] from the tips" make it "exciting" "every time" you tee off, even if once you land on the greens, you find they still "need another year to mature."

La Cantera, Resort   27 | 26 | 26 | 20 | $130
16641 La Cantera Pkwy.; 210-558-4653; 800-446-5387;
www.lacanteragolfclub.com; 7004/4953; 72.5/67.1; 134/108
■ The home of the PGA Tour's Valero Texas Open is "an excellent challenge" "with dramatic elevation changes"; the "great starting hole" is "a real eye-opener at over 600 yards", but no matter how wide you wrench those lids, the "many blind shots" might prove "too tricky", and the "ticket" might be too "dear" – if you warm up at "perhaps the best public practice facility in the state", maybe, just maybe, your score will be "worth the price" of the round, but even if it's not, the resort's "convenience" to the Alamo and other tourist spots can help you forget your foozles.

Pecan Valley   25 | 19 | 18 | 23 | $90
4700 Pecan Valley Dr.; 210-333-9018; www.thetexasgolftrail.com;
7010/5335; 73.9/65.7; 131/118
■ Reviewers are nuts about this "parkland classic" whose "great history" includes the 1968 "PGA Championship, when Julius Boros

beat Arnold Palmer"; as The King well knows, though it's "fairly flat", this "great, old-fashioned layout" "with pecan trees outlining holes" is "a difficult test"; moreover, a recent, "terrific restoration" has "brought back up to tournament level" a course that's "much better, if not as pretty as, other, more expensive tracks in town."

Quarry

25 | 22 | 22 | 21 | $110

444 E. Basse Rd.; 210-824-4500; 800-347-7759; www.quarrygolf.com; 6740/4897; 73.4/67.4; 128/115

■ It's two, two, "two courses in one" at this "memorable" San Antonio "must-play": a "kind of plain" "Scottish links wanna-be" on the "front side lulls you to sleep, only to be slapped [awake] when you get to No. 10", where the layout descends into "an old granite quarry, providing a fun change from traditional Texas courses"; for "beautiful vistas and challenging carries", "play the back nine twice" stammer stone-cutting strokers, but "don't go in the summer, when it can get sweltering."

Silverhorn

▽ 23 | 14 | 17 | 18 | $65

1100 W. Bitters Rd.; 210-545-5300; 6922/5271; 73.1/66.4; 129/109

■ It's "a super joy" to tee it up on what grooming groupies gush is "the most well-manicured course in San Antonio", a traditional track that "plays long" and where "getting it down the middle will pay benefits"; it's got "some fun holes", and as the low voter turnout for this one suggests, "it's usually easy to get on when others are full."

Tyler

Garden Valley, Dogwood ⌂

▽ 27 | 18 | 20 | 25 | $59

22049 FM 1995, Lindale; 903-882-6107; 800-443-8577; www.gardenvalleygolfresort.com; 6754/5532; 72.4/72.5; 132/130

■ Well, it's "not quite Augusta National in Texas, but it's pretty and fun" and "worth the drive from Dallas" nonetheless, woof the small pack of dogs who've dug up the fairways at this resort course where putting pups can rent a house by one of the holes; it's a "great value", though perhaps they should charge more and sink some dollars back into maintenance, yap yipsters who say the "conditioning can be suspect at times"; N.B. if you've only got time for a quickie, buzz about on the nine holes of its little sister, the Hummingbird track.

U.S. Virgin Islands

St. Croix

Carambola Golf Club

– | – | – | – | $100

72 Estate River, Kingshill; 340-778-5638; www.carambolagolf.com; 6843/5425; 72.7/71.0; 131/123

"Come for the views alone" at this secluded resort "challenge" implore offshore shotmakers of this "Robert Trent Jones Sr. design that will test and delight" you over rolling terrain best known for its strong collection of par 3s and variety of flora and fauna; those not 'Bola-ed over say the "boring, brown and not terribly difficult, wide-open track" "is not what you'd expect from a Caribbean paradise" – "when in St. Croix", the sticklers "stick to the diving."

St. Thomas

Mahogany Run Golf Club ▽ 19 | 14 | 16 | 15 | $115

No. 1 Mahogany Run Rd. N.; 340-777-6006; 6022/5739; 70.1/72.6; 123/119

☑ "Get off the ship and play the Devil's Triangle" beckon putting pirates of the "spectacular" stretch from the 13th through the 15th at this "not long but memorable" mountain "beauty" where "the views are the juice", but you shouldn't get so drunk on them that you "wander off the fairway into the dense vegetation" or off a cliff; conditions can vary from "bad" to "much better", so sometimes you're "better off going to the beach or shopping."

Utah

Salt Lake City

Homestead Golf Club & Resort ▽ 18 | 21 | 22 | 21 | $55

700 Homestead Dr., Midway; 435-654-1102; 888-327-7220; www.homesteadresort.com; 7040/5091; 73.0/68.8; 135/118

☑ Happy homesteaders hail this "beautiful course" with "lots of water" on a "unique layout" in the "pretty" Snake Creek Valley, where "you should stay the night and have dinner at the resort's great restaurant"; raiders wreck its rep, razzing "look up, dummy! – why play a flat valley track in the midst of the Wasatch" range with the state park tracks "right across the road (at half the price)"?

Thanksgiving Point 27 | 25 | 25 | 20 | $78

3003 Thanksgiving Way, Lehi; 801-768-7400; www.thanksgiving-point.com; 7714/5838; 76.2/72.8; 140/135

■ "The closed-on-Sunday policy is a real bummer", as is the "no-alcohol" rule at this family-style daytime resort, but otherwise golfers give thanks for an "interesting design" that's "long and challenging" but "high enough in altitude that you truly feel like Tiger when you tee off" into those "incredible views"; "it will be one of the best around when it matures", but even in its youth, "it makes excellent use of the terrain, with blind shots, dramatic elevation changes and forced carries" – as those squeaky-clean Mormons would say, "oh, my heck, it's fun!"

Valley View – | – | – | – | $22

2501 E. Gentile, Layton; 801-546-1630; 6652/5755; 71.0/73.2; 123/125

"Imagine playing a course where you hit every club in the bag and never have the same shot twice"; "it's one of the best-conditioned layouts ever, you're treated like royalty – and you're paying only $22"; to boot, this "championship" track from the almost-too-good-to-be-true school of golf is set in a valley with the Wasatch Mountains rising around it for "scenery that can't be beat."

Wasatch Mountain State Park, – | – | – | – | $25
Lakes Course

975 W. Golf Course Dr., Midway; 435-654-0532; www.utahfairways.com; 6942/5573; 72.0/71.5; 128/123

The Mountain's older, soupier sister is another "amazing" Ute beaut; water on 16 holes partially accounts for why this course in the Heber Valley tucked amid the Wasatch Mountains 45 minutes from Salt Lake City is "so gorgeous and tough"; try it in the fall, when the trees are ablaze.

Wasatch Mountain State Park,　— | — | — | — | $36
Mountain Course 🏌
*975 W. Golf Course Dr., Midway; 435-654-0532; www.utahfairways.com;
6459/5009; 70.4/67.4; 125/119*
"The beauty of this course and its high altitude make for a fabulous
round" "with lots of great views and very challenging holes" at a
very unchallenging price; "it's best not to play here in late June
through late July" or "the deer flies" will extract an extra greens
fee in blood; N.B. the size of this family of tracks might double if
plans go through for 36 more holes by 2004.

St. George

Coral Canyon 🕐　　　　▽ 29 | 26 | 25 | 24 | $85
*1925 Canyon Greens Dr., Washington; 435-688-1700;
www.coralcanyongolf.com; 7029/5026; 73.0/69.1; 137/122*
■ There's "not one brown spot on the whole" of this "absolutely
wonderful course", and that's "a great feat considering" it's near
Zion National Park in the Southwestern desert; a "beautiful layout"
with "diverse and interesting" holes set amid lakes, dry washes and
red-rock outcroppings, it's "very well maintained" by "nice people"
in a planned community just north of the ski town of St. George.

Entrada at Snow Canyon　　28 | 20 | 20 | 22 | $80
*2511 Entrada Trail; 435-674-7500; www.golfentrada.com;
7262/5454; 74.4/71.2; 127/127*
■ "Lava fields provide a new breed of hazard" at this "Mauna Lani
of the Southwest", where the "breathtaking" views of canyons,
arroyos and cliffs "would cost you $200 if it were in California"; it's
"worth the two-hour drive from Las Vegas" gush gambling golfers
whose enthusiasm erupts for a "challenge" – just "bring your
straight ball" because this is one of "the hardest you'll ever play."

Vermont

Northern Vermont

Sugarbush Golf Club　　　▽ 19 | 12 | 17 | 17 | $48
*2405 Sugarbush Access Rd., Warren; 802-583-2301; 800-537-8427;
www.sugarbush.com; 6464/5231; 71.7/70.5; 128/129*
■ They should "put chains on the cart wheels" at this vertigo-
inducing, "fun mountain" track where "Mother Nature only adds
to the challenge" laid down by Robert Trent Jones Sr., with
"beautiful scenery throughout and some pretty good holes to
go along with it"; though its Facilities rating isn't so hot, Service
ranks better, according to those teeing it up under the aegis of
the "greatest starter."

Vermont National 🕐　　　▽ 21 | 22 | 21 | 17 | $120
*1227 Dorset St., South Burlington; 802-864-7770; www.vnccgolf.com;
7035/4966; 73.6/69.2; 133/116*
☑ "Play it while it's still [somewhat] public" burble Burlingtonians
blown away by this "nice Nicklaus classic", an "exciting" design
that's "not easy but very fair"; naysayers natter that "hole layouts
that don't work" and "don't fit the landscape" "aren't worth the
money", or the hassle of very restrictive, non-member tee times.

Southern Vermont

Equinox, Gleneagles   23 │ 20 │ 21 │ 17 │ $99

108 Union St., Manchester; 802-362-4700; 800-362-4747;
www.equinoxresort.com; 6423/5082; 71.3/65.2; 129/117

■ "Any time in autumn is awesome", but the "heavenly" views of the Green Mountains and "steeples rising from Manchester's village center" ain't bad in spring and summer either at this "classic layout" where the "bouncy, well-kept", "wide-open" fairways and "undulating greens" are "playable for all levels", particularly after you "get your bearings" on the "downhill par-4 starting hole"; non-golfers can go for birdies at the falconry school at The Equinox resort, where the new "great spa" rounds out a "fancy, fun and relaxing" retreat.

Green Mountain National   25 │ 18 │ 18 │ 20 │ $89

Barrows Towne Rd., Killington; 802-422-4653; 888-483-4653;
www.gmngc.com; 6589/4740; 72.6/68.0; 138/118

■ "Make sure to ring the bell as you pass around certain corners, or you may find a ball flying over your head" because "there's lots of blind uphill and downhill shots" on this "true Vermont gem" that's "challenging in every respect with sand, hills, water" and a "brutally" "bearish" back nine; "mud will eat your ball early in the season" but "it's in way-fantastic condition during late fall."

Okemo Valley Golf Club   ▽ 23 │ 23 │ 21 │ 19 │ $66

89 Fox Ln., Ludlow; 802-228-8871; 6400/5100; 71.1/70.1; 130/125

■ "Many of the holes are works of art" at this "relatively new" "mountain golf" "favorite" where a "diverse layout" and "trying rough put a premium on accuracy"; "beautiful and well-kept", with "great views of Mt. Okemo", it's particularly "scenic" if you "play it in fall", when the foliage lights up the links – after that, the snow starts falling, and cross-country skiers make tracks where you made par.

Stratton Mountain Country Club   20 │ 19 │ 19 │ 18 │ $99

Stratton Mountain Rd., Stratton Mountain; 802-297-2200; 800-787-2886;
www.stratton.com
Forest/Lake: 6526/5153; 71.2/69.8; 125/123
Lake/Mountain: 6602/5410; 72.0/71.1; 125/124
Mountain/Forest: 6477/5163; 71.2/69.9; 126/123

☑ "On a warm, early October morning, as the multi-colored leaves form a mosaic in the spectacular surrounding hills, it's the most beautiful place in the world" waxes one poetic putter penning a paean to a place perhaps primarily prominent for its "excellent golf school" but possessing a track that's hosted six LPGA Tour events with "a good mix" of "demanding" holes amid a "breathtaking backdrop"; less laudatory linksters lament a "touristy" trap that, "given its location" at a sky-high resort, "should be more inspiring" and "better maintained."

Woodstock Country Club   19 │ 20 │ 20 │ 19 │ $82

14 The Green, Woodstock; 802-457-6674; www.woodstockinn.com;
6053/4924; 69.0/69.0; 121/113

■ In 1961, Robert Trent Jones Sr. redesigned this "quaint" 1895 "gem" at a historic resort purchased by a Rockefeller, and he made it "a delight to play on and be a part of"; with "tees so close to the greens that you hear 'fore!' all day long", it's "short but sweet", with "small streams across many fairways", so "bring your ball retriever", and after your round let the "knowledgeable staff" at the "beautiful facility pamper you" with fine dining, spa services and a host of other amenities.

Virginia

★ **Best in State**

28 Homestead, Cascades, *Roanoke*
27 Golden Horseshoe, Gold, *Williamsburg*
   Kingsmill Resort, River, *Williamsburg*
26 Augustine, *Washington, D.C.*
   Kingsmill Resort, Woods, *Williamsburg*

Charlottesville

Birdwood   22 | 17 | 17 | 21 | $50

R.R. 250 W.; 434-293-4653; www.boarsheadinn.com;
6820/5047; 73.4/72.4; 132/122

■ "Young people looking at colleges should select UVA simply to play Birdwood at student rates" recommend alums of the university's "long", "gorgeous" resort course where the "front is traditional Virginia golf and the back goes up into the hills", with "terrain changes but no blind shots" and views of the Blue Ridge Mountains – "there's nothing like playing it on a fall day with the turning leaves", long before you're stressing out over finals.

Keswick Club   – | – | – | – | $110

701 Club Dr., Keswick; 434-923-4363; www.keswickclub.com;
6307/4879; 68.9/65.2; 126/114

If you're not a member, you have to check into Keswick Hall to play this "first-class course", but that's ok because you're in for an elegant vacation "at a deluxe resort" when you do; the "classic Palmer layout" in a "marvelous setting on 600 acres" is attached to a "gorgeous clubhouse and locker room", a fine restaurant with "great food", a spa and fitness center, tennis courts, swimming pools and a library, all amid the "beauty" of the Blue Ridge.

Wintergreen Resort, Devil's Knob 22 | 20 | 20 | 20 | $95

Rte. 151, Wintergreen; 434-325-8250; 800-325-8200;
www.wintergreenresort.com; 6576/5101; 72.4/68.6; 126/118

■ True to the name, "the greens are evil" at this "steep", "tight", "true mountain" monster where you're gonna "wish the cart had a first gear"; "lots of altitude changes" "take advantage of a terrain" with "spectacular views", requiring "accuracy, not length", which is "fantastic if you hit straight" – if not, "bring lots of balls", and bless a "friendly" staff that helps make the experience "superb."

Wintergreen Resort, Stoney Creek 25 | 22 | 22 | 20 | $95

Rte. 151, Wintergreen; 434-325-8250; 800-325-8200;
www.wintergreenresort.com
Monokan/Shamokin: 7005/5500; 74.6/71.8; 132/127
Shamokin/Tuckahoe: 6998/5594; 73.8/72.4; 130/128
Tuckahoe/Monokan: 6951/5462; 74.0/71.6; 130/129

■ "Exquisitely cared for from tee to green" by a "laid-back staff" whose "Southern hospitality makes you feel like you belong", this "scenic, well-manicured and wonderfully diverse" 27-holer is "one of the best in Virginia"; Monokan/Shamokin, "the original 18 holes, should be played together if possible", though "replays are a great value", so try them all, since the newer "Tuckahoe nine features bentgrass fairways and greens" with "spectacular views"; by the way, the resort is a "nice place to stay" as well.

DC Metro Area
(see also Maryland)

Augustine
| 26 | 22 | 21 | 22 | $79 |

76 Monument Dr., Stafford; 540-659-0566; www.augustinegolf.com; 6850/4838; 74.3/68.2; 142/119

■ "The toughest opening holes ever played" by plenty of politicos hint that this "hidden gem" named after our Founding Father's father "intends to take a bite out of any golfer's ego", and with "fast, sloping greens" and "some awesome tee shots", its teeth sure aren't wooden; senators from the Peach State sigh "when the flowers are in bloom, it feels like Augusta" at "one of the nicest courses in the DC area", though all of Congress kvetches that "play is very slow", as is the drive here through "I-95 traffic."

Gauntlet 🏌
| 20 | 18 | 17 | 21 | $66 |

18 Fairway Dr., Fredericksburg; 540-752-0963; 888-755-7888; www.golfgauntlet.com; 6857/4955; 72.8/69.8; 137/126

☑ "Lots of memorable" "risk/reward challenges" lie in wait amid a "great combination of water and woods holes with excellent par 5s" at this "really fun", tight suburbanite in a "great location" "around a small lake" south of the DC Beltway; suffering an "elevated level of frustration", a few foes throw down the gauntlet thusly: "all that's missing from this tricked-up course is the windmill putt-putt hole."

Lansdowne Resort 🏌
| 24 | 26 | 23 | 18 | $105 |

44050 Woodridge Pkwy., Lansdowne; 703-729-8400; 800-541-4801; www.lansdowneresort.com; 7057/5213; 74.6/70.6; 139/124

■ With "the best finishing stretch in Northern Virginia" "punctuated by an old wall" from the Civil War era, "the back nine will humble you after the front elevates your ego" at this RTJ Jr. "beauty" that's so "well maintained" the "zoysia fairways practically tee up your ball"; "a great business destination with superb facilities and a super staff", it caters to DC-area suits, so beware "corporate outings that run long" and "delay your tee time."

Meadows Farms
| 19 | 12 | 20 | 25 | $39 |

4300 Flat Run Rd., Locust Grove; 540-854-9890; www.meadowsfarms.com
Island Green/Longest Hole: 7005/4541; 73.2/65.3; 129/109
Island Green/Waterfall: 6058/4075; 68.9/62.8; 123/110
Longest Hole/Waterfall: 6320/4424; 69.6/65.1; 125/105

☑ "If the longest hole in the U.S. doesn't getcha, the church-pew bunkers will bring back bad Sunday school memories" at the "funnest course" for fetishists in the DC area, with three nines sporting "lots of memorable" spots, namely that 841-yard par 6; "traditionalists may find it quirky, but the quirks are entertaining if you keep an open mind" rave radicals, while conservative club-wielding critics crank "if you like to play in cow pastures, this is for you" because, despite the "considerate grounds personnel", it's "not in very good condition."

Westfields   26 | 21 | 22 | 17 | $95
13940 Balmoral Greens Ave., Clifton; 703-631-3300;
www.westfieldsgolf.com; 6897/4597; 72.7/65.9; 136/114
■ There are "no houses", but there are "lots of traps", "trees everywhere" and "a lot of employees around", though hopefully not in the way of your ball at this "definite must-play" "built for [architect] Fred Couples' length"; if you can concentrate over the "airplane noise", "you really have to think your way around" "undulating greens that require good iron play", and though putters pinching pennies pout that it's "pretty pricey", those ubiquitous staffers really do "take care of your every need."

Front Royal

Shenandoah Valley Golf Club   20 | 16 | 17 | 25 | $50
134 Golf Club Circle; 540-636-2641; www.svgcgolf.com
Blue/Red: 6399/5000; 71.1/67.8; 126/116
Red/White: 6121/4700; 69.6/66.3; 122/114
White/Blue: 6330/4900; 70.7/66.2; 122/113
■ "For the price, you can't beat" this dirt-cheap track the "entire family can enjoy" for a song ('Oh, Shenandoah', perhaps?); it's "short and sans water, but it's beautiful", with views of the Blue Ridge, and even if conditions waver from "spectacular" to "not good", a "nice differentiation from hole to hole" at "a great value", plus lodging in a 1785 inn is "worth the hour-plus drive from DC."

Leesburg

Bull Run   23 | 19 | 19 | 20 | $88
3520 James Madison Hwy., Haymarket; 703-753-7777; 877-753-7770;
www.bullruncc.com; 7009/5069; 73.0/68.3; 134/110
◪ Swinging soldiers battling it out on this "horticulturally lovely layout" near the site of those famous Civil War tangles say it's a "great" round and an even better stroll, so "if your game doesn't make an appearance, you can still have a wonderful walk", though it's more like a run because the "fine staff" keeps up an "excellent pace of play"; bull, say critics, it's just "another overpriced track" "in bad shape", with "a few shortish par 3s."

Raspberry Falls   26 | 23 | 21 | 19 | $94
41601 Raspberry Dr., Leesburg; 703-779-2555; www.raspberryfalls.com;
7191/4854; 75.6/67.8; 140/113
■ "Be warned, it's like Paris – you hate it the first time but fall in love the second" say berry happy hookers of this "outstanding" "rustic and scenic" "Virginia horse country" linkster that "rewards good shots and penalizes bad ones, as it should"; climb aboard the "elevated, testosterone-pumping tees" and sail out onto "rolling fairways that make it seem as if you're at sea", but avoid sinking into "deep bunkers that make you feel as if you're underwater", and you're sure to have a "very enjoyable round", even if some salty swingers give it raspberries for being "S-L-O-W" and "a tad pricey."

Stonewall Golf Club 🏠   ▽ 29 | 27 | 25 | 20 | $105
15601 Turtle Point Dr., Gainesville; 703-753-5101;
www.stonewallgolfclub.com; 7002/4889; 74.1/67.9; 142/114
■ The "beautiful course" at this "country club for the rest of us" "rivals its cross-water neighbor, the [private] Robert Trent Jones

Club", say the few fortunate flubbers who've found it on the banks of Lake Manassas; on a "spectacular", "tough layout" "with generous landing areas" "in immaculate condition", "every hole is interesting" every time you play it, but they are at their most "scenic" "in autumn when the leaves are changing colors"; parched putters press "please, please, please get some drinking water on the track."

Virginia National   ∇ 20 | 12 | 17 | 19 | $68

1400 Parker Ln., Bluemont; 540-955-0796; 6800/5000; 73.3/68.3; 137/116
■ "As it matures", this "picturesque" toddler "will become a great course" forecast fans of the "beautiful river and mountain scenery" and "really nice layout" at what is quite possibly "the best deal in Northern Virginia"; give it a whirl while it's still on training wheels, just "don't hit your driver too often if you want to score", and "play in spring or fall", unless you like "gnats disrupting your round."

Richmond

Crossings   18 | 16 | 16 | 19 | $63

800 Virginia Center Pkwy., Glen Allen; 804-266-2254;
www.thecrossingsgolf.com; 6659/5625; 71.5/73.2; 128/128
◪ "Watch out for the bugs because they'll eat you alive", but beyond the bites, you're in for a "good experience, good value and good service" at this "very solid if unspectacular" layout amid the Civil War battlefields of suburban Richmond; warring wood-wielders whine it's "pricey" for an area where "you can find better" bargains.

Independence Golf Club,   – | – | – | – | $79
Championship Course

600 Founders Bridge Rd., Midlothian; 804-594-0261;
www.independencegolfclub.com; 7127/5022; 74.2/64.0; 137/112
The Virginia State Golf Association Foundation enlisted Tom Fazio to come up with an 18 that wanders along rolling terrain through woodlands with several tee boxes and lots of bunkering to make it interesting to all skill levels; the club also offers a nine-hole short course and houses the Museum of Virginia Golf History within its clubhouse, the Charles House, which is modeled after Thomas Jefferson's Monticello.

Roanoke

HOMESTEAD, CASCADES   28 | 25 | 25 | 20 | $210

Homestead Hotel, Hot Springs; 540-839-7739; 800-838-1766;
www.thehomestead.com; 6679/4967; 73.0/70.3; 137/124
■ "One of America's oldies" but "greatest" goodies, the state's No. 1–ranked Course "lives up to its reputation and its history" as a "true champion" "challenge"; the octogenarian host to seven USGA tournaments boasts "incredible views" and "all the amenities of a fine resort" that, despite its National Historic Landmark status, "combines grace and friendliness without pretension"; tee off where George Washington wiggled toes in local hot springs, but "bear in mind you're playing on the side of a mountain", so the difference between an "A-grade caddie and a B-grade caddie" can "make your round."

Homestead, Lower Cascades | 22 | 22 | 24 | 20 | $130 |
Homestead Hotel, Hot Springs; 540-839-7739; 800-838-1766;
www.thehomestead.com; 6579/4686; 72.2/65.5; 127/116

☑ "The golf is outstanding" throughout this "great" Relais &
Châteaux resort, as are the rooms, spa, dining and shopping;
however, 'lower' doesn't just refer to its geography, but to its
status – though weekenders welcome it as "a pleasant middle-
ground diversion from the challenge of playing" its storied sibling,
low-handicappers say it's a "good" 18, "but play the Cascades
again before this one", and after some sweet swinging, toast a
"tribute" to late resident pro and PGA Tour legend Slammin' Sam
Snead at the namesake pub across the road.

Homestead, Old | 20 | 25 | 26 | 22 | $130 |
Homestead Hotel, Hot Springs; 540-839-7739; 800-838-1766;
www.thehomestead.com; 6211/4852; 69.0/67.7; 129/116

■ "Given its age" (the first tee is 110 years old), the granddaddy
of this "top-flight" retreat is a "fascinating course"; one of "the
only places to play a configuration of equal numbers of par 3s, 4s
and 5s", it's "especially suited to couples" – just make sure your
shutterbug sweetheart "brings a camera to catch" you when you
are putting on the "wonderfully kept greens" against "magnificent
views" of the Allegheny Mountains; now, "after an extensive
renovation" by Rees Jones, the "huge surprise" is that some
players find it "more enjoyable than either of the Casades."

Virginia Beach

Bay Creek Golf Club   ▽ | 28 | 23 | 28 | 28 | $67 |
One Clubhouse Way, Cape Charles; 757-331-9000; www.bay-creek.com;
7204/5229; 75.2/69.8; 142/119

■ Go hungry to this "super new track" over the Bridge-Tunnel
because "it will hand you your breakfast, lunch and dinner" all in
one "blast"; "the front nine [starts] on the Chesapeake" and turns
toward the marsh, where the "back nine, no slouch either, has
several holes along Plantation Creek", so there's lots of "scenic"
water to swallow your shot, but its "forgiving fairways" are "not
too intimidating", and neither are "the cutest girls in the world
taking your bags from the car"; N.B. a clubhouse and a Nicklaus
course are in the works.

Hell's Point Golf Course | 19 | 15 | 16 | 18 | $62 |
2700 Atwoodtown Rd.; 757-721-3400; 888-821-3401; www.hellspoint.com;
6766/5003; 73.3/71.2; 130/116

☑ It ain't the Garden of Eden, despite the "cottonmouth snake [you
might] come across while looking for a lost ball" in the "often-
marshy, wooded" purgatory edging the fairways of this "swampy"
but "lovely" "secluded" layout; "some standard Rees Jones
tricks such as doglegs around lakes" make for an "interesting"
"but not outstanding design" that's a "monster from the tips" but,
like its namesake hot spot, might just be "living on its reputation."

TPC at Virginia Beach   ▽ | 24 | 23 | 23 | 17 | $117 |
2500 Tournament Dr.; 757-563-9440; 877-484-3872; www.tpc.com;
7432/5314; 75.8/70.1; 142/114

☑ "Beautiful" and "in great shape" if "a bit overpriced", this Virginia
Beacher is for lovers of "good greens" and "difficult" play; the

unenamored yammer that the "uninspired Pete Dye design" is "pancake-flat and boring" "with holes so similar they run together in the mind", making it the "lemon on the TPC tree", where the "distracted staff" might not be of much help if you're hoping to make lemonade.

Williamsburg

Golden Horseshoe, Gold   27 | 24 | 23 | 20 | $145
401 S. England St.; 757-220-7696; www.history.org;
6817/5168; 73.8/69.8; 144/126
■ "Feel the history" – no, not of the 1760s, but of the 1960s at Robert Trent Jones Sr.'s "excellent traditional layout" in Colonial Williamsburg, home of the venerable Williamsburg Inn; "one of the classic courses in the country", it sports "a variety of lies and shots" and "the best quartet of par 3s to be found", including the island-green 16th; it's "at its scenic best in springtime", its "best value in winter" and its most "difficult in fall, when fallen leaves make a three-ft. blooper in the middle of the fairway impossible to find."

Golden Horseshoe, Green   26 | 24 | 24 | 22 | $95
401 S. England St.; 757-220-7696; www.history.org;
7120/5348; 75.1/70.5; 138/120
◪ "In a beautiful setting" "carved through the trees" "hidden" away from the tourists in tricornered hats is this Williamsburg "gem" where "each hole is almost secluded from the others" so that "you feel as if just your foursome is playing the course"; though mystics muse that it's "missing the intangible feeling" of its "more famous sibling", its "forgiving fairways" and fees make it the "more golfer-friendly" "value of the two."

Kingsmill Resort, Plantation   22 | 27 | 24 | 20 | $110
1010 Kingsmill Rd.; 757-253-3906; 800-832-5665; www.kingsmill.com;
6543/4880; 71.3/67.9; 119/116
◪ "Anheuser-Busch runs one heck of a resort" for "golfers of any ability", where the "beautiful clubhouse", excellent spa and other "wonderful facilities" rate No. 1 in the state, the "friendly staff" is "always looking for a better way to serve you" and the "serene", "rolling" Arnold Palmer/Ed Seay design is "not as difficult" as its cousins; "bring the entire family" to frolic amid the old plantation ruins, despite better ball hitters blubbering that "the most exciting feature is finding [PGA Tour professional] Curtis Strange's home on the course."

Kingsmill Resort, River   27 | 26 | 24 | 19 | $155
1010 Kingsmill Rd.; 757-253-3906; 800-832-5665; www.kingsmill.com;
6837/4646; 73.3/65.3; 137/116
■ "From the drive in to sitting with a Budweiser" and a plate of "good food" at the 19th hole, golfers gush over this longtime host of the PGA Tour's Michelob Championship, a "first-rate" "thinking course" that makes "great use of the natural terrain" to "challenge the best"; it's "less extreme than most Pete Dye designs", and it may be "misnamed", since the James River "is seen on only the two" finishing holes, but "A-gamers" say it's "worth every penny", even if overnighters find "variances in the quality" of the resort's villas.

Kingsmill Resort, Woods
| 26 | 24 | 24 | 22 | $120 |

*1010 Kingsmill Rd.; 757-253-3906; 800-832-5665; www.kingsmill.com;
6784/5140; 72.7/68.7; 131/120*

■ "Shhh . . . it's better than the River" say some wanna-be Tigers of the Woods, which fans call "quiet", "lovely" and "playable" with "a lot of little surprises all over", i.e. "my idea of golf heaven"; since not every demon driver deigns to enter its pearly gates, it's "usually not crowded", and of course, "you can't say enough about" the "helpful, friendly" angels at the newly redone, "great clubhouse."

Kiskiack
| 21 | 16 | 17 | 20 | $75 |

8104 Club Dr.; 757-566-2200; 6775/4902; 72.5/67.8; 134/112

☑ "It's easy to get to off I-64, but it's a challenge not to take a big number somewhere" on the water-rimmed holes at this "better-than-average" woodlander where "you can't beat the twilight discount price"; "fun", "fair", affordable and accessible, it's also (surprise, surprise) "always overcrowded."

Royal New Kent
| 24 | 21 | 21 | 22 | $75 |

*5001 Bailey Rd., Providence Forge; 804-966-5359; 888-253-4363;
www.traditionalclubs.com; 7291/5231; 76.5/72.0; 147/130*

☑ "Play from the tips and may the force be with you" on this "Scotland-on-steroids" "wild Mike Strantz" "masterpiece" "that gives you blind shots and eye-popping scenery" but "little margin for error"; it's a "visually stunning" "must-play for serious golfers", but hackers who find it "impossible" caution "count your lost balls, not your score", and "use that yardage book" on "a tricked-up track" where "six-hour rounds" aren't out of the question.

Tradition at Stonehouse
| 24 | 22 | 22 | 21 | $75 |

*9700 Mill Pond Run, Toano; 757-566-1138; 888-825-3426;
www.stonehouseva.com; 6963/5013; 75.0/69.1; 140/121*

☑ It's "interesting", it's "extreme", it's even "bizarre", but there are folks who "love Mike Stranz's unforgiving, imaginative" design; surely, it's "best suited for better golfers, while high-handicappers should bring a couple dozen balls", nerves of steel and a periscope to peer around all those "blind tee shots"; the "sloped" "three-putt greens" on the "ridiculous" layout might have critics itching to burn this 'House down, but at least the "new, lowered greens fee" won't burn a hole in their pockets.

Washington

Bremerton

Gold Mountain, Cascade
| ▽ 25 | 19 | 22 | 26 | $32 |

*7263 W. Belfair Valley Rd.; 360-415-5432; www.goldmt.com;
6707/5306; 72.1/70.3; 120/117*

■ Ship-to-shore shotmakers say it's "amazing to see a Navy town embrace golf", but Bremerton's civilians do just that at "the best municipal facility in the state", where this "nice complement" to the Olympic course might be "overshadowed" by its sister, but it's "amazing for the money" nonetheless, with a "hilly, well-treed", "really exciting" layout; club-wielders clamor for its "country-club greens" and "great visuals" of Pacific Northwest wilderness, so it's "difficult to get on in the summertime" – "plan accordingly."

GOLD MOUNTAIN, OLYMPIC
28 | 17 | 20 | 28 | $50

7263 W. Belfair Valley Rd.; 360-415-5432; www.goldmt.com;
7035/5220; 73.5/69.5; 131/120

■ "Views and more views" of the "magnificent Olympic Mountains" highlight the "incredible experience" of a round on Washington's No. 1–rated Course and Top Value; the "mountain-climbing" links-style layout is so "awesome", it's "worth every penny" of the few you dish out and more; "it plays a little slow on weekends", particularly in high season, but it's "excellent in winter", and "the new clubhouse should put it over the top as a complete golf venue" year-round.

McCormick Woods
25 | 23 | 22 | 23 | $59

5155 McCormick Woods Dr. SW, Port Orchard; 360-895-0130;
800-373-0130; www.mccormickwoodsgolf.com;
7040/5758; 74.6/73.6; 136/131

■ It's "O.B. everywhere, so keep it straight" and "bring extra balls if you're not accurate" to this "fantastic" woodlander in a "lovely" spot below Mount Rainier with "beautifully maintained fairways and greens" tucked in amid "old-growth timber and water"; it just might be that the "twilight rates are the best deal in the Seattle area" and "the staff the friendliest in the state", but a few foozlers are still fussing that it's "a little overpriced for what you get": "wanna-be country club" "surrounded by too many homes."

Trophy Lake Golf & Casting
▽ 21 | 20 | 19 | 18 | $70

3900 SW Lake Flora Rd., Port Orchard; 360-874-8337;
www.trophylakegolf.com; 7206/5342; 74.3/70.3; 137/125

■ "Where else can you golf and fish?" wonder sportsmen who sigh "it does not get any better" than this club that lures swingers with "deals" and hooks them "with a great finishing hole" and views of Mount Rainer and the Olympic Range; if you think it's a "nice track but a bit expensive", you obviously haven't discovered "the e-mail newsletter: sign up for it and you'll find out about hidden specials."

Seattle

Apple Tree
▽ 25 | 24 | 23 | 23 | $55

8804 Occidental Ave., Yakima; 509-966-5877; www.appletreegolf.com;
7001/5428; 74.2/72.0; 132/124

■ Golfers discover the gravity of the 17th, a "terrific signature" island "green in the shape of an apple", followed by "a closing hole that will give you a nosebleed" at this "wonderful place to play in sunny Yakima (the Palm Springs of Washington State)"; the "killer" is "a little spendy on weekends", but it's "a fantastic value for seniors", and "in season, the apples are delicious."

Druids Glen
▽ 21 | 11 | 15 | 16 | $55

29925 207th Ave. SE, Kent; 253-638-1200; www.druidsglengolf.com;
7200/5354; 74.9/70.6; 135/128

☒ A coven of club-wielders bubble, bubble, toil and trouble with glee over the "superb par 3s" on this "lovely layout" that casts its spell as possibly "the best public course within 40 minutes of Seattle", where mystics marvel over "views of Mount Rainier" and "look out for elk and deer, and their tracks"; druidic detractors dis "the biggest rip-off in the state with lumpy greens, horrible drainage and snooty employees."

Golf Club at Newcastle, China Creek ⚐
▽ 19 | 28 | 26 | 8 | $95

15500 Six Penny Ln., Newcastle; 425-455-0606; www.newcastlegolf.com; 6416/4566; 71.4/76.7; 126/137

◪ The adjective must be a Seattle slang staple, 'cause swingers say there's "awesome golf", "awesome service" and "awesome views" of the skyline at this . . . um . . . awesomely "nice track" where amenities include "the region's best practice facilities" and "a terrific clubhouse and restaurant"; nevertheless, it's up a creek for critics who crab that "the immature, boring course" is "too expensive for what you get", which seems to be encroaching "construction", so "watch out" or "an errant shot could put you on a field of plastic."

GOLF CLUB AT NEWCASTLE, COAL CREEK ⚐
20 | 28 | 27 | 9 | $150

15500 Six Penny Ln., Newcastle; 425-455-0606; www.newcastlegolf.com; 7024/5153; 74.7/71.0; 142/123

◪ Repetitious roundsmen rate this "incredible course" with an "incredible clubhouse" and "incredible views" "incredibly pricey", but "worth it" at least "once a year" for "tough-as-they-come" play, "a great pro shop" and an "excellent" grill where you can compensate for your splurge on the course with a "moderately priced" meal; for picky putters, it remains to be seen whether this "marginal" track is a diamond in the rough, as "this second 18 hasn't grown in yet."

Harbour Pointe
19 | 17 | 16 | 17 | $55

11817 Harbour Pointe Blvd., Mukilteo; 425-355-6060; 800-233-3128; www.harbourpt.com; 6861/5320; 73.0/71.5; 137/123

◪ "A difficult front nine" points toward a "tough" round "from the get-go" for hookers working these "great holes" with "lotsa water" and "fantastic views of Puget Sound"; those harboring resentment sputter "it's not all it's cracked up to be" – with "few amenities", "too many houses" and "too many mediocre" moments, it's a "slow waste of money."

Washington National
22 | 17 | 20 | 16 | $90

14330 SE Husky Way, Auburn; 253-333-5000; www.washingtonnationalgolfclub.com; 7304/5117; 75.6/70.3; 141/118

◪ Husky hackers hoorah the University of Washington's "U.S. Open–quality layout", rating it a "well-maintained", "links-style" "must-play when in the Northwest" "where each hole offers its own drama"; some of the hubbub comes from female golfers throwing fits at "tricks and intimidation" on what they say is one of "the least friendly courses to women" at "waaay" too "pricey" a fee.

Tacoma

Classic Country Club
▽ 20 | 11 | 14 | 22 | $34

4908 208th St. E., Spanaway; 253-847-4440; 6793/5580; 73.6/73.3; 133/128

■ It's "not great amenities but great golf" that gets 'em in gear for the drive to this "out-of-the-way" walkable traditional; "in the region, "nothing's more true" than its "fast, hard, undulating greens" surrounded by "many grassy pot bunkers" at the tail end of "narrow fairways", and nothing's more "reasonable" than prices kept down by the "smart, new ownership."

Vancouver Area

Resort Semiahmoo, Semiahmoo Course   ▽ 25 | 25 | 24 | 21 | $59

8720 Semiahmoo Pkwy., Blaine; 360-371-7005; www.semiahmoo.com; 7005/5288; 74.5/71.6; 130/126

☑ Admirers checked into this resort at a nature preserve on a Puget Sound peninsula call its tree-lined Palmer design "a really fun challenge" through cedar and birch forest with views of Mt. Baker and water on five holes; critics counter "it's getting old" – "15 years ago it felt like you were playing in church, now you feel like you're on parade"; at the end of your long march, get away from it all in a sailboat at the facility's marina.

Wenatchee

Desert Canyon 🏌   27 | 26 | 24 | 23 | $85

1201 Desert Canyon Blvd., Orondo; 509-784-1111; www.desertcanyon.com; 7217/5407; 73.9/70.6; 134/115

■ Anomalous as it might seem in the soggy "Pac Northwest", this "total golf experience" with "some of the best views" "overlooking the majestic Columbia River" sports a "terrific desert layout"; just like farther south, you'll wanna "stay away from the waste areas and the snakes", and you'll also wanna "stay out of the wind" to hit the "wicked greens" on the "pretty wide-open target-style" spread; it's "hard to locate due to limited signage on the roads", but keep your eyes peeled, and you're in for "fun, fun, fun."

West Virginia

Elkins

Raven at Snowshoe Mountain   – | – | – | – | $85

10 Snowshoe Dr., Snowshoe; 304-572-1000; www.snowshoemtn.com; 7045/4363; 74.9/65.4; 139/113

"The most beautiful mountain 18 played" by a handful of alpine aces is also "one of the best values" for a sky-high adventure; at a popular ski resort, it boasts 200-ft. drops from tee to fairway and it's teeming with deer, fox, geese, bears (so don't wander into the woods without a club) and fish too – water's in play on eight holes.

White Sulphur Springs

GREENBRIER, GREENBRIER COURSE 🏌   26 | 29 | 28 | 20 | $300

300 W. Main St.; 304-536-1110; 800-624-6070; www.greenbrier.com; 6675/5095; 73.1/69.8; 135/118

■ Whee doggie! – the "caddie gave me a recipe for squirrel gravy (no kidding)" croons one city-slicker at this "old-world charmer" that hosted the 1979 Ryder Cup; "unfortunately, you'll no longer have the chance to get hustled for lessons from Slammin' Sammy Snead", who was a fixture at the grand old place before he passed away in May 2002, so you'll have to make your own uneducated way across this "beautiful course" with "breathtaking mountain views" before you "follow up with a dip in the springs" at "one of America's finest resorts" "for a vacation" with the kinfolk.

GREENBRIER, MEADOWS ♟   21 | 28 | 27 | 21 | $300
300 W. Main St.; 304-536-1110; 800-624-6070; www.greenbrier.com;
6807/5001; 72.4/68.5; 132/115
■ "The perfect complement to Old White and the Greenbrier" might
be lofters' "least favorite at this resort, but it's still better than 99
percent of the courses in the United States"; it's a "fun" meander
among streams and trees, with a view of Whiterock Mountain, but
"it's way overpriced, so play it off-season or on a package" deal
that includes unlimited rounds and practice sessions, club
cleaning and storage, a golf clinic, a swank room and lavish
breakfasts and dinners.

GREENBRIER, OLD WHITE ♟   25 | 28 | 28 | 20 | $300
300 W. Main St.; 304-536-1110; 800-624-6070; www.greenbrier.com;
6652/5123; 72.2/69.7; 131/119
■ "If you like 'em old and classical", this Scots-style octogenarian
"delivers", beginning with its "fantastic starting hole"; "just
tough enough, perfectly maintained" and "steeped in tradition and
panoramas", it's "mountain golf at its best", with "caddies as
good as they come", even if newfangled foozlers feel that the
"musty" hotel adjacent to the course is "a little over the top",
labeling it "Martha Stewart on steroids", which is a moniker
that might actually please the budding chefs enrolled in the
resort's culinary classes.

Wisconsin

★ **Best in State**
29 Whistling Straits, Straits, *Kohler*
  Blackwolf Run, River, *Kohler*
27 University Ridge, *Madison*
26 Blackwolf Run, Meadow Valleys, *Kohler*
  Whistling Straits, Irish, *Kohler*

Central Wisconsin

Lake Arrowhead, Lakes   ▽ 23 | 19 | 21 | 25 | $62
1195 Apache Ln., Nekoosa; 715-325-2929; www.lakearrowheadgolf.com;
7105/5272; 74.8/71.1; 140/124
■ All arrows point to this "hidden gem in the middle of Wisconsin",
"one of the state's best-kept secrets", where tight, tree-lined
fairways and bunker-guarded greens are tucked amid eight small
lakes and a waterfall cascades into a pond by the 3rd green; cheer
cheeseheads chipping on the cheap, "for the money, you won't
find many better that match design with dollar."

Lake Arrowhead, Pines   ▽ 26 | 19 | 21 | 25 | $49
1195 Apache Ln., Nekoosa; 715-325-2929; www.lakearrowheadgolf.com;
6625/5213; 72.1/70.1; 132/122
■ Stop complaining about the schlep from Madison or Green Bay –
"just make your plans and play it" press putters pining for the Lake
Arrowhead twins, "one of the best 36-hole combinations in the
Midwest"; with bentgrass fairways and greens closely guarded
by bunkers, the Lakes' sister ambles through big timber country
near the historic re-enactment settlement of Point Basse – it's an
area known for its cranberries, but it'll only cost you a few of those
to enjoy a round here.

Kohler

BLACKWOLF RUN, MEADOW VALLEYS ⚐
| 26 | 28 | 28 | 22 | $148 |

1111 W. Riverside Dr.; 920-457-4446; 800-618-5535;
www.blackwolfrun.com; 7142/5065; 74.7/69.5; 143/125

■ The other half of one half of Kohler's Blackwolf Run/Whistling Straits "golf mecca" "ain't the River, but it ain't chopped liver" either; in fact, it's "the best bang for the buck on earth" huzzah hyperbolic hookers; "stay at the American Club" in the all-inclusive resort village, feast in the many restaurants, shop till you drop, chill at the spa and play this "links-styler" as a "good warm-up for the best golf package I know of", suggest vacationers – just do it soon 'cause "reservations are nearly impossible and prices are rising."

BLACKWOLF RUN, RIVER ⚐ ⏱
| 29 | 28 | 27 | 22 | $173 |

1111 W. Riverside Dr.; 920-457-4446; 800-618-5535;
www.blackwolfrun.com; 6991/5115; 74.9/70.7; 151/128

■ "Play it before you die and again after you die" gush besotted ballers at Pete Dye's "magical" "mix of natural beauty and precision landscaping"; "a great combination of long, short, strategic and impossible holes" with "meandering streams", it's so "awesome, it's almost overpowering", so "bring your straight game" and "avoid the tips 'cause they're in a different time zone"; at a resort that "gives Midwest hospitality new meaning", "it's hard to consider $173 a good value, but compared to Pebble Beach, it's a bargain!"

WHISTLING STRAITS, IRISH ⚐
| 26 | 29 | 28 | 21 | $196 |

N8501 County LS, Sheboygan; 920-457-4446; 800-618-5535;
www.whistlingstraits.com; 7201/5109; 75.6/70.0; 146/126

■ "Pete Dye plays with your mind" on this "striking course" where "sheep roam the mountain overlooking the lake", bleating as you bleed in "bunker city"; the designer "never moved dirt so well", except on the "last three holes, which ruin near perfection" and make this "gentler", "faster play" and "better value" "slightly less spectacular" than its sibling; in other words, "can you get any closer to heaven" than this? – "yes, at the Straits next door."

WHISTLING STRAITS, STRAITS ⚐ ⏱
| 29 | 28 | 28 | 22 | $248 |

N8501 County LS, Sheboygan; 920-457-4446; 800-618-5535;
www.whistlingstraits.com; 7343/5381; 76.7/72.2; 151/132

■ "The pros will have all they can handle" when the "world-class American Club resort" hosts the 2004 PGA Championship because lurking on the "beautiful lakefront" is a "brutal test that's all about long, forced carries, tons of bunkers" and blusters – "when the wind gets up off the water, fuhgeddaboudit"; so take a "helpful caddie" "who knows every bunker" to guide you on the state's Top-rated Course, and "bring lots of balls, literally and figuratively."

Lake Geneva

Abbey Springs ⚐
| ▽ 22 | 18 | 18 | 20 | $90 |

1 Country Club Dr., Fontana; 262-275-6113; www.abbeysprings.com;
6468/5338; 71.4/72.4; 135/131

☑ Medium-length and heavily wooded, with views of Lake Geneva and a watery grave lurking on nearly half the holes, this tree-laced track "is a great deal of fun to play, with the chance to hit each club in the bag" according to regulars like course record-holder, Wisconsin's own PGA Tourist, Steve Stricker; "the pro shop staff makes you feel at home", though this house is a little decrepit, with facilities that are "getting old" and "in need of improvement."

Geneva National, Gary Player 🏌⏱ ▽ 25 | 25 | 21 | 21 | $125
1221 Geneva National Ave. S.; 262-245-7022;
www.genevanationalresort.com; 7018/4823; 74.2/68.4; 139/120
■ "The newest of the three at Geneva National" is "an excellent", "playable" Player set on a combo of parkland, woodland and lakefront terrains, all "quite well conditioned" and "challenging, with some long forced carries from the back tees"; despite the ratings and the fact that haute Hunt Club restaurant serves as this course's halfway house, a sprinkling of killjoys complain "don't be surprised by the lack of service", which is particularly "shoddy during value times" at early-bird and twilight hours.

Geneva National, Palmer 🏌⏱ ▽ 26 | 25 | 21 | 22 | $110
1221 Geneva National Ave. S.; 262-245-7022;
www.genevanationalresort.com; 7177/4892; 74.7/68.5; 140/122
■ "Incredible forests and views" of Lake Como highlight "a design as good today as it was 10 years ago" exclaim Arnie's Army of this "tops-in-every-way" layout; "the 17th hole is one to remember", "a great par 5 with water all the way down the left", followed by a "quite strong uphill close" per Palmer's partisans, or a "finishing fiasco" á la critics; "play before Memorial Day or after Labor Day for a great value", and try to ignore those "distracting kids" frolicking "by the homes" lining the fairways.

Geneva National, Trevino 🏌⏱ ▽ 24 | 24 | 21 | 23 | $110
1221 Geneva National Ave. S.; 262-245-7022;
www.genevanationalresort.com; 7116/5261; 74.2/70.2; 135/124
■ "Being a left-to-right player has its advantages" on this "typical Trevino design", so "play your fade" and avoid the big ol' oak, hickory and walnut trees that line the fairway; detail-oriented drivers declare "the front nine is more memorable than the back, except for No. 14", a 414-yard par 4, "which is the best hole of all 54 at the facility", where stay-and-plays at the on-site lodge or neighboring inns make the most of your weekend.

Grand Geneva Resort, Brute 🏌 25 | 21 | 23 | 18 | $130
7036 Grand Geneva Way; 262-248-2556; 800-558-3417;
www.grandgeneva.com; 6997/5244; 73.8/70; 136/129
■ "Aptly named" "but not so hard as to suck the joy out of the game", this Brute is "long and tough with lots of elevation changes" and "sprawling greens and wide fairways"; "if you like teeing it up above the hole and letting it rip into wonderful vistas, make plans to play the beauty" of a beast that's "always in super shape" and where "rangers keep play moving."

Grand Geneva Resort, Highlands 🏌 ▽ 19 | 22 | 22 | 19 | $115
7036 Grand Geneva Way; 262-248-2556; 800-558-3417;
www.grandgeneva.com; 6633/5038; 71.5/68.3; 125/115
◪ Fans say for an "easy and entertaining course at a down-home resort" recently enhanced with a new 10,000-sq.-ft. spa and

activities center and newly renovated rooms, try this "great" links-style layout; those who knew it when say "it was better before the redesign" "a few years" back because "all the Irish/Scottish influence is gone" now.

Madison

Lawsonia Resort, Links ⛳   24 | 20 | 22 | 22 | $75

W2615 N. Valley View Dr., Green Lake; 920-294-3320; 800-529-4453; www.lawsonia.com; 6764/5078; 72.8/68.9; 130/114

☒ The former estate of Chicago publishing magnate and Associated Press co-founder Victor Lawson is now owned by the American Baptist Assembly, and it's "one of the most beautiful, serene environments you'll ever play golf in", where a "nice", "neat old" linkster with "difficult greens" and views of Green Lake dates to the 1930s, when the place was a playground for privileged pigeons and pros; today's critics crank it's a "not-all-that-difficult", "tired track" with "nonexistent rough", so "skip it" and "play the Woodlands course here" instead.

Lawsonia Resort, Woodlands ⛳   25 | 19 | 22 | 22 | $75

W2615 N. Valley View Dr., Green Lake; 920-294-3320; 800-529-4453; www.lawsonia.com; 6618/5106; 71.5/69.1; 129/120

☒ "Get away" to this "beautiful" "golf paradise" where "holes with dramatic elevation drops" are "carved out of the Wisconsin forest" swoon wooed woodland wallopers who swear it's "definitely" "worth the travel" to be "playing in another world"; nevertheless, a few fussy flubbers remain unmoved over what they feel is a "neglected, overused" course where the "greens are normally not in very good shape."

Sentryworld Sports Center ⛳   ▽ 26 | 23 | 21 | 21 | $74

601 Michigan Ave., Stevens Point; 715-345-1600; www.sentryworld.com; 6951/5108; 74.4/71.0; 142/126

■ "Have you ever seen more flowers?" huzzah horticultural hackers tiptoeing around the 90,000 annuals bordering the 16th green, the highlight of "beautifully manicured landscaping" that is most "breathtaking in the spring", "when in full bloom"; as for the golf itself, "who'd have thought you'd find a layout this nice in central Wisconsin?" – "challenging" and "pretty long", it's a "must-play if you are even close to Stevens Point", where stay-and-play packages are on offer at local hotels.

Trappers Turn Golf Club   24 | 21 | 21 | 20 | $79

652 Trappers Turn Dr., Wisconsin Dells; 608-253-7000; 800-221-8876; www.trappersturn.com
Arbor/Lake: 6738/5000; 73.3/69.7; 133/123
Canyon/Arbor: 6759/5017; 72.8/69.4; 133/122
Lake/Canyon: 6831/5000; 72.9/69.5; 133/122

■ North of Madison "in the middle of waterpark Vegas for children is this incredibly beautiful, well-maintained course" laid down on land carved by glaciers that's a "moss-ridden beauty" with "a hole in a canyon"; it's a "fun frolic" "for mid-handicap" hooch sippers, where "good service" includes tending to "the best Bloody Mary ever, bar none", but apparently not ordering merchandise "for petite people", as a pro shop that caters to the cheese-and-beer Wisconsin crowd carries "everything in large."

University Ridge   27 | 23 | 23 | 24 | $72
9002 County Hwy. PD, Verona; 608-845-7700; 800-897-4343;
www.uwbadgers.com; 6888/5005; 73.2/68.9; 142/121
■ "You don't have to be a UW alum to appreciate" this "cheesehead treat", a college course as "jaw-droppingly pretty" as any Madison coed, all of whom play at a discount, while even drop-out duffers "get a free sleeve of balls with a round"; Robert Trent Jones Jr. "shows what you can do with a lot of space", laying down a "links front nine with lots of rough" and a "tree-lined, North Woods–type back" with "a good finisher" on a "nice, hilly" site; the Badgers "team should be real good" after workouts on "some of the best practice facilities around."

Milwaukee

Bog, The   ▽ 25 | 22 | 24 | 19 | $125
3121 County Hwy. I, Saukville; 262-284-7075; 800-484-3264;
www.golfthebog.com; 7110/5110; 74.9/70.3; 142/124
■ "Be accurate here" blubber ball bangers bogged down by "plenty of trouble and quite a few blind shots" at this "real test" of a woodlander with views of the enormous Cedarburg Bog; it's got "fabulous greens" because "it was one of the first facilities in the area to ban metal spikes from day one", but a few bloaks are boggled by "obnoxious rangers."

Bristlecone Pines 🏌   ▽ 20 | 17 | 18 | 18 | $79
1500 E. Arlene Dr., Hartland; 262-367-7888; www.golfbristlecone.com;
7005/4853; 74.1/69.4; 138/120
☑ It's "a little hard to find this place, but once you do you'll be happy" comment coneheads pining for the "very good holes" on this "nice", "well-maintained" track that's hosted a U.S. Open qualifier; its broad fairways are laid out in a "nice setting" edged by sandy waste areas and tall, thick native fescue grasses, with a creek meandering through 11 holes; it's slated to go private in five years' time, even though some swinging snobs bristle that it's just "average."

Brown Deer Park   24 | 15 | 17 | 23 | $79
7835 N. Green Bay Rd.; 414-352-8080; 6759/5861; 72.9/73.8; 133/132
■ Home of the PGA Tour's Greater Milwaukee Open, "the Bethpage Black of Wisconsin" is "an outstanding course with typical county park facilities", which means its "amenities are limited", but it "rivals Torrey Pines for a public, and tee times are much easier to obtain" shout deer-ly beloved fans of the "great, classic" "bargain" that "plays like a country club"; "with impeccable groundskeeping, heavy woods and enough challenges for pros", it's a "true gem" that manages to be "forgiving enough to keep the weekend [duffer] coming back."

Country Club of Wisconsin   ▽ 24 | 21 | 19 | 22 | $50
2241 Hwy. W., Grafton; 262-375-2444; 7049/5463; 74.5/72.3; 136/126
■ "A poor man's Bog", this soupy bargain is "one of the best values in the state", "isolated" as it is north of Milwaukee just inland from Lake Michigan, with water on 13 holes; it's in "very good condition", but the "amenities are few", so reviewers up for roughing it say "I'd like to return soon", while luxe-lovin' lofters "feel it is not enjoyable."

Naga-waukee

– | – | – | – | $42

1897 Maple Ave., Pewaukee; 262-367-2153; 6830/5817; 71.8/72.4; 125/125
From this woodland muni set on 200 acres of Kettle Moraine forest backdropped by the gorgeous Pewaukee Lake, "the views are unbelievable", but so are "its condition and the service in the pro shop"; in fact, "it's all so nice that you don't even realize it's county-owned", except when you pay your greens fee, which is a government-issued bargain.

Wyoming

Jackson

Jackson Hole Golf & Tennis

∇ 25 | 20 | 17 | 17 | $145

5000 Spring Gulch Rd.; 307-733-3111; www.gtlc.com; 7168/6036; 72.3/73.2; 133/125
■ "Love the moose-logo balls" say swingers at this "beautiful course" redesigned in 1967 by Robert Trent Jones Jr., with jaw-dropping vistas of the Grand Tetons from every hole; it sports water in play on two-thirds of its layout, offers four sets of tee boxes and is located right in the national park, where resort accommodations and activities abound, including tennis on courts next to the course.

Private Courses

Private courses are members-only, but guests of members may have access to play at a club.

Aronimink Golf Club
3600 Saint Davids Rd., Newtown Square, PA, 610-356-8000
Restored to its original Donald Ross design, this 1962 PGA Championship host features rugged par 4s with elevated greens.

Atlanta Country Club
500 Atlanta Country Club Dr., Marietta, GA, 770-953-2100
The showstopper at the PGA Tour's 1967–1996 Atlanta home is No. 13, with pines, wildflowers, a waterfall and covered bridge.

Atlantic Golf Club
Scuttle Hole Rd., Bridgehampton, NY, 631-537-1818
Rees Jones' spiritual cousin to England's Royal Birkdale links is buffeted by ocean breezes and framed in native grass mounds.

Augusta National Golf Club
2604 Washington Rd., Augusta, GA, 706-667-6000
Home to the Masters Tournament, this hilly beauty at a men-only club is rich in trees, flowers, creeks and ponds.

Baltimore Country Club, East
11500 Mays Chapel Rd., Timonium, MD, 410-561-3381
A.W. Tillinghast crafted this host of the 1928 PGA Championship, 1932 U.S. Amateur, 1965 Walker Cup and 1988 U.S. Women's Open.

Baltusrol Golf Club, Lower
Shunpike Rd., Springfield, NJ, 973-376-1900
An hour from Manhattan, this club has hosted seven U.S. Opens, four on the Lower course, which closes with back-to-back par 5s.

Bel-Air Country Club
10768 Bellagio Rd., LA, CA, 310-472-9563
At this celeb-studded enclave, holes hopscotch barrancas, as at the 10th, which golfers cross via the famed "Swinging Bridge."

Bellerive Country Club
12925 Ladue Rd., St. Louis, MO, 314-434-4400
The 1965 U.S. Open and 1992 PGA Championship were played on Robert Trent Jones Sr.'s elevated, fiercely trapped greens here.

Black Diamond Ranch Golf & Country Club, Quarry
2600 W. Black Diamond Circle, Lecanto, FL, 352-746-3440
Thirty- to 40-ft. elevation changes and holes that play up, down and around an old quarry make for a striking back nine on this Tom Fazio design.

Butler National Golf Club
2616 York Rd., Oak Brook, IL, 630-990-3333
Brutal par 3s led the pros to rate this course "the toughest on Tour" when the Western Open was held at its men-only club 1974–1990.

Camargo Club
8605 Shawnee Run Rd., Indian Hill, OH, 513-561-9292
Golden Age architect Seth Raynor crafted a wonderful variety of ravine-skirting par 3s and par 4s on this 1926 course.

Canterbury Golf Club
22000 S. Woodland Rd., Beachwood, OH, 216-561-1000
Jack Nicklaus broke Bobby Jones' record for majors when he won
the 1973 PGA Championship on this 1922 woodlander.

Castle Pines Golf Club
1000 Hummingbird Dr., Castle Rock, CO, 303-688-6000
At 7,559 yards, one of PGA Tour's longest tracks is a 1982 Nicklaus
design with sharp downhills framed in pines and wildflowers.

Cherry Hills
4125 S. University Blvd., Englewood, CO, 303-761-9900
President Eisenhower's home away from home in the Rockies has
hosted numerous championships, including the 1960 U.S. Open.

Chicago Golf Club
25W253 Warrenville Rd., Wheaton, IL, 630-668-2000
American golf royalty, this 1892 classic was the first 18-holer in the
country and hosted U.S. Opens in 1897, 1900 and 1911.

Colonial Country Club
3735 Country Club Circle, Ft. Worth, TX, 817-927-4200
Ben Hogan won the PGA Tour's Colonial National Invitational five
times here, earning the track its nickname, "Hogan's Alley."

Congressional Country Club, Blue
8500 River Rd., Bethesda, MD, 301-469-2000
This host of the 1964 and 1997 U.S. Opens was redone by Robert
Trent Jones Sr. and son Rees in 1960 and 1989 respectively.

Country Club, The, Clyde/Squirrel
191 Clyde St., Brookline, MA, 617-566-0240
A high-society Boston enclave for more than 100 years, this tree-
lined layout hosted three U.S. Opens and the 1999 Ryder Cup.

Country Club of Fairfield
936 Sasco Hill Rd., Fairfield, CT, 203-259-1601
Seth Raynor's 1914 breeze-fueled classic serves up a stout
collection of par 4s and handsome views of Long Island Sound.

Creek Club
1 Horse Hollow Rd., Locust Valley, NY, 516-676-1405
Wooded and links holes, an island green and lovely views of Long
Island Sound are on offer at this short but exciting 1923 layout.

Crooked Stick Golf Club
1964 Burning Tree Ln., Carmel, IN, 317-844-9938
Pete Dye's first true championship track hosted overnight sensation
John Daly's 1991 PGA Championship upset.

Crystal Downs Country Club
1286 Frankfort Hwy., Frankfort, MI, 231-352-9933
Atop a bluff between Lake Michigan and Crystal Lake, Alister
MacKenzie's windswept gem is thick with native roughs.

Cypress Point Club
3150 17 Mile Dr., Pebble Beach, CA, 831-624-6444
Alister MacKenzie's seasider, five minutes from Pebble Beach
Resort, hosted the PGA Tour's Bing Crosby National Pro-Am.

Desert Forest Golf Club
37207 N. Mule Train Rd., Carefree, AZ, 480-488-4589
Fairways and back-to-front sloping greens hemmed in by cacti
demand accuracy on this desert beauty with mountain views.

Double Eagle Club
6025 Cheshire Rd., Galena, OH, 740-548-4017
This Weiskopf/Morrish design boasts dual fairways and
conditioning so superb that the tee boxes could double as greens.

East Lake Golf Club
2575 Alston Dr. SE, Atlanta, GA, 404-373-5722
Bobby Jones' boyhood playground is reborn with a Rees Jones
redesign and a caddie program for local underserved youth.

Estancia Club
9801 E. Dynamite Rd., Scottsdale, AZ, 480-473-4400
Tom Fazio set tee boxes and greens on high desert rock
outcroppings at this enclave that climbs Pinnacle Peak.

Eugene Country Club
255 Country Club Rd., Eugene, OR, 541-345-0181
In 1967, Robert Trent Jones Sr. reversed the tees and greens and
enlarged the water hazards on this 1924 tree-laden track.

Firestone Country Club, South
452 E. Warner Rd., Akron, OH, 330-644-8441
RTJ Sr.'s redesign has hosted PGA Championships, the 2002 Senior
PGA Championship and the World Series of Golf.

Fishers Island Club
Fishers Island, Fishers Island, NY, 631-788-7221
At a high-society retreat afloat in Long Island Sound, this 1926 Seth
Raynor links design is known for its Atlantic shore vistas.

Forest Highlands Golf Club
657 Forest Highlands Dr., Flagstaff, AZ, 928-525-5200
Par 5s over 600 yards long are made more manageable by the
7,000-ft. altitude of this Weiskopf/Morrish design.

Garden City Golf Club
315 Stewart Ave., Garden City, NY, 516-746-2880
The 1902 U.S. Open host, Long Island's men-only institution plays
like a British links, with tall fescues, bunkers and sea breezes.

Golf Club, The
4522 Kitzmiller Rd., New Albany, OH, 614-855-7326
Hidden at a men-only club, this early Pete Dye challenges with tall
native roughs, clever bunkers and outstanding par 5s.

Grandfather Golf & Country Club, Grandfather
Hwy. 105, Linville, NC, 828-898-4531
In a high Blue Ridge valley next to the Linville River, this hilly design
looks up through the pines at Grandfather Mountain.

Hazeltine National Golf Club
1900 Hazeltine Blvd., Chaska, MN, 952-448-4929
Designed by RTJ Sr. and reworked by son Rees, this farm/forest
blend hosted the 1991 U.S. Open and 2002 PGA Championship.

Honors Course
9603 Lee Hwy., Ooltewah, TN, 423-238-4272
Tiger Woods' winning final-round 80 at the 1995 Men's NCAA
Championship testifies to the difficulty of this Pete Dye design.

Interlachen Country Club
6200 Interlachen Blvd., Edina, MN, 952-929-1661
Bobby Jones skipped his second shot across the pond at the 9th
on this track to win the 1930 U.S. Open in his Grand Slam year.

Inverness Club
4601 Dorr St., Toledo, OH, 419-578-9000
Donald Ross' 99-year-old remains a superb test; just ask Bob Tway, who holed a sand shot to win the 1986 PGA Championship.

Jupiter Hills Club, Hills
1800 SE Hill Club Terrace, Tequesta, FL, 561-746-5228
Bob Hope and auto exec William Clay Ford were among founders of this track with 70 feet of elevation changes amid hardwoods.

Kinloch Golf Club
1100 Hockett Rd., Manakin-Sabot, VA, 804-784-8000
Near Richmond, this millenial collaboration from Lester George and Vinny Giles offers multiple avenues of play on nearly every hole.

Kittansett Club
11 Point Rd., Marion, MA, 781-631-2800
On windy Buzzards Bay lies the 1953 Walker Cup Match host, where No. 3 plays to an island green encircled by sand.

Laurel Valley Golf Club
Rte. 711 S., Ligonier, PA, 724-238-9555
On an old pheasant-hunting preserve is this host of the 1965 PGA Championship, 1975 Ryder Cup Match and 1989 U.S. Senior Open.

Long Cove Club
44 Long Cove Dr., Hilton Head Island, SC, 843-686-1000
This 20-year-old is a stew of Pete Dye design with live oaks, palmettos, waste bunkers and an amazing variety of holes.

Los Angeles Country Club, North
10101 Wilshire Blvd., Los Angeles, CA, 310-276-6104
George Thomas' layout sits on pricey real estate at the meeting of Wilshire and Santa Monica Boulevards near Beverly Hills.

Maidstone Club
Old Beach Ln., East Hampton, NY, 631-324-0510
The 19th-century links design at this tony Hamptons club is washed in sea breezes that make it play longer than its yardage.

Medalist Golf Club, Medalist
9908 SE Cottage Ln., Hobe Sound, FL, 561-545-9600
Pete Dye and Greg Norman co-created this beauty with sea breezes, Pinehurst-style chipping areas and vast sand hazards.

Medinah Country Club, No. 3
6N001 Medinah Rd., Medinah, IL, 630-773-1700
Site of the 1999 PGA Championship, this brute with par 3s playing over Lake Kadijah will be longer when it reopens in a 2003 redo.

Merion Golf Club, East
450 Ardmore Ave., Ardmore, PA, 610-642-5600
Bobby Jones clinched his Grand Slam in 1930 at the "Babbling Brook" hole at this Mainline Philadelphia classic.

Milwaukee Country Club
8000 N. Range Line Rd., River Hills, WI, 414-362-5200
The host to the 1969 Walker Cup Match features a well-wooded back nine that tumbles down to the Milwaukee River.

Muirfield Village Golf Club
5750 Memorial Dr., Dublin, OH, 614-889-6700
Jack Nicklaus designed this track to host his own Memorial Tournament, won by Tiger Woods in 1999, 2000 and 2001.

Myopia Hunt Club
435 Bay Rd., South Hamilton, MA, 978-468-4433
The hilly host of four U.S. Opens 1898–1908 provides a solid, old-style test, thanks to bunkering and vexing putting surfaces.

Nantucket Golf Club
250 Milestone Rd., Siasconset, MA, 508-257-8500
Golfers maneuver in coastal gusts to avoid the numerous bunkers and tall rough on this British links-style Rees Jones design.

National Golf Links
Sebonac Inlet Rd., Southampton, NY, 631-283-0410
This 90-year-old on Great Peconic Bay is the work of Charles Blair Macdonald, who modeled creations after the British Isles' best.

NCR Country Club, South
4435 Dogwood Trail, Dayton, OH, 937-299-3571
Dick Wilson sculpted the bold bunkering of this home of the 1969 PGA Championship and 1986 U.S. Women's Open.

Newport Country Club
280 Harrison Ave, Newport, RI, 401-846-0461
Site of the first U.S. Open in 1895, this founding member of the USGA serves up sea breezes, fast fairways and cunning traps.

Oak Hill Country Club, East
Kilbourn Rd., Rochester, NY, 585-586-1660
Host to three U.S. Opens and the 1995 Ryder Cup Match, Donald Ross' 1920s design calls for long, accurate shotmaking.

Oakland Hills Country Club
3951 W. Maple Rd., Bloomfield Hills, MI, 248-644-2500
Ben Hogan called this track a "monster", but he tamed its undulating greens and many bunkers to win the 1951 U.S. Open.

Oakmont Country Club
1233 Hulton Rd., Oakmont, PA, 412-828-8000
A seven-time U.S. Open site, this 99-year-old has the most bunkers and the largest, fastest greens in championship golf.

Oak Tree Golf Club
1515 W. Oak Tree Dr., Edmund, OK, 405-348-2004
Amid prairie gusts, Pete Dye dishes up undulations, moguls and superb variety for events like the 1988 PGA Championship.

Ocean Forest Golf Club
200 Ocean Rd., Sea Island, GA, 912-638-5834
On an Atlantic island, Rees Jones' fairly flat mix of wooded holes and windy, open links hosted the 2001 Walker Cup Match.

Olympia Fields Country Club, North
2800 Country Club Dr., Olympia Fields, IL, 708-748-0495
Seventy-five years after the North first hosted the U.S. Open, Tiger Woods will attempt to defend his crown here in 2003.

Olympic Club, Lake
524 Post St., South San Francisco, CA, 415-587-4800
On a clear day, you can see the Golden Gate Bridge from the 3rd tee of this pine-, cedar- and cypress-lined four-time U.S. Open site.

Peachtree Golf Club
4600 Peachtree Rd. NE, Atlanta, GA, 404-233-4428
A one-time-only Bobby Jones/RTJ Sr. co-design, this hilly, forested Southerner boasts broad fairways and huge greens.

Pete Dye Golf Club
801 Aaron Smith Dr., Bridgeport, WV, 304-842-2801
Routed over a former strip coal mine, this undulating namesake
forces healthy carries across the Simpson River.

Pine Valley Golf Club
E. Atlantic Ave., Pine Valley, NJ, 856-783-3000
This brutal but beautiful favorite dishes out multiple forced carries
on holes hopscotching from one island of turf to the next.

Piping Rock Club
150 Piping Rock Rd., Locust Valley, NY, 516-676-2332
Near where Matinecock Indians smoked peace pipes, this 1912
design retooled in the '80s pays homage to the British best.

Plainfield Country Club
1591 Woodland Ave., Plainfield, NJ, 908-757-1800
Host of the 1978 U.S. Amateur and 1987 U.S. Women's Open, this
classic sports cross bunkers and contoured greens.

Point O'Woods Golf & Country Club
1516 Roslin Rd., Benton Harbor, MI, 616-944-1433
Tom Weiskopf, Ben Crenshaw and Tiger Woods are among champs
of the Western Amateur, played here since the '60s.

Prairie Dunes Country Club
4812 E. 30th Ave., Hutchinson, KS, 620-662-0581
Amid sandhills, yucca and plum thickets, this rolling, windswept
layout proved a formidable test at the 2002 U.S. Women's Open.

Pumpkin Ridge, Witch Hollow
12930 NW Old Pumpkin Ridge Rd., North Plains, OR, 503-647-9977
The 1996 site of Tiger Woods' third U.S. Amateur win hosted Nancy
Lopez's heartbreaking loss at the '97 U.S. Women's Open.

Quaker Ridge Golf Club
146 Griffen Ave., Scarsdale, NY, 914-725-1100
Hidden next to Winged Foot, this A.W. Tillinghast design boasts
outstanding par 4s and was host to the 1997 Walker Cup Match.

Quarry at La Quinta, The
1 Quarry Ln., La Quinta, CA, 760-777-1100
Every hole offers scenic desert backdrops at this Palm Springs–
area Tom Fazio course draped across mountain slopes.

Ridgewood Country Club, East/West
96 W. Midland Ave., Paramus, NJ, 201-599-3900
A.W. Tillinghast's 27-holer hosted the 1935 Ryder Cup, 1990 U.S.
Senior Open and 2001 Senior PGA Championship.

Rim Golf Club
300 S. Clubhouse Rd., Payson, AZ, 928-472-1431
The boulder escarpment backdropping the par-5 13th is just one
high desert wonder on this final Weiskopf/Morrish design.

Riviera Country Club
1250 Capri Dr., Pacific Palisades, CA, 310-454-6591
Host for the PGA Tour's Los Angeles Open, this eucalyptus-lined
track sits in a canyon south of Sunset Boulevard.

Robert Trent Jones International Golf Club
1 Turtle Point Dr., Gainesville, VA, 703-754-4050
Named for the dean of U.S. golf architects, this Presidents Cup
host is chock-full of water hazards and puzzle-piece bunkers.

Sahalee Country Club, North/South
21200 NE Sahalee Country Club Dr., Sammamish, WA, 425-868-8800
Meaning "high, heavenly ground" in Chinook, this 1998 PGA Championship site is bracketed by cedars, firs and hemlocks.

Salem Country Club
133 Forest St., Peabody, MA, 978-538-5400
Amid maples, oaks and pines, this Donald Ross design has hosted three U.S. Women's Opens and the 2001 U.S. Senior Open.

Sand Hills Golf Club
Hwy. 97 Mile Marker 55, Mullen, NE, 308-546-2237
A noteworthy post–World War II design, this Ben Crenshaw/Bill Coore links takes full advantage of sandy, rolling terrain.

Sand Ridge Golf Club
12150 Mayfield Rd., Chardon, OH, 440-285-8088
A modern classic amid aged beauties, this 1999 Tom Fazio design is dotted with strategically deployed, white sand bunkers.

San Francisco Golf Club
Junipero Sierra Blvd. & Brotherhood Way, San Francisco, CA, 415-469-4100
A.W. Tillinghast designed this quiet beauty that features massive cypresses, sensational bunkering, but nary a water hazard.

Scioto Country Club
2196 Riverside Dr., Columbus, OH, 614-486-4341
Jack Nicklaus learned to play on this classic that's hosted the U.S. Open, Ryder Cup, PGA Championship and U.S. Senior Open.

Seminole Golf Club
901 Seminole Blvd., North Palm Beach, FL, 561-626-1331
At a posh retreat in the Atlantic, this Donald Ross masterpiece challenges golfers with sea grape bushes, palms, ocean breezes and nearly 200 bunkers.

Shinnecock Hills Golf Club
200 Tuckahoe Rd., Southampton, NY, 631-283-1310
Wedged between the Atlantic Ocean and Great Peconic Bay, this links was the site of the U.S. Open in 1986 and 1995 and will host it again in 2004.

Shoal Creek
100 New Williamsburg Dr., Shoal Creek, AL, 205-991-9000
The 1984 and 1990 PGA Championships were played on this Nicklaus course carved from dense forest.

Shoreacres
1601 Shore Acres Rd., Lake Bluff, IL, 847-234-1470
On Chicago's North Shore, this short but sweet 1921 Seth Raynor masterpiece offers several exciting shots over steep ravines.

Somerset Hills Country Club
180 Mine Mount Rd., Bernardsville, NJ, 908-776-0043
Near the USGA headquarters sits this A.W. Tillinghast design featuring a well-bunkered front nine and a heavily wooded back.

Southern Highlands Golf Club
1 Robert Trent Jones Ln., Las Vegas, NV, 702-263-1000
The final Robert Trent Jones Sr. and Jr. collaboration co-hosts the Invensys Classic, with sprawling bunkers and a series of wonderful watery closing holes.

Southern Hills Country Club
2636 E. 61st St., Tulsa, OK, 918-492-3351
Bermuda rough, prairie wind and challenging bunkers made this Perry Maxwell parklander a solid test for the 2001 U.S. Open.

Stanwich Club
888 North St., Greenwich, CT, 203-869-0555
Fast greens, large bunkers, multiple water hazards and double-dogleg par 5s make this 1960 design the state's toughest course.

Troon Golf & Country Club
25000 N. Windy Walk Dr., Scottsdale, AZ, 480-585-4310
This Weiskopf/Morrish debut is a desert target track sporting a "Cliff" 14th amid boulders, with McDowell Mountain views.

Valhalla Golf Club
15503 Shelbyville Rd., Louisville, KY, 502-245-4475
The bluegrass rough and split fairways of this Kentucky thoroughbred hosted Tiger Woods' 2000 PGA Championship win.

Valley Club of Montecito
1901 E. Valley Rd., Santa Barbara, CA, 805-969-2215
Amid sycamore and eucalyptus groves, this 1929 Alister MacKenzie design offers stylish bunkering and superior par 3s.

Victoria National Golf Club
2000 Victoria Blvd., Newburgh, IN, 812-858-8230
Tom Fazio transformed an old strip mine into a gorgeous layout with lush mounding weaving through small ponds.

Wade Hampton Golf Club
Hwy. 107 S., Cashiers, NC, 828-743-5465
In the Smoky Mountains, Tom Fazio's 1987 design winds through a valley heavy with pines and crisscrossed by clear streams.

Wannamoisett Country Club
96 Hoyt Ave., Rumford, RI, 401-434-1200
Donald Ross' rare par 69 is crammed into 104 acres yet still packs a wallop with long, strong par 4s and speedy, undulating greens.

Whisper Rock Golf Club
32002 N. Old Bridge Rd., Scottsdale, AZ, 480-575-8700
Lined in saguaro, prickly pear and ocotillo, Phil Mickelson's debut offers superb par 4s and risk/reward par 5s.

Winged Foot Golf Club, East
Fennimore Rd., Mamaroneck, NY, 914-698-8400
West's shorter sister sports handsome par 3s and a tournament pedigree, including the inaugural U.S. Senior Open in 1980.

Winged Foot Golf Club, West
Fennimore Rd., Mamaroneck, NY, 914-698-8400
A.W. Tillinghast designed this four-time U.S. Open test with pear-shaped greens and deep bunkers on rolling parkland.

Yeamans Hall Club
900 Yeamans Hall Rd., Hanahan, SC, 843-744-5555
Tom Doak restored this layout to its 1925 glory with huge square greens and yawning traps amid aged oaks and magnolias.

Urban Driving Ranges

Within a short ride from a major business district

Atlanta

Charlie Yates Golf Course
10 Lakeside Village; 404-373-4655;
www.charlieyatesgolfcourse.com

City Club Golf Academy
2400 Defoors Ferry Rd.; 404-351-5331; www.cityclubgolf.com

Eagle Golf Club
460 Morgan Falls Rd.; 770-390-0424

Golf Tec
3655 Roswell Rd; 404-760-9919; www.golftec.com

Boston

Boston Golf Driving Range at The Radisson Hotel
200 Stuart St.; 617-457-2699; www.bostongolfacademy.com

City Golf Boston
38 Bromfield St.; 617-357-4653; www.citygolfboston.com

Chicago

Diversey Driving Range
141 W. Diversey Ave.; 312-742-7929;
www.diverseydrivingrange.com

Family Golf Center
221 N. Columbus Dr.; 312-616-1234

Dallas

Hank Haney City Place Golf Center
3636 McKinney Ave.; 214-520-7275; www.hankhaney.com

North Texas Golf Center
2101 Walnut Hill Ln.; 972-247-4653; www.northtexasgolf.com

Denver

All Golf at Overland
1801 S. Huron St.; 303-777-7331

Kennedy Family Golf Center
10500 E. Hampden Ave.; 303-755-0105; www.allgolf.com

Houston

Clear Creek Golf Club
3902 Fellows Rd.; 713-738-8000; www.clearcreekclub.com

Memorial Park Golf Course
1001 Memorial Loop E.; 713-862-4033;
www.houstonmunicipalgolf.org

Las Vegas

Angel Park
100 S. Rampart Blvd.; 702-254-4653; www.angelparkgolfclub.com

Badlands Golf Club
9119 Alta Dr.; 702-242-4653; www.americangolf.com

Los Angeles

Griffith Park Golf Courses
4900 Griffith Park Dr.; 323-663-2555

John Wells Golf Driving Range
11501 Strathern St.; 818-767-1954

La MA Golf Driving Range
2793 W. Olympic Blvd.; 213-365-9090

Rancho Park Golf Course
10460 W. Pico Blvd. (Patricia Ave.); 310-839-4374

New Orleans

Bayou Oaks Golf Facility
1 Palm Dr.; 504-483-9396; www.neworleanscitypark.com

New York City

Chelsea Piers Golf Club
Pier 59 (at West End Hwy.); 212-336-6400; www.chelseapiers.com

Randall's Island Driving Range
1 Randall's Island (north of Downing Stadium); 212-427-5689

Philadelphia

FDR Golf Club
Patterson & 20th Sts.; 215-462-8997; www.golfphilly.com

Karakung at Cobb's Creek Golf Club
Lansdowne Ave. & 72nd St.; 215-877-8707; www.golfphilly.com

San Diego

Bonita Driving Range
3631 Bonita Rd.; 619-426-2069

Stadium Golf Center
29-90 Murphy Canyon Rd.; 858-277-6667

Seattle

Interbay Golf Center
2501 15th Ave.; 206-285-2200; www.interbaygolf.com

Jefferson Park Golf Club
4101 Beacon Ave. S.; 206-762-4513; www.jeffersonparkgolf.com

Washington, DC

East Potomac Park Golf Course & Driving Range
972 Ohio Dr. SW; 202-554-7660

Indexes

Properties in indexes are followed by nearest major city.

Indexes list the best of many within each category.

Budget

($40 and under)

Baker National, *Minneapolis, MN*
Bethpage, Black, *Long Island, NY*
Bethpage, Blue, *Long Island, NY*
Bethpage, Green, *Long Island, NY*
Bethpage, Red, *Long Island, NY*
Blue Hill, *NYC Metro Area*
Bretwood, North, *Keene, NH*
Buffalo Run, *Denver, CO*
Chena Bend, *Fairbanks, AK*
Chenango Valley State Park, *Finger Lakes, NY*
Classic Country Club, *Tacoma, WA*
Crestbrook Park, *Waterbury, CT*
Eagleglen, *Anchorage, AK*
En-Joie, *Finger Lakes, NY*
Forest Akers MSU, East, *Lansing, MI*
George Wright, *Boston, MA*
Gold Mountain, Cascade, *Bremerton, WA*
Halifax Plantation, *Daytona Beach, FL*
Heritage Hills, *North Platte, NE*
Hermitage, General's Retreat, *Nashville, TN*
Heron Lakes, Great Blue, *Portland, OR*
Heron Lakes, Greenback, *Portland, OR*
Hickory Valley, Ambassador, *Philadelphia, PA*
HIdden Valley, *Pittsburgh, PA*
H. Smith Richardson, *Danbury, CT*
Indian Peaks, *Boulder, CO*
Jimmie Austin Course, *Oklahoma City, OK*
Juniper Hill, Lakeside, *Boston, MA*
Les Bolstad Course, *Minneapolis, MN*
Lockeford Springs, *Stockton, CA*
Los Verdes, *Los Angeles, CA*
Mariana Butte, *Denver, CO*
McCann Memorial, *Hudson Valley, NY*
Meadows Farms, *DC Metro Area*
Montauk Downs State Park, *Long Island, NY*
Murphy Creek, *Denver, CO*
Old Works, *Butte, MT*
Pacific Grove, *Monterey Peninsula, CA*
Papago Municipal, *Phoenix, AZ*
Piñon Hills, *Albuquerque, NM*
Rail, The, *St. Louis Area*
Rams Hill, *San Diego, CA*

Ridgeview Ranch, *Dallas, TX*
Riverdale, Dunes, *Denver, CO*
Rolling Meadows, *Topeka, KS*
Saddle Rock, *Denver, CO*
Smithtown Landing, *Long Island, NY*
Stoneybrook West, *Orlando, FL*
Swan Lake, *Long Island, NY*
Tokatee, *Eugene, OR*
Valley View, *Salt Lake City, UT*
Vineyard, *Cincinnati, OH*
Wachusett, *Worcester, MA*
Walking Stick, *Colorado Springs, CO*
Wasatch Mtn. State Park, Lakes Course, *Salt Lake City, UT*
Wasatch Mtn. State Park, Mountain Course, *Salt Lake City, UT*
Wasioto Winds, *Lexington, KY*
Whiteface Club, *Adirondacks, NY*
Wild Horse, *North Platte, NE*
Woodland Hills, *Lincoln, NE*

Bunkering

Bandon Dunes, Bandon Dunes Course, *Coos Bay, OR*
Bandon Dunes, Pacific Dunes, *Coos Bay, OR*
Bethpage, Black, *Long Island, NY*
Blue Heron Pines, East, *Atlantic City, NJ*
Cambrian Ridge, *Montgomery, AL*
Challenge at Manele, *Lanai, HI*
Cog Hill, No. 4 (Dubsdread), *Chicago, IL*
Colony West, Championship, *Ft. Lauderdale, FL*
Cuscowilla, *Lake Oconee, GA*
Desert Willow, Firecliff, *Palm Springs, CA*
Diamondback, *Orlando, FL*
Doral Resort, Blue Monster, *Miami, FL*
Doral Resort, Great White, *Miami, FL*
El Diablo, *Ocala, FL*
Estrella Mtn. Ranch, *Phoenix, AZ*
Gateway, *Naples, FL*
Grand Cypress, New, *Orlando, FL*
Harborside Int'l, Starboard, *Chicago, IL*
La Costa, South, *San Diego, CA*
Lakewood Shores, Gailes, *Bay City, MI*
Legends, Heathland, *Myrtle Beach, SC*
Links/North Dakota, *Williston, ND*

Indexes

Hyatt Dorado Beach, East, *Dorado, PR*
Hyatt Dorado Beach, West, *Dorado, PR*
Hyatt Regency Cerromar Beach, North, *Dorado, PR*
Hyatt Regency Cerromar Beach, South, *Dorado, PR*
Incline Village, Championship, *Reno, NV*
Inverrary, East, *Ft. Lauderdale, FL*
Kaanapali, North, *Maui, HI*
Lely Resort, Flamingo, *Naples, FL*
Lyman Orchards, Robert Trent Jones, *Danbury, CT*
Mauna Kea, *Big Island, HI*
MetroWest, *Orlando, FL*
Montauk Downs State Park, *Long Island, NY*
Otter Creek, *Indianapolis, IN*
Oxmoor Valley, Ridge, *Birmingham, AL*
Oxmoor Valley, Valley, *Birmingham, AL*
Palmetto Dunes, Robert Trent Jones, *Hilton Head, SC*
Rail, The, *St. Louis Area*
SCGA Members Club, *San Diego, CA*
Seven Oaks, *Finger Lakes, NY*
Silver Lakes, *Anniston, AL*
Spyglass Hill, *Monterey Peninsula, CA*
Sugarbush Golf Club, *Northern Vermont, VT*
Tamiment Resort, *Poconos, PA*
Tanglewood Park, Championship, *Winston-Salem, NC*
Treetops, Robert Trent Jones Masterpiece, *Traverse City, MI*
Wigwam, Blue, *Phoenix, AZ*
Wigwam, Gold, *Phoenix, AZ*
Woodstock Country Club, *Southern Vermont, VT*

Tom Fazio

Amelia Island Plantation, Long Point, *Jacksonville, FL*
Amelia Island Plantation, Ocean Links, *Jacksonville, FL*
Barefoot Resort, Fazio, *Myrtle Beach, SC*
Barton Creek, Fazio Canyons, *Austin, TX*
Barton Creek, Fazio Foothills, *Austin, TX*
Belterra, *Cincinnati Area, IN*
Branson Creek, *Springfield, MO*

Champions Club/Summerfield, *Palm Beach, FL*
Cordillera, Valley, *Vail, CO*
Dancing Rabbit, Azaleas, *Jackson, MS*
Dancing Rabbit, Oaks, *Jackson, MS*
Edgewood Tahoe, *Reno, NV*
Emerald Dunes, *Palm Beach, FL*
Gateway, *Naples, FL*
Glen Club, *Chicago, IL*
Grayhawk, Raptor, *Scottsdale, AZ*
Hartefeld Nat'l, *Philadelphia, PA*
Independence Golf Club, Championship Course, *Richmond, VA*
Karsten Creek, *Stillwater, OK*
Kiawah Island, Osprey Point, *Charleston, SC*
Legacy/Alaqua Lakes, *Orlando, FL*
Mahogany Run Golf Club, *St. Thomas, USVI*
Missouri Bluffs, *St. Louis, MO*
Nevele Grande, *Catskills, NY*
Oak Creek, *Orange County, CA*
Oyster Bay Town, *Long Island, NY*
Pelican Hill, Ocean North, *Orange County, CA*
Pelican Hill, Ocean South, *Orange County, CA*
PGA Golf Club, North, *Port St. Lucie, FL*
PGA Golf Club, South, *Port St. Lucie, FL*
PGA National, Champion, *Palm Beach, FL*
PGA National, Haig, *Palm Beach, FL*
PGA National, Squire, *Palm Beach, FL*
Pine Hill, *Cape May, NJ*
Pinehurst Resort, No. 4, *Pinehurst, NC*
Pinehurst Resort, No. 6, *Pinehurst, NC*
Pinehurst Resort, No. 8, *Pinehurst, NC*
Porter's Neck, *Myrtle Beach Area*
Primm Valley, Desert, *Las Vegas, NV*
Primm Valley, Lakes, *Las Vegas, NV*
Reynolds Plantation, National, *Lake Oconee, GA*
Ridgefield Golf Course, *Danbury, CT*
Sawmill Creek, *Cleveland, OH*

subscribe to zagat.com

        subscribe to zagat.com

Turtle Creek, *Philadelphia, PA*
Twelve Bridges, *Sacramento, CA*
Wailea, Gold, *Maui, HI*
Westin Mission Hills, Pete Dye, *Palm Springs, CA*
Whistling Straits, Straits, *Kohler, WI*
White Columns, *Atlanta, GA*
Wild Wing Plantation, Hummingbird, *Myrtle Beach, SC*
Wolf Creek, *Las Vegas, NV*
Woodlands Resort, TPC, *Houston, TX*
World Woods, Rolling Oaks, *Tampa, FL*
Yankee Trace, *Dayton, OH*

Environmentally Friendly

(Recognized by Audubon International, Golf Course Superintendents Association of America or another certifying organization)
Amelia Island Plantation, *Jacksonville, FL*
Baker National, *Minneapolis, MN*
Bald Head Island, *Myrtle Beach Area*
Bandon Dunes, *Coos Bay, OR*
Barefoot Resort, *Myrtle Beach, SC*
Barton Creek, *Austin, TX*
Bog, The, *Milwaukee, WI*
Broadmoor, *Colorado Springs, CO*
Cape May National, *Cape May, NJ*
Carolina Club, The, *Pinehurst, NC*
Champions Club at Summerfield, *Palm Beach, FL*
Desert Willow, *Palm Springs, CA*
Glen Annie, *Santa Barbara, CA*
Glen Dornoch Waterway, *Myrtle Beach, SC*
Golden Bear at Keene's Point, *Orlando, FL*
Gray Plantation, *Lake Charles, LA*
Harbor Links, *Long Island, NY*
Hermitage, *Nashville, TN*
Hidden Valley Resort, *Pittsburgh, PA*
Kelly Plantation, *Panhandle, FL*
Kiawah Island, *Charleston, SC*
Kingsmill, *Williamsburg, VA*
Legacy Club at Alaqua Lakes, *Orlando, FL*

Longaberger, *Columbus, OH*
Lost Key, *Panhandle, FL*
Memorial Park, *Houston, TX*
Olde Scotland Links, *Boston, MA*
Orange County National, *Orlando, FL*
Pasatiempo, *Santa Cruz, CA*
Pebble Beach, *Monterey Peninsula, CA*
PGA Golf Club, *Port St. Lucie, FL*
Pinehills, *Boston, MA*
Pinehurst Resort, *Pinehurst, NC*
Pumpkin Ridge, *Portland, OR*
RedHawk, *San Diego, CA*
Regatta Bay, *Panhandle, FL*
Resort At Squaw Creek, *Lake Tahoe, CA*
Reynolds Plantation, Oconee, *Lake Oconee, GA*
Running Y Ranch Resort, *Klamath Falls, OR*
Saddle Rock, *Denver, CO*
Sandestin, *Panhandle, FL*
San Juan Oaks, *San Jose, CA*
Spanish Bay, *Monterey Peninsula, CA*
Stevinson Ranch, *Stockton, CA*
St. James Plantation, *Myrtle Beach Area*
Strawberry Farms, *Orange County, CA*
Sunriver Resort, *Bend, OR*
TPC at Sawgrass, *Jacksonville, FL*
Westin Stonebriar, *Dallas, TX*
Widow's Walk, *Boston, MA*

Exceptional Clubhouses

Arcadia Bluffs, *Traverse City, MI*
Bay Hill, *Orlando, FL*
Bear's Best Las Vegas, *Las Vegas, NV*
Bear Trace At Chickasaw, *Memphis, TN*
Boca Raton Resort, *Palm Beach, FL*
Boulders, *Scottsdale, AZ*
Breakers, The, *Palm Beach, FL*
Bridges, The, *Gettysburg, PA*
Buffalo Run, *Denver, CO*
Caledonia Golf & Fish Club, *Pawleys Island, SC*
Camelback, *Scottsdale, AZ*
ChampionsGate, *Orlando, FL*
Crumpin-Fox Club, *Berkshires, MA*
Edinburgh U.S.A., *Minneapolis, MN*

Expense Account

($200 and over)

Junior-Friendly

Links-Style

Arcadia Bluffs, *Traverse City, MI*
Bandon Dunes, Bandon Dunes Course, *Coos Bay, OR*
Bandon Dunes, Pacific Dunes, *Coos Bay, OR*
Bay Harbor, *Petoskey, MI*
Beechtree, *Aberdeen, MD*
Blue Heron Pines, East, *Atlantic City, NJ*
Chaska Town, *Minneapolis, MN*
Crystal Springs, Ballyowen, *NYC Metro Area*
Currituck Club, *Outer Banks, NC*
Cuscowilla, *Lake Oconee, GA*
Half Moon Bay, Ocean, *SF Bay Area, CA*
Harborside Int'l, Port, *Chicago, IL*
Heather Glen, *Myrtle Beach, SC*
Keystone Ranch, Ranch Course, *Vail, CO*
Lawsonia Resort, Links, *Madison, WI*
Legends, Heathland, *Myrtle Beach, SC*
Links/Hiawatha Landing, *Finger Lakes, NY*
Links/Lighthouse Sound, *Ocean City, MD*
Links/Union Vale, *Hudson Valley, NY*
Long Island Nat'l, *Long Island, NY*
Maumee Bay Resort, *Toledo, OH*
Murphy Creek, *Denver, CO*
Okemo Valley Golf Club, *Southern Vermont, VT*
Pebble Beach, *Monterey Peninsula, CA*
Polo Trace, *Palm Beach, FL*
Samoset Resort, *Portland, ME*
Sandpines, *Eugene, OR*
Spanish Bay, *Monterey Peninsula, CA*
Spyglass Hill, *Monterey Peninsula, CA*
St. Ives Resort, Tullymore, *Grand Rapids, MI*
Tribute, *Dallas, TX*
Twisted Dune, *Atlantic City, NJ*
Waikoloa Beach Resort, Kings, *Big Island, HI*
Whistling Straits, Straits, *Kohler, WI*
Wild Dunes, Links, *Charleston, SC*

Newcomers

Architects, *Trenton, NJ*
Barona Creek, *San Diego, CA*

Bay Creek, *Virginia Beach, VA*
Bear's Best Atlanta, *Atlanta, GA*
Bear's Best Las Vegas, *Las Vegas, NV*
Bear Trace/Ross Creek Landing, *Nashville, TN*
Belterra, *Cincinnati Area, IN*
Black Gold, *Yorba Linda, CA*
Branton Woods, *Hudson Valley, NY*
Breckenridge Golf Club, *Vail, CO*
Cowboys, *Dallas, TX*
CrossCreek, *San Diego, CA*
Crystal Springs, Wild Turkey, *NYC Metro Area*
Eagle Ranch, *Vail, CO*
Falcon Crest, *Boise, ID*
Glen Club, *Chicago, IL*
Grande Dunes, *Myrtle Beach, SC*
Great River, *Danbury, CT*
Independence Golf Club, Championship Course, *Richmond, VA*
Legacy, The, *Des Moines, IA*
LochenHeath, *Traverse City, MI*
Lost Canyons, Shadow, *Los Angeles, CA*
Lost Canyons, Sky, *Los Angeles, CA*
Marriott's Wildfire, Faldo Championship, *Phoenix, AZ*
Pinehills, Jones, *Boston, MA*
Pinehills, Nicklaus, *Boston, MA*
Prairie Highlands, *Kansas City, KS*
Ranch, The, *Berkshires, MA*
Redlands Mesa, *Grand Junction, CO*
Reynolds Plantation, Oconee, *Lake Oconee, GA*
RiverTowne, *Charleston, SC*
Saratoga Nat'l, *Albany, NY*
Sea Island, Retreat, *Lowcountry, GA*
Shepherd's Hollow, *Detroit, MI*
St. Ives Resort, Tullymore, *Grand Rapids, MI*
Stonewall, *DC Metro Area*
Talega, *Orange County, CA*
Twisted Dune, *Atlantic City, NJ*
We-Ko-Pa, *Scottsdale, AZ*
Wilderness Ridge, *Lincoln, NE*
Wolf Creek, *Las Vegas, NV*

19th Holes

Avalon Lakes, *Cleveland, OH*
Aviara, *San Diego, CA*
Bay Hill, *Orlando, FL*
Boulders, *Scottsdale, AZ*

Bowling Green, *NYC Metro Area*
Capitol Hill, *Montgomery, AL*
Crumpin-Fox Club, *Berkshires, MA*
Crystal Springs, *NYC Metro Area*
Desert Falls, *Palm Springs, CA*
Desert Willow, *Palm Springs, CA*
Doral, *Miami, FL*
Emerald Dunes, *Palm Beach, FL*
Golden Horseshoe,
    Williamsburg, VA
Golf Club At Whitehawk Ranch,
    Lake Tahoe, CA
Grand Cypress, *Orlando, FL*
Grayhawk, *Scottsdale, AZ*
Great River, *Danbury, CT*
Half Moon Bay, *SF Bay Area, CA*
Harbour Town, *Hilton Head, SC*
Hawk Hollow, *Lansing, MI*
Heritage Club, *Pawleys Island, SC*
Homestead, *Roanoke, VA*
Kiawah Island, *Charleston, SC*
Kingsmill Resort, *Williamsburg, VA*
Kiva Dunes, *Mobile, AL*
Landmark at Oak Quarry,
    Riverside, CA
La Paloma Country Club,
    Tucson, AZ
Legacy at Lakewood Ranch,
    Sarasota, FL
Lost Canyons, *Los Angeles, CA*
Maderas, *San Diego, CA*
Murphy Creek, *Denver, CO*
Ojai Valley Inn and Spa, *Los
    Angeles, CA*
Orange County National,
    Orlando, FL
Oyster Bay Town Golf Course,
    Long Island, NY
Pasatiempo, *Santa Cruz, CA*
Pebble Beach, *Monterey
    Peninsula, CA*
Pelican Hill, *Orange County, CA*
PGA National, *Palm Beach, FL*
PGA West, *Palm Springs, CA*
Phoenician, The, *Scottsdale, AZ*
Pine Barrens, *Trenton, NJ*
Pine Needles Lodge, *Pinehurst, NC*
Poppy Hills, *Monterey
    Peninsula, CA*
Reynolds Plantation, Oconee,
    Lake Oconee, GA
Ridge at Castle Pines North, The,
    Denver, CO
Rocky River at Concord,
    Charlotte, NC
Sedona Golf Resort, *Phoenix, AZ*
Seven Bridges, *Chicago, IL*
Seven Oaks, *Finger Lakes, NY*

Spanish Bay, *Monterey
    Peninsula, CA*
SunRidge Canyon, *Scottsdale, AZ*
Sunriver Resort, *Bend, OR*
Talega, *Orange County, CA*
Torrey Pines, *San Diego, CA*
TPC at Sawgrass, *Jacksonville, FL*
Troon North, *Scottsdale, AZ*
Twelve Bridges Golf Club,
    Sacramento, CA
Ventana Canyon, *Tucson, AZ*
We-Ko-Pa, *Scottsdale, AZ*
Westin Innisbrook, *Tampa, FL*
Whistling Straits, *Kohler, WI*
World Golf Village, *Jacksonville, FL*

Opening Holes

Arizona Biltmore, Adobe,
    Phoenix, AZ
Arizona National, *Tucson, AZ*
Atlantic Golf At South River, *DC
    Metro Area*
Augustine, *DC Metro Area*
Bay Creek, *Virginia Beach, VA*
Bay Hill, *Orlando, FL*
Beaver Creek Golf Club, *Vail, CO*
Bethpage, Red, *Long Island, NY*
Boulders, South, *Scottsdale, AZ*
Broadmoor, West, *Colorado
    Springs, CO*
Cambrian Ridge, *Montgomery, AL*
Capitol Hill, Judge,
    Montgomery, AL
Capitol Hill, Legislator,
    Montgomery, AL
Colony West, Championship,
    Ft. Lauderdale, FL
CrossCreek, *San Diego, CA*
Desert Willow, Firecliff, *Palm
    Springs, CA*
Diamondback, *Orlando, FL*
DragonRidge, *Las Vegas, NV*
El Diablo, *Ocala, FL*
Equinox, Gleneagles, *Southern
    Vermont, VT*
Four Seasons/Las Colinas,
    Cottonwood Valley, *Dallas, TX*
Garrison, *Hudson Valley, NY*
Glen Annie, *Santa Barbara, CA*
Golf Club/Whitehawk Ranch,
    Lake Tahoe, CA
Grand Cypress, New, *Orlando, FL*
Grayhawk, Talon, *Scottsdale, AZ*
Great Gorge, *NYC Metro Area*
Greenbrier, Old White, *White
    Sulphur Springs, WV*
Keystone Ranch, Ranch Course,
    Vail, CO

Keystone Ranch, River, *Vail, CO*
La Cantera, Resort, *San Antonio, TX*
Lake Powell National, *Flagstaff, AZ*
La Quinta, Dunes, *Palm Springs, CA*
Murphy Creek, *Denver, CO*
Pasatiempo, *Santa Cruz, CA*
PGA Golf Club, Pete Dye, *Port St. Lucie, FL*
Poipu Bay Resort, *Kauai, HI*
Poppy Hills, *Monterey Peninsula, CA*
Raven/Snowshoe Mtn., *Elkins, WV*
Sagamore, The, *Adirondacks, NY*
Sandestin, Burnt Pines, *Panhandle, FL*
Seven Oaks, *Finger Lakes, NY*
Silver Lakes, *Anniston, AL*
Spanish Bay, *Monterey Peninsula, CA*
Spyglass Hill, *Monterey Peninsula, CA*
Tahoe Donner, *Lake Tahoe, CA*
Talamore, *Pinehurst, NC*
Tamarron Resort, *Durango, CO*
TPC at Sawgrass, Valley, *Jacksonville, FL*
Walt Disney World, Magnolia, *Orlando, FL*
We-Ko-Pa, *Scottsdale, AZ*
Wente Vineyards, *SF Bay Area, CA*
Westin Innisbrook, Island, *Tampa, FL*
World Woods, Pine Barrens, *Tampa, FL*

Pace of Play

Balsams Panorama, *Colebrook, NH*
Boulders, North, *Scottsdale, AZ*
Boulders, South, *Scottsdale, AZ*
Broadmoor, East, *Colorado Springs, CO*
Broadmoor, West, *Colorado Springs, CO*
Bull Run, *DC Metro Area*
Butternut Farm, *Worcester, MA*
Diablo Grande, Legends West, *Sacramento, CA*
Diablo Grande, Ranch, *Sacramento, CA*
Great River, *Danbury, CT*
Heritage, *Atlanta, GA*
Links/Union Vale, *Hudson Valley, NY*
Los Caballeros, *Phoenix, AZ*
Mare Island, *SF Bay Area, CA*

Mauna Lani, South, *Big Island, HI*
Nutters Crossing, *Baltimore, MD*
Orange County Nat'l, Panther Lake, *Orlando, FL*
PGA Golf Club, North, *Port St. Lucie, FL*
Red Hawk Ridge, *Denver, CO*
Robinson Ranch, Mountain, *Los Angeles, CA*
Sand Barrens, *Cape May, NJ*
Silverhorn Golf Club, *San Antonio, TX*
Sonnenalp, *Vail, CO*
Tiffany Greens, *Kansas City, MO*
World Woods, Pine Barrens, *Tampa, FL*
World Woods, Rolling Oaks, *Tampa, FL*
Worthington Manor, *Frederick, MD*

Par 3s

Amelia Island Plantation, Long Point, *Jacksonville, FL*
Amelia Island Plantation, Oak Marsh, *Jacksonville, FL*
Arizona Biltmore, Links, *Phoenix, AZ*
Arrowhead, *Denver, CO*
Barefoot Resort, Norman, *Myrtle Beach, SC*
Boca Raton Resort, Resort Course, *Palm Beach, FL*
Capitol Hill, Judge, *Montgomery, AL*
Carambola Golf Club, *St. Croix, USVI*
Chaska Town, *Minneapolis, MN*
Coeur D'Alene Resort, *Coeur d'Alene, ID*
Druids Glen, *Seattle, WA*
Eagle Ridge, *Freehold, NJ*
Eagle Ridge, South, *Galena, IL*
Glenwood Country Club, *Hot Springs, AR*
Golden Horseshoe, Gold, *Williamsburg, VA*
Harbour Town, *Hilton Head, SC*
Horseshoe Bay, Applerock, *Austin, TX*
Horseshoe Bay, Ram Rock, *Austin, TX*
Inn/Mtn. Gods, *Las Cruces, NM*
Island's End, *Long Island, NY*
Kapalua, Bay, *Maui, HI*
Kiawah Island, Cougar Point, *Charleston, SC*
Kiawah Island, Ocean, *Charleston, SC*

Cog Hill, No. 2, *Chicago, IL*
Coyote Lakes, *Phoenix, AZ*
Doral Resort, Great White, *Miami, FL*
Doral Resort, Red, *Miami, FL*
Eaglesticks, *Columbus, OH*
Farmstead, *NYC Metro Area*
500 Club, *Phoenix, AZ*
Forest Akers MSU, East, *Lansing, MI*
Gold Mountain, Cascade, *Bremerton, WA*
Great Gorge, *NYC Metro Area*
Greystone, *Finger Lakes, NY*
Heritage Palms, *Palm Springs, CA*
Hickory Valley, Ambassador, *Philadelphia, PA*
Hyannis Golf Club, *Cape Cod, MA*
Indian Wells, West, *Palm Springs, CA*
Island's End, *Long Island, NY*
Kingsmill Resort, Plantation, *Williamsburg, VA*
Les Bolstad Course, *Minneapolis, MN*
Long Island Nat'l, *Long Island, NY*
Nutters Crossing, *Baltimore, MD*
Oak Brook, *Chicago, IL*
Ocean City Golf & Yacht Club, Seaside, *Ocean City, MD*
Pacific Grove, *Monterey Peninsula, CA*
Pinehurst Resort, No. 1, *Pinehurst, NC*
Pinehurst Resort, No. 3, *Pinehurst, NC*
Rail, The, *St. Louis Area*
Rookery, The, *Rehoboth Beach, DE*
Schaumburg, *Chicago, IL*
Stow Acres, South, *Worcester, MA*
Swan Lake, *Long Island, NY*
Tahquitz Creek, Legend, *Palm Springs, CA*
TPC of Scottsdale, Desert, *Scottsdale, AZ*
Windham, *Catskills, NY*
Wizard, The, *Myrtle Beach, SC*
Woodstock Country Club, *Southern Vermont, VT*

Practice Facilities

Birkdale, *Charlotte, NC*
Black Lake, *Traverse City, MI*
Blackthorn, *South Bend, IN*
Bretwood, *Keene, NH*
Country Club of Hilton Head, *Hilton Head, SC*

Cypresswood, *Houston, TX*
Dunes at Maui Lani, *Maui, HI*
Forest Akers MSU, *Lansing, MI*
Forest Lake, *Orlando, FL*
Four Seasons Las Colinas, *Dallas, TX*
Golf Club at Newcastle, *Seattle, WA*
Golf Club At Whitehawk Ranch, *Lake Tahoe, CA*
Grand View Lodge, *Brainerd, MN*
Grayhawk, *Scottsdale, AZ*
Great River, *Danbury, CT*
Greenbrier, *White Sulphur Springs, WV*
Harborside International, *Chicago, IL*
Heritage Palms, *Palm Springs, CA*
Iron Horse, *Dallas, TX*
Jimmie Austin University of Oklahoma Golf Course, *Oklahoma City, OK*
La Cantera, *San Antonio, TX*
Legacy Club at Alaqua Lakes, *Orlando, FL*
Legends, *Myrtle Beach, SC*
Legend Trail, *Scottsdale, AZ*
Longaberger, *Columbus, OH*
LPGA International, *Daytona Beach, FL*
Lyman Orchards, *Danbury, CT*
Marriott Shadow Ridge, *Palm Springs, CA*
Murphy Creek, *Denver, CO*
Oak Creek, *Orange County, CA*
Palm Valley, *Phoenix, AZ*
Peninsula Golf & Racquet, *Mobile, AL*
PGA Golf Club, *Port St. Lucie, FL*
PGA West, *Palm Springs, CA*
Pinehills, *Boston, MA*
Pinehurst, *Pinehurst, NC*
Pine Needles Lodge, *Pinehurst, NC*
Pinewild, *Pinehurst, NC*
Possum Trot, *Myrtle Beach, SC*
Rancho San Marcos, *Santa Barbara, CA*
Remington, *Orlando, FL*
Robinson Ranch, *Los Angeles, CA*
Ruffled Feathers, *Chicago, IL*
Rum Pointe Seaside Golf Links, *Ocean City, MD*
Singing Hills, *San Diego, CA*
Springhouse, *Nashville, TN*
Starr Pass, *Tucson, AZ*
StoneWater, *Cleveland, OH*
Tiffany Greens, *Kansas City, MO*
TPC at Sawgrass, *Jacksonville, FL*

TPC of Scottsdale, *Scottsdale, AZ*
TPC of Tampa Bay, *Tampa, FL*
Tradition Club, The, *Pawleys Island, SC*
University Ridge, *Madison, WI*
Waverly Oaks, *Boston, MA*
We-Ko-Pa, *Scottsdale, AZ*
Westin Mission Hills, *Palm Springs, CA*
World Golf Village, *Jacksonville, FL*
World Woods, *Tampa, FL*
Yankee Trace, *Dayton, OH*

Private Functions

Arizona National, *Tucson, AZ*
Bay Hill, *Orlando, FL*
Bear's Best Las Vegas, *Las Vegas, NV*
Black Gold, *Yorba Linda, CA*
Boca Dunes, *Palm Beach, FL*
Boulders, *Scottsdale, AZ*
Bridges, The, *Gettysburg, PA*
Buffalo Run, *Denver, CO*
Caledonia Golf & Fish Club, *Pawleys Island, SC*
ChampionsGate, *Orlando, FL*
Country Club of New Seabury, *Cape Cod, MA*
Dancing Rabbit, *Jackson, MS*
Desert Willow, *Palm Springs, CA*
Edgewood Tahoe, *Reno, NV*
Glen Club, The, *Chicago, IL*
Golf Club At Bradshaw Farms, *Atlanta, GA*
Golf Club at Newcastle, *Seattle, WA*
Grayhawk, *Scottsdale, AZ*
Greystone, *Baltimore, MD*
Heatherwoode, *Dayton, OH*
Heritage Club, *Pawleys Island, SC*
Keswick Club, *Charlottesville, VA*
Keystone Ranch, *Vail, CO*
Kingsmill Resort, *Williamsburg, VA*
Ko Olina, *Oahu, HI*
La Quinta, *Palm Springs, CA*
Las Vegas Paiute Resort, *Las Vegas, NV*
Laurel Springs, *Atlanta, GA*
Legacy Golf Club, The, *Las Vegas, NV*
Lone Tree, *Denver, CO*
LPGA International, *Daytona Beach, FL*
Marriott Shadow Ridge, *Palm Springs, CA*
Mission Inn, *Orlando, FL*
Ocotillo Golf Club, *Phoenix, AZ*
Palos Verdes Golf Club, *Los Angeles, CA*

Pelican Pointe, *Sarasota, FL*
Peninsula Golf & Racquet, *Mobile, AL*
Pevely Farms, The Golf Club at, *St. Louis, MO*
Pine Hill, *Cape May, NJ*
Player's Club At Deer Creek, *Omaha, NE*
Porter's Neck Plantation, *Myrtle Beach Area*
Quicksilver, *Pittsburgh, PA*
Ranch, The, *Berkshires, MA*
Reynolds Plantation, Oconee, *Lake Oconee, GA*
Robinson Ranch, *Los Angeles, CA*
Royal American Links, *Columbus, OH*
Siena, *Las Vegas, NV*
StoneTree, *SF Bay Area, CA*
StoneWater, *Cleveland, OH*
Tiffany Greens, *Kansas City, MO*
Tribute, *Dallas, TX*
Troon North, *Scottsdale, AZ*
Trophy Club, The, *Indianapolis, IN*
Twelve Bridges Golf Club, *Sacramento, CA*
Ventana Canyon, *Tucson, AZ*
Vineyard, *Cincinnati, OH*
We-Ko-Pa, *Scottsdale, AZ*
Wilderness Ridge, *Lincoln, NE*

Pro-Event Hosts

Bay Hill, *Orlando, FL*
Bethpage, Black, *Long Island, NY*
Brown Deer Park, *Milwaukee, WI*
Callaway Gardens, Mountain View, *Columbus, GA*
Cog Hill, No. 4 (Dubsdread), *Chicago, IL*
Cypress Creek, *Orlando, FL*
Doral Resort, Blue Monster, *Miami, FL*
Dragon Ridge, *Las Vegas, NV*
Dunes Club, *Myrtle Beach, SC*
En-Joie, *Finger Lakes, NY*
Four Seasons/Las Colinas, Cottonwood Valley, *Dallas, TX*
Four Seasons/Las Colinas, TPC, *Dallas, TX*
Greenbrier, Greenbrier Course, *White Sulphur Springs, WV*
Harborside Int'l, Port, *Chicago, IL*
Harbour Town, *Hilton Head, SC*
Homestead, Cascades, *Roanoke, VA*
Kapalua, Plantation, *Maui, HI*
Kapolei, *Oahu, HI*
Kemper Lakes, *Chicago, IL*

Putting Courses

Horseshoe Bay Resort, *Austin, TX*
Legend Trail, *Scottsdale, AZ*
Marriott Desert Springs, *Palm Springs, CA*
Orange County National, *Orlando, FL*
Ponce De Leon Resort, *Jacksonville, FL*
Ravines Inn, *Jacksonville, FL*
RedHawk, *San Diego, CA*
Running Y Ranch Resort, *Klamath Falls, OR*
Timberton, *Jackson, MS*
Turtle Creek, *Philadelphia, PA*
World Golf Village, *Jacksonville, FL*
World Woods, *Tampa, FL*

Replicas

Bear's Best Atlanta, *Atlanta, GA*
Bear's Best Las Vegas, *Las Vegas, NV*
Boyne Highlands, Donald Ross, *Petoskey, MI*
Grand Cypress, New, *Orlando, FL*
Royal Links, *Las Vegas, NV*
Tour 18/Dallas, *Dallas, TX*
Tour 18/Houston, *Houston, TX*
Tribute, *Dallas, TX*

Resort

Amelia Island Plantation, *Jacksonville, FL*
Arizona Biltmore, *Phoenix, AZ*
Aviara, *San Diego, CA*
Balsams Panorama, *Colebrook, NH*
Bandon Dunes, *Coos Bay, OR*
Barton Creek, *Austin, TX*
Bay Harbor Resort, *Petoskey, MI*
Bay Hill, *Orlando, FL*
Beaver Creek Golf Club, *Vail, CO*
Belterra, *Cincinnati Area, IN*
Blackwolf Run, *Kohler, WI*
Boca Raton Resort, *Palm Beach, FL*
Boulders, *Scottsdale, AZ*
Boyne Mountain Resort, *Petoskey, MI*
Breakers, The, *Palm Beach, FL*
Broadmoor, *Colorado Springs, CO*
Callaway Gardens, *Columbus, GA*
Camelback, *Scottsdale, AZ*
Carmel Valley Ranch, *Monterey Peninsula, CA*
Challenge at Manele, *Lanai, HI*
Chateau Elan, *Atlanta, GA*
Coeur D'Alene Resort, *Coeur d'Alene, ID*

Cordillera, *Vail, CO*
Country Club of Hershey, *Harrisburg, PA*
Crystal Springs, *NYC Metro Area*
Doral Resort, *Miami, FL*
Eagle Ridge, *Galena, IL*
Edgewood Tahoe, *Reno, NV*
Equinox, Gleneagles, *Southern Vermont, VT*
Experience at Koele, *Lanai, HI*
Four Seasons at Las Colinas, *Dallas, TX*
Gold Canyon, *Phoenix, AZ*
Golden Horseshoe, *Williamsburg, VA*
Grand Cypress, *Orlando, FL*
Grand Geneva Resort, *Lake Geneva, WI*
Grand Traverse, *Traverse City, MI*
Grand View Lodge, *Brainerd, MN*
Greenbrier, *White Sulphur Springs, WV*
Homestead, *Roanoke, VA*
Homestead Golf Club & Resort, *Salt Lake City, UT*
Hualalai Golf Club, *Big Island, HI*
Hyatt Hill Country Golf Club, *San Antonio, TX*
Indian Wells, *Palm Springs, CA*
Kapalua, *Maui, HI*
Kauai Lagoons, *Kauai, HI*
Keswick Club, *Charlottesville, VA*
Keystone Ranch, *Vail, CO*
Kiawah Island, *Charleston, SC*
Kingsmill Resort, *Williamsburg, VA*
La Cantera, *San Antonio, TX*
La Costa, *San Diego, CA*
La Paloma, *Tucson, AZ*
La Quinta, *Palm Springs, CA*
Legends, *Myrtle Beach, SC*
Links at Lighthouse Sound, *Ocean City, MD*
Los Caballeros, *Phoenix, AZ*
Makena, *Maui, HI*
Marriott Desert Springs, *Palm Springs, CA*
Mauna Kea Resort, *Big Island, HI*
Mauna Lani Resort, *Big Island, HI*
Mid Pines Inn, *Pinehurst, NC*
Mission Inn, *Orlando, FL*
Nemacolin Woodlands, *Pittsburgh, PA*
Nevele Grande, *Catskills, NY*
Ojai Valley Inn and Spa, *Los Angeles, CA*
Pala Mesa Resort, *San Diego, CA*
Pebble Beach, *Monterey Peninsula, CA*

Toughest

(Courses with the highest slope
ratings from the back tees)

subscribe to zagat.com

St. James Plantation, Gauntlet, *Myrtle Beach Area*
St. James Plantation, Players Club, *Myrtle Beach Area*
Sugarloaf, *Central ME*
Sunriver Resort, Crosswater, *Bend, OR*
Sycamore Ridge, *Kansas City, KS*
Tiburon, Black, *Naples, FL*
Timberton, *Jackson, MS*
Tobacco Road, *Pinehurst, NC*
TPC at Sawgrass, Stadium, *Jacksonville, FL*
TPC of Myrtle Beach, *Myrtle Beach, SC*
Treetops, Robert Trent Jones Masterpiece, *Traverse City, MI*
Troon North, Monument, *Scottsdale, AZ*
Troon North, Pinnacle, *Scottsdale, AZ*
Twelve Bridges, *Sacramento, CA*
Ventana Canyon, Mountain, *Tucson, AZ*
Vistoso, *Tucson, AZ*
Wente Vineyards, *SF Bay Area, CA*
Whistling Straits, Irish, *Kohler, WI*
Whistling Straits, Straits, *Kohler, WI*
Willinger's, *Minneapolis, MN*
Wolf Creek, *Las Vegas, NV*

University

ASU Karsten, *Tempe, AZ*
Duke University Golf Club, *Raleigh-Durham, NC*
Forest Akers MSU, *Lansing, MI*
Jimmie Austin University of Oklahoma Golf Course, *Oklahoma City, OK*
Seven Oaks, *Finger Lakes, NY*
University of Maryland Golf Course, *DC Metro Area*
University of New Mexico Championship Golf Course, *Albuquerque, NM*
University Ridge, *Madison, WI*

Walking Only

Bandon Dunes, Bandon Dunes Course, *Coos Bay, OR*
Bandon Dunes, Pacific Dunes, *Coos Bay, OR*
Bethpage, Black, *Long Island, NY*
Whistling Straits, Straits, *Kohler, WI*

Women-Friendly

Amelia Island Plantation, Ocean Links, *Jacksonville, FL*
Baywood Greens, *Rehoboth Beach, DE*
Big Run, *Chicago, IL*
BlackHorse, North, *Houston, TX*
Boulders, South, *Scottsdale, AZ*
Boyne Highlands, Heather, *Petoskey, MI*
Broadmoor, East, *Colorado Springs, CO*
Camelback, Resort, *Scottsdale, AZ*
Challenge at Manele, *Lanai, HI*
Chateau Elan Course, Woodlands, *Atlanta, GA*
Coral Canyon, *St. George, UT*
Cowboys, *Dallas, TX*
Coyote Hills, *Orange County, CA*
Cypress Creek, *Orlando, FL*
Desert Willow, Firecliff, *Palm Springs, CA*
Eagle Ridge, *Freehold, NJ*
Emerald Dunes, *Palm Beach, FL*
Golf Club/Newcastle, China Creek, *Seattle, WA*
Grand Cypress, New, *Orlando, FL*
Grand Cypress, *Orlando, FL*
Greenbrier, Meadows, *White Sulphur Springs, WV*
Kapalua, Bay, *Maui, HI*
Kapalua, Village, *Maui, HI*
Kapolei, *Oahu, HI*
Keystone Ranch, River, *Vail, CO*
Kiawah Island, Ocean, *Charleston, SC*
Kingsmill Resort, Plantation, *Williamsburg, VA*
La Cantera, Resort, *San Antonio, TX*
Legacy, *Pinehurst, NC*
Legacy Ridge, *Denver, CO*
Los Caballeros, *Phoenix, AZ*
Lost Canyons, Shadow, *Los Angeles, CA*
LPGA International, Champions, *Daytona Beach, FL*
LPGA International, Legends, *Daytona Beach, FL*
Mesquite, *Palm Springs, CA*
Mission Inn, Las Colinas, *Orlando, FL*
Monarch Beach, *Orange County, CA*
Myrtle Beach Nat'l, Kings North, *Myrtle Beach, SC*
Nemacolin Woodlands, Mystic Rock, *Pittsburgh, PA*

Alphabetical
Page Index

Private courses are listed beginning on page 240.

Alphabetical Page Index

Alphabetical Page Index

Alphabetical Page Index

Alphabetical Page Index

Alphabetical Page Index

Alphabetical Page Index

Alphabetical Page Index

Alphabetical Page Index

Alphabetical Page Index

Alphabetical Page Index

Alphabetical Page Index